FALLEN PILLARS
U.S. Policy towards Palestine and Israel since 1945

Donald Neff

Also by Donald Neff
WARRIORS AT SUEZ
WARRIORS FOR JERUSALEM
WARRIORS AGAINST ISRAEL

FALLEN PILLARS
U.S. Policy towards Palestine
and Israel since 1945

Donald Neff

Institute for Palestine Studies
Washington, D.C.

Map is from *The Birth of Israel: Myths and Facts* by Simha Flapan. Copyright © 1987 by Simha Flapan. Reprinted by permission of Pantheon Books, a division of Random House, Inc.

Portions of this book are taken from articles by the author that appeared in the *Journal of Palestine Studies* XXIII, nos. 1–4. Copyright © 1993, 1994 by the Institute for Palestine Studies.

Library of Congress Cataloging-in-Publication Data

Neff, Donald, 1930 –
    Fallen pillars : U.S. policy towards Palestine and Israel since
  1945 / Donald Neff.
      p. cm.
    Includes bibliographical references and index.
    ISBN 0-88728-262-8. -- ISBN 0-88728-259-8
    1. United States--Foreign relations--Palestine. 2. Palestine-
  -Foreign relations--United States. 3. United States--Foreign
  relations--Israel. 4. Israel--Foreign relations--United States.
  5. United States--Foreign relations--1945-1993. 6. United States-
  -Foreign relations--1993- 7. Jewish-Arab relations--1949-
  I. Title.
  E183.8.P19N43 1995
  327.73056'09'04--dc20
                                                        95-19904
                                                           CIP

Printed in the United States of America

CONTENTS

To three good men
George W. Ball, J. William Fulbright and Merle Thorpe Jr.

ACKNOWLEDGMENTS

Some of the material in this book first appeared in the *Journal of Palestine Studies*. I want to express my deep appreciation to the *Journal*'s Associate Editor, Philip Mattar, for his consistent support and kindnesses, and to Managing Editor Linda Butler, who wields an editor's blue pencil with enviable talent and patience. The same is true of Eric Hooglund, who edited this book. I would like to salute Dr. A. Afifi and the Diana Tamari Sabbagh Foundation, which a number of years ago gave me a research grant. Although this book was not what we had in mind at the time, it is the direct result of the studies that the grant allowed me to conduct. A salute is also due to my old friends Jim Abourezk and Murray Gart; my sister Mary Neff Somers; Braxton and Chase, the newest of the clan, and as always, to wonderful Abigail Trafford.

LIST OF APPENDICES

[All appendices come from the official Foreign Relations of the United States *[FRUS] compiled by the State Department. The cited volumes are 1945: Volume VIII, The Near East and Africa; 1946: Volume VII, The Near East and Africa; 1947: Volume V, The Near East and Africa; 1948: Volume V, The Near East, South Asia and Africa, Part 2; 1949: Volume VI, The Near East, South Asia and Africa; and 1955: Volume XIV, Arab-Israeli Dispute 1955. All footnotes in appendices appear in the originals.]*

PREFACE
The Six Pillars
of U.S. Policy, 1897–1995

IT WAS LATE IN 1975 when the U.S. State Department announced that "in many ways, the Palestinian dimension of the Arab-Israeli conflict is the heart of that conflict."[1] What was remarkable about the statement is that it had taken Washington so long to recognize the reality publicly.

The Palestinians, after all, were the victims and the warriors on the home front with Israel. It was their land and their homes, their flocks and businesses that were lost in 1948 with the establishment of Israel. That event resulted in well more than half of the Palestinians becoming stateless refugees and more than three-quarters of the land of Palestine falling under Israeli control. Nineteen years later, Israel captured the rest of Palestine and the remaining Palestinians fell under military occupation or joined the list of refugees. Even after Egypt, Jordan and other Arab states made peace with Israel or publicly accepted the Jewish state, it was the Palestinian claim to justice that kept the conflict simmering.

The magnitude of the Palestinian *nakba*, the catastrophe, as the Palestinians call it, can hardly be exaggerated, nor the uniqueness by which such a fate befell them. Within the span of one lifetime, the Arab majority in Palestine was dispersed or under military occupation or confined to second class citizenship in Israel and immigrant Jews, who had numbered no more than seven percent of the population at the beginning of the twentieth century and owned no more than one percent of the land, ruled supreme over all of Palestine by mid-1967.[2]

The point made by the 1975 State Department declaration, often forgotten, was that the core of what is usually called the Arab-Israeli conflict is in its essentials the Palestinian-Israeli conflict. Confusion about the origins of the conflict all too often has obscured Americans' understanding of its true dimensions. It began as a conflict resulting from immigrants struggling to displace the local majority population. All else is derivative from this basic reality.

This is true of the general misperception that the conflict resulted from aggressive actions by Israel's Arab neighbors, thus transforming the conflict into a war between states. But the Arab-Israeli conflict was a byproduct, not the primary cause, of the struggle over Palestine, a symptom rather than the disease. So too was the widely held misperception between the 1950s and the demise of the Soviet Union in 1991 that the conflict arose as a result of Cold War competition. True, these various aspects of the conflict took on a life of their own over the years, thereby adding complicating dimensions to the conflict that greatly confused the basic issue. But at its heart, and during the whole of its nearly century-old course, the essence of the conflict has remained the same: a struggle between the original Palestinian majority of Arabs to retain their status and land against waves of immigrant Jews laying a claim to their biblical heritage.

That underlying reality forms the backdrop to the efforts by the United States to play a moderator's role in negotiations on the final status of the fundamental issues that divide the two people. Under the Declaration of Principles on Interim Self-Government Arrangements signed by Israel and the Palestine Liberation Organization on 13 September 1993 at the White House, the Palestinians were promised self-rule in the Israeli-occupied Gaza Strip and Jericho as the first step in an arduous five-year agenda "leading to a permanent settlement based on Security Council Resolutions 242 and 338." Although the timetable has lagged, the declaration calls for final status talks to "commence as soon as possible, but not later than the beginning of the third year of the interim period."

If there are not too many delays, Israelis and Palestinians should be sitting down sometime in 1996 with the United States on the sidelines urging them on. But what kind of advice will Washington be offering?

* *

Over nearly a century and under eighteen presidents, the United States has wrestled with itself over a policy toward Palestine. In the first half of the century, the focus was on whether or not to support a Jewish homeland in Palestine. That was the aim of the new creed called Zionism, a political movement dedicated to founding an independent state for Jews. As the argument heated up, the government polarized between the politicians represented by the president and Congress on one side against the experts of the State Department on the other. Over the decades support for a Jewish state ebbed and flowed inconclusively until 1947 when President Harry S. Truman cut the Gordian Knot and threw America's support behind partitioning of British-ruled Palestine into an Arab and a Jewish state. Within less than a year, Israel was established and the majority of Palestinians were expelled from their homeland.

After that traumatic event, U.S. policy became more complex to face the new realities emerging in the former British mandate now unevenly divided between Palestine and Israel. Over the last half of the century, these resolved them-

selves into basic policy pillars on arms, borders, Jerusalem, Palestinians and refugees. One more pillar emerged after 1967 covering settlements. In total these policy
pillars number six. All except the one on arms will constitute the cluster of core
issues to be resolved in the permanent status talks.

U.S. policy has by no means remained stagnant on these core issues. It
has evolved, quite dramatically in most cases, since the 1947 UN partition plan for
Palestine. The evolution of policy has been almost invariably in a direction leading
to a closer embrace of Israel's policies at the expense of the Palestinians. This has
been true under Democratic as well as Republican presidents, except for the notable exception of Dwight Eisenhower, and whether or not the chief executive
himself was an enthusiastic supporter of Zionism.

The change in the relationship with Israel is among the most extraordinary in America's history. Its trajectory goes from official opposition to Zionism at
the beginning of the century to 1947, when the experts of the State Department,
the Defense Department and the Central Intelligence Agency fervently opposed
creation of Israel on grounds that it would be a dangerous source of trouble in the
future. The trajectory concludes in today's policy in which the Jewish state is officially regarded as a strategic ally worthy of the largest proportion of U.S. foreign
aid funds, massive transfers of American technology, and special military and diplomatic protection.

America's original policy pillars were defined in 1947 as a result of the
need to consider all the basic issues involved in establishing a new country in a
foreign land with an indigenous majority population. Under this pressure, Washington spelled out its policy on the fundamental problems facing the world community. America's position on partition represents the earliest and most complete
formulation of official U.S. policy on the Palestinian-Israeli conflict. It stands as a
soundingboard to chart subsequent policy, and for that reason deserves detailed
attention.

In broad outline, U.S. policy pillars have evolved in the following ways
since 1947:

•   Arms policy between 1947 and 1961 rested on a total embargo on
selling weapons to Israel as well as the Arabs. Since then, the United States has
provided Israel with nearly all of its most advanced weapons and publicly pro-
claims a policy to assure Israel of a "qualitative edge" over all its Arab foes. Despite America's worldwide opposition to the proliferation of nuclear weapons,
Washington tacitly has tolerated Israel's development of a nuclear arsenal reputed
to be among the largest in the world.

•   Borders policy changed from originally accepting a Jewish state within
an area comprising about 55 percent of Palestine, as defined in the 1947 partition
plan, to an area of around 77 percent, the area Israel controlled after the fighting of
1948. UN Resolution 242 of 1967 committed the United States to a land-for-peace
policy, meaning it opposed Israel's conquests except for "minor border modifications." By 1993, Washington was referring to Arab East Jerusalem and all of the
West Bank, except for Jericho, as "disputed" rather than "occupied" territory, indi-

cating that Israel has as much claim to the captured territory as the Palestinians.

• Jerusalem policy originally posited that the Holy City belonged to neither Arab nor Jew but was an international city that should come under governance of a special international regime. This changed in 1967 to a formula where the holy places were to be under international protection and the fate of the city was left up to negotiations between Israelis and Arabs. With the coming of the Clinton Administration in 1993, Washington began funding construction of Jewish housing in a vastly expanded area called Greater Jerusalem and appears to accept Israel's claim to the city as its "united and eternal capital."

• Refugee policy began as an endorsement of the right of displaced Palestinians to return to their homes or to receive compensation and resettlement. Although later administrations continued to support that formulation in resolutions passed almost annually by the UN General Assembly, none of them made a serious effort to carry it out. After the coming to office of the Clinton Administration, Washington discontinued its traditional support of the refugees in the United Nations.

• Settlement policy opposed Israeli occupation of Palestinian land taken over by Israelis in 1948 and, more forcefully, actively opposed new Israeli settlements in territories occupied by Israel in 1967. The policy has since gone from considering settlements "illegal" under Jimmy Carter to "obstacles to peace" under Ronald Reagan to "complicating factors" under Bill Clinton. In fact, since the waning days of the Bush Administration, Washington has agreed to help finance some settlement construction with U.S. funds, in effect doing a complete about face and endorsing Israel's right to establish settlements on occupied Palestinian territory.

• Palestinian policy has been the only area where Washington moved in a direction opposite that espoused by Israel and actually influenced Israel to accept the U.S. position. U.S. policy originally contained no recognition of the Palestinians as a separate people. They were lumped together as Arabs whose fate best would be resolved by resettlement in Arab states. Then between 1948 and 1974, Washington considered Palestinians as refugees or terrorists or occupied civilians. It was only with the 1975 State Department declaration that Washington signalled its recognition of the Palestinians as a people. However, the United States has never gone so far as to espouse their cause in the United Nations, to grant them the right of self-determination or to endorse their claim to a Palestinian state.

These changes in policy did not occur overnight or in a political vacuum. Observers on both sides of the conflict, whether pro-Israel or pro-Palestinian, agree that the greatly altered policy pillars came about largely as a result of successful efforts by what has become known as the Israeli lobby. Whether or not the new policies are in America's interests is a different question, and a hotly disputed one between partisans. But that they mainly resulted from an alert and energetic effort by Israel's supporters to influence the White House and the Congress is clear from the record of nearly a century of intense lobbying on behalf of Zionism. The success of the pro-Israel lobby has become a source of pride for Israel and its supporters, and of despair for the Palestinians.

The interaction between the pro-Israel lobby and the State Department, the policy struggles among the White House and the Congress and the Zionists and the diplomats, the public posturing and the bureaucratic infighting, the international efforts over nearly a century of struggle, with its resulting impact on U.S. national policy—all this is just part of the complex dynamics that makes the Israeli-Palestinian conflict the most intriguing in American diplomatic history. It promises to continue to both astound and absorb America's interest as the new century dawns.

1 | ZIONISM
Jewish Americans and the State Department, 1897–1945

"[The] problems of Zionism involve certain matters primarily related to the interests of countries other than our own."
Secretary of State Philander C. Knox, 1912[1]

"Fellow Zionists...I am here as George Bush's vice president to underscore his commitment to Israel."
Vice President J. Danforth Quayle, 1992[2]

AT THE END OF THE NINETEENTH CENTURY, Palestine emerged as an issue engaging the attention of world Jewry and the State Department. The rising interest in this eastern Mediterranean province of the Ottoman Empire resulted from the official establishment of the new political creed of Zionism in 1897 at Basle, Switzerland. The delegates, 204 Jews from fifteen countries, agreed that "Zionism aims at the creation of a home for the Jewish people in Palestine to be secured by public law" and to that end they would encourage emigration to Palestine.[3] At the time, Arabs represented 95 percent of Palestine's roughly half-million people and they owned 99 percent of the land.[4]

That same year, 1897, the first Zionist Federation was established in the United States. It attracted few followers, either from the established Jewish community in America or among the hundreds of thousands of new Jewish immigrants flocking to east coast cities to escape East European anti-Semitism and pogroms. The settled and prosperous upper class Jews of German origin believed in social assimilation. Their social position and wealth proved to them that the American melting pot worked. The last thing they wanted was to embrace an ideology that advocated establishment of a foreign country specifically for Jews, thereby bringing into question their loyalty to the land that had brought them a comfortable and secure life.

By contrast, Zionism openly rejected assimilation and the whole melting pot metaphor. As explained by Theodore Herzl when he first formulated its purpose and aims in early 1896 in his seminal pamphlet *Der Judenstaat*: "We have sincerely tried everywhere to merge with the national communities in which we live, seeking only to preserve the faith of our fathers. It is not permitted us."[5]

At its heart, this was the fundamental rationale of Zionism: a profound despair that anti-Semitism could not be eradicated as long as Jews lived among gentiles. Out of this dark vision came the belief that the only hope for the survival of the Jews lay in the founding of their own state.

Such stalwart leaders of the U.S. German-Jewish establishment as financier Jacob Schiff and Rabbi I.M. Wise instantly denounced Zionism. Wise pronounced: "Zion was a precious possession of the past...but it is not our hope of the future. America is our Zion." Schiff thought it was a "sentimental theory."[6] It came as no surprise, then, that uptown New York Jews founded in 1906 the American Jewish Committee (AJC). While not specifically formed to oppose Zionism, its establishment offered a different vision. It was an organization designed to assure that its kind of American Jews would be urbane, well educated and socially assimilated.[7]

In this quest the elitists of AJC would try to deal with the huge problems posed by the massive influx of often illiterate and isolated Eastern European Jews in a subtle and soft-spoken way. Its central strategy was to employ the medieval Jewish tradition of the *shtadlan*, the "court Jew" who served as adviser to *goyim* (non-Jewish) governments and powerful families. These were wealthy and talented Jews who had earned the trust of gentile masters and in turn could influence them on behalf of the Jewish community.[8] This determinedly low profile approach was typified at the Jewish-owned *New York Times*, where Jewish-sounding bylines were disguised by substituting initials.[9]

AJC depended on the social standing and influence of its well connected members to pursue its vision rather than on a mass membership. When one AJC officer was asked how many members the group had, he replied: "We don't count AJC members...we weigh them."[10]

Opposition to Zionism in America extended to Jewish socialists and workers, who disdained it as a form of bourgeois nationalism, while ultraorthodox religious groups considered Zionism "the most formidable enemy that has ever arisen among the Jewish people" because it sought to do God's work through politics.[11] Not even the new immigrants streaming out of Eastern Europe were immediately attracted to Zionism, as was obvious from the fact that most of them chose to bypass Palestine in favor of going to the United States and other Western countries.

With the Jewish community so divided, the State Department dismissed Zionism as merely a minority political group and essentially an internal Jewish affair. But as Zionism gained ground in Europe in the first decade of the century, it also began attracting a select group of new converts in the United States. Though small in number, probably less than 20,000 of the 2.5 million Jewish community before World War I, the new Zionists began counting among their ranks lawyers, professors and businessmen. They were slowly becoming a group that Congressmen, particularly in the eastern cities, began to listen to, if not yet closely.[12]

Still, up to World War I, American Zionism remained, in the words of a pro-Zionist writer, "a small and feeble enterprise. It provided an outlet for some thousands...who met in their societies like votaries of some bizarre cult....The movement remained an 'East Side affair,' which meant that it had no money or influence or social prestige."[13]

The State Department established a Near East Division in 1909. This was not because of an especially acute interest in Palestine and Zionism but because of America's world-view at the time. The new division had as its bailiwick an enormous region that included Russia, Germany, Austria-Hungary, the Balkans and the Ottoman Empire plus far-flung areas stretching from Persia to Abyssinia. Among such nations and the problems they posed for the United States, Palestine was not highly visible. If anything, it was becoming an annoyance. Rising Zionist demands for support of a Jewish nation were increasingly resented among U.S. diplomats, who saw such requests "as an illustration of the purely Hebraic and un-American purposes for which our Jewish community seek to use this government," in the words of one U.S. diplomat.[14]

The State Department defined its chief function as protecting and promoting American interests abroad, not in endorsing or encouraging the efforts of a small group of Americans to help found another nation in a foreign land. In the eyes of the State Department, this would be interfering in another country without any obvious U.S. interest at stake and with a good chance of worsening relations. This was especially so with the Ottoman Empire, where relations were never easy and Zionist agitation against Ottoman rule in Palestine raised suspicions in Constantinople about broader U.S. policies and goals, complicating the State Department's daily chores.

Nor did reports over the decades about the Jewish community in Palestine incline the State Department to encourage Jews to go there or to support their effort to do so. The Jews living in Palestine in the last half of the nineteenth century and the early twentieth century—about 25,000 among 500,000 Arabs[15]—were generally poor, living in squalid, crowded city housing and dependent for their sustenance on donations from Jews living abroad. After small groups of Jews fleeing the Russian Pale of Settlement began arriving in the early 1880s, they tried setting up agricultural settlements but these often proved unsuccessful. A report on one settlement by the U.S. Consul in Jerusalem, Selah Merrill, who served in Palestine, with intervals away, between 1882 to 1907, said that in 1891 he found one of the largest settlements with "houses broken...and patched, windows were stuffed with rags, yards were covered with litter, outhouses and fences were neglected, crops were poorly cultivated and weeds were growing abundantly everywhere."

Merrill's conclusion was that "Palestine is not ready for the Jews. The Jews are not ready for Palestine." He reported that conditions were so difficult in Palestine that at times as many Jews left as arrived.[16]

Although Merrill regarded the Jews of Palestine with coolness, his reports were not unique. Other consuls and travelers reported on the harshness of life in Palestine, the filth and poverty of the cities and the destitution of the Jewish community. Moreover, from the State Department's view, Palestine was foreign territory over which America had no control and in which there was already an indigenous population far surpassing in number and longevity of residence the Jews. Why create more problems with the Ottoman Empire than necessary?

Among all of its challenges around the globe, the State Department had little reason to devote much attention to Zionism or, when it did, to support Zionist goals. The aloof tone of the State Department's attitude was illustrated in 1912 when the Zionist Literary Society sought a public endorsement from President William Howard Taft. Secretary of State Philander C. Knox turned it down by replying that "problems of Zionism involve certain matters primarily related to the interests of countries other than our own...and might lead to misconstructions."[17]

Paradoxically, that same year Zionism received its greatest boost in its short history in America, an event that was to become pivotal in the founding of a Jewish state in Palestine. Louis Dembitz Brandeis, son of middle class immigrants from Prague, a brilliant attorney who had graduated at the top of his law class at Harvard, converted to Zionism. The date was 13 August 1912.[18] Brandeis was 56 years of age, a wealthy Bostonian, a political progressive, a tireless reformer and one of the most famous lawyers in the country, known as the People's Attorney because of his successful litigation against the major financiers and industrialists. He was disliked heartily by the business establishment, including the wealthy Jewish communities of New York and Boston.

What made Brandeis' conversion so surprising was that he was a non-observant Jew who believed firmly in America's melting pot and had grown up "free from Jewish contacts or traditions," as he put it.[19] It was not until he was in his fifties that Brandeis began paying attention to the Jewish experience. Rising anti-Semitism in America, exposure to Zionists and the new immigrants, and estrangement from the Brahmin society of Boston because of his espousal of populist causes all combined to sharpen his sense of ethnic kinship. Then in August 1912 Brandeis met Jacob de Haas, editor of the Boston *Jewish Advocate* and, a decade earlier, an aide to Zionism's founder Theodore Herzl. Intrigued by de Haas' tales of Herzl and the beginnings of Zionism, Brandeis hired de Haas to instruct him in Zionism over the 1912–13 winter.[20]

Within two years, on 30 August 1914, Brandeis became head of the Provisional Executive for General Zionist Affairs, making him the leader of the Zionist Central Office, which had been moved from Berlin to neutral America just before the outbreak of World War I. At the time, Zionism in America was described by a historian of the movement as still "small and weak, in great financial distress, and low in morale."[21] To invigorate Zionism, the great man, as Brandeis was considered by many, especially among young law students, attracted to the movement a brilliant group of professionals, especially from the Harvard Law School.

With his conversion came changes in Brandeis' idea about the American melting pot. He now embraced the "salad bowl," a belief in cultural pluralism in which ethnic groups maintained their unique identity. Brandeis explained:

America...has always declared herself for equality of nationalities as well as for equality of individuals. America has believed that each race had something of peculiar value which it can contribute....America has always believed that in differentiation, not in uniformity, lies the path of progress.[22]

As for the nagging question of dual loyalty, a central concern of many Jews and the gentiles' supreme suspicion about Zionism, Brandeis insisted there was no conflict between being an American and a Zionist:

Let no American imagine that Zionism is inconsistent with patriotism. Multiple loyalties are objectionable only if they are inconsistent....Every American who aids in advancing the Jewish settlement in Palestine, though he feels that neither he nor his descendants will ever live there, will likewise be a better man and a better American for doing so....There is no inconsistency between loyalty to America and loyalty to Jewry. The Jewish spirit, the product of our religion and experiences, is essentially modern and essentially American.[23]

He linked Zionism with the early New England Puritans, declaring that "Zionism is the Pilgrim inspiration and impulse over again. The descendants of the Pilgrim fathers should not find it hard to understand and sympathize with it." To Jewish audiences he said: "To be good Americans, we must be better Jews, and to be better Jews, we must become Zionists."[24]

Brandeis' Zionism, clearly, was different from the passionate and messianic Zionism of Europe, driven as it was by pessimism about the enduring anti-Semitism of the world against Jews. His was an ethnic philanthropic vision, a desire to help needy Jews set down in a kind of New England town in the Middle East—but with no intention of going to Palestine to live among them. This concept remained a central tenet of American Zionism and helps explain why through the years so few Jewish Americans have emigrated to Israel.[25]

To European Zionists, it was a pale and anemic version of their life's passion, "Zionism without Zion," they grumbled.[26] However, Brandeis would achieve what probably no other Zionist could have—exerting major influence in gaining the support of the United States for a Jewish state in Palestine. Brandeis accomplished this feat by using his friendship with President Woodrow Wilson to advocate the Zionist cause, and by serving as a conduit between British Zionists and the president. Wilson was a ready listener. He was the son of a Presbyterian minister and a daily reader of the Bible. Although not particularly interested in the political ramifications of Zionism, he shared the vague sentiment of a number of Christians at the time that there would be a certain biblical justice to have the Jews return to Palestine.

Wilson thought so highly of Brandeis that he appointed him to the Supreme Court on 28 January 1916, thereby enormously increasing Brandeis' prestige and his influence in the White House. In turn, Brandeis resigned from all the numerous public and private clubs and organizations he belonged to, including, reluctantly, his leadership of American Zionism.

His resignation, however, did not mean Brandeis had deserted Zionism. Behind the scenes he continued to play an active role. At his Supreme Court chambers in Washington he received daily reports on Zionist activities from the New York headquarters and issued orders to his loyal lieutenants now heading American Zionism.[27] When the Zionist Organization of America (ZOA) was newly reorganized in 1918, Brandeis was listed as its "honorary president." Through his lieutenants, he remained the power behind the throne.

In the same year as Brandeis ascended to the high court, David Lloyd George became prime minister of Great Britain and Arthur James Balfour foreign secretary. It was a change as advantageous for the Zionists in Britain as Brandeis' appointment was in the United States. Both Lloyd George and Balfour favored Zionism though neither of them was Jewish. Balfour once had confided to Brandeis that "I am a Zionist," while Welshman Lloyd George was a firm believer in the Old Testament's claim to the right of the Jews to Palestine.[28]

Both men shared a common concern for gaining U.S. entry into the war and support of Britain's post-war goals in dividing up the Ottoman Empire, including the ambition of taking over Palestine as part of Britain's security zone for protecting the Suez Canal, the lifeline to its colony in India. In this, they were advised by the British embassy in Washington that Britain could be helped in achieving U.S. backing by finding favor with Jewish Americans: "They are far better organized than the Irish and far more formidable. We should be in a position to get into their good graces."[29]

Although that advice failed to reflect the rifts and competing power centers within the Jewish community, it was not as misleading as it might seem. There was emerging a growing consensus among Jews and other Americans in support of a Jewish homeland in Palestine, if not for Zionism as such, and thus a British declaration favoring such a homeland was certain to be popular among a sizable number of Americans. For instance, the Presbyterian General Assembly passed a resolution in 1916 favoring a Jewish homeland in Palestine and the American Federation of Labor endorsed the idea.[30] These supporters in turn could be expected to add their influence for closer relations between London and Washington.

But there was a major problem. The State Department and its secretary, Robert Lansing, remained distinctly cool toward Zionism but not to the plight of Jews in general. Although the department was scrupulous in expending efforts to protect the rights of Jews in Palestine who were American citizens, it avoided all association with Zionists. Moreover, in the spring and summer of 1917, Lansing and his department were focused on trying to arrange a separate peace with Turkey. The thorny question of the post-war status of the empire's various minorities was not high on their priority list.[31]

Lansing was a proud, upright attorney from New York who had become an expert on international law before being appointed secretary of state by Wilson in June 1915. He had neither a close relationship with Wilson nor shared the confidence the president placed in Edward M. House, a reserve colonel from Texas who had no title or staff but wielded considerable influence as Wilson's closest adviser.[32]

At this point, the behind-the-scene actions of a Russian-born Jewish chemist living in Britain became pivotal. He was Chaim Weizmann, a persistent and persuasive leader of Zionism in Britain who later would become Israel's first president. He was a tireless toiler for Zionism and enjoyed easy access to both Lloyd George and Balfour. Aware of their desire for U.S. support, Weizmann sought a backdoor past the State Department to the White House via Brandeis. On 8 April 1917, Weizmann cabled Brandeis, advising that "an expression of opinion coming from yourself and perhaps other gentlemen connected with the Government in favor of a Jewish Palestine under a British protectorate would greatly strengthen our hands."[33]

A month later, following America's entry into World War I, Brandeis had a forty-five minute meeting with Wilson on the president's views of Palestine. Afterwards, Brandeis was convinced that Wilson was "entirely sympathetic to the aims of the Zionist Movement" and favored a British protectorate in Palestine. However, he concluded Wilson did not want to make a public declaration because of the international complications such a statement would cause, not least of them the futile hope that Turkey still could be persuaded to quit the war.[34]

Another attempt in mid-September by London to gain from Wilson support of a declaration backing the Zionist movement, this time of a specific draft statement endorsing a Jewish homeland in Palestine, similarly was rebuffed. Wilson ordered Colonel House to tell the British that "the time was not opportune for any definite statement further, perhaps, than one of sympathy, provided it can be made without conveying any real commitment."[35]

In desperation, Weizmann cabled Brandeis that it "would greatly help if President Wilson and yourself would support the text. Matter most urgent. Please telegraph."[36] Brandeis was able to use his access to the White House to meet with Colonel House and together they assured Weizmann that

> from talks I have had with President and from expressions of opinion given to closest advisers I feel I can answer you in that he is [in] entire sympathy with declaration quoted in yours of nineteenth as approved by the foreign office and the Prime Minister. I of course heartily agree.[37]

Weizmann felt more was needed to counteract anti-Zionist sentiment in Britain, where there was strong opposition to Zionism, particularly from the only Jew in the Lloyd George Cabinet, Edwin Montagu, the secretary of state for India. Montagu had weighed in with a strong anti-Zionist assessment by one of the greatest Arabists of the time, Gertrude Bell, a colleague of T.E. Lawrence and currently involved in British intelligence in Cairo. She wrote that

> two considerations rule out the conception of an independent Jewish Palestine from practical politics. The first is that the province as we know it is not Jewish, and that neither Mohammedan nor Arab would accept Jewish authority; the second that the capital, Jerusalem, is equally

sacred to three faiths, Jewish, Christian and Muslim, and should never,
if it can be avoided, be put under the exclusive control of any one loca-
tion, no matter how carefully the rights of the other two may be safe-
guarded.[38]

To appease the anti-Zionists, the British Cabinet drafted a revised declaration. It specifically addressed Montagu's concern about non-Zionist Jews living
outside of Palestine by adding a final clause that said the establishment of a Jewish
national home would not prejudice the "rights and political status enjoyed in any
other country by such Jews who are fully contented with their existing nationality."[39]

Once again, Weizmann turned to Brandeis to help get Wilson's endorsement of the new text. In a long letter on 7 October, Weizmann wrote that "I have no
doubt that the amended text of the declaration will be again submitted to the President and it would be most invaluable if the President would accept it without res-
ervation and would recommend the granting of the declaration *now*.[40] [Italics in
original.]

When the British Foreign Office sent the draft to Wilson at about the
same time, he turned it over to Brandeis for his comments. The Justice and his
aides redrafted it in slightly stronger and cleaner language, substituting "the Jewish people" for "the Jewish race"—thereby muting the vexing question of who's-
a-Jew—and making the final clause read that there would be no prejudice to the
"rights and political status enjoyed by Jews in any other country," thus assuaging
the concern of assimilated Jews about dual loyalty.[41]

Colonel House sent the revision onto Wilson, but, in the midst of world
war, he felt no urgency about the matter. It was not until 13 October that he sent a
memo to House saying:

I find in my pocket the memorandum you gave me about the Zionist
Movement. I am afraid I did not say to you that I concurred in the
formula suggested by the other side [Britain]. I do, and would be obliged
if you would let them know it.[42]

Thus, in the most off-handed way possible, Wilson lent the enormous
weight of the United States to supporting the Zionist dream of a Jewish state in
Palestine. He did this without informing Lansing or seeking the advice of the State
Department, a snub they were not soon to forget. Although Wilson declined at the
time actually to make a public endorsement, his private agreement provided Lloyd
George the backing in the cabinet that he needed to issue a declaration. Wilson's
seemingly casual action was to have a profound effect on Middle East history and
on the daily lives of Palestinians.

Its immediate result came on 2 November 1917, when Britain issued the
fateful statement that was to become known as the Balfour Declaration. It came in
the form of a personal letter from Foreign Secretary Balfour to a prominent British
Jew, Lionel Walter, the second Lord of Rothschild:

Foreign Office,
November 2nd, 1917
Dear Lord Rothchild,
I have much pleasure in conveying to you, on behalf of His Majesty's
Government, the following declaration of sympathy with Jewish Zionist aspirations which has been submitted to, and approved by, the Cabinet:
"His Majesty's Government view with favour the establishment in Palestine of a national home for the Jewish people, and will use their best
endeavours to facilitate the achievement of this object, it being clearly
understood that nothing shall be done which may prejudice the civil
and religious rights of existing non-Jewish communities in Palestine,
or the rights and political status enjoyed by Jews in any other country."
I should be grateful if you would bring this declaration to the knowledge
of the Zionist Federation.
Yours,
Arthur James Balfour[43]

Arabs and anti-Zionists could not help noting the totally pro-Zionist content of the declaration. It failed to mention Christians or Muslims, Arabs or Palestinians, even though they remained by far the majority population in Palestine. At
the time, there were about 55,000 Jews and nearly 600,000 Palestinians in Palestine.[44] Yet, the Balfour Declaration spoke of a Jewish homeland, which was widely
understood to mean a Jewish state, although many Zionists continued to deny that
was their goal. Also, it pledged actively to help Jews while merely promising to
protect the rights of "the non-Jewish communities."

Lansing and the State Department had been humiliated by being bypassed.
Insult was added when Wilson waited until 14 December to inform his secretary of
state of his support of the Balfour Declaration. The occasion was prompted by a
letter Lansing had sent the day before to Wilson reporting that there was mounting
pressure from Zionists for the United States to issue its own declaration supporting
a Jewish homeland. Lansing included a detailed analysis of the issue:

My judgment is that we should go very slowly in announcing a policy
for three reasons. *First*, we are not at war with Turkey and therefore
should avoid any appearance of favoring taking territory from that
Empire by force. *Second*, the Jews are by no means a unit in the desire
to reestablish their race as an independent people; to favor one or the
other faction would seem to be unwise. *Third*, many Christian sects and
individuals would undoubtedly resent turning the Holy Land over to
the absolute control of the race credited with the death of Christ.

For practical purposes, I do not think that we need go further
than the first reason given since that is ample ground for declining to
announce a policy in regard to the final disposition of Palestine.[45]

The next day Wilson handed back to Lansing his letter. Lansing filed it
with a note: "The President returned me this letter at Cabinet Meeting, December

14, 1917, saying that very unwillingly he was forced to agree with me, but said that he had an impression that we had assented to the British declaration regarding returning Palestine to the Jews."[46]

Nonetheless, Wilson continued to refuse to make a public endorsement of the Balfour Declaration, with the result that Lansing continued to act as though the president's private support had no weight. On 28 February 1918, Lansing wrote to Wilson opposing a request by the Zionists to be issued passports to take part in a Zionist commission sponsored by Britain to tour Palestine. In his letter, Lansing wrote that the United States never had accepted the Balfour Declaration and should not sponsor an organization with distinctly political goals. Wilson agreed with his secretary of state.[47]

By this time Wilson was being hailed among Jews around the world as a lover of Zion on the basis of leaks about his private support of the Balfour Declaration. But, in fact, pro-Zionism was not official U.S. policy nor had Wilson yet uttered a single public word of support. It was only after a personal meeting with crusading Zionist Rabbi Stephen S. Wise in August 1918 that Wilson finally took the plunge, albeit in a very circumspect way. It was in the form of a Jewish New Year's greeting to the Jews praising the work of a Zionist commission currently investigating conditions in Palestine.

> I have watched with deep and sincere interest the reconstructive work which the Weizmann Commission has done in Palestine at the instance of the British Government, and I welcome an opportunity to express the satisfaction I have felt in the progress of the Zionist Movement in the United States and in the Allied countries since the declaration by Mr. Balfour on behalf of the British Government, of Great Britain's approval of the establishment in Palestine of a national home for the Jewish people, and his promise that the British Government would use its best endeavors to facilitate the achievement of that object, with the understanding that nothing would be done to prejudice the civil and religious rights of non-Jewish people in Palestine or the rights and political status enjoyed by Jews in other countries.[48]

While Zionists exultantly hailed this letter as America's commitment to the Balfour Declaration, the State Department denied that it expressed official policy. The department had not taken part in its drafting and therefore in its view the letter was little more than an expression of Wilson's personal sentiments. As diplomatic historian Frank E. Manual observed: "[Such presidential letters] have a peculiar status in American foreign policy. They are expressions of [presidential] attitude, and the degree to which they may be formal commitments of any sort, especially when they do not pass through the State Department, remains dubious."[49]

As late as 26 May 1922, the head of the Near East Division, Allan W. Dulles, later to become one of America's spymasters, wrote: "Ex-President Wilson is understood to have favored the Balfour Declaration, but I do not know that he ever committed himself to it in an official and public way."[50]

Such divisions and confusion between the State Department and the White

House and Congress as well were to remain a distinct feature of U.S. policy toward Palestine. While the politicians over the decades were quick to issue vague letters and declarations of support for various Zionist enterprises, the experts of the State Department resisted change and clung to a strict interpretation of policy. The resulting confusion more often then not left all sides in doubt about what U.S. policy at any one time actually was.

The final achievement of Brandeis and American Zionism in the post-war period was the passage by Congress on 11 September 1922 of a joint resolution favoring a Jewish homeland in Palestine. The words of the resolution practically echoed the Balfour Declaration.

> *Resolved by the Senate and House of Representatives of the United States of America in Congress assembled,* That the United States of America favors the establishment in Palestine of a national home for the Jewish people, it being clearly understood that nothing shall be done which may prejudice the civil and religious rights of Christian and all other non-Jewish communities in Palestine, and that the Holy places and religious buildings and sites in Palestine shall be adequately protected.[51]

The Zionists loudly trumpeted the resolution as another Balfour Declaration, evidence that their quest had official support. After all, it had been sponsored by Senator Henry Cabot Lodge and Representative Hamilton Fish and signed by President Warren G. Harding. However, during the debate leading up to passage of the resolution, a number of speakers had emphasized that it was merely an expression of sympathy by the Congress and that the resolution in no way would involve the United States in foreign entanglements. This was the interpretation adopted by the State Department. Like Wilson's 1918 letter endorsing Balfour, the department simply ignored it. When an Italian diplomat directly asked a State Department officer whether the resolution represented the official policy of the United States Government, the diplomat merely smiled.[52]

Passage of the congressional resolution was the height of Brandeis' brand of American Zionism, and also the end of its heroic period. Under Brandeis the Zionist membership had burgeoned tenfold, reaching around 200,000 after the heralded victory of the Balfour Declaration. The momentum of that historic event carried over into the halls of Congress and resulted in the joint resolution. But a year before the resolution became a reality, Brandeis himself was swept from power in Zionist councils in a showdown with Weizmann. Brandeis' tepid form of Zionism was simply too emotionalless and sterile for the crusader from Pinsk, the Russian town Weizmann called his birthplace. In a final confrontation in the spring of 1921, Weizmann declared: "There is no bridge between Washington and Pinsk."[53]

Under Weizmann's assault, Brandeis's leadership was repudiated by the American Zionist Organization at its 24th convention in Cleveland in June 1921. Brandeis quit the movement, taking with him some of his most brilliant lieutenants, among them his protege Felix Frankfurter, who was to become a justice on the Supreme Court. Brandeis' participation in the internecine politics of Zionism was at an end, although not his avid interest in the goals of Zionism. He remained committed to a Jewish home in Palestine until his death at age 84 in 1941.[54]

The blow to American Zionism caused by Brandeis' ouster was devastating. By 1929, there were no more than 18,000 members left in the ZOA.[55] It was not until the rise of Hitler and then the horrific stories of his "final solution," which began leaking out of occupied Europe in the early 1940s, that American Zionism again became a potent force, this time far stronger and more influential than Brandeis—much less the experts at the State Department—ever could have envisioned.

* *

Zionists were quick to impute anti-Semitism to explain the enduring opposition to Zionism by the State Department and succeeding secretaries of state, both Democratic and Republican, during the first half of the twentieth century. While no doubt some American diplomats reflected a distrust of Jews prevalent among the genteel society of the time and some few even might have harbored anti-Semitic emotions, the department's attitude was grounded in rational geopolitical reasons beyond racism.

Foremost, the State Department believed it had no business supporting the narrow political platform of a small sect that sought foreign territory. In effect, the Zionists were pursuing their own foreign policy. To take two major examples: It was not in U.S. interests to anger Constantinople during the war years when Washington was seeking a separate peace with Turkey. Nor, as the economic importance of oil grew, was it in Washington's interests to anger the Arabs. Yet, the Zionists not only pressed ahead with their program to establish a Jewish state in Palestine but they repeatedly sought to pressure through flattery or threat the president, the Congress and the State Department to support them.

There was also the question of Americans sending money overseas to aid a foreign project. As State Department lawyers observed: "It requires little discussion" that the proper function of government does not include "encouraging its nationals to deplete the national wealth by contributions of funds or investment of funds in foreign countries."[56] Implicit in this observation was the troubling question of dual loyalty.

Clustered with the issue of dual loyalty was the romance of the American melting pot. As the Civil War brutally had proved, the majority of Americans believed their nation was indivisible and should share a common cultural milieu. Religious diversity was a right, but ethnic exclusivism was widely perceived as a threat to the common fabric holding together a nation of immigrants. The Zionists' desertion of the melting pot for a salad bowl of ethnic groups was an affront to many Americans, including the traditionalists who guided the State Department.

Finally, there were the troubling facts about Palestine. The Arabs were the majority community, and had been for well over a millennium. Palestinians were a recognizable separate people with their own institutions, traditions and cultural uniqueness. Yet, Zionists were proposing not only to deny Arabs their Wilsonian right of self-determination—a cherished U.S. ideal—but to displace them as the major ethnic group. It was clear to nearly all observers that this could happen only by force, yet it was equally obvious that war and instability in the region were not in America's interests.

It was from these analyses that the State Department's coolness to Zionism derived. Policymakers were not necessarily anti-Semites, as Zionists charged, just because they believed support of Zionism was not in U.S. interests. Nonetheless, the Zionists were not mistaken in feeling a resentment and even hostility against them in the State Department.

Simply in terms of human relations, shorn of all questions of anti-Semitism, the department had ample reason to distrust the Zionists. The success of Brandeis and the Zionists in gaining the ear of the president and the Congress for projects opposed by the department was at best irritating. The diplomats did not consider it gentlemanly or fair for the Zionists to go behind their back and manipulate vote-conscious political leaders. As in the case of Wilson's support of the Balfour Declaration, this often occurred without the department even knowing what was going on until after it had already happened. Such tactics raised the ire of the proud diplomats, who perceived the Zionists as meddling in their elitist preserve, which of course it was.

Probably no tactic employed by the Zionists caused greater resentment than their efforts directly to intimidate the State Department and its staff. One such effort serves to demonstrate the Zionist technique. It was a highly effective tactic, and continues to be, and it goes far in explaining why the professionals at the State Department and successive secretaries of state harbored various degrees of animosity towards the Zionists.

The case involved an urbane and highly successful diplomat, Hugh Gibson. At the age of 36 in 1919 he was the newly installed ambassador to Poland, or to use the grandiose title of the day, the envoy extraordinary and minister plenipotentiary. Post-war Poland was home to one of the largest and least assimilated Jewish communities in Europe and their troubles were trumpeted by the Zionists as an example of ruthless anti-Semitism. In fact, anti-Semitic incidents were common, but not as common in Gibson's view as claimed by American Zionists. To his mother he wrote: "These yarns are exclusively of foreign manufacture for anti-Polish purposes."[57]

Gibson's skeptical reports to the State Department about the troubles of Polish Jews came to the attention of Brandeis. On 24 June 1919, Gibson was called by Colonel House to a meeting with the fabled justice and his protege, Felix Frankfurter. Gibson not only was at a disadvantage because of Brandeis' exalted status but also because his appointment as ambassador to Poland had yet to be confirmed by the Senate.

In Gibson's words, the two Zionists opened what the young diplomat later called the "prosecution" by saying that

> I had done more mischief to the Jewish race than anyone who had lived
> in the last century. They said...that my reports on the Jewish question
> had gone around the world and had undone their work....They finally
> said that I had stated that the stories of excesses against the Jews were
> exaggerated, to which I replied that they certainly were and I should
> think any Jew would be glad to know it.

Frankfurter claimed that Gibson "had no right to make reports to the department in regard to Jewish matters and should have 'refused' on the ground that I could not possibly learn enough about them to make even general observations." Frankfurter then hinted that if Gibson continued his reports that Zionists would block his confirmation as ambassador to Poland by the Senate.

Gibson was so furious by the confrontation that he wrote a twenty-one page letter about it to his friends in the State Department, including Frankfurter's claim that Gibson should not report on Jews. Nothing is more disconcerting or insulting to a diplomat than to have his reporting questioned, much less to be advised that he had no "right" to report on certain matters. Reporting is the secret heart of the diplomat's art, a talent especially valued in Washington where officials in those pre-television days depended on it as their window to the world beyond. Frankfurter could hardly have raised a more sensitive question or one more certain to raise the hackles of diplomats. Gibson went further in his letter than just describe his encounter. He also shared his suspicions of what the Zionists were trying to accomplish—"a conscienceless and cold-blooded plan to make the condition of the Jews in Poland so bad that they must turn to Zionism for relief."

The State Department in those days was a far more closed and clubby establishment of upper class scions than after 1945. This attack on one of its own was highly resented. A rising star of the foreign service had been humiliated and threatened by a justice of the Supreme Court acting as a spokesperson for a narrow Jewish group not even accepted by most Jews. Rancor was particularly strong in the Warsaw embassy, where it lingered for years. In 1923, Vice Consul Monroe H. Kline reported: "It is common knowledge that this race of people [Jews] are continually and constantly spreading propaganda, through their agencies over the entire world, of political and religious persecution." He added: "The Jew in business oppresses the Pole to a far greater extent than does the Pole oppress the Jew in a political way."

One of the consequences of the Gibson case, and similar if less dramatic ones over the years, was that Zionism would have few good friends, high in the State Department until Henry A. Kissinger became Secretary of State in 1973. As for Gibson, he went on to serve honorably as an ambassador in various posts until his retirement on the eve of World War II. Despite his early promise, however, he never became one of the department's principal officers.

* *

American Zionism awakened from its long slumber in 1935 with Stephen

S. Wise's assumption of the leadership of the Zionist Organization of America. An immigrant from a notable family in Budapest, Wise was a tireless reformer, a crusading liberal and a rabbi well respected among Christians. In his youth he had met Theodore Herzl and been inspired by his vision. But when Brandeis left the Zionist organization in 1921 Wise was one of the brainy members who went with him. Wise's return to organized Zionism marked a period where American Zionism again began regaining respect and influence, although most of America's four million Jews still rejected the political creed. Wise was very much in the Brandeis mode in terms of quietly promoting the cause with influential political leaders. In this he was highly successful because he enjoyed the friendship of President Franklin D. Roosevelt and, like Brandeis before him, had easy entree into the White House.

The State Department in the pre-war years remained opposed to Zionism, although Roosevelt himself was a supporter for most of his presidency until his ideas changed toward the end. Roosevelt actively encouraged the British to remain committed to the Balfour Declaration and not to cut back on Jewish immigration into Palestine. In the late 1930s and early 1940s, he even considered a plan to place all of Palestine under Jewish control and move the entire Palestinian population to Iraq. In a February 1940 meeting with Weizmann, Roosevelt reportedly said to the world leader of Zionism: "What about the Arabs? Can't that be settled with a little baksheesh?" Weizmann took his meaning to be that the Palestinians should be paid off as an incentive to leave the land.[58]

At about the same time, a voice harsher than Wise's began to be heard in American Zionism. It was Abba Hillel Silver, a former protege of Wise, who began speaking out in uncompromising words demanding Jewish rights. In 1940 he declared a "maximalist" Zionist position: "We'll force the President to swallow our demands! The gentle, patient and personal diplomatic approach of yesterday is not entirely adequate for our days."[59] He also advised: "Put not your faith in princes."[60] It was a tone usually missing from the rhetoric of American Zionists and it soon caught attention, propelling Silver into the national realm of Zionist politics.

Silver was an aggressive and pugnacious native of Lithuania who arrived in America at age nine, son of a rabbi and a future rabbi himself in the prestigious Congregation Tifereth Israel in Cleveland. He was a fierce foe of assimilation and, in fact, preached the opposite creed—to be "more" Jewish rather than less: "We are going to respond to every attack upon our people, to every libel and every slander, by more Jewishness, by more schools and synagogues and by more intensive and loyal work in Palestine."[61]

While Silver's stirring oratory and defiant ways brought Zionism great victories, it left him largely unloved even among his followers. Roosevelt did not like him and Truman despised him so much that he barred him and all Zionists from the White House. As Nahum Goldmann, one of world Zionism's leaders, said: "He was an Old Testament Jew who never forgave or forgot....He could be extremely ruthless in a fight, and there was something of the terrorist in his manner and bearing."[62] Silver's belligerent, in-your-face Jewishness strongly contributed to the emergence of Zionism's "loud diplomacy" that has since marked the ugly side of the Zionist lobby.[63]

Despite its lack of finesse, or perhaps because of it, the Israeli lobby was born under Silver's leadership of American Zionism. Silver's stature was greatly enhanced at the 1942 extraordinary convention of Zionists at the Hotel Biltmore in New York. Along with 586 delegates from around the nation were two foreign guests, Weizmann, now the grand old man of world Zionism, and David Ben Gurion, head of the Jewish Agency—the de facto Jewish government in Palestine—and the crusty leader of Palestine's Jewish community. Weizmann by now had mellowed and represented the minimal Zionist position, urging cautious steps toward establishing a Jewish state. The leader of American Zionism, Stephen Wise, also embraced this position. Ben Gurion represented Abba Hillel Silver's maximalist demand for a "Jewish commonwealth," the new code word for a state that was adopted so as not to cause undue concern among Arabs and their supporters.

While Weizmann and Wise espoused a cautious course, Ben Gurion demanded a postwar Palestine in which there was adherence to the Balfour Declaration and active Zionism, by which he informed the delegates he meant "nation-building, state-building."[64] Silver joined Ben Gurion, saying: "We must make [the Christians] understand that...the ultimate solution to the Jewish problem must finally be sounded, and the ultimate solution is the establishment of a Jewish nation in Palestine."[65]

The conference overwhelmingly supported Ben Gurion and Silver, passing on 11 May what later became known as the Biltmore Declaration. It called for the founding of a "Jewish commonwealth" in Palestine.[66] The Biltmore Declaration marked the beginning of the changing of the guard in American and world Zionism. The torch was being passed from Weizmann and Wise, the minimalists, to Ben Gurion and Silver, the maximalists. Silver's ascension was essentially secured the next year at a meeting called by the American Jewish Conference in New York on 22 August 1943.

The Jewish Conference embraced the most representative gathering of Jewish Americans ever held up to that time. All told, 8,486 local groups elected 379 delegates in all forty-eight states and the District of Columbia representing 1.5 million Jewish Americans. Another 125 delegates were chosen by sixty-four national Jewish organizations.[67]

Stories of the horrors of the holocaust enveloping the Jewish community of Europe were by now rife within the American community, and the 504 delegates at the Waldorf-Astoria in New York were not in a timorous mood. When Silver heard that Wise failed even to mention a "Jewish commonwealth" in his speech, he confronted the old Zionist veteran, his senior by nineteen years, and upbraided him so viciously that a witness said it was embarrassing to watch.[68]

Silver took the dais and delivered a thundering speech. "Why has there arisen among us today this mortal fear of the term Jewish commonwealth?....How long is the crucifixion of Israel to last?....Enough! There must be a final end to all this, a sure and certain end." By which he meant the earliest possible establishment of a Jewish state.[69]

The cheering delegates gave Silver a standing ovation, broke into the Zionist anthem of *Hatikvah* and endorsed the Biltmore Declaration by a vote of 480 to 4 with others abstaining. Silver emerged the hero of the meeting and a power in American Zionism challenging the dominance that only Wise had enjoyed in recent years. When Wise encountered Silver in a corridor, he pleaded: "Rabbi Silver, I am an old man, and have had my moment in the sun. You are a young man, and will have your proper share of fame. It is not necessary for you to attack me." Silver walked away without a word.[70]

While Silver was not loved and "rarely recognized peers," in the words of one of his employees, he was considerate of his staff and a superb organizer, as the emerging Jewish lobby proved.[71] Silver's spurt in prominence brought him to the co-chairmanship with Wise of the American Emergency Committee for Zionist Affairs (AECZA), an umbrella group representing the Zionist Organization of America, Hadassah and two smaller groups representing religious and labor Zionists.[72] Silver immediately became the dominating force, changed AECZA to AZEC, the American Zionist Emergency Council, and energetically embarked on what his public relations aide Si Kenen called without exaggeration "a political and public relations offensive to capture the support of congressmen, clergy, editors, professors, business and labor."[73]

In the process he created the modern Israeli lobby, the most pervasive and powerful special interest group in foreign affairs in the United States.[74] AZEC's budget soared from $100,000 to $500,000 and activists were instructed that "the first task is to make direct contact with your local Congressman or Senator." Others were targeted too: union members, wives and parents of servicemen, Jewish war veterans. Form letters were provided so local activists could commend, or condemn, newspaper articles and editorials. Schedules of anti-Zionist lecture tours were provided so the events could be picketed or otherwise opposed.[75]

Zionist action groups were organized at the grassroots with more than 400 local committees under seventy-six state and regional branches. These volunteers carried out the local campaigns and even funded groups to visit Washington where they met with Congressmen. When called on, they flooded with letters the White House and State Department. Millions of leaflets and pamphlets poured out of the Zionist offices. Books, articles and academic studies, often by non-Jews, were funded by the AZEC, including Walter Clay Lowdermilk's *Palestine, Land of Promise*, which became a best-seller in 1944. Massive petition and letter-writing campaigns were undertaken. One such petition, supporting the Biltmore Declaration, was signed by more than 150 college presidents and deans and 1,800 faculty members from 250 colleges and universities in forty-five states.[76]

Christian support was actively enlisted. The American Palestine Committee, an elitist Protestant group, was revived with secret Zionist funds, eventually reaching $150,000 in 1946.[77] "In every community an American Christian Palestine Committee must be immediately organized," ordered Silver's headquarters.[78] Another group, the Christian Council on Palestine, was formed among clergymen. It grew to 3,000 members by the end of the war. The aim of both groups was to "crystallize the sympathy of Christian America for our cause," in the words of an internal AZEC memo. How completely they were controlled by the Zionists became clear when the Christians felt it necessary to complain that AZEC was making statements in their names without prior consultation.[79]

The support of American labor also was enlisted through the founding of the American Jewish Trade Union Committee for Palestine. Its honorary chairmen were the heads of the CIO and AFL and the vice chairmen numbered nearly every important labor leader in America. The chairman was Max Zaritsky, president of the Hatters Union, who later would testify before the House Committee on Foreign Affairs: "American organized labor—twelve million strong—unreservedly and unequivocally supports the aspiration of the Jewish people for the establishment of their homeland in Palestine."[80]

Newspaper ads were taken out to support the cause, massive demonstrations held—including at New York's Madison Square Garden—and even pageants produced. Playwright Ben Hecht, a radical Zionist who thought Silver too moderate, wrote a 1943 hit called *We Will Never Die*. He enlisted Billy Rose to produce, Moss Hart to direct and Kurt Weill to do the music and such stars as Edward G. Robinson and Paul Muni to act in it as well as a young upcoming actor, Marlon Brando. The play toured the country, drawing in big crowds; in Washington Eleanor Roosevelt and most of the Supreme Court justices attended.[81]

Such activity was not exclusively the work of Silver and his AZEC group but all of it was motivated by the broad spectrum of American Jewry supporting a homeland. Membership in major Zionist groups soared, more than doubling to 400,000 by 1945.[82] The results of their efforts were impressive. By 1944 more than 3,000 non-Jewish organizations ranging from the Elks to the Grange passed pro-Zionist petitions and backed them up with petitions and letters to Washington. Such distinguished Protestant theologians as Paul Tillich and Reinhold Niebuhr actively supported the Zionists. Statements of support came from 411 of the 535 members of the Senate and House.[83]

In 1944, for the first time, both political parties had planks endorsing a commonwealth in Palestine. The Republicans called for unlimited Jewish immigration and the establishment of "a free and democratic commonwealth" while the Democrats were more specific and mentioned a "Jewish commonwealth."[84]

Zionism, fueled by the horrors of the holocaust against European Jews, had come of age in American domestic politics. Yet this development appears to have had little impact on President Roosevelt's ideas about Palestine and the Jews. It was the broader strategic realities that captured his attention. As the war years went by and the support of the Arabs, particularly Saudi Arabia and its oil, became more important, Roosevelt's concern about the negative geopolitical implications of Zionism grew. By 1943 he appears to have deserted the Zionist platform in favor of a scheme by which the holy land would be controlled jointly by Arabs, Christians and Jews. A report to the State Department from Colonel Harold B. Hoskins, a presidential agent who served as Roosevelt's private adviser and intelligence gatherer on the Middle East, said Roosevelt told him:

This concept to be successful would, he realized, have to be presented as a solution larger and more inclusive than the establishment of an Arab state or of a Jewish state. He realized that this idea, of course, required further thought and needed to be worked out in greater detail, but at least that was the line along which his mind was running.[85]

That same year Roosevelt privately assured Saudi Arabia and other Arab nations that the United States would not act on Palestine's future without consulting with both Arabs and Jews. These assurances were not leaked by any of the Arab countries or Washington. It was not until after Roosevelt's meeting with Saudi King Abdul Aziz ibn Saud on 14 February 1945 in the middle of the Suez Canal aboard a U.S. warship, the cruiser *Quincy*, that he repeated his promise of prior consultation. He officially put it in writing in a letter to his "great and good friend" the king on 5 April 1945:

> Your majesty will recall that on previous occasions I communicated to you the attitude of the American Government toward Palestine and made clear our desire that no decision be taken with respect to the basic situation in that country without full consultation with both Arabs and Jews. Your Majesty will also doubtless recall that during our recent conversation I assured you that I would take no action, in my capacity as Chief of the Executive Branch of this Government, which might prove hostile to the Arab people.[86]

The letter was made public six months later by the State Department at the urging of Saudi Arabia.[87]

Unfortunately for anyone trying to make sense of U.S. policy on Palestine, only the month before, on 16 March, Roosevelt had bowed to Zionist complaints about his meeting with Ibn Saud and authorized Rabbi Wise to issue a public statement that the president continued to believe in both unlimited Jewish immigration and establishment of a Jewish state. Now, with Roosevelt's pledge to Ibn Saud, the State Department was left trying to reconcile Roosevelt's contradictory pledges. An internal State Department memorandum written on 6 April, the day after Roosevelt's letter to Ibn Saud, laid out the problem:

> We secured the President's approval to a message to our Near Eastern posts explaining that while the President did authorize Rabbi Wise to make this statement, it referred only to possible action at some future date and that the President of course had in mind his pledges to the Arabs that they as well as the Jew would be consulted. This reply will probably not satisfy the Arabs, but it seemed to be the only constructive course of action open to us. In our opinion the situation is so serious, and the adverse effect upon our long-term position in the Near East so likely, that we should reconsider the entire position, adopt a definite policy on Palestine, and obtain the President's concurrence, with the hope of averting any future misunderstandings as to what our policy actually is...Of course, if we were actually to implement the policy which the Zionists desire, the results would be disastrous.[88]

The memorandum reflected a pattern of conciliation by an anxious bureaucracy trying to wed presidential political statements to statecraft and American interests. For the diplomats this was an essentially hopeless effort, because the reality was that presidents did not understand the true dimensions of the Palestinian question and, moreover, were blinded to it by the lures of domestic politics. They treated the Zionist dream at best as a ticket to election and in some cases overladen, as with Wilson, with a Christian sympathy for the Jewish association with the holy land. They failed to understand the enormous complexities of Zionism's international ramifications, and certainly none of them understood or sympathized with the unique predicament of the Palestinians.

Despite his sophistication, Roosevelt, like the presidents before and after him, suffered this myopia. For Roosevelt, his eyes were opened to Arab concerns during his meeting with Ibn Saud. It was the first meeting between a U.S. president and an Arab leader, and it shed a new light onto the issue.

Roosevelt came away from the session deeply impressed by the profound hostility of the Arabs to Zionism and the certain belief that a Jewish state could not be founded without force. On the way home, Roosevelt confided to Secretary of State Edward R. Stettinius that he "must have a conference with Congressional leaders and re-examine our entire policy in Palestine." In an address to Congress, he said that "I learned more about that whole problem, the Muslim problem, the Jewish problem, by talking with Ibn Saud for five minutes than I could have learned in the exchange of two or three dozen letters." He summoned Judge Joseph Proskauer of the American Jewish Committee and told him to try to dampen Jewish hopes for a homeland because such an effort would certainly lead to war or a pogrom. In the circumstances, he added, a Jewish homeland was absolutely impossible at the present time.[89]

On the last day of his life, 12 April 1945, Roosevelt sent telegrams to both Iraq and Syria repeating his pledge about consultation. A similar message was sent by the secretary of state to Lebanon.[90] Three hours after his last telegram was cabled, Roosevelt was dead at age 63.

Now the vice president, Harry S. Truman, not only would inherit the presidency but also the attention of a Zionist lobby determined to marshal all of its vast resources and energies to secure a Jewish homeland in Palestine.

2 | PARTITION
The Division of Palestine, 1945–1948

"...the creation of a viable Jewish state...in an adequate area of Palestine instead of in the whole of Palestine [would be acceptable]."
President Harry S. Truman, 1946[1]

"My administration would not support the creation of any Palestinian entity that would jeopardize the security of our strategic ally, Israel."
Presidential candidate George Bush, 1988[2]

HARRY S. TRUMAN HAD BEEN PRESIDENT less than a week when Secretary of State Edward R. Stettinius Jr. sent him a memorandum warning that Zionists probably would seek to get from him a commitment to establishing a Jewish state in Palestine. At the time, it was a popular position. The horrors and the dimensions of the holocaust that had nearly destroyed European Jewry were becoming clearer every day as World War II entered its final gasp. Zionists were joined by millions of Americans in their revulsion at the Nazi genocide, lending sympathy, however indirectly, for the main Zionist aim of securing Palestine for Jews. It was an issue that was persistently forcing itself on the White House and could not be ignored by the new president, as Stettinius' 18 April 1945 memo made clear.

> Dear Mr. President:
> It is very likely that efforts will be made by some of the Zionist leaders to obtain from you at an early date some commitments in favor of the Zionist program which is pressing for unlimited Jewish immigration into Palestine and the establishment there of a Jewish state.
> As you are aware, the Government and people of the United States have every sympathy for the persecuted Jews of Europe and are doing all in their power to relieve their suffering. The question of Palestine is, however, a highly complex one and involves questions which go far beyond the plight of the Jews of Europe. If this question shall come up, therefore, before you in the form of a request to make a public statement on the matter, I believe you would probably want to call for

27

full and detailed information on the subject before taking any particular position in the premises. I should be very glad, therefore, to hold myself in readiness to furnish you with background information on this subject any time you may desire.

There is continual tenseness in the situation in the Near East largely as a result of the Palestine question and as we have interests in that area which are vital to the United States, we feel that this whole subject is one that should be handled with the greatest care and with a view to the long-range interests of this country.[3]

Two days later, Rabbi Stephen S. Wise, still a major figure in American Zionism and the one most admired by Christians, arrived at the White House for a courtesy call. When he left fifteen minutes later, Wise had no reason to be disappointed. Truman assured him that he had read the Balfour Declaration and Roosevelt's statements on Palestine, that he was concerned about the welfare of Europe's displaced Jewish population and—perhaps the best news of all for Wise—that he was "skeptical...about some of the views and attitudes assumed by the 'striped-pants boys' in the State Department. It seemed to me that they didn't care enough about what happened to the thousands of displaced persons who were involved."[4]

Here were three themes that would remain central in the mind of the new president from Missouri with little foreign experience when he considered Palestine: the suffering of Jewish displaced persons—DPs in the parlance of the day; dislike boarding on distrust of the State Department, and belief in the Balfour Declaration.[5] He had little or no understanding of Palestine itself or of the Palestinians and their own increasingly desperate plight. He similarly seemed to have little feeling for Jews in general. Ultimately, he came to absolutely despise Zionists. But he believed the Balfour Declaration promised Jews a Palestinian homeland and, in his words, it was a "promise [that] should be kept."[6]

A fourth consideration, one that came to dominate Truman's thinking as elections loomed, was the 5-million strong Jewish American community. As it became more powerful through its lobbying organizations and more unified in favoring a Jewish state in Palestine, Truman came increasingly to look at the Jewish lobby as a source of organized strength to counterbalance his numerous political foes.[7] He planned to seek election on his own as the Democratic standard bearer in 1948. But he was detested by the right of his own party, distrusted by the left and under suspicion in the traditionally Democratic south.[8]

Truman received political advice from Judge Samuel I. Rosenman, whom he had inherited from Roosevelt as a speech writer and adviser. While not a Zionist himself, Rosenman was important to Truman for his contacts with the Jewish community and he was active in furthering Jewish causes. When Rosenman left in mid-1946, he was replaced by an ardent supporter of Zionism whom Truman came to depend on heavily for political advice. He was a fellow Missourian, Clark Clifford, a non-Jewish young lawyer who had signed on as a special presidential counsel. Clifford strongly believed that Truman's road to success included the Jewish vote and its generous contributions. He was close to the Zionist community, and his advice to Truman on Palestine usually reflected its views—and opposed those of the State Department.[9]

Another important promoter of Zionist aspirations was White House administrative assistant David K. Niles, a secretive naturalized Polish Jew who had grown up in Boston and was devoted to politics and Zionism.[10] He was a holdover from the Roosevelt Administration. While Clifford was the political operative, Niles was the behind-the-scene liaison between the White House and Zionists. Both Clifford and Niles were regularly briefed by Eliahu Epstein, head of the Zionist Organization's Washington office and later, under the name of Elath, Israel's first ambassador to Washington. The two men were, in the opinion of Secretary of Defense James Forrestal, an anti-Zionist, the principal architects of Truman's pro-Zionist policy that was based on "squalid political purposes." Forrestal added that "United States policy should be based on United States national interests and not on domestic political considerations."[11]

For its part, the State Department remained opposed to Zionism's goal of founding a Jewish state, as it had been since the beginnings of Zionism. If anything, it had become more opposed than ever under the unrelenting lash of the Zionist lobby, which tirelessly belabored the department to change its policy, and of the doleful events unfolding in Palestine where Jewish terrorists were attacking British and Arabs with indiscriminate violence. It was obvious that deep trouble was brewing there with still unforeseen but ominous implications. Throughout the Middle East, American diplomats regularly were quizzed by concerned Arab governments about U.S. policy toward Palestine, and were being warned about a bloodbath that would accompany attempts to found a Jewish state.

The State Department had been relieved in April 1945 with the letter of President Roosevelt to Saudi King Ibn Saud and other Arab governments pledging that the United States would take no action in Palestine without consulting the Arabs as well as the Jews. It was a promise well received not only in Arab capitals but in the department itself, since it meant that U.S. policy retained some independence from the Zionist program. But still there was a suspicion that Truman favored the Zionist goal of a Jewish homeland, and so the department set out to make sure the new President was aware of the latest twist in U.S. policy.

On 1 May, Joseph C. Grew, the acting secretary of state, sent a memorandum to Truman about Palestine:

> In this connection I thought you would like to know that although President Roosevelt at times gave expression to views sympathetic to certain Zionist aims, he also gave certain assurances to the Arabs which they regard as definite commitments on our part. On a number of occasions within the past few years, he authorized the Department to assure the heads of the different Near Eastern Governments in his behalf that 'in the view of this Government there should be no decision altering the basic situation in Palestine without full consultation with both Arabs and Jews'. In his meeting with King Ibn Saud early this year, moreover,

> Mr. Roosevelt promised the King that as regards Palestine he would make no move hostile to the Arab people and would not assist the Jews as against the Arabs.[12]

Two weeks later the State Department found a reason to remind Truman about the matter and to nudge him into signing on to Roosevelt's commitment. On 14 May, Grew wrote Truman that the department had just received a letter from King Abdullah of Transjordan inquiring about U.S. policy. Grew suggested that Truman repeat the Roosevelt promise to Abdullah of "full consultation with both Arabs and Jews."[13] Truman did on 17 May, and on 4 June sent a similar reassuring letter to Egypt.[14]

Hearing that Zionist leaders were hoping to meet soon with Truman, Grew sent another memo to the president on 16 June, reminding him that

> you may recall that our basic attitude on Palestine is that it is one of the problems which should come up for settlement after the war through the United Nations Organization, and that in any event no decision regarding it should be taken without full consultation with both Arabs and Jews. It does not seem, therefore, that you need go any further, unless you care to do so, than to thank the Zionists leaders for any material which they may give you and to assure them that their views will be given your careful consideration.[15]

Meanwhile, a new secretary of state, James F. Byrnes, had been appointed in July, meaning the State Department's Near East office was faced not only with educating Truman about U.S. policy but the new secretary as well. Byrnes was a veteran of both houses of Congress, a former justice of the Supreme Court and, during the war years, Roosevelt's White House assistant in charge of war mobilization. But despite that impressive resume, he knew little more about foreign affairs than Truman.[16]

On 24 August, Loy W. Henderson, the director of the Office of Near Eastern and African Affairs, sent Byrnes a long memorandum outlining four possible plans for settling the Palestine problem. These included making Palestine into a Jewish state, an Arab state, partitioning it or placing it under an international trusteeship. Henderson and his experts clearly favored the trusteeship idea, since it would be least detrimental to U.S. interests or Arab objections and might even be embraced by non-Zionist Jews as "a reasonable compromise solution." They felt an all-Arab or Jewish state would be impossible to found without massive misery and that partition "would be likely to arouse widespread discontent in the Arab and Muslim worlds which would be somewhat unfavorable to American interests."[17]

But before getting to discussion of these plans, the memo observed:

> We are aware that Palestine has become a problem in American internal politics as well as one in the field of foreign relations. The President and his political advisers are in a much better position than we to evaluate the domestic political factors involved and, therefore, we do no presume to give advice in this regard.

> We feel, however, that we would be derelict in our responsibility if we should fail to inform you that in our considered opinion the active support by the Government of the United Sates of a policy favoring the setting up of a Jewish State in Palestine would be contrary to the policy which the United States has always followed of respecting the wishes of a large majority of the local inhabitants with respect to their form of government. Furthermore, it would have a strongly adverse effect upon American interests throughout the Near and Middle East....At the present time the United States has a moral prestige in the Near and Middle East unequaled by that of any other great power. We would lose that prestige and would be likely for many years to be considered as a betrayer of the high principles which we ourselves have enunciated during the period of the war.[18]

Whether Byrnes bothered passing this considered message on to Truman is unclear. But one thing that already was becoming obvious was Truman's disdain for the State Department and its "striped-pants boys," as he referred to them. Without even informing the Near East office, much less seeking its advice, Truman took it on himself to send a personal letter to Prime Minister Clement Attlee urging Britain to allow "as many as possible" of the Jewish displaced persons in Europe to enter Palestine.[19]

Truman did not mention a precise figure, but a highly sympathetic report on DPs, the Harrison report, which he had enclosed with his letter, alluded to something under 100,000 DPs wanting to go to Palestine.[20] Simultaneously, the Zionists were pressing to have 100,000 Jews allowed to migrate to Palestine. Thus, the figure 100,000 came into being as the one proposed by Truman and he never contradicted it. In fact, he later used it himself and it became the rallying cry in the verbal battle leading up to partition.

News of the letter soon leaked and caused a firestorm. The British were upset because they had promised in their White Paper of 1939 that Jewish immigration would be limited to 15,000 a year and, after 1944, that the Arabs would have a de facto veto over Jewish immigration into Palestine. Land purchases by Jews would be severely restricted and in ten years Palestine would be granted independence.[21] But now, with all the unspeakable details of the holocaust coming into public view, the concentration camps and crematoria, the astounding figure of 6 million dead, the Jews were demanding an open gate to Palestine.

Many Christians sympathized with them and London was under tremendous pressure to change its policy. However, this would have the effect of nullifying the 1939 White Paper, which was what the Zionists wanted but which the Arabs strongly opposed. Moreover, the Arabs made a strong argument by pointing out that in the two decades of Britain's mandate over Palestine it had allowed so many Jews entry that the Palestinian majority had been reduced from ten to one to two to one. The balance would shift even more dramatically if unlimited Jewish immigration were allowed.

Complained the Arab League: "Any attempt to renew Jewish immigration into Palestine will no doubt change the basic situation in that country and the

Arab States cannot agree to any decisions that change the standing policy pledged in that respect by the White Paper of 1939 and consider it inconsistent with undertakings given by both U.S. and British Governments."[22]

Arabs were also upset by Truman's letter because for the first time it linked European Jewry to the Palestine question as though they were parts of the same problem. Arab newspapers lashed out at Truman, calling his letter "aggression" and "frank hostility." The embassy in Iraq reported that one newspaper "with sarcasm and venom rips into America for holding itself out as protector of Four Freedoms while supporting imperialistic Zionism."[23]

As the Arabs, British and Jews all descended on the State Department demanding to know what was going on, the American diplomats could only grit their teeth in silence. Among themselves they fumed because they had not been consulted before Truman sent off his letter. One of Henderson's deputies handwrote him a note: "It seems apparent to me that the President (and perhaps Mr. Byrnes as well) have decided to have a go at Palestine negotiations without bringing NEA into the picture for the time being....I see nothing further we can appropriately do for the moment except carry on our current work, answering letters and telegrams, receiving callers, etc., as best we can...."[24]

Such suspicions were not misplaced. Secretary of State Byrnes later confided: "For the past year President Truman has had personal charge of the Palestine problem. Communications between the British Government and the United States Government have been carried on by the President and Mr. Attlee—not by Mr. [Foreign Secretary Ernest] Bevin and me."[25] Even earlier the British Foreign Office had observed that the State Department was having problems, noting in an internal memorandum: "The State Department seems to be caught between its own Middle East representatives and the President's political advisers."[26]

On 1 October 1945, Henderson finally sent a memorandum to Acting Secretary of State Dean Acheson pointedly reminding him that U.S. policy was to consult with both Arabs and Jews. Implicit was the message that the Near East office also should be consulted before the president acted in such sensitive matters.

> We are deeply concerned at the repercussions resulting from reports which are being widely disseminated to the effect that the President, without consultation with either Jews or Arabs, is bringing pressure upon the British Government to arrange for the immediate admission of 100,000 Jewish refugees to Palestine....In the case of the Arab world, unrefuted allegations are being made that the United States is not living up to [its] pledges....We feel that our good name is at stake in the Near East and elsewhere and we sincerely hope that before any further moves are taken by this Government in the matter of Palestine we shall be in a position to reassure the Arab Governments as well as the Jews that we intend to live up to our promises of consultation. We also hope that if we decide, regardless of reactions in the Near East, to embark upon a policy which seems likely to alter the basic situation in Palestine we shall actually consult with Arabs and Jews before taking any steps towards adopting and implementing that policy.[27]

As a final thought, the memo rather hopefully added: "If you would like to bring our views expressed herein to the attention of the President or the Secretary, we should be glad to repeat them in whatever form you may consider appropriate."

In fact, Acheson the next day did send on to Truman a summary of the memo, which boldly pointed out to the president that his proposal to Attlee

> would, if adopted, constitute a basic change in the Palestine situation, and it is already clear from the violent reaction of the Arabs that it would in fact make an immediate issue out of the Palestine question....President Truman's proposal would involve the abrogation of a cardinal feature of the British White Paper policy. The disposition on our part to fail to carry out our promises would constitute the severest kind of blow to American prestige not only in the Near East but elsewhere.[28]

This undisguised rebuke could hardly have made for pleasant reading by the prickly and thin-skinned new president, and he completely ignored the advice. However, it does help explain why he had such a dislike of the State Department. No president likes to be lectured by the bureaucrats, especially at a time when he was the butt of a witticism going around the capital that "to err is Truman."[29]

Truman's mood was not improved a fortnight later when Britain sent a report to the State Department admitting that "Palestine is a terrible legacy," but then criticizing Truman's endorsement of immigration to Palestine: "His Majesty's Government would be lacking in frankness if they did not make it clear that the approach to the problem in the United States is being most embarrassing to them and is embittering relations between the two countries at a moment when we ought to be getting closer together in our common interests."[30]

In an effort to defuse the issue, the British suggested forming a joint Anglo-American Committee of Inquiry to determine how many Jews Palestine could absorb. The intent of the proposal was to delay any major decisions for as long as possible. Truman balked, insisting that the committee produce "speedy results."[31] For good measure, he added he that he still believed the gates of Palestine should be opened to the Jews of Europe.[32]

He confided in his memoirs: "In my own mind, the aims and goals of the Zionists at this stage to set up a Jewish state were secondary to the more immediate problem of finding means to relieve the human misery of the displaced persons."[33] Truman's focus, in other words, was on the humanitarian efforts to aid the DPs, not on the political ambitions of Zionism to establish a Jewish state.

This split between goals, humanitarian versus political, was clearly revealed by reaction to the Anglo-American Committee. The Zionists opposed it, despite Truman's support for increased immigration, charging that it would delay a solution of the Palestine problem. They called for immediate abrogation of the 1939 White Paper, the entry of 100,000 Jews into Palestine, reaffirmation by Britain and the United States of the Balfour Declaration and appointment of an Anglo-

American commission to implement the above recommendations.[34]

The Arabs also opposed it, since they wanted no change in the White Paper and no more Jewish immigrants. By this point King Ibn Saud in Saudi Arabia was becoming suspicious of Truman's tendency to conduct policy toward Palestine out of his hip pocket. Twice in August, at a press conference on the 16th and in his letter to Attlee, Truman bluntly had supported increased migration into Palestine despite his pledge of consultation. "We want to let as many Jews into Palestine as is possible," he said at his press conference.[35]

As rumors circulated with increasing velocity about Truman's pro-Zionism, Ibn Saud cabled Truman on 2 October seeking his permission to release Roosevelt's April letter pledging full consultation with Arabs and Jews. It was a transparent way to remind the new president of that commitment, and also to reveal it to the world. The king added that it "is impossible that [the United States] would support the expulsion of a nation from its country so as to replace it with another nation by means of might and force, and under the protection of military forces."[36]

There was little Truman could do to halt Ibn Saud, and on 18 October the two countries jointly released the letter. In a press release accompanying the letter, Secretary of State Byrnes said: "The substance of this Government's position has been that this Government would not support a final decision which in its opinion would affect the basic situation in Palestine without full consultation with both Jews and Arabs."[37] A short time later he advised U.S. embassies in the Middle East:

> In discussing this Government's Palestine policy with Arab or other leaders you should make it plain that full 'consultation' with both Jews and Arabs...does not mean prior 'agreement' with Jews and Arabs. It is obvious that if no basic change could be made without the full agreement of both Jews and Arabs very little if any progress could be achieved in the direction of a solution at this time.[38]

By now the extremist Zionists in Palestine no longer were willing to wait for the great powers to decide their fate. On the night of 31 October–1 November 1945 as many as 3,000 Jews launched a coordinated campaign and attacked Palestine's railway system, cutting all lines in fifty places from Acre to Wazzan, from Affula to Haifa and from Lydda to Jerusalem. An attack also was made on the Lydda railway station and the refinery at Haifa was blown up. The casualties were six killed, mainly British police and troops.[39]

The attacks came on the eve of the anniversary of the issuance of the Balfour Declaration on 2 November 1917 and were meant to show Jewish impatience. The declaration now left a bitter taste for the Jews who charged that Britain, by restricting immigration, was not living up to its commitment to aid establishment of a Jewish national home. The bombing of the rail system was a virtual declaration of war by Jewish terrorists against British rule. The Jewish-owned *Palestine Post* in Jerusalem editorialized: "There have been suggestions that the elements in the Yishuv [Jewish community] dedicated hitherto to the defense of Jewish life and property despising aggression and rejecting retaliation have now been impelled toward direct action."[40]

Arabs marked the date with demonstrations and riots. In Alexandria, Egyptian police opened fire on rampaging mobs, killing ten and wounding 300.[41] That same month, Saudi Foreign Minister Faisal ibn Abdul Aziz warned the United States:

> Your Government has permitted itself to be placed in the position of urging the British to break their pledges to us. I assure you that the British are now telling us officially that they favor the Arab case against Zionism but they are being pushed by you into pro-Zionist moves....We Arabs would rather starve or die in battle than see our lands and people devoured by the Zionists as you would do if we were giving them one of your own states for a nation.[42]

Despite such complaints, the Congress on 19 December 1945 passed a joint resolution calling for "free entry of Jews into [Palestine] to the maximum of its agricultural and economic potentialities...so that they may freely proceed with the upbuilding of Palestine as the Jewish National Home, and in association with all elements of the population, establish Palestine as a democratic commonwealth in which all men, regardless or race or creed, shall have equal rights."[43] This was considerably less than what the Zionists wanted, since it merely called for a democratic commonwealth open to all people instead of a Jewish state. The Arabs protested anyway, because it also called for maximum immigration. However, in the end the congressional action had little effect beyond allowing the politicians to assure their Jewish voters that they were thinking of them.

Meanwhile, months of haggling between Washington and London finally had resulted in agreement on composition of the inquiry to be conducted by the Anglo-American Committee. On 10 December, Truman announced the six American members of the committee: Judge Joseph C. Hutcheson of Texas, the U.S. chairman; Dr. Frank Aydelotte, director of the Institute for Advanced Study at Princeton; Frank W. Buxton, editor of the *Boston Herald*; William Phillips, a former undersecretary of state; James G. McDonald, former League of Nations high commissioner for refugees and later the first U.S. ambassador to Israel, and Bartley C. Crum, a California attorney. Half of the U.S. delegation was Zionist or pro-Zionist: Buxton, Crum and McDonald. In the months ahead, these three would keep Zionists monitoring the committee's work informed of its attitudes and activities. Crum had received his appointment through his friendship with David Niles despite the opposition of Loy Henderson. That opposition was later to cost Henderson because Crum conducted a crusade against him as being anti-Zionist and demanded his resignation, thereby focusing more pressure on the State Department and on Henderson personally.[44]

It was no oversight that the American delegation contained no Congressmen, although the British had three members of Parliament.[45] Its duties were bound to be so controversial that Byrnes had written to Truman that "it really is not a friendly service to a Senator or Congressman to appoint him to this Commission."[46]

The committee's writ was to examine the merits of the positions of the Arabs and Jews, to determine the desires of the displaced Jews in Europe and to investigate conditions in Palestine. It was then to recommend the best course of action by both countries, all this to be completed within 120 days. The committee began its work in early January 1946 with hearings in Washington, D.C., where one of the British members, Labor Member of Parliament Richard Crossman, gained a deep insight to the roots of support for Zionism by American gentiles. He saw it as a reflection of the "frontier mentality":

> Zionism after all is merely the attempt by the European Jew to rebuild his national life on the soil of Palestine in much the same way as the American settler developed the West. So the American will give the Jewish settler in Palestine the benefit of the doubt, and regard the Arab as the aboriginal who must go down before the march of progress. After all he only achieved his own freedom by a war of independence against George III and if the Jew in Palestine comes into conflict with George III's successors in colonial administration he is bound to win an instinctive American sympathy.[47]

There can be little doubt that to a large extent President Truman shared this general American attitude. But as anti-Zionists pointed out, the problem with the frontier mentality was that it was an antiquated attitude no longer applicable to the modern world. The day of the "march of progress" by trampling over aborigines was over. Moreover, the Palestinian Arabs were hardly aborigines. They had been settled for at least 1,300 years in Palestine—some would argue for at least twice that time—and they were not without sophistication and cultural achievements, much less undeserving of the human rights that World War II was supposed to have assured them.

* *

The new year, 1946, heralded mid-term elections with all their sensitivity to things political. Politics especially interfered in relations between Washington and Britain, particularly over Palestine policy. All year long Truman and British leader Clement Attlee struggled to keep their relations cordial. But it was a fruitless effort. Each leader had enormous political forces working on him to take actions that were bound to increase the strains on the other and only complicate the Palestine problem.

Truman was determined to help European Jewry by increasing immigration to Palestine, a position from which he refused to budge. This caused Attlee and his colleagues endless headaches in Britain's relations with the Arabs. Foreign Minister Ernest Bevin was reported to have been driven into his "blackest rages" by Truman's constant reiteration of the 100,000. At one point he declared: "I hope

I will not be misunderstood in America if I say that this [100,000] was proposed with the purest motives. They did not want too many Jews in New York."[48]

Attlee tried to explain to his American counterpart the varied and complex problems that Palestine caused Britain. Foremost, an infusion of new Jews into Palestine certainly would amount to a basic change in policy because it would have a profound effect on the demographic equation, which now stood at around 1.2 million Palestinians against less than 600,000 Jews. Moreover, it would have other reverberations. The new immigrants could be expected to join the Jewish underground army or the Jewish terrorist gangs, thereby threatening the security of the British and Palestinian civilians. British soldiers were already being killed routinely by Jewish terrorists and London did not want fresh Jewish recruits arriving in Palestine. There was also the question of finances. Who would pay to transport the DPs and then aid them with housing and other necessities once in Palestine?

There were also strategic considerations for Britain. Egypt had been Britain's linchpin in its security for the Middle East and the lifeline to India for nearly a century. Now Egypt was pressing for the withdrawal of all British forces throughout the country and concentrating them in bases in the Suez Canal zone. The Chiefs of Staff looked to Palestine as a fallback position where Haifa could replace Alexandria as a major naval base, a strategic air base could be located in the interior and garrisons scattered throughout.[49]

These were only part of Britain's problems. After three decades of cynically offering Arabs and Jews contradictory pledges in pursuit of empire, London now was faced with irreconcilable promises. In addition, since it held major oil concessions in the Arab states and was maneuvering to supplant the United States in the rich Saudi Arabian oil fields, Britain did not want to alienate the Arabs. The empire, moreover, contained 80 million Muslims. It had been depleted by the war and was in dire financial straits. The empire was crumbling under the centrifugal forces of the postwar world. Its statesmen were desperate and confused and frustrated.

So too was Truman. From the time of his move into the White House he had been under attack and given little chance of ever gaining the presidency on his own. Even though presidential elections were more than two years away, the midterm elections of 1946 would be the first national report card on his record. Truman needed all the support he could get. He especially was in no position to alienate the Zionist lobby, and certainly not in this highly emotional period when many ordinary Americans sympathized with the Zionist dream and the commiserated with the misery of the European displaced persons. (In the event, the Democrats lost both Houses, but not because of a lack of effort by Truman.)

In these conflicting circumstances, it was inevitable that Attlee and Truman would clash. But for the moment they held their breath and waited for the conclusions of the Anglo-American Committee. The twelve members of the committee, after considerable argument among themselves, came in right on schedule with a unanimous report on 30 April 1946. It satisfied no one.

It contained ten points and proposed three principles:

I.   That Jew shall not dominate Arab and Arab shall not dominate Jew in Palestine.

II.   That Palestine shall be neither a Jewish state nor an Arab state.

III. That the form of government ultimately to be established shall, under international guarantees, fully protect and preserve the interests in the Holy Land of Christendom and of the Muslim and Jewish faiths.[50]

It then added a bombshell. The committee recommended as two of its points the elimination of restrictions on Jewish land purchases and the immediate entry of 100,000 Jews into Palestine.[51]

Truman immediately went public and announced—without consulting Britain—that he supported that part of the report dealing with the land restrictions and the 100,000 immigrants. Truman's statement mollified many Jewish Americans, as it was meant to do, if not extremist Zionists. However, the Zionists remained restrained because two of the committee's Zionist members, Crum and McDonald, had returned early to Washington and convinced firebrand Zionist leader Abba Hillel Silver that to denounce the report would increase Truman's growing resentment of Zionist pressure. Instead, it was better to have Truman's support for ending restrictions on land purchases and the entry of 100,000 Jews into Palestine, a position supported by White House Zionist David Niles.[52]

The British were furious. Attlee privately complained that he was annoyed because "the Americans...forever lay heavy burdens on us without lifting a little finger to help."[53] Publicly, he pointed out in the House of Commons that "the report must be considered as a whole in all its implications....His Majesty's Government wish to be satisfied that they will not be called upon to implement a policy which would involve them single-handed in such commitments and in the course of joint examination they will wish to ascertain to what extent the Government of the US would be prepared to share the resulting additional military and financial responsibilities."[54] He particularly wanted an agreement to disarm the Jewish underground army and terrorists, which were taking a toll on the two and a half British divisions now needed in Palestine to keep the peace.[55]

Complaints from the Arab nations was "swift and alarming," in the words of the Near East division. "The Arabs have singled out the recommendation for putting 100,000 Jews into Palestine for criticism of the strongest kind, and they give every indication of the intention to resist."[56] From Syria and Lebanon there was reported the emergence of intense anti-Americanism: "Disillusionment is particularly bitter as regards American Government attitude as voiced in Mr. Truman's statement..."[57] The reaction in Egypt was "bitterly critical....newspapers almost without exception, attack report as disastrous and in complete variance with justice for Arab rights."[58] It was the same everywhere in the Arab world. Old King Ibn Saud was reported to have taken the report and Truman's remarks "very bad."[59]

While the Anglo-American report stirred up tremendous emotions, it

solved nothing. The report had no official standing. It was merely a recommendation that neither government immediately accepted as policy. The Near East division urged adoption of the entire report—not just parts of it like the 100,000—as
official policy "at the earliest possible moment." However, it pointed out that consultations first would have to be held with the British, as well as the Arabs and
Jews. It also threw cold water on the prevalent idea that moving 100,000 DPs to
Palestine would solve Europe's problem. It described this action as "a temporary
solution at best" because tens of thousands of DPs were moving westward from
the Russian zones and they would "soon fill the vacuum."[60]

On 9 May, Secretary of State Byrnes sent Truman a memorandum relay-
ing London's view of the problems Britain would face if the report were adopted.
These were mainly military and financial, which Britain now made known it would
expect the United States to share, including deployment of troops that would be
"sustained at full strength so long as the commitment in Palestine last. A token
contingent would not be sufficient." The costs of security and housing for the
100,000 would not be cheap. The British put a conservative estimate at 60 million
to 70 million pounds sterling over two years. If the commitment lasted ten years,
the cost would rise to 115 million to 125 million pounds.

Byrnes added: "If the US Government is unable to agree to assist in implementing the report the British Government will have to consider what its future
policy in Palestine is to be."[61]

Truman and Attlee agreed on a two-track approach to their problems.
They would formally begin the promised consultations with Arabs and Jews, and
at the same time they would appoint a committee of experts to iron out the numerous technical and practical details that would be involved in adopting the Anglo-
American report as policy. The first setback came when the Arabs unanimously
turned down a 21 May invitation by Washington to submit their views within thirty
days on the report. While the Jews agreed to attend, the Arab Higher Committee,[62]
the organization led by the Mufti of Jerusalem that represented Palestinians, replied that it rejected the invitation "completely....[The Arabs of Palestine are] the
sole people to decide on their fate and they reject any foreign intervention in their
country."[63]

The British had no more luck. The Arabs agreed, since Britain was the
mandatory power, but the Jews refused because the report had ruled out a Jewish
state. However, the Jews did meet unofficially with British officials and the London conference actually dragged on from mid-September 1946 to mid-February
1947 without any achievement beyond reinforcing the growing conviction that a
joint solution by Britain and America was not possible.[64]

Nor were London and Washington any more successful on the second
track. The effort to find practical ways to carry out the Anglo-American report was
filled with difficult decisions and pitfalls. As the weeks passed, disputes and suspicions led the two countries into one of the angriest and bitterest periods in their
long relations.

The man chosen to head the small U.S. delegation on the technical talks was veteran diplomat Henry F. Grady, who had served as ambassador in Asia and Greece but never in the Middle East. His group arrived in London on 12 July with its negotiating options fairly restricted because Truman had determined that he would not commit any U.S. troops to Palestine and would not join Britain in sharing responsibility for a trusteeship over the area. On the other hand, he offered to pay for the transport and housing of 100,000 DPs to Palestine, to give up to $300 million in economic aid and loans, and to ask Congress to admit 50,000 DPs to America. [65] These offers were hardly tempting to the British since they opposed the 100,000 transfer in the first place and the offer of allowing half that number into the United States did not strike them as especially generous given the comparative sizes of America and Palestine.

Nonetheless, by 24 July, the two negotiating teams had come to a quick agreement. Their recommendations became known as the Morrison-Grady Report, Morrison being Member of Parliament Herbert Stanley Morrison who presented the report to Parliament. The central features very much favored the British position, especially in its recommendation to delay movement of 100,000 Jews to Palestine. The report said this would be done within one year, but added that the start would not begin until all sides agreed on a form of government, not likely to occur quickly under even the best of circumstances. Morrison-Grady recommended dividing Palestine into four areas comprising limited autonomy for Arab and Jewish provinces and separate districts for Jerusalem-Bethlehem and the Negev desert. Britain would remain the trustee and administrating authority with control over foreign affairs, defense, justice, taxation and, significantly, immigration.[66]

Attlee was so pleased with the agreement that he cabled Truman praising the American delegates for "their energy and cooperative spirit."[67] The Jews, however, felt betrayed and, as the mid-term elections loomed closer, they turned up the political heat on Truman. They charged that he would be turning Palestine into another Jewish "ghetto" if he accepted Morrison-Grady. Influential Republican Senator Robert A. Traft denounced the report as a sellout to the British.

The militant and impatient mood of the extreme Zionists had been dramatically demonstrated on 22 July with the blowing up of the British military headquarters in the King David Hotel in Jerusalem, killing ninety-one people—forty-one Arabs, twenty-eight British and seventeen Jews.[68] Whatever the great powers decided, the Jews of Palestine increasingly were taking matters into their own hands. By the time Truman met on 30 July with his Cabinet to discuss the report he was so exasperated by the mounting violence in Palestine and criticism at home that he blurted out: "Jesus Christ couldn't please [the Jews] when He was here on earth, so how could anyone expect that I would have any luck?"[69]

That same day, Truman had another bombshell for Attlee. He sent Acting Secretary of State Dean Acheson to explain to the British Ambassador in Washington that with "the greatest reluctance and regret" he could not endorse the Morrison-Grady report. Acheson was candid, explaining that "in view of the extreme intensity of feeling in centers of Jewish population in this country neither political party would support this program...."[70] Attlee responded to Truman by expressing his "great disappointment" but vowing to go ahead and try to get Arabs and Jews to accept a modified form of the plan with the changes mainly having to do with economic development and the "tempo and extent" of immigration.[71]

The implicit threat of slowing immigration was no doubt a goad to make Truman reconsider. However, he found this impossible to do politically. In the words of Acheson: "President feels that in view opposition to Plan, he would not be able to prevail on Congress to agree to financial contributions for its implementation nor to rally sufficient public support to warrant undertaking by the Government to give plan in its present form moral backing."[72]

* *

With London and Washington deadlocked and the Arabs demanding acknowledgment of their majority status while Zionist extremists engaged in a terror campaign against British rule, moderate Zionists of the Jewish Agency decided to put forward their own plan. It called for partition of Palestine into independent Arab and Jewish states. Nahum Goldmann, one of the Jewish Agency's moderate and most persuasive advocates, flew to Washington in early August and through the good offices of David Niles in the White House arranged to meet with Acting Secretary of State Acheson.[73] Goldmann said he could guarantee support of the majority of Jewish Americans for a plan that partitioned Palestine, ended the British government there, granted the Jewish state full autonomy and control over immigration, including the immediate entrance of 100,000 Jews.[74]

Acheson liked the idea and, along with David Niles, presented it personally to Truman. He accepted it on 9 August. Niles was so thrilled that he rushed to Goldmann's hotel room, threw himself on the bed and exclaimed in Yiddish: "If my mother could hear that we are going to have a Jewish state."[75]

With rumors swirling that his expected Republican rival in 1948, Thomas E. Dewey, was about to issue a pro-immigration statement of his own, Truman decided to announce his interest, if not outright support, of partition on the eve of Yom Kippur, which that year fell on 4 October. The State Department opposed, but it was only a month away from mid-term elections and Truman was being urged on by the Zionists. He sent a draft of his statement the day before to Attlee, only to have the British leader plead by urgent return cable for Truman to delay "at least for the time necessary for me to communicate with Mr. Bevin."[76] Truman refused, saying it was "imperative I make my position clear today."[77] Today, of course, was Yom Kippur, when a presidential message of support of the Jewish quest for a state in Palestine would be greatly appreciated among Jews in the electorate.

Truman made a lengthy summary of his pro-Zionist actions, urging once again immediate immigration of a substantial number of Jews to Palestine and adding that "the creation of a viable Jewish state in control of its own immigration and economic policies in an adequate area of Palestine instead of in the whole of Palestine" might serve as a bridge to finding a solution.[78] While Truman had not come out directly supporting partition—he said it might help in "bridging the gap" between British and Zionist proposals—the subtlety of his wording was completely ignored. Not only Jews but the American media hailed Truman for his "support of the Jewish state."[79]

The timing of Truman's remarks was not lost on Attlee. He was once again feeling betrayed, believing that Truman was playing domestic politics with an issue of enormous peril to British interests. He responded with an angry and tart message:

> When just after midnight last night I received the text of your proposed statement on Palestine, I asked you at least to postpone its issue for a few hours in order that I might communicate with Mr. Bevin in Paris....I have received with great regret your letter refusing even a few hours grace to the Prime Minister of the country which has the actual responsibility for the government of Palestine in order that he might acquaint you with the actual situation and the probable results of your action. These may well include the frustration of the patient efforts to achieve a settlement and the loss of still more lives in Palestine....
>
> I shall await with interest to learn what were the imperative reasons which compelled this precipitancy.[80]

In a long cable trying to justify his action, Truman explained that he had chosen Yom Kippur in order to "alleviate their plight" because it had been a "year and a half since their liberation with no decision on their future" and the Jews' sense of "depression and frustration...[was] intensified by the approach of their annual Day of Atonement, when they are accustomed to give contemplation to the lot of the Jewish people."[81]

Truman also had to make explanations to the Arabs. In an unusually sharp letter from King Ibn Saud, the Saudi Arabian leader expressed his "great astonishment" about Truman's new position, adding:

> I am confident that the American people who spent their blood and their money freely to resist aggression, could not possibly support Zionist aggression against a friendly Arab country which had committed no crime except to believe firmly in those principles of justice and equality, for which the United Nations, including the United States, fought, and for which both your predecessor and you exerted great efforts....I am certain that Your Excellency and the American people cannot support right, justice, and equity and fight for them in the rest of the world while denying them to the Arabs in their country, Palestine, which they have inherited from their ancestors from Ancient Times.[82]

These thoughts were not too far from the thinking of Gordon P. Merriam, the head of the State Department's Division of Near Eastern Affairs, a subdivision of Henderson's Office of Near Eastern and African Affairs. Merriam wrote:

> U.S. support for partition of Palestine as a solution to that problem can be justified only on the basis of Arab and Jewish consent. Otherwise we

should violate the principle of self-determination which has been written into the Atlantic Charter, the Declaration of the United Nations, and the United Nations Charter—a principle that is deeply embedded in our foreign policy. Even a United Nations determination in favor of partition would be, in the absence of such consent, a stultification and violation of UN's own charter.

He added that without consent "bloodshed and chaos" would follow without any benefit to the United States. When Acheson saw the memo he declared it so explosive that he ordered Merriam to destroy all copies except the original for his own files.[83]

After Merriam argued in another memo that "our policy is one of expediency, not of principle," Henderson commented in a note to Acheson: "Of course we have practically been forced by political pressure and sentiment in the U.S. in the direction of a 'viable Jewish state.' I must confess that when I view our policy in the light of the principles avowed by us I become uneasy."[84]

Despite these concerns in the Near Eastern office, Truman did not change his mind. He responded to Ibn Saud's message with a long and placating cable, trying to justify U.S. policy on the humanitarian ground of helping Jews brutalized by the war in Europe. Truman went on to assure the Saudi king that the Arabs did not have to fear that the Jews would launch "aggressive schemes" against the Palestinians, adding: "I may add, moreover, that I am convinced that responsible Jewish leaders do not contemplate a policy of aggression against the Arab countries adjacent to Palestine."[85]

Ibn Saud's tart response came as no surprise to the old hands in Near Eastern Affairs, who were familiar with his thinking and to a large degree agreed with it. The king noted with irony that "in the name of humanity it is proposed to force on the Arab majority of Palestine a people alien to them, to make these new people the majority, thereby rendering the existing majority a minority." He added:

> Your Excellency will agree with me in the belief that no people on earth would willingly admit into their country a foreign group desiring to become a majority and to establish its rule over that country. And the United States itself will not permit the admission into the United States of that number of Jews which it has proposed for entry into Palestine....I believe that after reviewing all the facts, Your Excellency will agree with me that the Arabs of Palestine, who form today the majority in their country, can never feel secure after the admission of the Jews into their midst nor can they feel assured about the future of the neighboring states.[86]

Truman did not brother trying to compose a detailed response to Ibn Saud. Meanwhile, the impatience and growing militancy of the Zionists was emphasized at the meeting from 9 to 29 December of the 22nd World Zionist Congress in Basle, Switzerland, the first since the outbreak of World War II. Venerable old Chaim Weizmann was shunted aside as too moderate under an assault by firebrand Abba Hillel Silver. The major issue separating the two men was whether to achieve a Jewish state by violence or compromise. Weizmann was openly scornful of Silver for offering "full political and moral support" of violence from the safety of the United States.

"Moral and political support is very little when you send other people to the barricades to face tanks and guns," said Weizmann. "The eleven new settlements in the Negev have, in my deepest conviction, a far greater weight than a hundred speeches about resistance—especially when the speeches are made in New York while the proposed resistance is to be made in Tel Aviv and Jerusalem." This was among the last times Weizmann appeared in his full vigor in Zionist gatherings.[87]

The new leadership was nearly unanimous in believing that the British had to be pushed out of Palestine, by violence if necessary, in order for the Jews to establish their own state and have free immigration. Weizmann was not re-elected but no new president was chosen to replace him. Nonetheless, Silver in the United States and David Ben Gurion in Palestine were now stronger than ever.[88] What the ascendancy of extremist leaders meant in life and death terms was ominous. Statistics showed that Jewish terrorists in Palestine had killed 373 people during 1946, 300 of them civilians.[89]

* *

Truman's repeated public endorsements of large-scale immigration left the British in an increasingly impossible public light, making them seem anti-Semitic, and the Zionists took adroit advantage of London's predicament. Soon after the end of World War II, they had begun sponsoring a major campaign of illegal immigration, hiring ships to send the tattered refugees from Europe into the paths of British ships patrolling off Palestine, where the media reported the spectacle of British sailors turning back crowded ships and denying Jews entry into Palestine.[90] The saga of homeless Jews fresh from Europe's death camps and bound for Palestine in barely seaworthy vessels was a running human interest story in the media throughout the immediate postwar years.[91]

Yet, Britain felt compelled to prevent the arrival of the illegal immigrants. This was because of its commitment to the Arabs to limit immigration and for its own security and that of the Palestinians. Little noted by the press was the fact that every able-bodied immigrant added to the military power of the Jews in Palestine. British Foreign Minister Bevin warned that new immigrants would be "the beginning of an army which would take Palestine away from the Arabs...."[92]

By early 1947, Britain was being pummelled by criticism on all sides. Finally, exasperated by Truman's refusal to withdraw his demand for immediate immigration of Jews to Palestine, unrelenting complaints from both Arabs and Jews, its bad image in the press over its efforts to halt illegal immigration—and on top of all that faced with granting freedom to India and withdrawal in Egypt—Britain angrily declared it had enough. On 14 February Britain announced it was turning over the whole question to the United Nations. Four days later, Foreign

Minister Ernest Bevin explained to the House of Commons that neither the Arabs nor the Jews could find a solution and that Britain had found that it was unable "to impose ourselves a solution of our own. We have, therefore, reached the conclusion that the only course now open to us is to submit the problem to the judgment of the United Nations."[93]

On 25 February, Bevin put much of the blame of Britain's predicament on Truman. He accused the President in the House of Commons of playing politics with the Palestine issue: "I begged that the statement [Truman's Yom Kippur statement on 4 October 1946] be not issued, but I was told that if it was not issued by Mr. Truman a competitive statement would be issued by Mr. [Thomas] Dewey. In international affairs I cannot settle things in if my problem is made the subject of local elections."[94]

Privately, Bevin explained to his ambassador in Washington, Lord Inverchapel: "I recognize that certain passages in this speech may give offense in the United States...but it was necessary to show the House of Commons how we have striven for American cooperation, and how the attitude of the United States has in fact complicated our problem."[95]

Truman was "outraged" by Bevin's remarks, and the White House issued a denial that it was letting politics interfere with foreign policy. But the British never withdrew the statement.[96]

* *

The United Nations assumed its responsibilities for Palestine by calling a special session of the General Assembly, starting 28 April 1947, to select yet another committee to study the problem. A Soviet proposal to establish a large committee with representatives from the major powers was rejected and instead on 13 May a special committee of eleven neutral states without vital interests in Palestine was chosen: Australia, Canada, Czechoslovakia, Guatemala, India, Iran, Netherlands, Peru, Sweden, Uruguay and Yugoslavia. The committee, named the United Nations Special Committee on Palestine (UNSCOP), was ordered to report back to the General Assembly on 1 September 1947. The basic choice facing UNSCOP was whether to partition Palestine into an Arab and a Jewish state or recommend some other solution.

The Zionists continued to favor partition while the Arabs unsuccessfully sought termination of Britain's mandate and a declaration of independence for the Arab majority in Palestine. To emphasize their contention that the United Nations had no authority to interfere in Palestine, the Arabs boycotted UNSCOP's deliberations.

Truman generally favored partition. He had indicated his favor ever since his Yom Kippur statement of 1946 but had taken no specific public position on partition as late as the summer of 1947. Among his concerns was the fear that the United States would be maneuvered into finding itself replacing Britain and taking over responsibility for maintaining law and order. At the time Britain had nearly

100,000 troops and policemen tied up in Palestine.[97]

On 31 August, UNSCOP issued its report unanimously calling for an end to the mandate. The majority—Canada, Czechoslovakia, Guatemala, Netherlands, Peru, Sweden and Uruguay—recommended the partition of Palestine between "an Arab state, a Jewish state and the City of Jerusalem" after a two-year transition period. Jerusalem was envisioned as an international zone under permanent UN trusteeship. The plan awarded Israel all of the Negev, most of the Mediterranean coast and eastern Galilee. The Arab state contained the mountainous heartland of Palestine, western Galilee and the Gaza Strip up to just north of Asdud. Jewish immigration would be a total of 150,000 over two years and thereafter 60,000 a year.[98]

The minority—India, Iran and Yugoslavia (Australia had abstained)—recommended an independent federal government with Jerusalem as its capital and divided into Arab and Jewish cantons that would govern over internal matters. Foreign relations, immigration and defense would be controlled by the central government, which would have a bicameral legislature. Jewish immigration would be restricted to the "absorptive capacity" of the Jewish areas, which was to be determined by an international commission. The Negev and Jaffa would go to the Arab canton rather than to the Jews as in the majority report.[99]

The conflicting recommendations left the General Assembly with the problem of reconciling both reports or deciding which to adopt. It was a process that took nearly three months. During that time, Arabs and Jews sought support for their sides. In the end, it would take a two-thirds majority of the assembly to adopt a plan.

The finding by the majority for partition of Palestine aroused passionate opposition within the State Department, and especially in the Office of Near Eastern and African Affairs. Henderson warned that partition, if adopted, would have to be implemented by force.[100] In addition, Henderson said he opposed partition because the UNSCOP plan was "not based on any principle" and was "full of sophistry."[101] In a detailed memorandum submitted to Secretary of State George C. Marshall on 22 September, Henderson launched a full-scale attack against partition. His views, he said, were shared by "nearly every member of the Foreign Service or of the department who has worked to any appreciable extent on Near Eastern problems." Among the points Henderson made in his memo:

> The UNSCOP Majority Plan is not only unworkable; if adopted, it would guarantee that the Palestine problem would be permanent and still more complicated in the future....The proposals contained in the UNSCOP plan are not only not based on any principles of an international character, the maintenance of which would be in the interests of the United States, but they are in definite contravention to various principles laid down in the Charter as well as to principles on which American concepts of Government are based. These proposals, for instance, ignore such principles as self-determination and majority rule. They recognize the principle of a theocratic racial state and even go so far in several

instances as to discriminate on grounds of religion and race against persons outside of Palestine. We have hitherto always held that in our foreign relations American citizens, regardless of race or religion, are entitled to uniform treatment. The stress on whether persons are Jews or non-Jews is certain to strengthen feelings among both Jews and Gentiles in the United States and elsewhere that Jewish citizens are not the same as other citizens....

We are under no obligations to the Jews to set up a Jewish state. The Balfour Declaration and the Mandate provided not for a Jewish state, but for a Jewish national home. Neither the United States nor the British Government has ever interpreted the term 'Jewish national home' to be a Jewish national state.[102]

As the days passed, Arabs, Jews and the world's nations began choosing sides, or in the case of Britain, neither side. London's disillusionment with Palestine was complete. It wanted out. But in the meantime Britain did not want the world community to assume that it would act as its policeman in Palestine. As Foreign Minister Bevin warned Secretary of State Marshall: "We will not play the role of providing what is virtually a mercenary army to be used to shoot either side in the name of law and order but which, in fact, is enforcing a settlement by force on one side or the other."[103]

On 26 September, Britain publicly announced that "in the absence of a settlement they must plan for an early withdrawal of British forces and of the British administration from Palestine." The effect was that Britain would end its mandate in mid-1948 but until then would not impose by force a solution that was not acceptable to Arab and Jew.[104]

Three days later, the Palestinians' representative, the Arab Higher Committee, rejected both the majority and minority plans, charging the United Nations had no rights in the matter.[105] Others soon announced their decisions: On 2 October the Jewish Agency for Palestine accepted the majority plan.[106] On 11 October, the United States announced in the General Assembly its support of partition on the orders of Truman despite fierce opposition in the State Department.[107] Two days later the Soviet Union supported partition.

Truman's decision won him the praise he sought. Jews in Palestine and the United States hailed the announcement. David Ben Gurion, chairman of the Jewish Agency Executive Committee, said the U.S. decision was an "important step toward establishment of a Jewish state." Rabbi Silver called the announcement "American statesmanship at its best and noblest."[108]

However, the most militant Jews continued to be strongly opposed to partition. Menachem Begin, the leader of the terrorist Irgun Zvai Leumi group, said: "We shall fight these plans, even if the majority of the Jewish Agency sees them as the solution of the Palestine issue. We shall never acquiesce in the partitioning of our homeland."[109] Begin and his followers, as well as the Stern Gang, an even more extreme Jewish terrorist group, were fighting for all of Palestine to be under exclusive Jewish rule, including Transjordan.[110] To such opposition, David

Ben Gurion had a pragmatic answer, pointing out that such agreements were never final, "not with regard to the regime, not with regard to borders, and not with regard to international agreements."[111]

Arabs condemned the announcement. Faris Khouri, Syrian ambassador to the UN, charged that "no election season ever passed without American political parties making solemn promises to enhance and support Zionist dreams. No inquiry commission for Palestine has ever been free from United States intervention, attempting to exert pressure to realize the absurd aspiration of Zionism."[112]

The Arab and Jewish sides presented their formal positions on 18 October before the General Assembly, now sitting as the Ad Hoc Committee on Palestine. Jamal Husseini, vice chairman of the Arab Higher Committee for Palestine, presented the Arab view while Chaim Weizmann, still with great moral force but no official Zionist position, spoke for the Jews. Said Husseini:

> Many people may be physically or morally homeless and they may covet the homes of others and love to have them for their own, but neither homelessness nor love can give a right to possess the homes of others....The right of self-determination in Palestine is our right and we shall stick to it....If it is thought that the Arab of Palestine, as a little child who is forced by his mother to take a bitter pill, will object a little and kick a little and then give way to a melting candy in his mouth, may I solemnly declare to this venerable body that this is a dangerously fallacious illusion. The Arabs of Palestine will never give way under any pressure to part with any portion of their country; with the land that is strewn with the graves of their fathers, with their monuments, their mosques and chapels, their brothers and sisters, who count in hundreds of thousands, to be trampled upon and dominated by Zionists.[113]

Weizmann said:

> A Jewish state in Palestine will in its own interests, as well as by its own ideals, seek close cooperation with the Arab states on its border....I retain my belief in the prospect of Arab-Jewish cooperation once a solution based on finality and equality has received the sanction of international consent. The Jewish State in Palestine may have a constructive message for its neighbors as well. The smallness of the state will be no bar to its full intellectual achievement. Athens was only one small state and the whole world is still its debtor. But this solution accomplishes something further as well. It has profound relevance to the Jewish problem which weighs so heavily upon the conscience of mankind....The Jewish problem in its most acute phase today is the problem of 1,000,000 Jews in Europe and the Orient who have no assurance of a secure existence. The proposed Jewish State by intensive agriculture and irrigation and by industrial development can provide homes for them all.[114]

On 22 October, the Ad Hoc Committee set up three subcommittees to study the UNSCOP reports, to hear more testimony and then present detailed proposals to the General Assembly. Subcommittee One was composed of nine members favoring partition, including the United States and the Soviet Union. Subcommittee Two similarly was constituted with those favoring federation, as was a third devoted to exploring the chances of finding a solution by conciliation. In the event, the latter two subcommittees were of little importance.[115]

After a month of study, testimony and negotiations, Committee One decided to make three major territorial changes in UNSCOP's majority report. It agreed that Jaffa would be assigned to the Arab state as an enclave on the Mediterranean coast and it awarded Beersheba and its environs to the Arab state as well as a strip of land on the western Negev along the Egyptian border. The United States had been planning to support giving all of the Negev to the Arab state since the desert had around 100,000 Bedouin and at most only 4,000 Jews.[116] However, a personal visit by Chaim Weizmann to Truman on 19 November convinced the president that the Jews should have most of the Negev.[117] Truman was no doubt unaware that the effect of this would be to cut off for the first time the Arabs of Africa from the Arabian peninsula, a strategic setback for Islam that not even the Crusaders had accomplished.

Interestingly, that same day Clark Clifford gave Truman a forty-three page memorandum on "detailed measures to restore the President's flagging popularity....[calling for] support for the Jewish cause in Palestine, a move calculated to win the backing of Jews and liberals," in the words of a U.S. official history of the office of the secretary of defense. To implement Clifford's proposals, Truman authorized creation of a Research Division, financed by the Democratic National Committee but under Clifford's personal supervision.[118]

With these territorial changes, the majority report was accepted by the nine members of Committee One and their report sent onto the General Assembly sitting as the Ad Hoc Committee on 19 November.[119] After further minor amendments, the Ad Hoc Committee was scheduled to vote on 25 November and then the General Assembly on 29 November. At this late date, the State Department still sought to change Truman's support of partition. On 24 November Loy Henderson circulated a strong anti-partition memorandum:

> I feel it again to be my duty to point out that it seems to me and all the members of my Office acquainted with the Middle East that the policy which we are following in New York at the present time is contrary to the interests of the United States and will eventually involve us in international difficulties of so grave a character that the reaction throughout the world, as well as in this country, will be very strong....I wonder if the President realizes that the plan which we are supporting for Palestine leaves no force other than local law enforcement organizations for preserving order in Palestine. It is quite clear that there will be widescale violence in that country, in both the Jewish and Arab sides, with which the local authorities will not be able to cope....It seems to me we ought to think twice before we support any plan which would result in American troops going to Palestine.[120]

The memorandum was read to Truman by Under Secretary of State Robert A. Lovett, but there is no evidence that it had any influence on the President.[121]

By this time Zionist pressure to support partition was at a fever pitch. Truman wrote in his memoirs: "I do not think I ever had as much pressure and propaganda aimed at the White House as I had in this instance."[122] To a friend he wrote: "I received about 35,000 pieces of mail and propaganda from the Jews in this country while this matter was pending. I put it all in a pile and struck a match to it."[123]

Other members of his administration testified to similar pressures. Under Secretary of State Robert A. Lovett reported that he had "never in his life been subject to as much pressure as he had been in the three days beginning Thursday morning and ending Saturday night [between 27 and 29 November]."[124] Lovett complained to Truman's private secretary that "our case is being seriously impeded by high pressure being exerted by Jewish agencies. There have been indications of bribes and threats by these groups."[125]

Records of communications—telegrams, letters, and so on—received by the White House in the last half of 1947 showed a dramatic increase in the public's interest in the Palestine question. In the third quarter of the year, 65,000 communications were received; in the fourth quarter, 70,000. There was no breakdown of positions taken in these messages but researchers concluded they resulted from an organized effort by Zionist groups in America.[126] At the time, there were about a million dues-paying Zionists in America, who represented a small but intensely dedicated and coherent group.[127] During this period Postmaster General Robert E. Hannegan, who was also chairman of the Democratic National Committee, brought up at Cabinet meetings the Palestine question in the context of the "very great influence" the administration's support of Zionism had on fund-raising for the party.[128]

On 25 November, the UN Ad Hoc Committee, in reality the General Assembly, voted on the report, 25 to accept with 13 against and 17 abstentions. The vote was one short of the two-thirds majority the partition plan would need to pass in the General Assembly, scheduled for four days later. Those four days were filled with a whirlwind of activity by Arabs and Jews and their supporters, including Zionists in the White House such as administrative aide David Niles. Historian William Roger Louis reported: "Through Niles' coordinating efforts at the White House the Zionists were able to launch a campaign that left the President and officials at the State Department reeling under a bombardment of letters, telegrams, and telephone calls."[129]

During the less than 100 hours leading up to the UN vote, American officials operating under White House orders exerted heavy pressure on non-Muslim nations to support partition. Among those nations who succumbed to the pressure were Ethiopia, France, Haiti, Liberia, Luxembourg, Paraguay and Philippines.[130] Former Undersecretary of State Sumner Welles, who was actively helping the Zionists, wrote: "By direct order of the White House every form of pressure, direct and indirect, was brought to bear by American officials upon those countries outside of the Muslim world that were known to be either uncertain or opposed to partition. Representatives or intermediaries were employed by the White House to make sure that the necessary majority would at length be secured."[131]

The day for the vote was a Saturday but the General Assembly nonetheless duly gathered at Flushing Meadows, as did a mass of 10,000 mainly Zionist spectators trying to get in. Among the observers was Harold Beeley, Britain's expert on Palestine. He described the scene to the Foreign Office with an acid pen:

> Cumulative effect of their [newspapers] articles on many Delegates must have been to convey the impression that an opponent of partition was an enemy of the American people. Final meetings...in the Assembly Hall at Flushing...were packed with an almost exclusively Zionist audience. They applauded declarations of support for Zionism. They hissed Arab speakers. They created the atmosphere of a football match, with the Arabs as the away team.[132]

When the vote came it was 33 to 13 with 10 abstentions and one absent (Siam), giving the resolution the necessary two-thirds majority in the 57-member world body. Passage was assured when seven countries that had abstained on 25 November switched their vote to affirmative: Belgium, France, Haiti, Liberia, Luxembourg, Netherlands and New Zealand. Voting against were Afghanistan, Cuba, Egypt, Greece, India, Iran, Iraq, Lebanon, Pakistan, Saudi Arabia, Syria, Turkey and Yemen. Abstaining were Argentina, Chile, China, Colombia, El Salvador, Ethiopia, Honduras, Mexico, United Kingdom and Yugoslavia.

Pandemonium broke out in the hall when the two-thirds was reached. Jews shouted with joy and hugged each other. The Arab representatives walked out en bloc.

The resolution, number 181, recommended partitioning Palestine into "independent Arab and Jewish states and the Special International Regime for the City of Jerusalem," making the Holy City a *corpus separatum*. [133] The Arabs immediately rejected partition, calling it unjust and an infringement on the rights of the majority in Palestine. The Arab League officially declared it illegal on 17 December.[134] The Jews accepted it officially, although considerable opposition to it continued within the Jewish community in Palestine. Among those Zionists opposed were all the religious parties and the major Jewish terrorist organizations, including the Irgun headed by Menachem Begin, who declared partition "illegal. It will never be recognized."[135]

The partition plan awarded the Jews 5,893 square miles, although at the time Jews owned only about 8.6 percent of the land.[136] The Arabs, who made up two-thirds of the population—608,000 Jews to 1,327,000 Arabs, including 90,000 Bedouin—received 4,476 square miles while the international district of Jerusalem was allotted sixty-seven square miles. These disproportionate figures help to explain why the Arabs at first had a hard time believing the seriousness of the UN action.

Sir Hugh Gurney, the chief secretary of the British Palestine government, reported: "The absence of any immediate reaction of the Arabs can be attributed to their incredulity." He said they had trouble taking the plan seriously because "it seems very possible that the Arabs would have a majority population within quite a short time if the present rate of natural increase continues."[137]

When they did finally begin to take partition seriously, Arab objections focused on the partition plan's award of 56 percent of Palestine to the minority population of Jews.[138] In the Arab state there would be 800,000 Palestinians and 10,000 Jews. The Jewish state would have 498,000 Jews plus 330,000 Palestinians and around 90,000 Bedouin, who had not been counted in the partition plan.[139] In Jerusalem there would be 105,000 Palestinians and 100,000 Jews.

Demographically, the Jewish community at the time of the partition plan was mainly concentrated in three major centers: 100,000 in Jerusalem, 213,000 in Tel Aviv plus 82,000 in surrounding settlements and 119,000 in Haifa and environs. These three areas accounted for 85 percent of the Jews with the other percent living in a few scattered sections of the north (Acre, Beisan, Nazareth, Safad and Tiberias, for a total of around 40,000) and in the single centrally located district of Ramle, with around 32,000. At most there were around 4,000 in the large Beersheba-Negev southern districts.[140] Statistically, there were six Jewish towns, 21 Jewish urban settlements and 266 Jewish rural settlements in the proposed Jewish state.[141]

The Jews were so thinly populated in most parts of Palestine that Foreign Minister Bevin complained that "it is impossible to find in all Palestine, apart from Tel Aviv and its environs...any sizable area with a Jewish majority."[142]

By contrast, the Palestinian community was located throughout the land. Only about one-third of the Palestinians lived in urban areas in seventeen wholly Arab cities (Acre, Beersheba, Beisan, Beit Jala, Bethlehem, Gaza, Hebron, Jenin, Khan Yunis, Lydda, Majdal, Nablus, Nazareth, Ramallah, Ramle, Shafa Amr and Tulkarm). In addition, there were four mixed cities: Safad with an Arab majority, and Haifa, Jerusalem and Tiberias with Jews predominating.[143] The rest of the Palestinians lived in 91 towns and 833 villages, all of them inhabited only by Palestinians.[144]

Palestinian scholar Walid Khalidi later summed up the Palestinian view:

> The Palestinians failed to see why they should be made to pay for the Holocaust....They failed to see why it was *not* fair for the Jews to be a minority in a unitary Palestinian state, while it *was* fair for almost half of the Palestinian population—the indigenous majority on its own ancestral soil—to be converted overnight into a minority under alien rule in the envisaged Jewish state according to partition.[145]

The partition plan was not a binding legal order. Rather it was a recommendation to Britain, the Mandatory Power, and other UN members that such a plan be carried out, with the Arab and Jewish states to come into being not later than 1 October 1948. In order to execute the plan, the UN Commission on Palestine of five members—Bolivia, Czechoslovakia, Denmark, Panama and Philippines—was chosen to take over administration progressively as the British withdrew, beginning at the Egyptian border and moving northward. The commission was to go to Palestine in late December and help the Arab Higher Committee and the Jewish Agency to liaison with the British and establish a Joint Economic Board to oversee the economic union of Palestine. Each of the two communities was to have an armed militia under the UN Commission. In addition, by 1 February Britain was to open a port to receive "substantial" Jewish immigration.[146]

Nothing came of the UN Commission. The British refused to have anything to do with implementing partition and so refused to deal with the commission. Within days of passage of the partition resolution London informed the world that it would surrender its mandate and withdraw its 100,000 troops and police from Palestine by 15 May 1948. Meanwhile, it strongly urged the UN Commission not to go to Palestine until 1 May lest the members' presence provoke Arab riots.[147] In fact, riots already had erupted throughout Palestine and the Arab world following adoption of the partition plan. In Palestine, seven Jews were killed and eight wounded in the first day.[148] The bloodiest riots elsewhere were in the British colony in Aden where more than 100 deaths, mainly Jews, were reported within a week.[149]

The partition resolution also created the Trusteeship Council to administer Jerusalem as a *corpus separatum* and to draft a Statute of Jerusalem. It completed drafting a detailed statute on 21 April, but nothing came of it or of the commission's other efforts because of objections by Arabs and Jews. Events after 1948 rendered the council powerless. It was dissolved in 1952.[150]

On 1 December 1947, the Jews in Palestine launched military Plan Gimmel (Plan C) aimed at buying time for the mobilization of Jewish forces to carry out Plan Dalet (Plan D), which was to expand Israel's borders. Aside from buying time, Plan Gimmel's aims were to seize strategic points vacated by the British, terrorize the Arab population into submission and maintain lines of communication through Arab areas between Jewish localities.[151]

On 2 December, Palestinians began a three-day strike throughout Palestine. Clashes with Jews resulted in eight Jews killed and six Palestinians.[152] By mid-December civil war was well underway. *The New York Times* reported on 12 December: "The Jews again appeared today to be on the offensive, roughly two-thirds of the incidents being initiated by them and in their operations they showed evidence of planning, something absent in general from the Arab attacks."[153] Lehi terrorists also took part, with British Major R.D. Wilson reporting that Lehi made "bestial attacks on Arab villages, in which they showed not the slightest discrimination for women and children, whom they killed as opportunity offered."[154]

British Jerusalem District Commissioner J.H. Pollock reported: "The political situation has deteriorated throughout the district and intercommunity strife may now be said to be in full swing."[155]

All of Palestine slowly descended into chaos. Palestinian diplomat Izzat Tannous recorded in his memoirs: "Gradually, all government services were interrupted. Electric wires were cut; water pipes were destroyed; post and telegraph services were severed and all communications between Arab and Jew in every part of Palestine were severed. Arabs in Jewish quarters moved to Arab quarters and vice versa."[156]

By early 1948, it was clear that the only way to prevent Arab and Jews from fighting each other was by armed intervention. If armed force was used, the United States, as the partition plan's major sponsor, would have to contribute troops and these troops could end up fighting Arabs to protect Jews, or Jews to protect Arabs. Realistically, given the political climate in America, there was little doubt that Americans would end up fighting Arabs to capture for the Jews what the United Nations had awarded them.

It was this prospect that made partition such a popular and emotional issue among America's supporters of the proposed Jewish state. However, it was precisely this dangerous possibility that caused analysts in the State and Defense Departments to worry about the enormous risks involved for the United States. Such armed intervention, the Policy Planning Staff warned, "would in Arab eyes be a virtual declaration of war by the U.S. against the Arab world."[157]

Thus, within two months after adoption of partition, it was shown to be a failure. On 6 February Loy Henderson wrote: "The Palestine Partition Plan is manifestly unworkable....I think that...by mid-April general chaos will reign in Palestine."[158] Five days later, Dean Rusk, the director of the State Department's Office of United Nations Affairs and future secretary of state, warned that partition is "unworkable without resort to war."[159]

If all-out war and great suffering were to be avoided, the United States would have to go back to the drawing board and find another policy.

3 | REFUGEES
The Uprooting of a People, 1947–1967

"The leaders of Israel would make a grave miscalculation if they thought callous treatment of [the fate of the Palestinian refugees] could pass unnoticed by world opinion."

Secretary of State George C. Marshall, 1948[1]

"We...believe that resolution language referring to 'final status' issues should be dropped, since these issues are now under negotiation by the parties themselves. These include refugees...."

U.S. Ambassador to the United Nations
Madeleine K. Albright, 1994[2]

IN THE EARLY MONTHS OF 1948 Palestine descended into a hell of chaos and violence. Law became increasingly lax and impotent. Government institutions and agencies broke down. Safe travel became impossible. A trickle of wealthy Palestinian families began leaving their homes to escape the ambushes and lightning attacks that marked the tactics employed by both sides.

The British had foreseen that partition of Palestine into Arab and Jewish states could not be imposed without force. London refused to authorize its 100,000 troops and police to effect partition by force. British rule was ending after three decades and soon its forces would be going home. The problems of Palestine would be someone else's, although it was not clear who that would be. No country was eager to send troops, especially the United States.

The British confined their role to trying to moderate the killing and maintain the status quo. Even this was asking a lot of troops who were furious at being the target of Jewish terrorist attacks. Still, they tried to preserve life. They prevented fights when they could and, when they could not, they tried to separate the combatants. By so doing they saved lives while risking their own. Ninety-two British policemen and soldiers were killed in the first three months after passage of the UN partition resolution.[3] It was a thankless task.

Casualties among Arabs and Jews were considerably higher, reported the

U.S. Consul General in Jerusalem, Robert B. Macatee. He informed Washington on 9 February 1948 that more than 1,000 Arabs and Jews had been killed and 2,000 wounded over the period since the partition resolution:

> This is a large number, but in considering it one should remember that these casualties have occurred with the British still doing a consider-able amount of interfering in Arab-Jewish melees. Whatever the Jews and Arabs may believe or say regarding British favoritism toward each other, practically all independent observers in the country will agree that if the British had not been here the casualty roll would have been much larger....A day without shooting or an incident or two in Jerusa-lem, for example, is now unknown. Rifle and machine gun fire and heavy explosions in the center of Jerusalem are commonplace, even in the daytime....Yet neither the Jewish nor Arab community shows any desire whatever to compromise.[4]

With the killings there emerged, slowly and barely noticed, an entirely unforeseen problem. Upper and middle class Palestinian families began to leave their homes in increasing numbers. As early as 11 December 1947 agents informed Jewish leader David Ben Gurion that "Arabs were fleeing from Jaffa [and] from Haifa. Bedouins are fleeing from the Sharon" (the Coast Plain). The movements were confused and without plan. Some city dwellers returned to their villages while others moved to such all-Arab cities as Hebron and Nablus. Others fled Palestine for neighboring Arab states. By the end of March at least 75,000 Palestinians, mainly from Haifa, Jaffa, Jerusalem and coastal and Jerusalem villages, had fled their homes.[5]

These refugees received no attention in the higher councils of the State Department or the Truman White House throughout the winter of 1948. Under any circumstances this would have not been unusual since Washington was largely responsible for creating the refugee problem by its advocacy of partition and no government is quick to claim credit for failure. In this case, however, the adminis-tration was totally engrossed in how to extricate itself from support of partition without seeming to. It was a delicate task and it consumed the attention of the top officials of the administration.

President Truman was determined not to renounce partition publicly and thereby add to his reputation for inconsistency, particularly not in 1948. Presiden-tial elections were scheduled for November and Truman's popularity was so low that even members of his own Democratic Party were challenging him. Truman could not afford to lose the support of the Jewish community, which continued strongly to support partition and was openly thankful to Truman for his policy. Campaign contributions and votes could be expected to follow.

The mood in the State Department was glum. It was obvious that Truman's policy was driven by domestic political considerations and that partition could not occur without violence. The escalating violence caused the department in the early months of 1948 to wage a paper battle to change Truman's position and adopt a new policy. In this campaign the State Department was helped by a new and impressive voice. It was that of George F. Kennan, the scholarly and perceptive foreign service officer whose reporting from the Moscow embassy in 1946 had provided the rationale for Washington's containment policy against the Soviet Union.

By 1948, Kennan was the State Department's director of Policy Planning, an office created to study long term policy. He and his staff agreed with the Office of Near Eastern Affairs that continuation of the partition policy represented disaster for the United States. In a long and thoughtful top secret document, "Report by the Policy Planning Staff on Position of the United States With Respect to Palestine," issued on 19 January, Kennan and his staff spelled out the perils raised by partition. These included, Kennan warned, risking significant economic and military losses, particularly in Saudi Arabia:

> King Ibn Saud values the friendship between his country and the U.S. and recognizes the significant financial aid to Saudi Arabia derived from oil royalties. He is reluctant to sever political and economic ties with the U.S. Nevertheless, he is under strong pressure from other Arab states to break with the U.S. Prince Faisal, his son and Foreign Minister, departed for Saudi Arabia from the UN General Assembly in a bitterly anti-American mood[6] and may give strength to a faction of less moderate elements which will force the King's hand. Important U.S. oil concessions and air base rights will be at stake in the event that an actively hostile Government should come into power in Saudi Arabia.

Other major points made by Kennan:

> Any assistance the U.S. might give to the enforcement of partition would result in deep-seated antagonism for the U.S. in many sections of the Moslem world over a period of many years....
> The USSR stands to gain by the partition plan if it should be implemented by force because of the opportunity thus afforded to the Russians to assist in "maintaining order" in Palestine....The presence of Soviet forces in Palestine would constitute an outflanking of our positions in Greece, Turkey and Iran, and a potential threat to the stability of the entire Eastern Mediterranean area....
> As a result of U.S. sponsorship of UN action leading to the recommendation to partition Palestine, U.S. prestige in the Moslem world has suffered a severe blow and U.S. strategic interests in the Mediterranean and Near East have been seriously prejudiced. Our vital interests in those areas will continue to be adversely affected to the extent that we continue to support partition....[7]

Behind these concerns was Kennan's suspicion that Truman already had committed so much to the Jews that if U.S. troops were sent to Palestine they would automatically end up throwing their full weight to the Jewish cause against the Arab majority. In a separate memorandum, he wrote:

> The pressures to which this Government is now subjected are ones which impel us toward a position where we would shoulder major responsi-

bility for the maintenance, and even the expansion, of a Jewish state in Palestine....If we do not effect a fairly radical reversal of the trend of our policy to date, we will end up either in the position of being ourselves militarily responsible for the protection of the Jewish population in Palestine against the declared hostility of the Arab world, or of sharing that responsibility with the Russians and thus assisting at their installation as one of the military powers of the area.[8]

The Kennan study was seconded by both the Central Intelligence Agency and the Defense Department. The CIA concluded in a major study of its own that the peaceful partitioning of Palestine was impossible:

It is apparent that the partition of Palestine...cannot be implemented. The Arabs will use force to oppose the establishment of a Jewish state and to this end are training troops in Palestine and other Arab states....Even among Jews there is dissatisfaction over the partition plan. Irgun Zvai Leumi and the Stern Gang, the two extremist groups, have refused to accept the plan and continue to claim all of Palestine (and even Transjordan) for the Jewish state.[9]

The Defense Department joined in opposition to sending troops to Palestine, writing:

The Joint Chiefs of Staff have emphasized their view that, of all the possible eventualities in the Palestine situation, the most unfavorable in the security interests of the United States would be the intrusion of Soviet forces and, second only to that, the introduction of U.S. troops in opposition to possible Arab resistance.[10]

The military leaders' concern was well founded. The U.S. army had declined from 3.5 million men and women in 1945 to only 400,000 in early 1948. Yet, by mid-February it was estimated that at least 80,000 troops, and probably as many as 160,000, were needed to implement partition by force.[11] Later studies showed that even if other nations joined the effort, the United States probably would have to contribute at least 50,000 troops, a number which would absorb, in the words of a message from the Secretary of Defense to the Secretary of State, "substantially our entire present ground reserve, both Marine and Army. In other words, there will be no troops available for deployment to any other area...."[12]

The Pentagon did not have to remind Truman in an election year about the political dangers involved in sending troops to Palestine. Among other reasons, such a course less than three years after World War II would be vastly unpopular among Americans embarked on peacetime lives. Whatever else had to be done, the one thing Truman was determined not to do was to risk the lives of American troops in Palestine.

Under the weight of these various studies, Truman and his advisers devised a two-part strategy to deal with Palestine. Its aim was to desert or suspend partition. The first part focused on undercutting the legal basis for armed intervention, thereby avoiding any possibility for the commitment of U.S. troops. Washington would maintain that the Security Council was not empowered to enforce partition since dividing up Palestine was merely a political recommendation by the General Assembly, not an order to be imposed by force.[13]

It was the second part of the strategy, however, that contained the core and the challenge of the matter. The strategy amounted to a subtle diplomatic ballet that had to be conducted with finesse if it was to be achieved without causing too much political harm to Truman. The execution rested on the shoulders of U.S. Ambassador to the United Nations Warren R. Austin. After accomplishing the first step by demonstrating that partition could not be imposed by force, there would come the denouement: gain the General Assembly's agreement to suspend partition in favor of a trusteeship to replace the British mandate. In the words of a State Department message to Truman, the U.S. argument would be that since it was "clear that Palestine is not yet ready for self-government...some form of United Nations trusteeship for an additional period of time will be necessary."[14]

In other words, the strategy was to throw the whole mess back to the General Assembly. Dean Rusk, the State Department's head of the Office of United Nations Affairs, tried to put the best face on it by saying the aim was to impose "a trusteeship for Palestine to replace the present mandate until such time as the Jews and Arabs could work out a modus vivendi."[15] The argument had the benefit of getting away from partition and perhaps even halting the slaughter going on in Palestine.

Truman agreed with this approach. But he insisted that adoption of a trusteeship was not an abandonment of partition. In the words of his memoirs, "This was not a rejection of partition but rather an effort to postpone its effective date until proper conditions for the establishment of self-government in the two parts might be established."[16] In a top secret message to Secretary of State George C. Marshall on 22 February, Truman wrote: "I approve in principle this basic position. I want to make it clear, however, that nothing should be presented to Security Council that could be interpreted as a recession on our part from the position we took in the General Assembly [on partition]."[17]

Truman's message made it clear that he was fully aware of what the State Department planned, and of its potentially disastrous political aftermath for his career if it was not handled with diplomatic delicacy. Thus, he cautioned that the proposal had to be presented in a way that could not be interpreted as abandoning partition. By taking this approach, Truman was covering his political flank, giving him plausible deniability. Indeed, he argued he merely was delaying partition until the bloodletting stopped and partition became practical.

Political pressure remained intense to support the Jewish state. Truman reported that it "did not diminish in the days following the partition vote in the UN. Individuals and groups asked me, usually in rather quarrelsome and emotional ways, to stop the Arabs, to keep the British from supporting the Arabs, to furnish American soldiers, to do this, that, and the other. I think I can say that I kept my faith in the rightness of my policy in spite of some of the Jews."[18]

By this time, in the early part of the year, Truman was so fed up with vociferous demands by Zionists that he barred them from the White House: "As the pressure mounted, I found it necessary to give instructions that I did not want to be approached by any more spokesmen for the extreme Zionist cause. I was even so disturbed that I put off seeing Dr. Chaim Weizmann."[19] Truman liked and admired the old Zionist, but his resentment at Zionist pressures was at a peak.

On 24 February, Ambassador Austin gently dropped the first shoe. He delivered America's interpretation of the Security Council's legal position as prohibiting the use of force. The maneuver was so subtle that it fell with barely a public ripple. In fact, it was so subtle that one official observed that the "kernel of our constitutional position requires considerable educative effort if it is to be got across to the people in plain English."[20] Subtle or not, it was an important bridge spanning the transition of U.S. policy from partition to trusteeship.

In order to halt the process unfolding in the United Nations, American Zionists and Clark Clifford persistently argued for keeping partition. As late as 6–8 March, two weeks after Austin's opening UN salvo, Clifford wrote two lengthy memoranda to the president offering an array of arguments justifying partition and creation of a Jewish state. "[P]artition is the only course of action with respect to Palestine that will strengthen our position vis-à-vis Russia....Jewish Palestine is strongly oriented to the United States, and away from Russia, and will remain so unless a military vacuum in Palestine caused by collapse of UN authority brings Russian unilateral intervention into Palestine."[21] He added that by drawing back from partition now,

> the United States appears in the ridiculous role of trembling before threats
> of a few nomadic desert tribes....Why should Russia or Yugoslavia or
> any other nation treat us with anything but contempt in light of our
> shilly-shallying appeasement of the Arabs?

Moreover, argued Clifford, concern about the Arab world was unnecessary because "...the Arabs need us more than we need them. They must have oil royalties or go bankrupt." Clifford went so far as to urge Truman to brand "the Arab states as aggressors" and to lift the U.S. arms embargo so that "the Jewish militia and Hagana...[will have] equal opportunity with the Arabs to arm for self-defense."[22] At the time the Palestinians and the Arab states were being denied weapons by all the major Western countries. No one, except the Zionists, was branding them the aggressors.

Partition was proving such a disaster that Truman ignored his political adviser and stuck, however reluctantly, with his diplomatic and military leaders. The increasing bloodshed in Palestine demonstrated that partition was failing, a failure for which Truman had to take the major blame.

On 19 March, Ambassador Austin dropped the second shoe. He announced in the Security Council that America believed partition was unworkable and that a UN trusteeship should be established to replace the British when they ended their withdrawal from Palestine on 15 May. The matter, he added, should go back to a special session of the General Assembly.

The reaction this time was deafening. Headlines screamed: "Ineptitude," "Weakness," "Vacillating," "Loss of American Prestige."[23] From Jerusalem, the consul general reported: "Jewish reaction...one of consternation, disillusion, despair and determination. Most feel United States has betrayed Jews in interests Middle Eastern oil and for fear Russian designs."[24] Even the Australian foreign minister declared that the United Nations had been "undermined by intrigues against the Jewish people."[25]

Truman was furious. The matter hardly had been handled with the sort of finesse that Truman had ordered. He felt that this clearly could be "interpreted as a recession on our part." The timing caused Truman extreme embarrassment not only because of the political uproar but because he had broken his own vow not to meet with Zionists and had seen Zionist leader Chaim Weizmann only the day before. Truman had given his personal word to Weizmann that the United States would not abandon its policy.[26] Now there was the public perception that he had. To his diary, Truman complained that the "State Department pulled the rug from under me today."[27]

That was an exaggeration, of course. Truman himself later admitted to Secretary of State Marshall, according to a memorandum from Marshall to one of his aides: "...He [Truman] said that the reasons he was so exercised in the matter was the fact that Austin made his statement without the president having been advised that he was going to make it at that particular time. He had agreed to the statement but said that if he had known when it was going to be made he could have taken certain measures to have avoided the political blast of the press."[28]

To make matters worse, the flap had occurred despite the fact that Truman had insisted on being personally involved on policy affecting partition and had essentially cut out the lower levels of the State Department. One internal message referred to partition as being "dealt with at the highest levels in Washington. They [State Department personnel] had strict orders to 'clamp down.'"[29] Nonetheless, it was the "middle levels" of the State Department that Truman henceforth blamed in public for the uproar.

Despite his embarrassment and the intense political heat, Truman stuck by the decision to drop partition and go to trusteeship. The new policy had the effect of throwing the whole question of partition and trusteeship back to the General Assembly on 15 April. It was still being discussed when the Jews declared a month later the establishment of Israel, rendering the questions of partition and trusteeship moot. Meanwhile, the slaughter and agony of civilians in Palestine did not pause. It grew worse.

* *

The flow of Palestinian refugees that had started as a trickle at the end of 1947 was becoming a stream by mid-April. The first hint of the flood to follow occurred on 18 April 1948 when Jewish forces launched an attack on Tiberias at the edge of the Sea of Galilee. In response, the town's estimated 5,300 Palestinian residents fled in terror.[30] The panicky flight of the Tiberians came only nine days after Jewish terrorists had slaughtered 254 men, women and children at the Palestinian village of Deir Yassin.[31] Rumors of the massacre were rife in the nervous Palestinian community, adding to the normal jitters of war.

In quick order, Haifa, with a slight Palestinian majority in its 150,000 population, fell on 22 April and Safad, with 9,500 Palestinians and 2,400 Jews, on 12 May. In both cases, the Palestinians fled en masse.

Up to this time, the major cities attacked by the Jews had been included as part of the Jewish state envisioned by the UN partition plan. However, in early May, Jewish forces began taking over cities and towns designated as part of the Arab state: Jaffa, an all-Palestinian city of 70,000, fell on 13 May, the day before Israel's founding. Western new Jerusalem, designated part of an international city and with around 30,000 Palestinians, mainly Christians, fell to Israeli forces on 14 May. As a result, when Israel came into being that same day, it already was well on its way to expanding its partition borders into the Palestinian community and cleansing the areas of Arabs.

Thus began in earnest "the Palestinian refugee problem." It was these refugees, eventually numbering 726,000 men, women and children, whose plight henceforth lay at the base of the Israeli-Palestinian conflict.[32] However, the enormity of the refugee problem did not attract high level attention in the spring of 1948. Truman and his advisers still were tied up with trying to abandon partition without appearing to, with the worrisome implications of the emerging state of Israel and, most compelling, with the presidential campaign. The plight of refugees in Palestine seemed remote.

* *

While the refugee flood was swelling in May, Truman was faced with another ticklish diplomatic problem that could have an enormous impact on the presidential campaign as well as Palestine. Even before they actually did so, the Jews had made it clear that they planned to proclaim their own state when the British finally withdrew in mid-May. The question facing the administration was whether to recognize the new state. The Zionists passionately supported immediate, or even earlier, recognition while the State Department thought it would be prudent to wait.

Domestic political considerations once again weighed heavily on Truman. The preconvention campaign was in its final months yet polls were showing he would lose against almost any Republican.[33] To review all aspects of the recognition matter, Truman called an extraordinary meeting in the White House on 12 May, two days before the end of Britain's withdrawal and Israel's self-proclaimed existence. The Secretary of State and other top officials were present, including presidential counselor Clark Clifford, who carried the White House political argument. Clifford charged the State Department was ignoring reality in opposing immediate recognition as soon as Israel was born. The only hope to gain advantage, he said, was for the United States to give prompt recognition to the inevitable Jewish state before the Soviet Union.[34]

Under Secretary of State Robert Lovett responded for the State Department, noting that "premature" recognition would be "buying a pig in a poke. How did we know what kind of Jewish state would be set up?" Clifford's recommendation, he charged, "was a very transparent attempt to win the Jewish vote...." Secretary of State Marshall agreed with Lovett. Marshall immediately after the meeting dictated his recollection of his acid comments:

> I remarked to the President that, speaking objectively, I could not help but think that the suggestions made by Mr. Clifford were wrong. I thought that to adopt these suggestions would have precisely the opposite effect from that intended by Mr. Clifford. The transparent dodge to win a few votes would not in fact achieve this purpose. The great dignity of the office of President would be seriously diminished. The counsel offered by Mr. Clifford was based on domestic political considerations, while the problem which confronted us was international. I said bluntly that if the President were to follow Mr. Clifford's advice and if in the elections I were to vote, I would vote against the President....the President terminated the interview by saying that he was fully aware of the difficulties and dangers in the situation, to say nothing of the political risks involved which he, himself, would run.[35]

Probably no senior aide had ever so directly insulted a president and retained his post. Marshall, however, was far too imposing a figure for Truman to discharge, particularly at this time when the beleaguered president was fighting for his political life. In fact, Marshall's strong opposition deterred Truman from taking an even more daring gesture than instant recognition of Israel. Clifford had wanted the president to make an early announcement of support of the establishment of a Jewish state even before the Jews had declared it. That would have had the effect of the United States officially encouraging the Jews to establish a state. Such an endorsement would have infuriated the Arabs. Marshall succeeded in convincing Truman not to go that far.

Nonetheless, as late as 14 May, just hours before the declaration establishing Israel, Clifford met with Lovett to try to sway the State Department behind recognition. He informed Lovett that recognition was "of the greatest possible importance to the President from a domestic point of view," adding: "The President was under unbearable pressure to recognize the Jewish state promptly." Lovett argued that recognition should be delayed but Clifford was firm, causing Lovett to observe wryly:

> My protests against the precipitate action and warnings as to consequences with the Arab world appear to have been outweighed by considerations unknown to me, but I can only conclude that the President's political advisers, having failed last Wednesday afternoon [12 May] to make the President a father of the new state, have determined at least to make him the midwife.[36]

That same day Truman gave *de facto* recognition to Israel at 6:11 p.m. Washington time. It was exactly eleven minutes after Israel proclaimed its existence on 14 May when the United States became the first nation to recognize the new state.[37] The transparency of Truman's political motives brought about nearly open revolt within the State Department. Disillusionment was already present, as demonstrated by the sarcastic tone in Lovett's memo on his conversation with Clifford. After Truman's recognition, the mood turned to despair. Kennan expressed it in a memorandum to Marshall on 21 May: "The Policy Planning Staff, while fully cognizant of the limitations on formulation of policy in the Department on the Palestine matter, wishes to record once more its deep apprehensions over the trend of U.S. policy."[38] By 24 May, Marshall informed Truman "of the difficulty we had in preventing a number of resignations among the members of our delegation to the United Nations and the State Department." To Lovett, Marshall observed: "He was unaware of this and seemed much perturbed at the possibility."[39]

As aggravating to the diplomats as Truman's bowing to domestic politics was the fact that since 1946 the State Department in general, and the Office of Near Eastern Affairs in particular, had been under unrelenting attack by the Zionists. Loy Henderson had become the bete noir of the Zionists, mainly as a result of Bartley Crum, the Zionist delegate on the old Anglo-American Committee whom Henderson had opposed. Crum in 1946 had accused Henderson of being an Arabist and demanded his resignation. The attacks had grown fiercer and more personal over the years, finally drawing in even such peripheral but influential figures as Eleanor Roosevelt against Henderson and his Division of Near Eastern and Africa Affairs. In opposing Henderson's early warnings about partition provoking violence, she had responded: "Come now, come, Mr. Henderson, I think you're exaggerating the dangers. You are too pessimistic....I'm confident that when a Jewish state is once set up, the Arabs will see the light; they will quiet down; and Palestine will no longer be a problem."[40]

Despite the Zionists charges of prejudice, the fact was that Henderson and his embattled colleagues were essentially Wilsonians, officials who believed in self-determination and majority rule. They were neither pro-Arab nor anti-Zionist. They did not oppose a Jewish state because it was Jewish but because, in Henderson's words, "it would be contrary to the policy which the United States has always followed of respecting the wishes of a large majority of the local inhabitants with respect to their form of government."[41] Although Truman for obvious reasons disliked him—Henderson knew the extent of the president's pandering to the Zionists—the diplomat was highly regarded by his colleagues. George Kennan wrote of him as a "man of so active an intelligence, such deep seriousness and impressive sincerity, and such unbending conscientiousness...that he left his impression on everyone who was associated with him."[42]

Regardless of the ceaseless attacks and the president's open scorn of their advice, Henderson and his small group hung on. They continued to serve Truman loyally, if with private reservations. If Henderson's advice had been followed, the United States would not have been branded as the country that aided and abetted the process of partitioning Palestine against the wishes of the Arab majority. Nor would it have shared responsibility for Israel's expansion at the cost of nearly three-quarters of a million uprooted Palestinians.

On the other hand, cynicism had its rewards. Truman reaped the benefits of his political ploys by gaining strong Jewish support to defy all predictions and getting elected in his own right as president of the United States.[43]

* *

The immediate result of Israel's declaration of a Jewish state in defiance of the Arab majority in Palestine was the entrance on 15 May of army units from five Arab countries: Egypt, Iraq, Jordan, Lebanon and Syria. The Arab troops invaded in order to prevent Israeli forces from continuing their conquest of Arab land beyond the UN partition plan, although other motives such as destroying the Jewish state or preventing Jordan from taking over parts of the West Bank were certainly at work. The State Department had predicted such an intervention less than two weeks before the British withdrawal. An internal memorandum observed that

> the Jews will be the actual aggressors against the Arabs. However, the Jews will claim that they are merely defending the boundaries of a state which were traced by the UN....In the event of such Arab outside aid the Jews will come running to the Security Council with the claim that their state is the object of armed aggression and will use every means to obscure the fact that it is their own armed aggression against the Arabs inside which is the cause of Arab counter-attack.[44]

Indeed, that was precisely what happened. As foreseen by the State Department, the Arabs were outgunned, outmanned and less organized than the Israelis. They never succeeded in carrying the battle into the Jewish state.[45]

Israeli forces were so strong that the presence of the Arab armies did not deter them from capturing Acre on 17 May. The coastal city had been designated as part of the Arab state. Its 1947 population of 16,000 included 13,000 Palestinian Muslims and Christians, and around 3,000 Jews. By May 1948, however, the fall of Haifa and surrounding Arab areas had turned the old fortress city into a refugee center, swelling the Arab population to 40,000. The Israeli conquest of Acre caused another mass evacuation.[46] Other Palestinian towns soon followed: Lydda and Ramle, all-Palestinian towns, fell on 11 July; all 70,000 Arab residents were forced to flee. Nazareth, all-Palestinian with 17,000 residents, was captured on 16 July. However, Palestinian residents were allowed to remain, the only major Palestinian town where this happened.[47] In most areas, the Palestinians were actively forced to flee or deliberately panic-stricken into fleeing with reminders of Deir Yassin.[48]

These dramatic events finally began catching the attention of Washington. By early May there began appearing references in dispatches to the State Department about "thousands Arabs fleeing country."[49] On 22 May, the consul general in Jerusalem reported that "now extremely difficult get in touch with prominent and representative Arabs...."[50]

The number of refugees grew exponentially. By 28 June, the State Department was using the preliminary figure of 300,000 as the number of Palestinians who were now refugees. Already there were reports that Israel would not allow them to return to their homes. The chargé in Egypt, Jefferson Patterson, advised the State Department that if Israel refused the return of the refugees it would prove to the Arabs that the "statements by Zionists that they seek Arab friendship have no basis in fact" and, moreover, the refusal would convince the Arabs that the "real intention of Jews is to dispossess refugee Arabs of property and enterprises in Israel in order to provide space and economic opportunities for Jewish immigrants."[51]

A week later the special UN Mediator in Palestine, Count Folke Bernadotte,[52] estimated there were as many as 400,000 Palestinian refugees whose condition "without food, clothing and shelter was appalling." In reporting Bernadotte's remarks, Patterson said Bernadotte had observed that the basic problem was whether the refugees eventually would be allowed by Israel to return to their homes. Added Patterson:

> In this connection, Bernadotte said PGI [provisional government of Israel] was 'showing signs of swell-head.' Shertok [Foreign Minister Moshe Sharett]...had indicated politically PGI could not admit Arab refugees as they would constitute fifth column. Economically PGI had no room for Arabs since their space was needed for Jewish immigrants....In regard to property Arab refugees, he [Bernadotte] said apparently most had been seized for use by Jews. He had seen Haganah organizing and supervising removal contents Arab houses in Ramle which he understood was being distributed among newly arrived Jewish immigrants.[53]

A week later, Sir Raphael Cliento, the Australian-born UN expert on refugees, reported the Palestinian homeless were "more helpless than anywhere else in the world except China."[54] By 19 August, the dimensions of the refugee problem finally came to Truman's direct attention. The State Department informed him that there were 330,000 refugees and their condition was pathetic:

> They are destitute of any belongings, are without adequate shelter, medical supplies, sanitation and food. Their average daily ration, made up exclusively of bread, is only 600 calories. Once the rainy season commences and winter sets in, tragedy on the largest scale will be inevitable unless relief is forthcoming. Thus far the Provisional Government of Israel has refused to admit the Arab refugees to their former homes, which have in some cases been destroyed by fighting and in other preempted by Jewish immigrants.[55]

On 16 September, Bernadotte bluntly warned the United Nations that "the choice is between saving the lives of many thousands of people now or permitting them to die." He urged the United Nations to expedite the return of the refugees to their homes from which they "fled or were expelled from," adding:

> It would be an offense against the principles of elemental justice if these innocent victims of the conflict were denied the right of return to their homes while Jewish immigrants flow into Palestine, and, indeed, at least offer the threat of permanent replacement of the Arab refugees who have been rooted in the land for centuries.[56]

Specifically he recommended that "the Arab refugees should be given the right to return to their homes or receive compensation and resettlement."[57]

A month later, after Jewish terrorists assassinated Bernadotte, which had the incidental effect of deflecting public attention away from the refugees, his replacement, Ralph Bunche, warned the world body that the refugees' plight had become "critical" and aid must be "greatly increased if disaster is to be averted."[58] At about the same time the State Department estimated the number of refugees at 468,000 and warned Truman that "the situation is daily more critical as cold weather sets in."[59] It advised him that there was a "desperate need for blankets and clothing in addition to larger quantities of food supplies."[60]

Israel, however, insisted the refugees were not its responsibility, that their number was far less than claimed by the United States and others, and it refused to take any action to help them. Its official position was that

> the Government of Israel must disclaim any responsibility for the creation of this problem. The charge that these Arabs were forcibly driven out by Israel authorities is wholly false; on the contrary, everything possible was done to prevent an exodus which was a direct result of the folly of the Arab states in organizing and launching a war of aggression against Israel.[61]

Despite numerous firsthand reports by disinterested observers, and the testimony of countless refugees, Israel largely succeeded in the public relations effort to convince the world that the refugees had fled by their own volition as a result of the 15 May attack by Arab armies and that Israel had no responsibility for them. When the U.S. Representative in Israel, James G. McDonald, began reflecting Israel's claim that the refugees were created by the Arab states' intervention, Secretary of State George C. Marshall himself set him straight:

> Arab refugee problem is one which, as you quote PGI [Provisional Government of Israel] as saying, did develop from recent war in Palestine but which also began before outbreak of Arab-Israeli hostilities. A significant portion of Arab refugees fled from their homes owing to Jewish occupation of Haifa on April 21–22 and to Jewish armed attack against Jaffa April 25....The leaders of Israel would make a grave miscalculation if they thought callous treatment of this tragic issue could pass unnoticed by world opinion.[62]

Despite the State Department's clear understanding of what really was going on, Israel continued its claims that it was not responsible for the refugees. Even as late as mid-1949, Chaim Weizmann assured Truman in a personal letter that the refugee problem "was not created by us. It was not the birth of Israel which created the Arab refugee problem, as our enemies now proclaim, but the Arab attempt to prevent that birth by armed force....They left the country last year at the bidding of their leaders and military commanders and as part of the Arab strategic plan."[63]

Nonetheless, the reality was well known at the United Nations by the fall of 1948. In order to try to pressure Israel, the United Nations' Ralph Bunche and U.S. and British officials began in mid-October working on a UN General Assembly draft resolution that recognized "the right of the Arab refugees to return to their homes in Jewish-controlled territory at the earliest possible date; and the right of adequate compensation for the property of those choosing not to return and for property which has been lost as a result of pillage or confiscation or of destruction not resulting from military necessity...."[64]

The latter part of the sentence referring to losses not resulting from combat was a reference to the pillage and widespread looting and destruction wreaked by Jewish troops on Palestinian property.[65] Indiscriminate plundering of Palestinian property by Jews was so common that it caused Prime Minister David Ben Gurion to confide to his diary that he was "bitterly surprised" by the "mass robbery in which all parts of the population participated." Indeed, the despoliation was not confined to soldiers. Israeli historian Tom Segev reported: "In Haifa, Jaffa and Jerusalem there were many civilians among the looters." Another Israeli writer, Moshe Smilanky, reported: "Individuals, groups and communities, men, women and children, all fell on the spoils. Doors, windows, lintels, brinks, roof-tiles, floor-tiles, junk and machine parts...." Segev commented that Smilanky "could have also added to the list toilet bowls, sinks, faucets and light bulbs."[66]

Indiscriminate killings of Palestinian civilians also occurred. At the village of al-Dawayima near Hebron, Israeli soldiers massacred at least 100—and perhaps more than twice that number—men, women and children. An Israeli eyewitness reported: "The children they killed by breaking their heads with sticks. There was not a house without dead....One soldier boasted that he had raped a woman and then shot her." At least two old women were locked in a house before it was blown up.[67] Villagers surviving such experiences—with the massacre of Deir Yassin still fresh in mind—soon joined the exodus of fleeing Palestinians.

On 17 October U.S. Representative in Israel McDonald reported urgently and directly to President Truman that the

> Arab refugee tragedy is rapidly reaching catastrophic proportions and should be treated as a disaster. Present and prospective relief and re-settlement resources are utterly inadequate....Of approximately 400,000 refugees approaching winter with cold heavy rains will, it is estimated, kill more than 100,000 old men, women and children who are shelterless and have little or no food.

In case his report be dismissed as being too emotional, McDonald added: "(All adjectives used above are realistically descriptive and are written out of fifteen years of personal contact with refugee problems.)"[68]

The central problem was that no country, especially the United States, was eager to help the mass of refugees and thereby assume a degree of responsibility for their uncertain future. Moreover, a survey of various U.S. embassies and legations in the region showed that there was little hope the Arab countries, even if they had felt responsible for the tragedy, could afford to support the refugees.

The Cairo embassy reported that if the 250,000 refugees held in the Gaza Strip were driven into Egypt the "result would be almost catastrophic for Egypt financially." The embassy in Amman reported that the presence of 80,000 in Jordan and 302,000 in Arab Palestine were a serious drain on "almost nonexistent resources" and that "money, jobs and other opportunities [were] scarce." The 90,000 in Lebanon were an "unbearable burden" on that government because of unemployment and the "sensitive balance that exists between Christians and Moslems." Syria had 80,000 to 100,000 but the government had "practically abandoned its relief expenditures as unsupportable budgetary drain."[69]

Despite their slender resources, the State Department reported that "the great brunt of relief expenditures has been borne, perforce, by the Arab States...." During the last nine months of 1948, the report added, the Arabs nations had donated $11 million to refugee aid. "This sum," said the report, "in light of the very slender budgets of most of these Governments, is relatively enormous." (At the time, Transjordan's total government budget was only $5 million.)[70] The report noted that "the total direct relief offered...by the Israeli Government to date consists of 500 cases of oranges."[71]

Beyond their financial inability to support the refugees, the Arab states feared the political instability a large infusion of restless, homeless people would cause their societies. One State Department official noted the refugees would constitute a "core of agitation" in any nation that accepted them.[72] Another report cautioned that the continuing presence of the refugees not only would undermine the economies of the Arab states but "may well provide the motivation for the overthrow of certain of the Arab Governments."[73]

This theme was elaborated on in yet another report:

> Since Egypt and Saudi Arabia have no refugees (Egypt has reportedly sent all of hers into Gaza Strip) and Iraq has only 4,000, figure of 800,000 [refugees] constitutes about one-tenth population remaining Arab states. Since they [are] generally more advanced than other Arabs they constitute potential core of dangerous agitators offering a threat to existence of Arab government. They also create, so Arab leaders here have told me, core of irredentist movement that will plague all Arab states and provide basis for continual agitation to point that there will be no possibility of having anything more than armistice in Middle East.[74]

In fact, refugees had added 21 percent to the population of Transjordan,

10 percent to Lebanon and 3.5 percent to Syria. In addition, Egypt was keeping 225,000 penned in the Gaza Strip, frightened to allow them into Egypt proper, and Transjordan was faced with 230,000 others remaining in areas under Amman's military control in Palestine. The refugees were not the type of healthy and potentially productive workers that most nations seek. The State Department estimated that 15 percent "are aged, sick, and infirm. It would appear that the able-bodied men and women amount to a maximum of 25 percent of the total, or 180,000." The rest of the refugees, the majority, were "infants, children, pregnant women, and nursing mothers."[75]

A study by the Israeli foreign ministry made equally grim reading: "The most adaptable [refugees] and best survivors would manage by a process of natural selection, and the others will waste away. Some will die but most will turn into human debris and social outcasts and probably join the poorest classes in the Arab countries."[76]

* *

In the fall of 1948, the Palestinian refugee problem arrived back at the doorstep of the United Nations, where its genesis had begun on 29 November 1947 with passage of General Assembly partition resolution 181. The tragic consequences of partition were clear to all: nearly three-quarters of the Palestinian community uprooted and scattered; 13,000 Palestinians, mainly civilians, had been killed, and 156,000 Palestinians left under Israeli military occupation in the guise of citizenship within Israel.[77] Refugees, huddled in caves and under trees, were dying daily in increasing numbers in the fall of 1948.[78]

The reaction of the General Assembly came on 19 November when it unanimously created the Agency for Relief for Palestine Refugees to organize and coordinate relief activities of various international humanitarian groups. Funds totalling $29.5 million were allocated to care for 500,000 refugees for a period of nine months, from 1 December 1948 to 31 August 1949, and an additional $2.5 million was allocated for administrative costs.[79] Second, the Assembly established a formula for resolution of the refugee problem: repatriation or resettlement and compensation. The formula was outlined in resolution 194 (III) passed on 11 December 1948.[80] Article 11 stated:

> *Resolves* that the refugees wishing to return to their homes and live at peace with their neighbors should be permitted to do so at the earliest practicable date, and that compensation should be paid for the property of those choosing not to return and for loss of or damage to property of which, under principles of international law or in equity, should be made good by the Governments or authorities responsible.
>
> *Instructs* the Conciliation Commission to facilitate the repatriation, resettlement and economic and social rehabilitation of the refugees and the payment of compensation, and to maintain close relations with the Director of the United Nations Relief for Palestine Refugees

and, through him, with the appropriate organs and agencies of the United Nations.

The vote was 35–15–8, with the United States voting with the majority, which was made up mainly of European and Latin nations. Those opposed were Islamic and Communist nations and the abstainers were Asian and Latin. Henceforth, resolution 194 embodied U.S. policy toward the refugees, becoming the official U.S. reference point for all questions concerning refugees.

Resolution 194 also established a three-member Conciliation Commission for Palestine (usually referred to in U.S. official documents as PCC) to "achieve a final settlement of all questions outstanding between" Arabs and Jews. In addition to the refugee problem, these were identified as finding peace between the parties and establishing an international regime over Jerusalem. The members were France (Claude de Boisanger), Turkey (Huseyin Cahit Yalchin) and the United States (Joseph Keenan, who lasted only two weeks and was replaced by Mark F. Ethridge). Two venues were involved in the PCC's efforts: Jerusalem to establish an international regime for that city, and Lausanne, Switzerland, where the members met unsuccessfully between 27 April and 15 September 1949 to resolve the refugee problem and achieve overall peace.[81]

At Lausanne, in addition to the three PCC members, was an Israeli delegation headed by Dr. Walter Eytan, a veteran negotiator, while the Arabs appeared as one body represented by Egypt, Lebanon, Syria and Transjordan. A "Palestinian adviser," Ahmad Shuqayri, was attached to the Syrian delegation—meaning the refugees did not have their own independent delegate in the discussions that were focused on their future.[82] This typified the general disregard at the time in Washington and elsewhere of the Palestinian community. Palestinians during this period and well into the 1960s generally were referred to merely as Arabs and lumped together with the larger Arab world without identity as a separate community.

* *

The prospect of forging peace treaties at Lausanne caused the State Department clearly to delineate U.S. Middle East policy on a number of basic issues, among them the U.S. attitude toward the refugee problem. The policy positions were spelled out in top secret instructions by Acting Secretary of State Robert A. Lovett on 19 January 1949 to U.S. Delegate to the PCC Mark Ethridge.[83] Under *Palestinian Refugees*, the instruction said: "You should be guided by the provisions of the General Assembly resolution [194] of December 11 concerning refugees." In other words, the Truman Administration affirmed its support of resolution 194's formula of repatriation or resettlement and compensation.

In espousing repatriation or compensation Washington was in direct opposition to Israel, which continued to maintain that it had no responsibility for the refugees and would not allow their return. Israel also resisted paying compensation. Unmentioned by Israel was the extent of its conquests or the fact that many of the abandoned Palestinian homes had already been taken over by Jews. Israel's conquests included not only such major cities as Jaffa, Lydda and Acre but also 418 Palestinian villages that were destroyed and another 100 villages that were occupied by Jews.[84] In all, Israelis took over more than 50,000 homes, 10,000 shops and 1,000 warehouses. It was estimated that about a quarter of the buildings in the new state were originally the property of Palestinians.[85]

Although reliable figures were lacking at the time, the PCC later determined that the value of lost Palestinian immovable property was at least $480 million in 1947 dollars; other estimates ranged many times higher.[86] One Arab estimate put the figure at $35 billion in 1990 dollars.[87]

* *

The bitter scene in Palestine in early 1949 was portrayed graphically by *New York Times* correspondent Anne O'Hare McCormick:

> [Palestine is] a vast camp, an armed camp on one side of the line and a refugee camp on the other....[Israel] is born at the expense of another people now fated to join the ragged ranks of the displaced. For good or ill, it is born to upset the equilibrium of an area so shaky that it trembles at a touch. This new nation, stronger and more unified than its neighbors, is bound to change the balance in this area, whether as a point of stability or a constantly disruptive element is the big question of the future....if Israel is a fact that must be recognized, so is the burning sense of invasion and usurpation the Palestinian Arabs feel. Of themselves, these people would not have waged this war. They had no leadership and until now no widespread hatred of their Jewish neighbors. The 750,000 who are displaced persons are too wretched and dispirited to cherish any thought of fighting now. Neither they nor the sullen Arab minority remaining under Israeli rule constitute a physical danger, but their resentment is as real and deep as the nation spirit of Israel.[88]

In another report she wrote: "So far no one here has expressed any sense of responsibility or sympathy for these wretched victims of the Palestine war, and [Foreign Minister Moshe] Sharett does not admit that Israel is in any way accountable for their flight."[89]

McCormick's reporting elicited a letter to the *Times* from Kermit Roosevelt, grandson of Theodore Roosevelt and an expert in the region who was later to become a legendary intelligence agent. He wrote that the Palestinian uprooting mainly was caused by excesses of the Jewish terrorists "such as the massacre of Deir Yassin, which most correspondents agree started off the main evacuation....Although Israeli officials indignantly repel the insinuation that the Arab evacuation was the result of a deliberate policy on their part, Mrs. McCormick notes 'they cheerfully acknowledge that they lost no time in taking advantage of it.'" Roosevelt added:

As Americans, we must ask ourselves: what will the creation of three-quarters of a million exiles do to the long-range prospects for peace in the Middle East? We cannot expect that these exiles will abandon willingly the goal of returning to their own homes. The lands into which they have been driven are shaky, both economically and politically; they are in no condition to cope with a refugee and resettlement problem as large as this. If our object is the establishment of peace and security in the Middle East, the solution of this refugee problem must be high on our agenda.[90]

Despite such public airing of the refugee problem, the U.S. media generally devoted little attention to it and subsequently most Americans remained ignorant of the tragedy unfolding in Palestine. This was documented by the State Department in a major study prepared in March 1949. According to this report the public in the United States

generally is unaware of the Palestine refugee problem, since it has not been hammered away at by the press or radio. Aside from *The New York Times* and *The Herald Tribune*, which have done more faithful reporting than other papers, there has been very little coverage of the problem. With the exception of a Sunday feature article by Max Boyd, the wire service stories, if filed, have not been used. Editorial comment is still more sparse. Freda Kirchwey in *Nation*, a few editorials in *America* (Catholic), an editorialized article in the *New Leader* and one editorial each in *The Baltimore Sun* and the *Des Moines Register* nearly exhausts the list. Most of the news articles and editorials have had a friendly slant, except for *The New York Post*, which was violently opposed to helping the Arabs.[91]

One explanation for the indifference of the media toward the fate of the Palestinian refugees was that memories of the mass suffering during World War II were still fresh. The world had been shocked at the slaughter of tens of millions in the war, including six million Jews. People remained stunned by the suffering revealed by the discovery of the Nazi death camps, the spectacle of piles of emaciated and rotting bodies and the uprooting of millions of people. At war's end in 1945, there were seven million "displaced persons," Europeans who had lost or been forced from their homes and had no shelter or food, among them tens of thousands of Jews too frightened or angry to return to their inhospitable homes in Germany and Poland.[92]

Beyond this, Israel still had not made known in public its stand on the refugees beyond repeated statements that it was not responsible for them and would not allow their return. Publicly, Israel based its argument on the claim that the Palestinians would be a security threat. There was no public relations gain in discussing the facts on the ground: Palestinian housing already was either destroyed or taken over by Jews.

While the refugees remained relatively pacific because they continued to believe that one day they would return to their homes, Washington realized that the prospects for their repatriation were inexorably diminishing with each passing day.[93] A February 1949 memorandum from McDonald, the U.S. representative in Tel Aviv, summarized the obstacles to the Palestinians' return:

> ...the unprecedentedly rapid influx of Jewish refugees during 1948 and the plan to admit a quarter of a million more in 1949 will, if carried out, fill all or almost all of the houses and business properties previously held by Arab refugees....Hence there will be almost no residence or business property and only a limited number of farms to which the Arab refugees can hope to return.[94]

In addition, a State Department study observed that "Israeli authorities have followed a systematic program of destroying Arab houses in such cities as Haifa and in village communities in order to rebuild modern habitations for the influx of Jewish immigrants from DP camps in Europe. There are, thus, in many instances, literally no houses for the refugees to return to. In other cases incoming Jewish immigrants have occupied Arab dwellings and will most certainly not relinquish them in favor of the refugees." The study added that "it is reasonable to assume that as many as 600,000 refugees will have to be permanently settled in the Arab states." Since the paper placed the total number of refugees at 725,000, this meant that Washington assumed, at most, that only 125,000 refugees could expect to return.[95] However, even 125,000 may have been an optimistic estimate. Jewish immigrants were pouring into the new country at the rate of 25,000 a month after May 1948.[96] Thus, by rejecting responsibility for the refugees and at the same time confiscating their property, Israel was solving its most pressing problem, housing for the new immigrants.

By the end of February the plight of the refugees was so enormous that the refugee problem itself had become the major impediment to any peace agreement. Beside the refugees, other areas of dispute between Jews and Arabs paled, in the opinion of U.S. officials. The consul in Jerusalem, William C. Burdett, cabled the State Department that

> immediate key to peace negotiations, if not to peace, is refugee problem. Arab League is not dead intellectually even if militarily ineffective. There was complete concert of approach to us with almost open request for imposed peace, for guarantees accompanying it and for beginning of solution of refugee problem as sine qua non of discussions of other questions.[97]

That same day, Mark Ethridge, the U.S. member of the Palestine Conciliation Commission, told Prime Minister David Ben Gurion that the "refugees were [the] main concern [for] Arab States." He added that they constituted "such human and psychological problem to them that if Israel could make advance gesture regarding refugees...general settlement would be greatly facilitated....Ben Gurion agreed but strongly stressed Israeli need for military security as well as peace."[98] In secret Ben Gurion repeated his position that "they may not return."[99]

In public the Israelis continued a Sphinx-like silence, as they did even in their confidential communications with the United States about their ultimate intentions toward the refugees. Israeli officials kept their American counterparts off balance by hinting broadly that eventually at least some of the refugees might be allowed to return. Thus, American officials anxiously held out hope that Israel could be persuaded to accept back some refugees. However, Ethridge reported in mid-March that "six weeks of effort to get the Israeli Government to commit itself on the refugee problem have resulted in not one single statement of position."[100]

Nonetheless, the Truman Administration devoted the first half of 1949 trying futilely to persuade Israel to relent, at least partially, on its inflexible attitude toward the Palestinian refugees. The main burden was carried by the PCC's Ethridge, a political appointee who had been publisher of the Louisville *Courier Journal* and a personal friend of Truman. He had no experience in Middle Eastern diplomacy, and therefore displayed a refreshing candor and impatience with the usual coded language that passed for diplomatic practice. It did not take the plain-speaking Kentuckian long to fathom the rigidity of Israel's position on the refugees. As early as 28 March 1949, he reported to the State Department:

> Failure of Jews to do so [settle the refugee problem] has prejudiced whole cause of peaceful settlement in this part of world....Since we gave Israel birth we are blamed for her belligerence and her arrogance and for cold-bloodedness of her attitude toward refugees....What I can see is an abortion of justice and humanity to which I do not want to be midwife....[101]

By April, Ethridge was completely disillusioned with the Israelis. On the 13th, he had a heated meeting with Prime Minister Ben Gurion over the refugee issue. In his report to the State Department, Ethridge wrote: "It is obvious that Israel has not changed position on refugee problem whatever....Israel does not intend to take back one refugee more than she is forced to take and she does not intend to compensate any directly if she can avoid it." Ethridge reported that Israel continued to insist that the number of refugees was exaggerated and that it "refuses to accept any responsibility whatever for creation of refugees," adding: "I have repeatedly pointed out political weakness and brutality of their position on refugees but it has made little impression."[102]

At the same time, Ethridge wrote a personal letter to his friend Truman:

> The Jews are still too close to the blood of their war...and too close to the bitterness of their fight against the British mandate to exercise any degree of statesmanship yet. They still feel too strongly that their security lies in military might instead of in good relations with their neighbors....The Arabs have made what the Commission considers very great concessions; the Jews have made none so far.[103]

By this time, President Truman himself was impatient with the Israelis. He cabled Ethridge on 20 April:

> Dear Mark....I am rather disgusted with the manner in which the Jews are approaching the refugee problem. I told the President of Israel in

the presence of his Ambassador just exactly what I thought about it. It
may have some effect, I hope so.[104]

Not only did Truman's message have no impact, but Israeli officials responded that "they intend to bring about a change in the position of the United
States Government...through means available to them in the United States." That
boastful message was contained in a memorandum from Acting Secretary of State
James E. Webb to President Truman.[105] It added that Ethridge and the UN Commission had "failed to obtain any concessions from the Israelis on a territorial
settlement or the refugee question." Its conclusion was that Israel "will do nothing
more concerning the Arab refugees at the present time." The memorandum informed the president that "the Department believes that the time has come to make
a basic decision concerning our attitude toward Israel." It urged that a strong message be sent to Israel, but cautiously added that the proposed message "would
arouse strong opposition in American Jewish circles" and suggested that Truman
first might like to check with his political advisers.

There is no record of Truman's response, but he was stung enough that
the next day the State Department sent to Tel Aviv the stiffest message since Israel's
existence. It warned that if Israel continued to ignore the advice of the United
Nations and the United States, "the US Govt will regretfully be forced to the conclusion that a revision of its attitude toward Israel has become unavoidable."[106]
Israel's response came a fortnight later. It was indirect but nonetheless rude. Israel's
delegate at the Palestine Conciliation Commission in Lausanne openly distributed
a news story in the *Palestine Post* saying, in the paraphrase of Ethridge, that "nothing has happened to alter the attitude of the Israeli Government in the slightest."[107]
Israel's official response was delivered to the State Department on 8 June, asserting disingenuously that Truman's note must have been "based on a misunderstanding" of Israel's true position and therefore, by implication, it was not a serious
matter.[108]

Such arrogance by a supposedly friendly state was not in the usual experience of the State Department, and U.S. officials at the time no doubt thought it a
simple enough matter to pressure a small country numbering less than a million
people. In retaliation, the State Department sought to pressure Israel by threatening to withhold $49 million of unallocated funds from a $100 million Export-
Import Bank loan to Israel. It was decided that the funds would not be delivered if
Israel did not take back at least 200,000 refugees. George C. McGhee, the newly
appointed U.S. coordinator on Palestine Refugee Matters, was chosen to deliver
the message to the Israeli ambassador in Washington.[109] According to McGhee's
account:

> I asked the ambassador [Eliahu Elath] to lunch with me at the Metro-
> politan Club and put our decision to him in the most tactful and objec-
> tive way I could....The ambassador looked me straight in the eye and
> said, in essence, that I wouldn't get by with this move, that he would
> stop it....Within an hour of my return to my office I received a message

from the White House that the President wished to dissociate himself from any withholding of the Ex-Im Bank loan.[110]

Even before this final humiliation, Israeli officials had made no attempt to hide their satisfaction with the power they wielded through the Jewish community in America. The U.S. consul in Jerusalem had reported in July during the middle of the dispute:

> Israel is convinced of its ability to "induce" the United States to abandon its present insistence on repatriation of refugees and territorial changes. From experience in the past, officials state confidently "you will change your mind," and the press cites instances of the effectiveness of organized Jewish propaganda in the U.S.[111]

As it turned out, the Israelis were right. Truman was "induced" to take no further action. Israel received its money without changing its policies. From Israel, Representative McDonald observed: "The [next] American note abandoned completely the stern tone of its predecessor....More and more, Washington ceased to lay down the law to Tel Aviv."[112]

For U.S. diplomats it was a humiliating experience. Stuart W. Rockwell, a member of the U.S. delegation in Lausanne, cabled the Secretary of State that Washington's capitulation "indicates a radical change in U.S. attitude toward Israel...There has been no alteration in position of Israeli delegation here on basic issues which would justify such change in U.S. policy. Announcement will place me in very awkward position vis-à-vis Israeli delegation, with members of which...I have been taking strong line....Announcement particularly unfortunate view possible effect on cooperation Arab states with U.S."[113]

It was a fateful capitulation by Truman, signalling to Israel that it literally could act as it wanted—or did not want—toward the refugees without undue worry about American protestations. It was a signal not lost on the Arab world. After this display of the power of the Israeli lobby, the Truman Administration made no further serious effort to exert overt pressure to bring Israel in line with U.S. policy.

The Lausanne peace talks ended 15 September in total failure. Ethridge placed the primary blame on Israel:

> If there is to be any assessment of blame for stalemate at Lausanne, Israel must accept primary responsibility....Her attitude toward refugees is morally reprehensible and politically short-sighted....Her position as conqueror demanding more does not make for peace. It makes for more trouble....There was never a time in the life of the commission when a generous and far-sighted attitude on the part of the Jews would not have unlocked peace.[114]

Instead, Israel ignored America's advice and imposed its rule in its expanded frontiers, tightening its grip on Jerusalem and publicizing its claim that the refugees were not its responsibility while settling Jewish immigrants in their homes. Not all Israelis, however, were blind to the tragedy unfolding before them. For example, Minister of Agriculture Aharon Cizling early warned his colleagues:

> We still do not properly appreciate what kind of enemy we are now nurturing outside the borders of our state. Our enemies, the Arab states, are a mere nothing compared with those hundreds of thousands of Arabs who will be moved by hatred and hopelessness and infinite hostility to wage war on us, regardless of any agreement that might be reached.[115]

Prime Minister David Ben Gurion had no time for such sentiments, particularly not during this period when Palestinian housing was urgently needed for Jewish immigrants arriving by the thousands. Ben Gurion's hard-line and the double failure of the Lausanne talks and of Truman's inability to get Israel to change its policy left the refugee problem unresolved. Sensing Washington's weakness, the UN General Assembly finally took a major action to aid the refugees. By a vote of 47–0–6, with the U.S. supporting, it established on 8 December 1949 the United Nations Relief and Works Agency (UNRWA) to give direct aid to the 726,000 Palestinian refugees.[116] The Assembly observed that UNRWA "is necessary to prevent conditions of starvation and distress" among the refugees.[117] UNRWA remained the primary agency caring for Palestinian refugees, who, with their descendants in 1993 totaled 2,797,279 persons registered with UNRWA, more than 1.8 million of them still in camps.[118]

* *

For the quarter-century after Truman's failed efforts to influence Israel to adopt a humane policy toward the refugees, U.S. policy nominally remained the same. Administrations from Eisenhower through Bush routinely supported General Assembly resolutions reaffirming resolution 194's call for repatriation or resettlement and compensation. That was the public policy. However, official concern for the refugees weakened in Washington as the years passed. Only in the Eisenhower and the Kennedy administrations were innovative strategies devised to address the refugee problem. After their failure, succeeding administrations seemed content to allow the issue to drift.

The Eisenhower Administration's strategy to break the refugee impasse centered on a regional scheme to share the waters of the Jordan Valley among Arabs and Israelis. It was an imaginative effort since Israel, Jordan, Lebanon and Syria all shared parts of the valley and, moreover, more than half of the Palestinian refugees uprooted by the 1948 war still remained in the region formed by the frontiers. The Jordan Valley Development Program envisioned the irrigation of land on which as many as 160,000 refugees could make a living and another 140,000 find work in businesses servicing the farmers.[119]

The man placed in charge of selling the program to the Arabs and Israel in the fall of 1953 was Eric Johnston. He explained his mission was to help the refugees:

> Today thousands of them are homeless, landless, penniless, and increas-

ingly hopeless. In the Jordan Valley, on lands watered through modern irrigation canals, many of these people could be given a new economic stake and the dignity of independence once again. While it would not solve the whole problem of the Arab refugees, who number more than 800,000, settlement in the Jordan Valley would at least ameliorate the tension. It would ease the burning sense of frustration and resentment they now feel after six long years of displacement and defeated hope.[120]

However, mutual Arab-Israeli suspicions, Israel's determination to go ahead with its own national water carrier project and cabinet crises in Lebanon and Syria all contributed to derailing Johnston's efforts, which lasted from October 1953 to October 1955.[121]

John Foster Dulles, Eisenhower's secretary of state, made a final effort in 1955 by offering significant U.S. aid to solve the refugee problem. On 26 August, Dulles called in a major speech for limited repatriation and resettlement as well as compensation, adding:

> Compensation is due from Israel to the refugees. However, it may be that Israel cannot, unaided, now make adequate compensation. If so, there might be an international loan to enable Israel to pay the compensation which is due and which would enable many of the refugees to find for themselves a better way of life. President Eisenhower would recommend substantial participation by the United States in such a loan for such a purpose. Also he would recommend that the United States contribute to the realization of water development and irrigation projects which would, directly or indirectly, facilitate resettlement of the refugees.[122]

Although Dulles had sought to placate Israel by saying that the dimension of repatriation of the refugees should only be "to such an extent as may be feasible," it was clear in Washington that this was an issue on which Israel was implacable. Thus in internal discussions, it was conceded, as it had been since 1949, that "it [is] clearly not possible for all or most of them [to] go back." [123] In fact, internal memos referred to only 75,000 refugees being repatriated over a five-year period.[124]

Similarly, Washington was ready to allow Israel to pay bargain basement prices for the property abandoned by the refugees. In concert with Britain, Washington secretly agreed that Israel would have to pay only $280 million. Moreover, it was agreed that Israel would have to raise only 30 percent of the funds, with the rest coming from long-term, low-interest loans, mainly from Britain and the United States.[125] Even these concessions, however, were not enough to induce Israel into modifying its policy against repatriating refugees. Moreover, on 27 September, a month after Dulles' speech, the focus of the region was dramatically shifted by Egypt's purchase of arms through Czechoslovakia, a development that sparked Israel's decision to go to war against Egypt.[126] The result was the Suez Crisis of 1956. It ended the Eisenhower Administration's efforts to solve the refugee problem.

* *

The last major U.S. effort to tackle the refugee problem came during the Kennedy Administration. It took place between 1961 and 1962 and was called the Johnson Plan, after the man chosen to negotiate with the parties, Joseph E. Johnson, a former diplomat and president of the Carnegie Endowment for International Peace.[127] In order to avoid embarrassment if the operation failed, it was classified top secret and the administration arranged for Johnson to become a special representative of the long dormant Palestine Conciliation Commission, technically making him a representative of the United Nations and not the U.S. Government, although he coordinated closely with the State Department.[128]

Operating under Article 11 of UN resolution 194, Johnson sought to find a way to apply the formula of repatriation or resettlement and compensation by allowing refugees to make their own choice on repatriation, providing UN aid for resettlement and establishing a special UN fund for compensation.[129] His efforts were criticized by both sides. Israel remained firmly opposed to repatriation. As before, it argued that a return of a large number of refugees would create a security problem. Prime Minister David Ben Gurion declared to the Knesset: "There is only one practical and fair solution for this problem of the refugees: to resettle them among their own people in countries having plenty of good land and water and which are in need of additional manpower."[130]

The Arab states—Egypt, Jordan, Lebanon and Syria—were no more enthusiastic. As usual, the Palestinians themselves had no direct involvement although it was their fate that was being discussed. The Arab states opposed having the refugee problem isolated from the other core issues of borders and security, fearing that "liquidation of the Palestinian problem," as they referred to it, would cement the status quo left by the 1948 fighting that had ended favoring only the Israelis.[131] Moreover, the Arabs were unmoved by promises of aid for resettlement since they feared that special help for the Palestinians would be perceived by their own masses as favoritism for aliens over local residents. Despite Ben Gurion's claim, none of the Arab countries was in short supply of manpower nor confronted by excessive supplies of good land or water, and their strained economies were in no position to absorb the burden of hundreds of thousands of additional needy people.

The Johnson Plan remained alive into the summer of 1962, with all sides continuing to talk with him. In August, the White House offered a tempting deal to Israel. It would for the first time offer it major weapons. Among the favors Washington wanted in return was Israel's acceptance of the Johnson Plan.[132] Israel accepted the weapons but remained adamantly opposed to accepting refugees.

Failure to receive any concessions from Israel on the refugee issue soured the Arabs, and on 6 October 1962 Syria announced its rejection of the Johnson Plan, saying it "paves the way for the liquidation of the Palestine problem in a final manner and in favor of Israel."[133] Leaks about the plan, including distortions of many of its details, were made by the American Zionist Council and resulted in

Jewish American opposition. The council was heavily subsidized by the Jewish Agency for Israel in Jerusalem. With opposition rising in America and none of the states involved signalling acceptance of the plan, President Kennedy and his advisers decided in early December that the Johnson effort would be "buried."[134]

So too was any further effort by the Kennedy Administration—or succeeding ones—to solve the refuge problem. A personal effort in 1963 by Prime Minister Ben Gurion to gain a commitment from the United States not to discuss the refugees in public was turned down by the State Department, leaving Washington in the position of talking about the problem even if it had no viable solutions.[135]

* *

The administration of Lyndon B. Johnson not only made no attempt to deal with the Palestinians, but it cemented their status as merely "refugees" in UN Security Council Resolution 242, passed after the 1967 war. The Palestinian community again had been shattered by the six days of fighting in June, which left in its wake 210,000 new refugees, and once again made homeless another 113,000 Palestinians who already had been refugees from the 1948 war.[136] By 1968, 1,364,294 Palestinians were registered with UNRWA as refugees.[137] Despite the new suffering, the furthest the Johnson Administration went on the issue was to refer to the need that there be "justice for the refugees." But the statement did not refer to the refugees as Arabs or Palestinians.[138]

The Nixon Administration similarly was uninterested, although President Richard M. Nixon's Secretary of State, William Rogers, mentioned in late 1969 the need for a "just settlement of the problem of those Palestinians whom the wars of 1948 and 1967 have made homeless." In 1971, Nixon himself referred to the "legitimate aspirations of the Palestinian people," a rare reference by a president to the Palestinians as a people.[139] But essentially, in the halls of the State Department and the White House, policy toward the Palestinian refugee problem remained ignored. No serious effort was made henceforth to repatriate them or resettle and compensate them.

In fact, quite the reverse occurred. With the coming to power of President Clinton, the United States embarked on a strategy that appeared aimed at downgrading the refugees from their international status as a ward of the United Nations to a strictly bilateral concern of Israel and the Palestinian National Authority created by the 1993 accord between the Palestine Liberation Organization and Israel. Attempts were being made by the United States to dissolve the United Nations Work Relief Agency, the organization that since 1949 had been aiding the refugees, and transfer its responsibilities to the Palestinian authority.[140]

The result of such a change would significantly alter the refugees' status. It would remove the refugee issue from the United Nations and leave the fate of the Palestinians up to negotiations between Israel and the Palestinian National Authority. After nearly a half-century, the refugees would cease to enjoy the moral and legal authority of the world community and become merely another problem to be dealt with on the local level.

4 | BORDERS
The Growth of Israel and Resolution 242, 1947–1967

"The Govt of Israel should entertain no doubt whatever that the US Govt...believes that it is necessary for Israel to offer territorial compensation for territory which it expects to acquire beyond the boundaries [of the UN partition plan]."
Acting Secretary of State James E. Webb, 1949[1]

"In 1948 Israel's Arab neighbors went to war rather than accept the Jewish state. In the '50s and '60s, some of them began to move toward accepting the '47 frontiers....In the '70s and '80s, the United States and some moderate Arab regimes...accepted the '67 frontiers, but once again balked at those that existed."
Former Secretary of State Henry A. Kissinger, 1992[2]

THE FAILURE OF THE 1947 UN PARTITION PLAN caused total disarray in U.S. policy toward Palestine. Partition had been exposed as unattainable, unrealistic and cynical. Yet, abandoning partition in favor of a trusteeship was clearly not adequate to stem the violence. No nation, especially the United States, wanted to take over the British burden, self-imposed as it was, of stationing troops in Palestine between the two warring sides. Clearly, the United States needed a new policy. At the same time, London shared Washington's quest for a workable policy. Looking after its self-interests, it sought a strategy that would assure that its withdrawal from Palestine did not leave it without some residual presence or direct influence in the immediate region around the Suez Canal.

To escape their mutual dilemma, the State Department and Britain's Foreign Office worked in great secrecy during the summer of 1948. At the end they came to a common, if once again cynical, agreement. They jointly concluded that the best solution was to deny completely the Palestinians their own state. Under the Anglo-American strategy, the Palestinians would simply disappear by being absorbed in neighboring Arab states, mainly Jordan, or Transjordan as it was known at the time. The mutual Anglo-American goal was for Jordan to take over most areas of Palestine not occupied by the Jewish state.

Such a conclusion required abrupt changes in the policies of both countries. For Washington, it meant not only deserting the basic premise of partition—the establishment of an independent Arab state along side a Jewish state—but also dropping trusteeship too, since the Palestinians as citizens of Arab states would not need the protection of foreign troops. That, of course, was the major advantage for Washington—not having to send troops to Palestine, particularly not in an election year, and especially if at the same time Washington could satisfy American Zionists by continuing support of the Jewish state. As an underdog in the presidential campaign President Truman recognized he needed the Jewish community's endorsement.

In contrast, for London the policy meant Britain would have to drop its total objection to partition and accept it to the extent of dividing Palestine into a Jewish state and an expanded Jordan. Ever since Britain had established Transjordan in 1922 under a League of Nations mandate, its expansion had been a goal for King Abdullah. The British-appointed monarch saw himself as ruler of a Greater Syria holding sway over Lebanon and Syria as well as part of Palestine. His ambitions enjoyed Britain's sympathetic attitude, at least as far as Palestine was concerned, and by 1948 Britain independently had come to the conclusion that it was in its urgent interests to place Arab Palestine under Abdullah. Under the changing circumstances of the region, Jordan had become vital to Britain's security in the Middle East. Sour relations with Iraq, rising demands for withdrawal of British troops from Egypt after a presence of nearly eighty years and the withdrawal from Palestine as of 14 May meant that Jordan had become Britain's best option for the stationing of troops in the immediate region of the strategic Suez Canal.

Although Jordan nominally had been granted its independence in 1946, it had signed that same year a mutual defense pact with Britain that essentially left the former mandatory power in charge of external affairs and internal administration. The Jordanian army, called the Arab Legion, was commanded and largely officered by British soldiers. British "advisers" worked in all government departments. British subsidies maintained the life-style of King Abdullah, however humble it was.[3]

Washington traditionally had acquiesced to British leadership in the eastern Mediterranean, except in Palestine, and it was content with Britain's choice of Jordan as a strategic asset. There followed from this attitude Washington's willingness not to oppose King Abdullah's ambitions towards Palestine. In this quest, Abdullah repeatedly had met with Zionist leaders and come to an agreement that his army would not attack the Jewish state if he was given freedom to act in the rest of Palestine. Britain fully joined in this strategy. By early 1948 the British Resident in Jordan, Sir Alec Kirkbridge, noted that

> Transjordan has best claim to inherit residue of Palestine...occupation
> of Arab areas by Transjordan would counteract chances of an armed
> conflict between a Jewish State and other Arab States....King Abdullah
> would be prepared to acquiesce in formation of a Jewish State provided
> Transjordan obtained the rest of Palestine.[4]

British Foreign Minister Ernest Bevin worked closely "with Abdullah to secure the expansion of his kingdom over most of Arab Palestine," in the words of historian Avi Shlaim. "...It is hardly an exaggeration to say that he colluded directly with the Transjordanians and indirectly with the Jews to abort the birth of a Palestinian state."[5]

No doubt, if the full record were known, the same could be said about the United States. This was because Washington not only took a benign view toward British ambitions in the eastern Mediterranean but also because of the pervasive influence of Zionists on the White House in matters affecting the Middle East. The Jews favored the British strategy and Abdullah's designs to the extent that it would prevent the establishment of an independent Palestinian state.[6]

This attitude was reflected in a memorandum written by Robert M. McClintock, a State Department UN specialist, five weeks after the withdrawal of British troops and Israel's establishment. McClintock observed that "it is now clear in the light of facts and events which have supervened that there will be no separate Arab State and no economic union as envisaged in the [1947] General Assembly resolution." He noted that the original borders of the partition plan had been impossibly complex, likened by some "to a portrait by Picasso," adding:

> In summary, therefore, a sensible territorial solution for the Palestine problem would be to re-draw the frontiers of Israel so as to make a compact and homogeneous state, the remainder of Palestine to go largely to Transjordan with appropriate transfers of populations where necessary; Jerusalem to remain an international entity with free access to the outside world; boundaries of the two new states [Israel and Transjordan] to be guaranteed mutually between themselves and the United Nations; and the economic prosperity of the region to be enhanced by customs union between Israel and Transjordan.
>
> This would be of particular advantage to the Arabs as 'freezing' the boundaries of Israel and thus affording protection to the Arab States against the wider pretensions of the Jewish revisionists and such fanatics as those of the Irgun who have pretensions to the conquest of Transjordan.[7]

McClintock noted in the memo that the British "Colonial Secretary, Sir Arthur Creech Jones has recently indicated his belief...that a deal is possible of arrangement between King Abdullah of Transjordan and the State of Israel for a territorial settlement similar to that outlined in the preceding paragraphs."

Thus, by late June 1948, both London and Washington independently were working their way toward a common view on the post-war nature of Palestine. The bitterness lingering between London and Washington from Truman's earlier support for entry of 100,000 Jewish displaced persons into Palestine and, especially, his support of partition, was disappearing. On 25 June 1948, Under Secretary of State Robert Lovett reported under Marshall's signature to Ambassador Lewis W. Douglas in London that the "'entente cordiale' has been reestablished" and thus the two governments again could "pull in tandem to assist in the constructive working out of this onerous Palestine." He named Douglas as the chief U.S. negotiator with the British to develop a joint policy toward Palestine, adding that "there is a very large measure of agreement between ourselves and British Foreign Office as to the most sensible arrangement of the Palestine issue, keeping always in mind the requirements of this government to maintain its recognition of the State of Israel."[8]

The impetus to find a new joint policy was in large part propelled by a truce between Israel and the five Arab armies that had entered Palestine on 15 May. The truce went into effect on 11 June. In the first round of fighting no land designated part of the Jewish state had been lost and a number of Arabs areas, mainly the Western Galilee and the city of Jaffa, had been captured by Israel. The truce was to last for one month. The time limit caused all parties to scurry for ways to extend it and find a final solution.

On 28 June, UN Mediator Count Folke Bernadotte moved ahead of London and Washington by proposing a "Union" of Palestine and Jordan "comprising two members, one Arab and one Jewish....The purposes and function of the Union should be to promote common economic interests, to operate and maintain common services, including customs and excise, to undertake development projects and to coordinate foreign policy and measures for common defense."[9] Other points of Bernadotte's proposal:

• The whole or part of the Negev would go to the Arabs, even though it had originally been awarded to the Jewish state.

• This was to be in return for granting the Jews all or part of Western Galilee, originally Arab.

• Jerusalem should go to the Arabs with the Jewish community enjoying municipal autonomy and special arrangements made for the protection of the Holy Places.

• Haifa would become a free port as would an airport at Lydda.

Neither the Arabs nor Israelis found Bernadotte's recommendations fair or worth pursuing. The Arabs recommended that all Palestine become a democracy with representation proportionate to each community's size. Israel urged Bernadotte to drop his proposals and consider a whole new approach.[10]

Washington did not like all of Bernadotte's plan either. While it accepted his suggestion to swap Western Galilee for the Negev, it opposed giving Jerusalem to the Arabs and it doubted the practicality of a union. Passions on both sides made the idea of Arabs and Jews working together unrealistic. Moreover, Israel made it plain that it would accept nothing less than full sovereignty, a position that an internal State Department report concluded that "opinion in this country will not permit any deviation from...." the Israeli position.[11]

With these serious reservations about Bernadotte's plan and with a sense of impatience and anxiety building as the month-long truce approached its expiry, pressures increased to form a solid U.S. policy. In a long memorandum at the end of June, Philip C. Jessup, the acting U.S. representative at the United Nations, noted that it was time to "make up our mind whether we favor establishment of a

Palestinian Arab state or extension of the boundaries of Transjordan to take in the Arab areas of Palestine as those areas may be determined. We favor the latter course...." The reason for that, he added, was because both Britain and Israel favored giving the Palestinian lands to Jordan and there existed "no apparent leadership among the Palestinian Arabs around whom could be built the nucleus of a Palestinian state."[12]

Meanwhile in Palestine, the month-long truce expired. Fighting resumed on 9 July with Israeli forces launching strong attacks in the north and south, as well as securing the Tel Aviv–Jerusalem road.[13] Under pressure from the United Nations, a second truce came into effect on 18 July. The brief interval of fighting had brought Israel substantial new gains. Its forces had conquered northern Galilee, secured communications between the coastal plains and Jerusalem and maintained a tenuous link to the isolated Jewish settlements in the Negev.[14] The Central Intelligence Agency reported:

> The [first] truce resulted in so great an improvement in the Jewish capabilities that the Jews may now be strong enough to launch a full scale offensive and drive the Arab forces out of Palestine. Events during the truce, and the enormous increase in Jewish strength resulting from them, considerably change the previously held estimate of the probable course of the war in Palestine. The Arabs' logistical position generally is very bad and their ammunition supply is exceedingly low. It is estimated that they could not continue to fight, even on the previous moderate scale, for more than two to three months.[15]

Israel's battlefield victories were imposing new facts on the map. These facts were steadily eroding the frontiers laid out in the partition plan, making more urgent than ever the need for a new policy. Yet, as late as 12 August, the administration had still not made up its mind. Marshall on that date referred to the future of Arab Palestine as being either part of Transjordan or a Palestinian Arab state.[16] The next day, 13 August, Marshall remarked that "top clearance from the White House has not yet been received at this stage in formulating opinion as to the most practical solution of the Palestine problem."[17]

Over the next two weeks London and Washington finally agreed on a joint policy that in broad outline gave Western Galilee to Israel and the Negev and the rest of Arab Palestine to Transjordan. On 1 September the policy was personally approved by President Truman.[18] That same day Marshall hinted at the new policy in a cable to the embassy in Israel, saying that

> the US feels that the new State of Israel should have boundaries which will make it more homogeneous and well integrated than the hourglass frontiers drawn on the map of the November 29 Resolution. Perhaps some solution can be worked out as part of any settlement with Transjordan which would materially simplify boundary problem. Specifically, it would appear to us that Israel might expand into the rich area of Galilee, which it now holds in military occupation, in return for relinquishing a large portion of the Negev to Transjordan. This would

leave the new State with materially improved frontiers and considerably enriched in terms of natural resources by acquisition of Galilee in return for the desert Negev.[19]

The trickiest part of the collusion by Britain and the United States was to hide the fact that they jointly had adopted a new policy. Specifically, they were concerned that their collusion would be perceived by the Arabs as aiding Israel and abetting King Abdullah's ambition to expand Jordan's borders into Palestine. The Arabs refused any recognition at all of Israel and they suspected Abdullah was plotting with the British, which he was, in order to expand his kingdom. The Arabs opposed what they called the aggrandizement of Abdullah. Ambassador Jessup at the United Nations observed:

> It might be argued...that the real reason for present Syrian extremism is not so much fear of Israel as fear of the expansion of Transjordan and increase in Abdullah's prestige in the light of his former Greater Syrian ideas.[20]

If it became known that the United States and Britain were behind the plan to link Arab Palestine to Jordan, the Arabs would protest strongly, perhaps violently. As a result, Washington and London conspired with Count Bernadotte to make their new policy seem the work of the UN Mediator. As Ambassador Douglas in London advised the State Department: "Officials feel it important that from moment proposals become known they should carry as label 'Mediator—made in Sweden.'"[21]

To make certain that the two countries and Bernadotte were in complete accord, the State Department dispatched UN specialist Robert McCormick to the mediator's headquarters in Rhodes. The British sent Sir John M. Troutbeck from the Cairo Embassy. Together the two officials went over Bernadotte's proposed list of new recommendations, which he planned to release in the next few days. Although McCormick later reported that there was general agreement with Bernadotte's ideas and "our conversations were devoted more to perfection of Bernadotte's first draft of the conclusions than to matters of substance," the fact was they spent two days together working on the proposals and a third day on how to present it. At the end McClintock wryly observed that the product of their efforts would probably wind up being called "the Bernadotte plan."[22]

Bernadotte sent his report to the United Nations on 16 September, recommending "revisions in the boundaries broadly defined in the resolution of the General Assembly of 29 November in order to make them more equitable, workable and consistent with existing realities in Palestine." His principal recommendations were:

1) All of Galilee to Israel and the Negev and most of the rest of Arab-controlled Palestine to Transjordan, "subject to such frontier rectifications regarding other Arab States as may be found practicable and desirable."

2) Faluja, Lydda, Majdal and Ramle would go to the Arabs and the line connecting those communities would describe the northern border of the Negev.

3)   No mention was made of Jaffa, but the United States supported its return to the Arabs.

4)   Haifa and the oil refineries and terminals would become a free port, as would the airport at Lydda.

5)   Jerusalem would become an international city "with maximum feasible local autonomy for its Arab and Jewish communities, with full safeguards for the protection of the Holy Places and sites and free access to them, and for religious freedom."[23]

Not unexpectedly, London and Washington immediately accepted Bernadotte's proposals "in their entirety," since the proposals were essentially theirs. Once again, however, the Arabs and Jews rejected them, charging they were unfair. The Egyptians quickly perceived the true British motives behind the plan. The ambassador to Egypt, Stanton Griffis, reported that there was a "widely held belief that British support for plan is based principally on desire secure merger Arab Palestine and Transjordan as step in enlarging their sphere of influence and toward creation Greater Syria." He then indicated how cynical the players had become: while Egypt officially opposed the plan it might accept it if Egypt were given Gaza and part of the Negev.[24]

Israel vehemently objected to the surrender of the Negev, arguing that it had been awarded to the Jewish state in the partition plan. However, the Western Galilee had been given the Arabs. But Israel, in insisting on keeping the Negev, did not offer the return of Western Galilee. Nonetheless, the Israeli argument quickly gained support among American Zionists. They went on the offensive and applied enormous pressure on President Truman, who was now less than two months away from elections. The extreme Zionists led by Abba Hillel Silver placed full-page ads in newspapers, attacking what they called, as predicted, the "Bernadotte plan," and charging Truman with desertion of the Democratic Platform. The platform had recognized the Jewish state within the boundaries of the partition plan, that is, including the Negev but—pointedly ignored by the Zionists—not the Western Galilee.

The attacks caught Truman while he was on a transcontinental railway campaign tour. The only telephones available were at various stops, such as Tulsa, Oklahoma, where Truman's political adviser, Clark Clifford, hopped off the train and made a call to Acting Secretary of State Lovett on 29 September. Clifford had found a phone in the Tulsa freight yards and his conversation was "punctuated by the whistles of on-coming trains."[25] In his memorandum of the conversation, Lovett recounted that Clifford told him "that the pressure from the Jewish groups on the President was mounting and that it was as bad as the time of the trusteeship suggestion." Clifford said the president was planning to issue a statement to the Zionists reversing his support for the Bernadotte plan. Lovett was horrified:

> I told Clifford that the consequences...would put the Secretary in an intolerable position and...would label this country as violating its agreements and as completely untrustworthy in international matters. The

consequences could be absolutely disastrous to us in the United Nations and elsewhere.[26]

In this case, Truman relented. But as the election grew closer, Truman's apprehensions that the State Department would say something to upset the Zionists grew greater. Through Clifford, he ordered Lovett to say nothing about the Bernadotte plan and suggested that a Zionist adviser be employed to help Marshall draft a statement on the plan. He was Benjamin V. Cohen, the retired counsel to the State Department who currently was serving as Alternative Representative to the U.S. Delegation at the first part of the Third Session of the General Assembly at Paris. Marshall was about to arrive in Paris and was planning to give out a statement saying the United States continued to support the Bernadotte plan "entirely." However, Clifford instructed: "We feel it would be most helpful if he would include Ben Cohen in such discussion [of Marshall's proposed statement] because of the latter's familiarity with our problems here."[27]

Marshall agreed, but in return he strongly advised Truman not to make any statements on the Bernadotte plan himself. In a top secret, NIACT (meaning "night action"), eyes alone message to Lovett he warned that he felt "certain that if President himself makes statement, as his political advisers no doubt insist, he will inevitably carry issue direct into political campaign as [Republican candidate Thomas E.] Dewey will certainly respond. Issue here will be thrown into confusion and possibility of settlement at least postponed and truce imperiled."[28]

The same advice, even more forcefully stated, came from Ambassador Douglas in London. He was a non-career political appointee, which perhaps explains his brutal candor:

> I most earnestly hope that if any statement at all is issued it will not come from the White House. I recognize, of course, that the intimate advisers of the President would much prefer that he, himself, make a pronouncement. But he himself would be the first to realize that no political position, however high—no public office, however great its prestige, is worth gambling with the vital interests of the US.[29]

Although Dewey and Truman had a gentleman's agreement not to outbid each other in pandering to the Jewish community, the Republican candidate broke it on 22 October, less than two weeks before election day. The occasion was so portentous that Lovett notified Marshall, still in Paris, by urgent cable, warning that "Dewey in effect repudiated Administration's Palestine policy with respect to the Bernadotte Plan." Lovett said Dewey did this by reaffirming the Republican Platform plank on Palestine which, like the Democratic plank, supported Israel's partition boundaries. On the surface, that seemed innocent enough. But the Zionists had so roiled the atmosphere that reaffirmation of the plank became a code action for supporting Israel's demand that it be allowed to keep the Negev as well as the Western Galilee.

Lovett informed Marshall that the "statement obviously designed to take advantage of widely publicized criticism of President for abandoning Palestine plank in Democratic Platform and timed specifically to embarrass President during his windup trip to Chicago, New York and Brooklyn next week." Lovett added that he expected his weekend to be "unhappy" because Truman's reaction would be "immediate and aggressive."[30]

Lovett was right on all counts. The reaction from Truman was instantaneous. In a public statement, he virtuously expressed regret that "the Republican candidate has seen fit to release a statement with reference to Palestine...[while] I had hoped our foreign affairs could continue to be handled on a non-partisan basis." He then not only reaffirmed his support of the Democratic Platform plank on Palestine but emphasized the plank's language that any border modifications should be made "only if fully acceptable to the State of Israel." It was a bizarre assertion, since it had been Israel which had changed the borders and the implication now was that Israel had to agree to the Arab demand for the return of their occupied territory.

Truman did not stop there. He pledged that as soon as Israel established a permanent government—it was still a provisional government pending convening of a representative assembly—"it will promptly be given *de jure* recognition." And he promised to expedite any loan applications from Israel.[31] There was thus little wonder that Lovett called this pre-election period the "silly season."[32] It got even sillier as election day loomed closer.

Meanwhile, the United Nations was meeting on the delicate subject of whether to condemn Israel for its latest aggression and perhaps even impose sanctions against it. In mid-October, Israel had broken the truce in effect since 18 July by sending forces southward in a well-coordinated plan. During six days of fighting Israel captured nearly all of the Negev, routing its Arab population.[33] The offensive created an estimated 130,000 new refugees.[34]

Israel followed its offensive in the Negev with a major operation in the Galilee that cleaned out all Arabs behind a fifteen-mile truce line between Nazareth and the south Lebanese border.[35] Now its grip on both the Negev and the Galilee was solid.

The White House dreaded that the Security Council might act against Israel before the 2 November election. Truman on 29 October personally warned the State Department not to take any position or make any statement without first getting his approval.[36] Two days later he directed Marshall through Lovett that "every effort be made to avoid taking position on Palestine [in the UN] prior to Wednesday." That was November 3, one day after the election. The message added: "If by any chance it appears certain vote would have to be taken on Monday or Tuesday he directs USDel to abstain....On Wednesday or thereafter proceed on understanding of American position previously taken as regards truce in May and July resolutions." That meant the State Department could then vote against Israel. Lovett added: "Any other matters relating Palestine should be reported and cleared until present restrictions removed."[37]

Meanwhile, on 30 October national polls predicted a substantial Dewey victory. Under Secretary of State Lovett already was thinking of a new administration taking over. In a somber cable to Marshall, he remarked:

> I am sure you agree that our past experience with formally approved
> positions and instructions which are subsequently and suddenly altered
> or revoked is increasingly dangerous and intolerable. I can imagine what
> you have been through in Paris. It has been absolute hell here. As I see
> it, the national election itself, regardless of its outcome, gives us a new
> chance to review our Palestine policy, agree on a bipartisan approach
> and plan a consistent course of action which we can stick to honorably
> and resolutely.[38]

Although Truman won, Lovett's hope for a new approach to the Middle
East did not materialize, neither then nor under most later administrations. Although the White House issued in mid-November new "principles applicable to
the U.S. position on the Palestine question before the General Assembly," they
were essentially the same as those worked out in the summer with Britain. The
major difference was that now they were more assertive that "Arab Palestine standing
alone could not constitute a viable independent state." The memorandum added
that "Israel should now be dealt with as a full-fledged member of the community
of nations. It follows that Israel should be entitled to the normal attributes of independent states; it should now, for example, have full control over immigration into
its territory...."[39]

On 20 December, Israel launched its final assault of the war. Although the
second truce officially remained in effect, Israel's air, land and sea forces destroyed
the isolated remnants of Egyptian forces in southern Palestine and then moved into
Egyptian territory, finally forcing Cairo to sue for a cease-fire and to agree to negotiate an armistice.[40] The attack brought a sharp condemnation from both the
United Nations and President Truman, demanding "an immediate withdrawal."[41]
The Israeli force was withdrawn on 4 January 1949 and on 7 January a new cease-
fire went into effect—ending the first Arab-Israel war.[42]

However, one final violent gesture lay in store. On the same day as the
cease-fire, Israeli warplanes flew over Egyptian territory where they shot down
five unsuspecting British aircraft. Israelis then removed some of the wreckage and
scattered it over Israeli territory to support their public claim that the dogfight had
occurred when the British violated Israeli airspace.[43] Ezer Weizman, later Israel's
commander of the air force and Israel's president, led the attack, explaining years
later that he had wanted "just one more victory to finish up the war."[44] That it came
against the British, whom many Israelis loathed, added to the Israeli delight.

* *

With the fighting ended, talks began. Armistice negotiations started between Israel and Egypt on 13 January with other Arabs following later. It was
Israel that spoke with the strongest voice as the undisputed victor. It had thoroughly defeated the Arab forces, uprooted and dispersed nearly three-quarters of
the Palestinian community, thereby changing the Palestinian majority status to one

of a minority, and it occupied 77.4 percent of Palestine, increasing its size from the 5,900 square miles granted by the UN partition plan to a total of about 7,800 square miles.[45] It had failed to capture the Old City of Jerusalem but it had placed West Jerusalem under military occupation as the first step in declaring Jerusalem the capital of Israel.[46]

Israel in 1949 held an area of Palestine that included 475 Palestinian towns and villages. This compared with a total of 279 Jewish settlements that were in existence as of the 29 November 1947 adoption of the UN partition plan.[47] In all, about a quarter of the buildings in use in the new state of Israel were originally the property of Arabs. [48] About 90 percent of Israel's olive groves were taken from the Arabs and 50 percent of the citrus orchards.[49] So massive was the confiscation of olive groves and citrus orchards that income from them was "instrumental in alleviating the serious balance-of-payments problem which Israel suffered from 1948 to 1953," according to scholar Ian Lustick.[50]

The reaction in the State Department to Israel's conquests was to continue to insist that the original borders laid out in the partition plan be re-established or, at most, modified by mutual exchanges of land. While the armistice talks were going on between Egypt and Israel in Rhodes under Acting UN Mediator Ralph Bunche, the State Department made a detailed review of U.S. policy:

> US favors incorporation of greater part of Arab Palestine in Transjordan. The remainder might be divided among other Arab states as seems desirable.
>
> If Israel desires additions to its territory...such as western Galilee and Jaffa, now under Israeli occupation, Israel should make territorial concessions elsewhere, i.e., the southern Negev. Israel is not entitled to keep both the Negev and western Galilee and Jaffa. If there is no agreement between the parties, the Israelis should relinquish western Galilee and Jaffa and the Arabs should relinquish the Israeli portion of the Negev. If Israel desires to retain western Galilee and Jaffa, the southern border of Israel should not be drawn further south than the thirty-first parallel [51] within the territory allotted to Israel under the resolution of November 29.[52]

The problem with this policy was that Israel had no intention of giving up any of its conquests. While Israel and American Zionists kept up a drumbeat of demands that the partition boundaries be honored, they actually meant that Israel be allowed to retain the Negev without alluding to its retention of Arab Western Galilee. They prevailed.

On 24 February Israel signed the first of the armistice agreements with Egypt, followed with Lebanon (March 23), Transjordan (April 3) and Syria (July 20). [3] Iraq was the only Arab state that had sent forces to Palestine that refused to sign an armistice. Although it was their fate being discussed, the Palestinians once again were not directly represented in the talks. Instead they were putatively represented by Jordan.

The armistices had the effect of confirming the battle lines as the *de facto* borders, meaning Israel would retain its conquests without surrendering any major areas of Arab land, until formal peace treaties could be achieved. The Israeli triumph at the negotiating table was every bit as impressive as had been its performance on the field of battle. British Lieutenant General Sir John Bagot Glubb, the legendary Glubb Pasha who commanded Jordan's Arab Legion, tartly commented:

> Where an area allotted to [the Israelis] in the partition plan was still occupied by Arab forces, they claimed that they were legitimately entitled to drive those forces out. The partition plan was here the touchstone. But where Israeli forces were in occupation of an area allotted to the Arabs by the United Nations, they were entitled to remain. In these circumstances, military occupation established a sufficient right.[54]

Some State Department observers were no more sympathetic with Israel's negotiating tactics than Glubb. One American official, Consul to Jerusalem William C. Burdett, reminded Washington that the agreements had been

> acquiesced in by Arab states under varying degrees of force or threat of force on part of Israel. Arabs realized [they] were defeated militarily, felt [they] could count on no action by UN or great powers to curb further aggression by Israel and thus must sign armistice on any terms. Use of blackmail particularly flagrant in case of Transjordan negotiations which UN official characterized as marked by 'utter perfidy on one side and utter stupidity on other.' Inevitable result has been storing up turbulent reservoir resentment against Israel, UN and US....Israeli actions including two offensives in Negev, attack in Galilee, seizure southern Negev, incursion into Syria and liberal use of big stick in armistice talks hardly support her claim to be 'peace-loving state.'[55]

While the State Department continued to insist that Israel would have to make fair exchanges of land with the Arabs, the fact was that Israel early on had decided not to limit its size. Prime Minister David Ben Gurion had explained to his colleagues at the time of the state's founding in 1948: "If the UN does not come into account...and they [the Arab states] make war against us and we defeat them...why should we bind ourselves?" As a result of Ben Gurion's arguments, Israel's Proclamation of Independence had not defined or even mentioned the boundaries of the new state.[56]

It was a compliment to how well Israel hid its true ambitions that the State Department was surprised when Israel finally revealed its determination to retain the conquered territory at peace talks at Lausanne in the spring. The State Department thought it was such dramatic news that it sent a special report to President Truman from Acting Secretary of State James E. Webb:

> (1) While Israel makes no demands upon Lebanon at present, it would later like a portion of southeastern Lebanon considered necessary to Israeli development plans. The Israeli delegate said Israel would be willing to compensate Lebanon for this territory, but he did not specify in what way this would be done;

(2) Israel desires to acquire from Egypt the Egyptian occupied Gaza strip, allotted to the Arabs under the partition resolution of November 29, 1947;

(3) Israel makes no demands upon Syria at present, but will accept the international frontier with the proviso, also to be applied to Lebanon, that if either state desires to open negotiations in the future for border rectification, this may be done;

(4) Israel will make further demands upon Transjordan for territory in Arab Palestine considered necessary to Israeli development plans. Israel has in mind giving Abdullah a few villages in return;

(5) Israel will retain occupied areas such as Western Galilee and Jaffa, Lydda and Ramle allotted to the Arabs under the partition plan;

(6) Israel will relinquish none of the Negev.[57]

Webb told Truman that it was important to solve the conflict to prevent "Soviet penetration and exploitation of the Near East. The present instability will certainly continue if the Lausanne [peace] talks break down as a result of the new Israeli position, which is susceptible of interpretation by the Arabs as confirming their constant fears of Israeli territorial expansionism. Failure of the Israelis to modify their present demands will inevitably aggravate Arab distrust of Israel and bring about renewed Arab charges that the United States remains passive no matter how unreasonable the demands of Israel."

Webb added:

> The Department believes that the time has come to make a basic decision concerning our attitude toward Israel....In the light of all the foregoing, the Department considers that it is now essential to inform the Israeli Government forcefully that, if it continues to reject the friendly advice which this Government has offered solely in the interest of a genuine peace in the Near East, this Government will be forced with regret to revise its attitude toward Israel....Although the Department of State is convinced of the necessity of carrying out this plan of action in the light of our national interest...the matter involves other important considerations, since the proposed course of action would arouse strong opposition in American Jewish circles. It is therefore suggested that you may wish to ask your advisers to give careful consideration to the possible implications of the above procedure.

Truman already had expressed impatience with Israel's inflexibility toward the refugees, and Webb's message obviously lacerated his feelings. The next day a strong message was sent to Tel Aviv, warning that the United States was "seriously disturbed by the attitude of Israel with respect to a territorial settlement in Palestine and to the question of Palestinian refugees....The US Govt is gravely concerned lest Israel now endanger the possibility of arriving at a solution of the Palestine problem in such a way as to contribute to the establishment of sound and friendly relations between Israel and its neighbors." It went on: "The Govt of Israel should entertain no doubt whatever that the US Govt...believes that it is necessary for Israel to offer territorial compensation for territory which it expects to acquire beyond the boundaries" of the UN partition plan. If Israel continued to ignore the advice of the United Nations and the United States, the message sternly warned, "the US Govt will regretfully be forced to the conclusion that a revision of its attitude toward Israel has become unavoidable."[58]

Israel essentially dismissed the message.[59] Four days later, Webb remarked to Secretary of State Dean Acheson that no one should "overestimate US influence with Israel. Past record suggests Israel has had more influence with US than has US with Israel...."[60]

Diplomats in the British Foreign Office had long held the same conclusion. In an internal 1949 memorandum in the Foreign Office, it was noted that Jewish influence on President Truman was considerable and resulted in consequent shifts in U.S. policy: "One way of explaining this is to point to the undoubted weakness of their President. Another way of explaining it is that each time the Jews have been permitted too much time so that they have been enabled to put the screw on Truman." The memo added: "As long as America is a major power, and as long as she is free of major war, anyone taking on the Jews will indirectly be taking on America."[61]

From Jerusalem, U.S. Consul Burdett reported that Israeli officials were openly bragging about the power of the Jewish American community to influence U.S. policy. He urged Washington either to put strong pressure on Israel to become conciliatory or to "admit that the US and UN are unable or unwilling to take the required measures and therefore that US policy on boundaries and refugees cannot be carried out." He left no doubt what he believed were Israel's territorial ambitions: "Israel eventually intends to obtain all of Palestine, but barring unexpected opportunities or internal crises will accomplish this gradually and without the use of force in the immediate future."[62]

In the end, Truman essentially followed Burdett's advice and conceded—but not publicly—that he did not have the political strength to stand up to Israel. U.S. efforts to get Israel to give up its conquered territory or relinquish some of its own in exchange soon petered out. No further serious effort was made by the United States to address the border issue until the Eisenhower Administration. Israel retained its conquests, and U.S. support as well.

The only aspect of U.S. policy that bore fruit was denying the Palestinians their own state. In 1950 King Abdullah annexed the Arab parts of Palestine left unconquered by Israel, a territory that became known as the West Bank. The United States did not follow Britain in officially recognizing the land-grab although it did not raise any loud protests. Nor did any other nation recognize the annexation except Pakistan.[63] The Palestinians considered Abdullah's action perfidy and he was assassinated the next year.[64]

* *

The Eisenhower Administration's effort to solve the vexing border problem came in the context of an ambitious joint U.S.–British program to find peace. It was a secret plan called Operation Alpha, and its unique feature was that Britain and the United States were ready to join in an international guarantee, presumably by the United Nations, of any new borders that could be agreed upon. [65] The reason for the secrecy was to prevent Arabs and Israelis from learning what solutions the two countries were planning to propose as a fair resolution and thereby have time to oppose them.

In the early period of their joint discussions at the beginning of 1955 it was agreed that "Israel must make concessions." But the point was quickly qualified: "However, we cannot expect large transfers of territory. The changes proposed should be such that in presenting them to Israel they can be made to appear as 'frontier adjustments' which [Prime Minister Moshe] Sharett has stated Israel would be prepared to make. From the Arab point of view they will reunite village lands."[66]

As the discussions progressed it soon became clear how small the return of land by Israel was expected to be—77.5 square miles out of its total of 7,805. Moreover, Jordan was expected to give up part of the Latrun Salient between Tel Aviv and Jerusalem so Israel could have a more direct route between the two cities. No mention was made of Western Galilee or Jaffa and other occupied Palestinian cities. However, Israel was expected to give up two small triangles of land in the southern Negev whose apexes would meet in the middle of the desert. Where the apexes touched there was to be a bridge or an underpass so that Arab and Israeli vehicles would not mingle. This ingenious plan was designed as a way to offer the Arabs an east-west land route between Africa and Arabia as well as Israeli access to its southern port at Aqaba.[67]

The Alpha border plan amounted to a much diluted rendition of the 1949 policy which demanded that Israel either return Western Galilee and Jaffa or surrender much of the Negev. Now it was being asked to give up only small triangles of the Negev and a small land swap with Jordan in return for an international guarantee of its borders. Whatever the outcome—acceptance of the Alpha plan or continuance of the status quo—Israel would be a major beneficiary since it would retain land that would have been denied it in the 1948–1949 period. However, even these minor demands on Israel were considered a political hot potato.

Secretary of State John Foster Dulles told President Dwight D. Eisenhower that he wanted to unveil the general outline, but not the details on borders, of the Alpha plan on 26 August 1955 because "we need to make such an effort before the situation gets involved in 1956 politics. Both [Vice President Richard M.] Nixon and [Attorney General Herbert] Brownell looked over the statement and think it is tolerable from a political standpoint."[68]

Still, Israel and the Arabs showed little interest and, despite the flurry of secret planning that had accompanied Operation Alpha over more than half a year, it suffered a quick death. This was in part because within barely a month of its introduction the region was plunged into crisis by Egypt's Czech arms deal, accelerating the path to war in another year.[69]

Although disappointed, Dulles was not surprised by the failure of Israel to accept the Alpha plan. He earlier had warned Eisenhower that "Israel does not want to consider any boundary adjustments. Rather it wants first of all a security treaty with the United States."[70]

Indeed, it was not borders that Israel wanted to talk about with Washington. It was a security guarantee from the United States. It wanted this without giving up its occupied territory, in essence meaning a U.S. guarantee of its expanded frontiers. That had been Israel's persistent theme since the beginning of the 1950s.[71] Prime Minister David Ben Gurion was enthusiastic enough about a defense pact with the United States that he was willing in return to grant America military bases in Israel.[72]

However, Dulles proved an adept diplomat in foiling Israel's requests, as Israeli Ambassador Abba Eban learned. In his memoirs, Eban recalled that Dulles agreed in principle with a guarantee of Israel's frontiers but then "reduced it to frustration by stating that the United States could not 'guarantee temporary armistice lines;' it could only guarantee permanent agreed peace boundaries."[73] Reports of Israel's quest became public in 1955, setting off concern in the Soviet Union. Moscow publicly warned in mid-1955 that a security treaty with the West would violate Israel's 1953 undertaking to Moscow that Israel would not "enter into any alliance or agreement that has aggressive aims against the Soviet Union."[74]

Israel's increased activity in 1955 in seeking the guarantee came as a result of a number of factors, including the establishment that year of the Baghdad Pact, a British-led bloc aimed at the Soviet Union that provided arms to Iraq but not Israel, and the Czech arms deal with Egypt. In a meeting on 2 October with Dulles, Eban had sought a "guarantee of the status quo" but Dulles declined, giving his reason as it "raises problems about [the] likely effect on [the] Arab world as whole. We do not want, and assume Israel does not want, [a] situation where USSR backing all Arabs and US backing Israel."[75]

But that was exactly what Israel sought, as Dulles himself later seemed to realize. On hearing that Israeli Foreign Minister Sharett was coming to the United States in mid-November on a speaking tour, Dulles warned that this was "a most serious problem. It is obviously an effort on his part to go over the heads of our government and the position I announced to him and to force administration into policy of supporting Israel to a degree and in a manner which will surely antagonize entire Arab world and allow Soviet Union to become dominant in that area."[76]

More than that, by pitting the United States against the Soviet Union, Israel would become a Cold War ally of America and thus justify its requests not only for a security guarantee but for arms, economic aid and diplomatic support as well.

Such an alliance remained a long term objective of Israeli policy, which was officially achieved with the 1981 agreement on strategic cooperation signed by the Reagan Administration. These efforts at entwining Israel's fate with that of the United States were unrelenting and continued beyond the strategic cooperation agreement. For instance, Israel's American lobbying arm, the American Israel Public Affairs Committee, in its 1985 policy statement listed the goal of enhancing the framework of strategic cooperation by "moving toward a full political-military alliance between the U.S. and Israel."[77]

* *

Israel dramatically expanded its border in 1956 when it attacked Egypt and captured the whole of the Sinai Peninsula. But the Sinai was not the limit of its ambitions. During a planning session in France where Israeli, British and French officials colluded to wage war against Egypt, Ben Gurion listed Israel's view of the future:

> Jordan has no right to exist and should be divided. East of the Jordan River, it will become part of Iraq, and Arab refugees will settle there. The West Bank will be annexed to Israel, as an autonomous region. Lebanon will get rid of its Muslim regions to assure stability based on the Christian part. Britain will hold sway over Iraq, including the East Bank, and the southern Arabian Peninsula. France—over Lebanon, perhaps Syria, with close ties to Israel. The Suez Canal will be internationalized, and the Red Sea straits will be under Israeli control.[78]

However, Ben Gurion had not counted on Dwight Eisenhower's toughness. The president adamantly insisted that Israel give up its Sinai gains, causing a backlash by Israel's supporters against his administration. The pressure became such that Secretary of State Dulles complained to friends in February 1957 that "I am aware how almost impossible it is in this country to carry out a foreign policy [in the Middle East] not approved by the Jews. [Former Secretary of State George] Marshall and [former Defense Secretary James] Forrestal learned that." In other conversations in mid-February, Dulles remarked about the "terrific control the Jews have over the news media and the barrage which the Jews have built up on congressmen....I am very much concerned over the fact that the Jewish influence here is completely dominating the scene and making it almost impossible to get Congress to do anything they don't approve of. The Israeli Embassy is practically dictating to the Congress through influential Jewish people in the country."[79]

The pressure became so great that Eisenhower felt it necessary to go on television on 20 February 1957 to explain the situation to the nation:[80]

> Should a nation which attacks and occupies foreign territory in the face of United Nations disapproval be allowed to impose conditions on its own withdrawal? If we agreed that armed attack can properly achieve the purposes of the assailant, then I fear we will have turned back the clock of international order. If the United Nations once admits that international disputes can be settled by using force, then we will have destroyed the very foundation of the organization and our best hope of establishing world order. The United Nations must not fail. I believe that in the interests of peace the United Nations has no choice but to

exert pressure upon Israel to comply with the withdrawal resolutions.[81]

On the same day Eisenhower privately sent a message to Ben Gurion warning of punitive actions by Washington if Israel did not withdraw from the Sinai Peninsula. He informed Ben Gurion that he would approve sanctions against Israel and also might cut off all private assistance to the country, which amounted to $40 million in tax-deductible donations and $60 million annually in the purchase of bonds. A week later, on 27 February, Israel announced it accepted the U.S. position and shortly would announce the beginning of its withdrawal. Finally, on 16 March, Israel withdrew from all the territory it had occupied in the Sinai Peninsula during its invasion the previous fall, thus abandoning all territorial gains by force of arms.[82]

But that was to change dramatically in another decade.

* *

Like a kaleidoscope, Israel's 1967 conquests suddenly altered the border issue into a completely different picture. Israel ended the war in control of 20,870 square miles of new territory. Thus Israel's control of Arab land had again increased, from the original size of Israel envisioned in the 1947 UN Partition Plan of 5,900 square miles, which Israel had increased to about 7,800 square miles in the 1948 fighting, to a new total of 28,870 square miles. This included 18,100 square miles in Egypt's Sinai, including 135 square miles of the Gaza Strip; 2,270 square miles in Jordan's West Bank, and 500 square miles in Syria's Golan Heights.[83]

Israel's conquests occurred at a time when the White House was sympathetic to its ambitions. President Lyndon B. Johnson, unlike Eisenhower, was a strong believer that Israel contributed to U.S. interests. Under Johnson's predecessor, John F. Kennedy, and under Johnson himself there had been no effort to address the borders. As a result of the 1967 war there now was an even more dramatic situation. But instead of serving as a catalyst for examining the whole borders issue the new borders obscured the old. From this time on, the borders issue focused on the new conquests. Ignored henceforth were Israel's conquests in 1948.

This shifting of the borders issue from the original conquests to the conquests of 1967 was cemented in passage of UN Security Council Resolution 242 on 22 November 1967. The United States, with the guidance of UN Ambassador Arthur J. Goldberg, played the leading role in getting the resolution accepted by privately assuring the Arabs that Israel would not be allowed to retain its new conquests. The implication, perhaps not widely understood at the time, was that the old conquests of 1948 were a fait accompli essentially beyond negotiation.

The resolution, unanimously passed by the United Nations Security Council on 22 November 1967, was deceptively simple and brief, 292 words.[84] If one more word had been added, much of the quarreling still going on about its meaning could have been avoided. That is the simple word "the" or "all." Instead, the resolution simply calls for "withdrawal of Israeli armed forces from territories." Failure to call for the withdrawal from "the" or "all" territories was considered at the time as an exercise in creative ambiguity, a hedge to give both parties a chance to straighten out awkward frontiers left by the 1949 armistices. Although most council members wanted to demand Israel's total withdrawal, Israel encouraged the idea, and the United States agreed, that the post-war period was a time when the frontiers could be rationalized to both sides' advantage with minor and reciprocal changes.

The United States gained Arab acceptance of the resolution by its repeated pledge that there would be only small and reciprocal border changes. This U.S. position was detailed in a secret State Department study completed in 1978:

> Support for the concept of total withdrawal was widespread in the Security Council, and it was only through intensive American efforts that a resolution was adopted which employed indefinite language in the withdrawal clause. In the process of obtaining this result, the United States made clear to the Arab states and several other members of the Security Council that the United States envisioned only insubstantial revisions of the 1949 armistice lines. Israel did not protest this approach.[85]

One example of how the United States sold the resolution to the Arabs involved the Latrun Salient, a small protrusion of land held by Jordan in the Latrun Plain that blocked direct motoring between Tel Aviv and Jerusalem through the Wadi el Bab. On 6 November, less than three weeks before the passage of 242, Secretary of State Dean Rusk privately assured King Hussein of Jordan in a Washington meeting that if Jordan gave up the Latrun Salient, "the United States would then use its diplomatic and political influence to obtain in compensation access for Jordan to a Mediterranean port in Israel."

Ambassador Goldberg gave Hussein similar assurances at the same time, also citing Latrun as the kind of minor change contemplated.[86] When Hussein met on 8 November with Lyndon Johnson, who had been briefed by Rusk on the U.S. interpretation, the Jordanian monarch asked how soon Israeli troops would withdraw from most of the occupied lands. The president replied: "In six months."[87] After these assurances from the top echelon of the government, King Hussein pronounced himself "extremely satisfied" with the U.S. interpretation of withdrawal by Israeli forces.[88]

Israel gave every indication in 1967 that it agreed with the U.S. interpretation. The 1978 State Department study reported: "There was no overt conflict between the United States and Israel over the U.S. views on withdrawal, and in several respects the U.S. position coincided with that of Israel....At no time during this period did Israel argue that it would withdraw only on selected fronts. To the contrary, in conversations with American officials the Israelis consistently discussed the concepts of withdrawal and secure borders in terms of three fronts."[89]

* *

Resolution 242 had barely passed before Israel began challenging its generally accepted meaning. Foreign Minister Abba Eban later argued that the issue of withdrawal was not really the "central and primary" concern of the resolution. Instead, he asserted, what was important was the need for a "just and lasting peace," while at the same time ignoring Israel's continuing military occupation. At another time Eban and other Israeli officials argued that the principle of the "inadmissibility of the acquisition of territory by war" was not relevant to Israel since the phrase appeared only in the preambular paragraph or, alternatively, because it applied only to wars of aggression. Israel's initiation of the 1967 war was ignored.[90]

A more forceful argument made by Eban and succeeding Israeli officials maintained that since the resolution allowed for "territorial revision" the scope and dimension of Israel's withdrawal was vague and undetermined, going so far as to claim that it was not "applicable to all the territories involved."[91] In reality, Eban had been involved directly in the U.S. discussions in New York prior to passage of the resolution and not only was aware of the U.S. interpretation but indicated that Israel agreed with it. Nonetheless, the alleged vagueness of the resolution remains to this day Israel's major argument for retaining occupied territory.

Surprisingly, the most successful Israeli argument turned out to be the assertion that the territories were not occupied. They were "liberated" from Jordan, which had no more right to them than Israel, meaning sovereignty over the territories was in dispute. Israel arrived at this interpretation by maintaining that Jordan's annexation of the West Bank in 1950 had been a unilateral act recognized by only two countries, Britain and Pakistan, leaving the implication that Arabs ruling Arabs under Jordan was no more legitimate than Israel's military occupation.

In large part, the reason Israel has been so successful was because of the refusal of Washington to take a public position on its own interpretation of resolution 242. It was only in late 1969 that the U.S. interpretation was detailed publicly. That was not only the first but also the last time the issue received detailed and public airing. The man who did it was Secretary of State William Rogers, notably evenhanded on the conflict. On 9 December 1969 Rogers remarked in an address that resolution 242

> calls for withdrawal from occupied territories, the non-acquisition of territory by war, and recognized boundaries. We believe that while recognized political boundaries must be established, and agreed upon by the parties, any changes in the preexisting lines should be confined to insubstantial alternations required for mutual security. We do not support expansionism.[92]

Other officials became candid and outspoken only after they were out of office. For instance, Dean Rusk, the secretary of state in 1967 who personally negotiated with King Hussein and approved passage of 242, later wrote: "Resolution 242 never contemplated the movement of any significant territories to Israel."[93] In his memoirs, Rusk repeated that formulation, explaining that "we thought...certain anomalies could easily be straightened out with some exchanges of territory, making a more sensible border for all parties."[94]

Similarly, Lord Caradon, the putative author of the resolution, wrote in 1981 long after his retirement:

> It was from the occupied territories that the Resolution called for withdrawal. The test was which territories were occupied. That was a test not possibly subject to doubt. As a matter of plain fact East Jerusalem, the West Bank, Gaza, the Golan and Sinai were occupied in the 1967 conflict; it was on withdrawal from occupied territories that the Resolution insisted.[95]

Even Henry Kissinger wrote in his memoirs: "Jordan's acquiescence in Resolution 242 had been obtained in 1967 by the promise of our United Nations Ambassador Arthur Goldberg that under its terms we would work for the return of the West Bank to Jordan with minor boundary rectifications and that we were prepared to use our influence to obtain a role for Jordan in Jerusalem."[96]

Despite such authoritative statements and the persuasive evidence of the 1978 State Department study on the meaning of resolution 242, Israel and its supporters have maintained that the resolution does not say, or does not mean, what it clearly does. Arthur Goldberg, an avowed Zionist, eventually even claimed that he and other officials never had supported the idea of minor and reciprocal changes.[97]

Clearly such statements did not result from a misunderstanding. They were a deliberate misrepresentation of the record by Israel and its supporters in an effort to justify Israel's continued occupation. Lucius D. Battle, who was the assistant secretary of state for the Middle East at the time and intimately involved in passage of 242, reaffirmed in an interview in 1993 the original U.S. interpretation. He added that Goldberg had proven over the years to be, on the issue of 242, "a slippery character."[98]

* *

Despite the continuing uncertainly about the original meaning of resolution 242, the United States has not enunciated its position since the Carter Administration. This came about largely because of President Jimmy Carter. There was a deep irony in this outcome because Carter came to office in 1977 talking publicly and loudly about resolution 242 and the U.S. interpretation. In his first months in office, Carter referred openly to minor and reciprocal border changes, the only president to do so.[99] Under Carter, resolution 242 once again took on renewed urgency and meaning. On 27 June 1977, Carter revealed his Middle East ideas by releasing a position paper that strongly endorsed 242. It said: "We consider that this resolution means withdrawal on all three fronts—that is, Sinai, Golan, West Bank–Gaza....no territories, including the West Bank, are automatically excluded from the items to be negotiated."[100]

But then he made a major miscalculation. Still relatively new in office, naive in foreign affairs, overly trusting, and desperately concerned to get re-elected, Carter sought to win the confidence of Israel's new leader, Menachem Begin, in their first meeting in 1977. In a private upstairs session at the White House on 19 July, Carter pleaded with Begin to halt the establishment of settlements in the occupied territories while Begin asked the president to stop talking in public about resolution 242 meaning minor adjustments to the frontiers. In a note on the meeting, Carter wrote that Begin "asks that we not use phrase 'minor adjustments' without prior notice to him—I agreed. He will try to accommodate us on settlements."[101] Begin's accommodation, it turned out, was an empty promise. Less than one week later, Begin's government conferred legal status on three Jewish settlements in the occupied territories. Despite Begin's reneging, Carter did not retaliate and kept his promise not to mention "minor adjustments."

Not even Israel's expansion into southern Lebanon in 1978 changed Carter's mind, although Israel effectively had taken over a six-mile deep self-described "security zone" that it placed under the control of its surrogate, the South Lebanon Army, which was supplied and trained by Israel.[102] (After Israel's 1982 invasion of Lebanon, Israel expanded the zone. As of 1995, it encompassed 348 square miles, nearly 10 percent of Lebanon, going up to twelve miles deep and encompassing eighty-five Lebanese villages with a population of 180,000.[103])

Instead of punishing Israel for its expansionism and for breaking its word on settlements, Carter kept his promise not to refer to the U.S. interpretation of resolution 242. The result of this willingness to keep only one side of a broken bargain was that Carter, and no president since him, has voiced in public that provocative phrase "minor border adjustments." When Arab and other interlocutors questioned various administrations over the years since 1977 about U.S. policy on withdrawal, they have been soothingly assured that "there is no change in policy." Thus Reagan, Bush and Clinton are on record as stoutly asserting that the United States stands firmly behind resolution 242 "as the foundation stone of America's Middle East peace effort," as Reagan once put it.[104] What, exactly, they have meant by that has remained hazy.

Just how effective Israel's borders strategy has been over the years was remarked upon by Henry Kissinger in 1992:

> Israel adopted procrastination as the best strategy....The way the peace process evolved seemed to confirm this judgment. In 1948 Israel's Arab neighbors went to war rather than accept the Jewish state. In the '50s and '60s, some of them began to move toward accepting the '47 frontiers but not those that existed....In the '70s and '80s, the United States and some moderate Arab regimes...accepted the '67 frontiers, but once again balked at those that existed. In the face of these constantly improving offers, Israel had nothing to lose and much to gain from procrastination.[105]

While perceptive, this analysis ignores the role of the United States. If Washington had not acquiesced in Israel's refusal to return Palestinian land it is doubtful that the Jewish state would have been successful in retaining it. Washington not only allowed Israel to retain its conquests but encouraged its most extreme political elements. The point was that if Washington was not going to take a hard-line against Israel's territorial claims, why should Israel's hard-liners themselves be more conciliatory? Faced with this logic, Israel's moderates were left stranded without serious argument against the most extreme territorial ambitions.

How successful Israel's maximal territorial strategy has been, and how compliant Washington's reaction has been, became more glaring than ever during the Clinton Administration. Under Clinton, it appeared that Washington was prepared to desert resolution 242 in its entirety. The suspicion arose because of the administration's refusal to follow the precedent of previous administrations in describing the territories as occupied. This was revealed in its two draft papers on an Israeli-Palestinian Declaration of Principles, submitted during the peace talks on 14 May and 30 June 1993—before the 1993 Israeli-PLO accord. In the papers, the United States made no mention of the occupation or, for that matter, of Israeli withdrawal, redeployment or an exchange of land for peace.[106]

In the 30 June draft the Clinton Administration wrote: "The two sides concur that the agreement reached between them on permanent status will constitute the implementation of Resolutions 242 and 338 in all their aspects." While the language was legalistically so ambiguous as to defy clear interpretation, certainly one reading of it is that the Clinton Administration has no position at all on the meaning of 242.

5 | PALESTINIANS
America Discovers
a People, 1947–1995

PALESTINIANS WERE KEENLY AWARE that it was not just the Jews who coveted their land. A threat also came from the east. That was where King Abdullah ibn Hussein, a descendant of the Prophet Mohammed and scion of the dispossessed Hashemites of Arabia, ruled over Jordan and dreamed arabesques of conquest. His transcen-dental vision was to achieve a Greater Syria under his sovereignty, an area that in his dreams stretched from Syria through Lebanon and into Palestine.

For a quarter-century Abdullah had suffered the restraints of his British mandate masters as well as the restrictions imposed by the limited resources of his arid kingdom. By late 1947, however, it was clear Britain's days in Palestine were ending and a Jewish state was going to emerge in Palestine. If he could not have Greater Syria, then Abdullah at least wanted whatever the Jews did not claim in Palestine.

Twelve days before the UN partition plan of 29 November 1947, Abdullah and the Jews made a partition pact of their own. Golda Meir, the acting head of the political department of the Jewish Agency, traveled to Naharayim near Abdullah's palace at Shuneh to meet with the king. They agreed that Jordanian troops would not attack Jewish forces and that only one state, Jewish, would be created in Pales-tine. In return, Abdullah would be allowed to annex the rest of Palestine.[3]

At first, the State Department was not enthusiastic about the entrance into Palestine of the Arab Legion, as Jordan's army under British command was called.

But as partition itself proved unworkable and Britain pushed its program to strengthen Jordan as a way to increase its own security, Washington slowly came around. The new U.S. attitude emerged not only because the Zionists favored Abdullah's plan but because the only major leader among the Palestinians themselves was highly detested by American officials.

He was Hajj Amin Husseini, the Mufti (chief Muslim religious authority) of Jerusalem since 1922, the same year that Abdullah had ascended the throne of Britain's newly established Jordan. The two leaders roundly despised each other. In fact, Abdullah—as well as the Zionists—had tried over the years to have Husseini assassinated.[4] As leader of the Palestinian community Husseini generally had worked amiably with the British until the sudden influx into Palestine of Jews from Hitler's Germany in the mid-1930s—61,854 in 1935 alone.[5] This intimidating surge in Zionist growth helped prompt a nationwide Palestinian strike in mid-April 1936 demanding a halt to immigration, banning land sales to Jews and establishing a Palestinian government.

On 25 April 1936 Husseini became head of the new Arab Higher Committee, a nationalist group comprised of all elements of Palestinian society united by their opposition to Zionism and British rule. Among his first acts was to spell out to British High Commissioner Sir Arthur Wauchope the frustrations of the Palestinian community. In a memorandum to Wauchope, Husseini stressed the following points:

1) The Jews always have declared their intention to make Palestine a homeland for all the Jews of the world.

2) Their increased immigration and land purchases are aimed at establishing a Jewish state.

3) Britain facilitates Jewish immigration and the usurpation of Arab lands.

4) Britain trespassed on Arab rights when it issued the Balfour Declaration, which affected a country not its own.

Husseini's memorandum added:

> The Arabs are of the strong belief that the continuation of the present policy will lead them to immediate annihilation. They find themselves compelled, moved by their struggle for existence, to defend their country and national rights.[6]

As was its habit, Britain at first ignored Husseini's complaints. By late May, however, the Palestinians' general strike had erupted into full scale insurrection. But instead of being its instigator, as alleged by his detractors, Husseini was essentially its captive. Wauchope reported to London in mid-May that the Arab leaders "are at present powerless to stop the strike unless immigration is suspended as the feeling of Arabs is now so strong."[7]

The Arab Revolt, as it became known, was a grassroots uprising that in its first phase lasted until October 1936, when Britain promised to send another committee to listen to Palestinian grievances. Called the Peel Commission after its head, Lord Robert Peel, grandson of the nineteenth century prime minister, it concluded in its report released on 8 July 1937 that many of the Palestinian complaints were justified and that the revolt had been caused by a fear of Zionism and "the desire of the Arabs for national independence."

The commission also concluded that differences between Arabs and Jews were irreconcilable and for the first time called for the partition of Palestine into a Jewish and an Arab state. However, there would not be a Palestinian state, but rather "an Arab state consisting of Transjordan and the Arab part of Palestine."[8]

Both sides rejected the Peel report. The Palestinians resumed their revolt, which continued into March 1939. The costs were high. More than 3,000 Palestinians, 2,000 Jews and 600 British were killed. The Palestinian community was left shattered, its leaders in exile or prison and its people largely unarmed by British confiscations of weapons.[9]

Among the victims of the 1936–39 Palestinian uprising was Hajj Amin Husseini. Although the Mufti was not injured physically, it was starting with this revolt that his reputation among Westerners was ruined. Zionists were particularly effective in demonizing this Palestinian nationalist, in much the same way they later did Yasser Arafat. Thus, by 1939, the monster image had become attached to Husseini, thanks mainly to the British who saw him as the enemy of their mandate and the Zionists who saw the Mufti as a leader charismatic enough to unite the Palestinians. One of the things the early Zionists feared most was the emergence of an Arab as a true leader capable of uniting the Palestinians and the Arab nation into an effective opponent. A similar fear caused the Israelis to go to war less than two decades later against Gamal Abdul Nasser of Egypt.[10]

Husseini abetted his enemies by fleeing from British authority and going to Germany, where he spent the war years. Because, to the Arabs, World War II was a strictly European affair, Husseini and a number of Arabs nationalists acted on the adage that the enemy of my enemy is my friend. Other Arab nationalists, including Anwar Sadat of Egypt, supported the Germans. Husseini traded his endorsement of Hitler for a promise of German support for the freedom of Palestine.

After the war, the Western Allies, and particularly Britain, publicly vilified Husseini as a collaborator, which he surely was. However, there is no evidence to buttress Zionist charges that he ever took part in or abetted atrocities against European Jews.[11] For Britain, focusing on Husseini as evil incarnate had the added advantage of fitting into its strategy to ignore Palestinian nationalism in favor of King Abdullah. Extravagant Zionist claims that Husseini's "hands...are drenched in the blood of millions of Jews" brought no public denials in Washington or London.[12] In the view of the West, Husseini was a Middle Eastern version of Hitler.

Given Britain's dominant position in the Middle East and America's superpower status, the demonization of Husseini had a chilling effect on Arab leaders' relations with him. They recognized that the more they associated with Husseini the less they would enjoy aid from the West. The Egyptian prime minister, Mahmud Nuqrashi, warned Husseini when he finally returned to the Middle East after the war not to try to head a Palestinian state because he "would never be accepted or trusted by the Western Powers."[13] There was, of course, a degree of self-interest in such advice. By weakening Husseini and Palestinian nationalism the neighboring Arab states anticipated that they might share in the dividing up of Arab Palestine themselves.

Husseini's return in mid-1946 was to Cairo, not Palestine. British officials had refused his entrance to Palestine, determined to freeze him out of any diplomatic role. Nonetheless, he remained enormously popular among Palestinians as well as in the wider Arab world. In recognition of his popularity, the Arab League, which had been created in 1945 by Egypt, Iraq, Jordan, Lebanon, Saudi Arabia, Syria and Yemen, established a new Arab Higher Committee and made Husseini its leader shortly after his arrival in Cairo.[14]

Husseini once again was a force with which to be reckoned. However, except for the masses, Arab leaders were no more eager than the Jews, British and Americans to see Husseini's stature increased. His reception by the Egyptians was cool. So was it by the Jordanians. When he sought to get closer to Palestine by seeking to move to Amman, the Jordanians turned him down.[15] The Jewish Agency let it be known that it would negotiate with any Arab leader except the Mufti.[16]

When war finally came in 1948, the Palestinians had no full-time military force, no military unit structure, no unified command and no on-site leader.[17] The Mufti remained in Cairo, essentially under town arrest by the cautious Egyptians.[18] Yet, reported the Consul General in Jerusalem, Robert B. Macatee, to the State Department, "No Arab approaches the Mufti's stature in the eyes of Palestinian Arabs. He is the central figure on the Arab stage."[19] Husseini was able to field a guerrilla force of only about 2,000 men in what was called the Holy War Army or variously the Holy War of Salvation and the Army of Salvation.[20] His guerrillas were quickly defeated.

With Jewish forces successful nearly everywhere on the battlefield, the Palestinians made one final, desperate effort to establish their own state. On 1 October 1948, the Arab League declared the establishment of the All Palestine Government, also called the Arab Government of Palestine, with its capital in Gaza.[21] Ahmad Hilmi Pasha was named prime minister and Husseini president of the Assembly, meaning he wielded the real power.[22]

In a message sent to the State Department, Hilmi explained that

> in virtue of the natural right of the people of Palestine for self-determination which principle is supported by the Charters of the League of Nations, the United Nations and others and in view of the termination of the British mandate over Palestine which had prevented the Arabs from exercising their independence, the Arabs of Palestine, who are the owners of the country and its indigenous inhabitants and who constitute the great majority of its legal population, have solemnly resolved to declare Palestine in its entirety and within its boundaries as established before the termination of the British mandate an independent state and constituted a government under the name of the All Palestine Government deriving its authority from a representative council based

on democratic principles and aiming to safeguard the rights of minorities and foreigners, protect the holy places and guarantee freedom of worship to all communities.

Hilmi sought "to establish relations of cordiality and cooperation" with the United States.[23]

The Lebanese foreign minister told U.S. officials that the "Gaza Government was set up as opposition to Abdullah...popular reaction is that other Arabs wish to thwart Abdullah's ambitions for federation of Arab regions with Transjordan [and] concomitant tacit recognition of Israel."[24]

However, like Husseini's lack of resources at the outbreak of war, the All Palestine Government had no civil service, no army, no money, no territory, and it had no more success than Husseini's guerrillas. Gaza was controlled by Egypt and the small part of Palestine not absorbed by Israel was under Jordan's Arab Legion. Nonetheless, the government had soaring ambitions. It announced its borders were "Syria and Lebanon in the north, Syria and Transjordan in the east, the Mediterranean in the west and Egypt in the south"—in other words, all of Palestine.[25]

The United States declared itself unimpressed and worked against the Palestinian entity simply by ignoring it. A number of motives prompted the U.S. attitude, including Washington's collusion with Britain to give Arab Palestine to Jordan, its opposition to the Mufti, and also a fear that Israeli extremists might use the All Palestine Government as a pretext to take over all of Palestine. Washington announced its formal refusal to recognize the All Palestine Government on 13 October 1948.[26] In a telegram to embassies in the region, the State Department advised that

US Govt considers establishment of "Arab Palestine Govt" under present circumstances prejudicial to successful solution Palestine problem as well as to best interests Arab States and Arab inhabitants Palestine. "Govt" apparently being set up without prior consultation wishes Arab Palestinians. Also appears dominated by Mufti, an adventurer, whose reprehensible wartime activities in association with our enemies cannot be forgotten or forgiven by US....By claiming speak for all Palestine "Govt" affords ready pretext to Jewish revisionists make similar claims for PGI [Provisional Government of Israel] control all Palestine.[27]

Predictably, King Abdullah, Britain and Israel also refused to recognize the government. Under active British pressure, even the Arab governments stalled until mid-October. By then Egypt had ordered Husseini and the rest of the cabinet out of Gaza. They would never return. In Cairo, the Palestinian leaders were isolated and unable to perform any official duties. Thus, within weeks, the All Palestine Government withered away.[28] The Palestinians' last chance in this period at forming their own state was lost. Within less than two years Arab Palestine, except for the Gaza Strip, would be part of Jordan and henceforth be called the West Bank. Suddenly, the ancient name of Palestine ceased to exist in most Western countries.

With the failure of the All Palestine Government and the annexation of the West Bank by Jordan, the only Palestinian claims recognized by the United States were those of the refugees. Thus, previous policy was abandoned. Up to the time of the 1947 partition plan, the State Department had traditionally acknowledged Palestinians' rights as the majority community, including the right of self-determination. Once partition failed and the United States began colluding with Britain to support Jordan's annexation of the abortive Arab state, all further references to Palestinian rights, and especially to their right of self-determination, disappeared from internal and external State Department documents. Henceforth, Palestinian national rights were no longer cited. For the next quarter-century, the United States essentially ignored the Palestinians.

* *

U.S. policy remained unchanged through the 1950s and 1960s. But little noted in Washington in this period was the emergence in the mid-1960s of a Palestinian nationalist movement determined to demonstrate that Palestinians not only were a nation but that their unresolved refugee status afforded them rights and legitimate claims. Abdullah's grandson, King Hussein, presaged the change by pointing out in Washington after meeting with President Johnson on 16 April 1964 that the Palestinian problem was at the center of the Middle East conflict:

> It is simply that the Israelis are refusing to restore the rights unlawfully wrested from the Arabs of Palestine—the inalienable right of those refugees to return to their ancestral land, to the properties that they have developed with the sweat of their brows and to their normal means of decent livelihood.[29]

Washington paid little attention to Hussein's words nor to a seminal event a month later: the founding of the Palestine Liberation Organization in Jerusalem on 28 May 1964, followed at the beginning of 1965 by the launching of guerrilla operations inside Israel by Fatah, the underground group founded by Yasser Arafat six years earlier. From this time forward the equation between Palestinians, Israelis and the rest of the world changed, albeit hesitantly. No longer were the Palestinians just refugees. They were a people demanding recognition of their losses and their nationhood.

In reaction to the Palestinians' new self-awareness, Israelis insisted with growing vehemence that Palestinians "did not exist," as Prime Minister Golda Meir once declared. She made the remark in 1969, two years after Israel's total occupation of the Palestinian community in the 1967 war. Her contention was that "there was no such thing as a Palestinian people....It was not as though there was a Palestinian people considering itself as a Palestinian people and we came and threw them out and took their country away from them."[30]

But, of course, that was exactly what had happened. The dispossession of their homeland was the essence of the Palestinian case against Israel. While Prime

Minister Meir was correct in noting that the Palestinians had not had their own country, they nonetheless had been recognized by the Ottoman Empire and later the British Empire as a distinct political entity.[31]

An unexpected byproduct of the shock of Israel's conquests in the 1967 war, with the entire Palestinian community coming under Israeli military occupation, was the focusing of increased attention on the question of who were the Palestinians. To the world at large, the PLO declared that Palestinians were a people who had "legitimate rights," as the PLO Charter of 1968 proclaimed.[32] But to the U.S. government they remained refugees or, now, a new type of Palestinian—the civilian under military occupation.

It took a period of brutal and highly visible terrorist attacks, starting in 1968 with the first skyjacking of an Israeli El-Al civilian jetliner, finally to make the world community recognize the Palestinians. George Habash, leader of the Popular Front for the Liberation of Palestine, one of the PLO's most radical factions and a leading practitioner of terrorist attacks, explained in 1969 that the importance of terrorism for the Palestinian cause resided in its "shock value....We had to shock both an indifferent world and a demoralized Palestine nation....The world has forgotten Palestine. Now it must pay attention to our struggle....What we are after is liberation of Palestine. If we must blow up a dozen El-Al planes, then we will."[33]

The terror campaign backfired in the United States. Washington refused to change its policy. Moreover, the brutal terror repulsed most Americans, who were ignorant of its causes. Not even passage of a series of resolutions by the United Nations General Assembly affirming Palestinian rights convinced Washington to recognize the Palestinians.

Starting in 1968, General Assembly resolutions established that the Palestinians were a separate people deserving all the rights due such groups. Over a six-year period, the UN through annual resolutions established the legal and moral framework for Palestinian nationalism. A number of pioneering resolutions were passed during this period, including the following:[34]

• In 1968, resolution 2443 (XXIII) established the Special Committee to Investigate Israeli Practices Affecting the Human Rights of the Population of the Occupied Territories.

• In 1969, resolution 2535 (XXIV) reaffirmed the "inalienable rights" of the Palestinians.

• In 1970, resolution 2672 (XXV) recognized that the "people of Palestine are entitled to equal rights and self-determination, in accordance with the Charter of the United Nations."

• In 1971, resolution 2787 (XXVI) confirmed the "legality of the peoples' struggle for self-determination and liberation from colonial and foreign domination and alien subjugation, notably in southern Africa...as well as the Palestinian people, by all available means consistent with the Charter of the United Nations."

• In 1972, resolution 2963 (XXVII) expressed concern that "the people of Palestine have not been permitted to enjoy their inalienable rights and to exer-

cise their right to self-determination."
- In 1973, resolution 3089 (XXVIII) declared that "full respect for and realization of the inalienable rights of the people of Palestine, particularly its right to self-determination, are indispensable for the establishment of a just and lasting peace in the Middle East...."
- In 1974, after the Arab states recognized the PLO as the "sole, legitimate representative" of the Palestinian people, the General Assembly awarded observer status to the organization. It also invited Chairman Yasser Arafat to address the United Nations, a dramatic event that signalled the Palestinians' recognition as a people nearly worldwide—except in the United States.[35]

The United States, in unity with Israel, opposed—and has continued to ever since—all of the above resolutions, including those echoing the "inalienable rights" proclaimed in the U.S. Declaration of Independence. However, as a result of the UN efforts on behalf of the Palestinians, it was no longer possible by the mid-1970s to ignore the fact that all those refugees and civilians under Israeli occupation were no more than just an amorphous mass. They were, as the world community acknowledged, a people with a distinct identity and with the rights accorded such groups.

Further abetting the perception of the Palestinians as a distinct people were the new circumstances resulting from the aftershocks of the 1973 war. For the first time the United States started dealing directly and seriously with Arab leaders after the war. Up to then, U.S. policy was essentially to ignore Egyptian and Syrian demands vis-à-vis Israel, as it did the Palestinians. King Hussein of Jordan was an exception. He was a welcome guest at the White House, although his advice was seldom acted upon. Otherwise, estrangement from the Arabs became the official policy of National Security Advisor and later Secretary of State Henry A. Kissinger from 1969 to 1973. He believed that the longer the Arabs were kept frustrated the sooner they would recognize that Arab-Israeli accommodation could only come via Washington.

In frustration, the leaders of Egypt and Syria chose a different route, war. While they were not ultimately successful on the battlefield, the global repercussions of the 1973 war shocked Kissinger into completely changing policy (see chapter 8). Immediately afterwards, he embarked on a vigorous new policy of step-by-step diplomacy involving in-depth talks with Arab leaders. One of the prices Kissinger had to pay was finally to listen to the Arab side of the conflict, a practically unique experience for an American official. Anwar Sadat of Egypt and Hafez Assad of Syria—and when they a had chance, King Hussein of Jordan and others—tirelessly lectured Kissinger during his visits in 1974 and 1975 that the core of the conflict was not the Soviet Union and the Cold War, as Kissinger believed, or the enmity of Arab states towards Israel. It was the Palestinian problem.

Since the message came from leaders with whom Kissinger had to bargain in order to pursue his diplomacy, the message could not be ignored. In the words of a Kissinger associate, Deputy Assistant Secretary of State Harold H. Saunders for Near Eastern and South Asian affairs, "He was confronted with a new reality."[36]

Israel was not blind to the growing recognition of Palestinians as a people, and it did what it could to prevent the spread of that perception. At Israel's insistence, Kissinger agreed in the Sinai II accord of September 1975 to a secret pledge that the United States would not recognize or negotiate with the Palestinians' representative, the Palestine Liberation Organization. This would not change until the PLO recognized "Israel's right to exist" and accepted UN resolutions 242 and 338, a particularly touchy issue for Palestinians since 242 referred only to "refugees" and neither resolution made any mention at all of Palestinians.[37]

Despite the anti-PLO pledge, the signing of Sinai II brought with it an another unexpected boost to Palestinian nationalism in an indirect way. It led to an invitation from Congress to the State Department to testify on the Hill to explain U.S. policy, an opportunity Kissinger used in order to perform something of a balancing act for his Arab negotiating partners. He instructed Hal Saunders and the Near Eastern affairs office to write a policy paper reassessing the role of the Palestinians in the conflict. It proved to be an historic occasion.

* *

The years since Loy Henderson and his stalwarts in the Near Eastern Affairs division had not been kind ones for Arab specialists in the State Department. The Eisenhower Administration (1953–1961) had been cool towards Israel, but not so cool as actually to oppose American Zionists and force the Jewish state to return its conquests of 1948 or to recognize the rights of the Palestinians. Then had come President Kennedy (1961–1963), who broke America's 1947 arms embargo and granted Israel for the first time U.S. weapons that greatly increased its military strength but did nothing for the Palestinians.

Lyndon Johnson (1963–1969) totally embraced Israel, becoming the most pro-Israeli president up to that time. During his term Israel completed its conquest of all of Palestine in the 1967 war, bringing it under total Jewish rule after seventy years of concerted effort by Zionists. However, Johnson showed little interest in making Israel return its conquests.

With the coming to power of Richard Nixon (1969–1974), America had a president who personally was skeptical of Israel's actions and ambitions, but who brought with him Kissinger, first as National Security Adviser and, after September 1973, Secretary of State. President Ford (1974–1977), cool to Israel but vulnerable to the lobby's pressures because of his political weakness, kept Kissinger as Secretary of State. In total, Kissinger served eight years at the center of U.S. policy-making.

Kissinger was a Jewish immigrant from Austria, extremely sympathetic to the Israelis, and he did more to aid Israel's long term power than any single individual before him. It was Kissinger who encouraged Nixon's superficial view that the Arab-Israeli conflict was a byproduct of the Cold War, and it was he who was instrumental in forming the embryonic perception that Israel was a strategic ally of the United States. In return, with the active cooperation of Congress, he was instrumental in giving to Israel unprecedented amounts of U.S. economic, military and diplomatic aid, vastly strengthening the Jewish state against its Arab neighbors.[38] In his memoirs, Israeli leader Yitzhak Rabin wrote: "The story of Kissinger's contribution to Israel's security has yet to be told, and for the present suffice it to say that it was of prime importance."[39]

* *

Over this span of presidents, life for the Arab specialists in the State Department had not been pleasant. Like Truman, subsequent presidents kept U.S. policy in the Middle East to themselves because of its exaggerated impact on domestic politics, leaving the counsel of the specialists more often ignored than not. Zionists had not relented in their attacks against the State Department after their victories under Truman. On the contrary, the Israeli lobby had grown more powerful under the name of AIPAC, the American Israel Public Affairs Committee. It emerged in 1959 as the successor of earlier Zionist advocacy groups and became an enormously effective voice for Zionism in Washington and the most powerful special interest group in the country.[40]

AIPAC published and distributed the *Near East Report*, a newsletter totally focused on Israeli interests and distributed free to all Congressmen and influential policymakers. It also operated a speaker's bureau, conducted special research on topics affecting U.S.-Israeli relations, actively campaigned around the country in Israel's cause, and kept track of personnel in the State Department and elsewhere in the government and out of it. AIPAC did not hesitate to identify officials and individuals by their attitude toward Israel. It became fiendishly adept at labeling anyone against Zionism as anti-Semitic, a malicious but effective charge that blurred the difference between opposing Zionism and the ugly racism of hating Jews in general.[41]

The willingness of some Zionists to besmirch reputations had a chilling effect, especially on State Department officials trying to guide U.S. policy in the Arab-Israeli conflict. Richard B. Parker, who worked in the Division of Middle Eastern Affairs during Nixon's presidency, later admitted that he and his colleagues "were afraid to speak out for fear of being accused of anti-Semitism."[42]

Nonetheless, that did not stop the Zionists from labeling Parker an Arabist. This was a code word employed in Zionism's smear campaign against the State Department specialists and other critics of Israel. On the surface it meant a specialist who was fluent in Arabic, conversant with Arab history and was intimately familiar with the Middle East. It should have stood as a proud label of cultural and professional accomplishment. As used by Zionists, however, it implied a biased, Arab-lover who hated Jews. In the Zionist lexicon, to be an Arabist was only one step up from being anti-Semitic.

A full blast of Zionist venom against the "Arabists" hit the State Department specialists in 1971 in a major article in *The New York Times Magazine* by columnist Joseph Kraft. He charged that "Arabists" in the State Department harbored a "basic bias" against Israel. Translated, that meant they were anti-Semites whether they themselves knew it or not.[43] The Kraft article marked the acceleration of the process of demeaning the Arabists. It eventually caused increasing numbers of career diplomats to abandon Arabic studies altogether because, as Professor Augustus Richard Norton later observed wryly, "to be labeled an Arabist is hardly career-enhancing."[44]

Given the siege mentality produced by such gratuitous attacks, it was not surprising that the Near Eastern Affairs Division had not been active in a decade in producing any pioneering recommendations on how to relieve the Palestinians' plight. Nonetheless, once they received Kissinger's 1975 order to take a fresh look at the issue, the analysts had no difficulty in formulating a new perspective. The new view marked the first time since Israel's founding that the U.S. position actually came close to describing the reality.

Saunders laid out the new view to the House of Representatives Foreign Affairs Subcommittee on the Middle East on 12 November 1975. It was the first extensive U.S. statement on the Palestinians by any administration. Saunders said:

> In many ways, the Palestinian dimension of the Arab-Israeli conflict is the heart of that conflict....The Palestinians collectively are a political factor....The legitimate interests of the Palestinian Arabs must be taken into account in the negotiating of an Arab-Israeli peace.[45]

The Saunders Document, as the statement became known, caused an uproar among American Zionists and in Israel, where the Cabinet expressed "grave criticism" and charged that it contained "numerous inaccuracies and distortions."[46] The opposition to Saunders' statement became so loud that Kissinger soon discounted it as an "academic and theoretical exercise"—even though Kissinger himself carefully had worked on it before Saunders' appearance.[47]

Although it soon became obvious that the Saunders Document represented no serious shift in U.S. diplomacy, it nonetheless signified an important landmark in the struggle.[48] After this, for the first time, U.S. analysts began identifying Palestinians as a people and not by their function or situation such as refugees, terrorists or Arabs under Israeli occupation. Henceforth the refugee problem became only one part of the broader spectrum of the Palestinian problem. Observed former Central Intelligence Agency analyst Kathleen Christison: "In many ways the statement changed the bureaucracy's way of looking at the Palestinian issue and set the stage for the Carter Administration's greater concern for Palestinians." [49]

* *

Jimmy Carter's administration (1977–1981) went farther than any other in espousing Palestinian rights, but achieved little. This was mainly because of Carter's political weakness and his fear of the influence of the Israeli lobby. A fairly typical example of Carter's political vulnerability was recounted by Egyptian Foreign Minister Ismail Fahmy, who said Carter confided to him in 1977: "President [Anwar] Sadat repeatedly asks me to exercise major pressure on Israel, but I want you to know that I simply cannot do it because it would be a personal political suicide for me."[50]

A short time after meeting with Fahmy, Carter met with Israeli Foreign Minister Moshe Dayan and openly sought his help in improving relations with Jewish Americans. Dayan laid down a number of conditions for agreeing to peace with Egypt and thereby earning Carter gratitude from Jews. Among the conditions was that Israel would not have to deal with the PLO about a Palestinian state. This verged on blackmail, in the opinion of some U.S. diplomats, but Carter did not protest.[51] On the other hand, he never did earn the gratitude of the Jewish community either.

In the first two years of his presidency, before he understood fully the great power of the Israeli lobby, Carter was outspoken about the rights of the Palestinians. He mentioned in public the need for a Palestinian "homeland," Palestinian "legitimate rights" and the Palestinian need "to participate in the determination of their own future."[52] Less than five months after taking office he declared:

> I don't think that there can be any reasonable hope for a settlement of the Middle Eastern question which has been extant now on a continuing basis for more than twenty-nine years without a homeland for the Palestinians. The exact definition of what that homeland might be, the degree of independence of the Palestinian entity, its relations with Jordan or perhaps Syria and others, the geographical boundaries of it, all have to be worked out by the parties involved.[53]

But at the same time Carter continued in general to side with Israel against UN resolutions supportive of the Palestinians, and he went out of his way to reassure the lobby by saying flatly on 9 March 1978: "We do not and never have favored an independent Palestinian nation."[54]

Carter refused to talk with the PLO unless it recognized Israel and UN resolution 242, even though the Kissinger pledge prohibited only negotiations, not exchanges of views. As Harold Saunders noted: "We could have talked if we wanted. The agreement said no negotiations, not no talks."[55]

Carter's cooling toward the Palestinians culminated at the historic Camp David meeting between him, Menachem Begin and Anwar Sadat in the fall of 1978. During the intense negotiations at the presidential retreat Carter essentially abandoned any effort to aid the Palestinians. While Israel promised "full autonomy" for the Palestinians in the accords signed 17 September 1978, the agreement ultimately turned out to be no more than the bilateral pact with Egypt that Begin had sought all along. There was no serious plan on how autonomy was to be achieved. Nor was there any mention of "self-determination" or "the inadmissibility of the acquisition of territory by war," although UN resolution 242 was cited as the basis of the accords. Finally, the PLO, the body designated by the Arab world to represent the Palestinians, was not mentioned anywhere in the accords. The Palestinians as usual were not represented in the talks.[56]

Although the Framework of the accords referred to "the legitimate rights of the Palestinian people and their just requirements," Begin renounced the clause the day after the signing of the accords. He told an Israeli television interviewer that "legitimate rights" really "has no meaning," saying he had accepted the phrase only to please Carter and Sadat "and because it does not change reality."[57]

Since the Palestinians had not been invited to the negotiations, Chairman Arafat described the accords as a "dirty deal." His judgment was widely shared within the Palestinian community and in the larger Arab world.[58] Palestinian outrage was so acute that the community failed to test just how far the United States might have been willing to go in pushing for their legitimate rights. Given Begin's inflexible ambitions, the Palestinian rejection probably did not affect substantially the future. But it was a missed opportunity to gain U.S. favor at Israel's expense.

On the other hand, the political costs to Carter of championing the Palestinians had already been significant. He was routinely being criticized in the media as anti-Israel and a number of influential Jewish Americans turned away from him. After the Israeli-Egyptian peace treaty was signed on 26 March 1979 in Washington, he essentially stopped his involvement in the conflict.

When Israeli intelligence discovered and leaked to the press that Carter's UN ambassador, Andrew Young, a personal friend, had met privately with the PLO's UN observer, Zehdi Labib Terzi, in New York on 26 July 1979, Carter immediately fired him for breaking the Kissinger pledge not to deal with the PLO.[59] He further tried to please the lobby by reaffirming his commitment not to deal with the PLO: "I...committed our nation to adhere to this commitment."[60]

As his National Security Council Middle East expert, William B. Quandt, observed, the president had "found that the constraints of the American political system came into play whenever he tried to deal with the Palestinian question. Even to refer to Palestinian rights or to a Palestinian homeland could set off shock waves within the American Jewish community. They would be instantly felt in Congress and relayed back to the White House. Before long Carter learned to say less in public...."[61]

* *

The decade of the 1980s was historic for Palestinians, both in rebellious action and political maturity. Although they were driven from Lebanon by Israel's 1982 invasion, the Palestinians recouped five years later by launching the intifada, the uprising that challenged the legitimacy of Israel's occupation and spotlighted its costs, both moral and financial. In 1988, the PLO renounced terror and vowed to trade peace for a bit of Palestinian land. These moves brought the PLO international acceptance and helped create the atmosphere that culminated in the Israeli-PLO accord in 1993.

The 1980s were even more historic for the Israeli lobby in America. AIPAC soared to unparalleled strength under President Ronald Reagan (1981–1989). He was a total supporter of Israel and appeared to have little appreciation of the Palestinian and Arab side of the conflict. During the Reagan Administration, AIPAC became practically a full partner in forming U.S. policy toward the Middle East.

This intimate relationship between a lobby promoting a foreign cause and the White House was embraced by Reagan's two secretaries of state during his eight years in office. The first secretary, Alexander Haig, a former Army general and bureaucratic infighter, lasted less than a year and a half. The other was George Pratt Shultz, who had served under Nixon as secretary of labor, director of the office of management and budget and as secretary of the treasury.

Under Haig, a "strategic relationship" between Israel and the United States was first announced on 10 September 1981, and on 30 November it was officially signed as the Memorandum of Understanding on Strategic Cooperation with Israel. [62] Like Kissinger, Haig considered the Arab-Israeli conflict a reflection of the Cold War and he had spearheaded the agreement as a way to deter the Soviet Union in the Middle East. The agreement called for U.S.-Israeli cooperation against threats in the Middle East "caused by the Soviet Union or Soviet-controlled forces from outside the region." It created a coordinating council and working groups on weaponry research, military cooperation, maintenance facilities and other areas of mutual interest. Haig pledged that the United States would buy up to $200 million a year worth of Israeli arms and extend military "cooperation in research and development, building on past cooperation in this area."

The pact angered Arabs, who charged the United States was directly helping Israeli "aggression and expansionism," a sentiment echoed at the United Nations and among Third World countries.[63] The Arabs believed their fears were borne out on 14 December when Israel annexed the Golan Heights, which it had captured from Syria in 1967. Israel declared, through a bill passed in parliament, that the "law, jurisdiction and administration of the state shall apply to the Golan Heights."[64]

The Israeli action was a violation of the UN Charter, the Geneva Convention and UN resolution 242. Moreover, Washington had not been warned. Its angry reaction was immediately to deplore Israel's annexation, calling it a violation of the Camp David peace accords.[65] In retaliation, Washington on 18 December suspended the Memorandum of Understanding on Strategic Cooperation with Israel.[66] When Prime Minister Begin was notified, he exploded:

> You have no moral right to preach to us about civilian casualties. We have read the history of World War Two and we know what happened to civilians when you took action against an enemy. We have also read the history of the Vietnam war and your phrase "bodycount"....Are we a vassal state? A banana republic? Are we fourteen-year-old boys, that if they don't behave they have their knuckles smacked?...The people of Israel has lived for 3,700 years without a memorandum of understanding with America—and it will continue to live without it for another 3,700 years.[67]

Despite such outbursts, the Reagan Administration eventually relented and two years later reinstated the pact.[68]

More important to Menachem Begin than the strategic alliance was getting rid of the representative of the Palestinian people, the Palestine Liberation Organization. Even more than its acts of terror, the PLO represented the most powerful expression of the Palestinians' claims against Israel. It was gaining in international recognition and was increasingly seen in Israel as a threat to the Jews' claims to all of Palestine. In June 1982 Israel launched a full-scale war against Lebanon to crush once and for all the PLO and at the same time eradicate the more than 400,000-strong Palestinian refugee community in Lebanon. Although thousands paid with their lives, the Palestinians remained in Lebanon. But Arafat and the 6,000-man PLO cadre were forced out, driven once again into exile, the fighters scattered among seven Arab states while Arafat and his headquarters staff landed in Tunis, nearly 1,500 miles from Palestine.[69]

The Israelis and others claimed the invasion was undertaken with Haig's agreement.[70] The volatile secretary of state, unpopular in the White House because of his incessant turf battles for more power, was asked to resign on 25 June 1982. In his place Reagan appointed George Shultz.[71] Shultz's attitude towards the Palestinians was dismissive and the record makes it doubtful that he ever read the Saunders Document. On the contrary, he ultimately orchestrated unprecedented transfers of U.S. wealth and technology to Israel while at the same time inextricably tying the economies, bureaucracies, diplomatic policies, and fortunes of the two countries closer than any others in the world.

Shultz at first seemed determined to be evenhanded in the Middle East. He helped negotiate an international agreement that ensured the safety of Arafat and his fighters when they left Beirut in late 1982, much to the dismay of Israel and the resentment of Israel's American supporters. Moreover, in his first nine months, the Reagan Administration twice invoked the Arms Export Control Act against Israel for improperly using U.S. weapons in its attack against Iraq's nuclear facility and in Lebanon.[72] He also put forth the Reagan peace plan, which was highly unpopular in Israel and among Jewish Americans.

By February 1983, Israeli Defense Minister Moshe Arens publicly complained that relations between the United States and Israel had deteriorated to the point that "the frustration and impatience and anger" in the relationship was perhaps the worst in history.[73] Soon the Reagan Administration was under broad media attack for its lack of successes in foreign policy, much of it because of the Middle East. *Time, Newsweek, The Washington Post,* and columnists Rowland Evans and Robert Novak, to name only some of the major critics, were especially harsh. *Time* talked about the "vacuum at state" and *The Post* wrote that "there is a growing body of thought that Shultz may be too quiet, that he may not be forceful enough."[74]

Behind much of the criticism was a constant drumbeat that Shultz was too harsh on Israel. Under such criticism, Shultz's attitude toward Israel underwent a transformation. Within two months the administration's relations with Israel improved so dramatically that Zionist William Safire, a columnist for *The New York Times,* was writing that "the Reagan Administration has suddenly fallen passionately in love with Israel."[75] After that the criticism of Shultz essentially ceased while Shultz's support of Israel grew greater. By mid-1984, Moshe Arens was describing relations between the two countries as "probably better" than ever before.[76] Media criticism of Shultz was henceforth muted.

Sources in Washington explained Shultz's sudden conversion not as the result of a divine revelation but as a deliberate tactic aimed specifically at escaping Zionist attacks by the media.[77] According to the sources, two of Shultz's closest colleagues, his new executive secretary Charles Hill, and Under Secretary of State for Political Affairs Lawrence Eagleburger, later secretary of state in the Bush Administration, called on him in the spring of 1983 and warned that unless he embraced Israel he would be driven from office by media and Zionist attacks. Whatever the facts, the record clearly shows that from this time forward Shultz never again seriously opposed Israel, or treated the Palestinians with anything more than contempt. For instance, when Israel's U.S.-built planes flew all the way to Tunisia in 1985 to bomb Arafat's home in a failed assassination attempt, the White House said the attack seemed to be a "legitimate response" against "terrorist attacks."[78] When Arafat sought to visit the United Nations in 1988, Shultz flatly turned down the Palestinian leader in violation of America's treaty to admit UN guests.[79]

At any rate, by 1985 Shultz was openly proclaiming his Zionist credentials. At AIPAC's annual conference, he declared:

> Our original moral commitment to Israel has never wavered, but over the years Americans have also come to recognize the enormous importance of Israel—as a partner in the pursuit of freedom and democracy, as a people who share our highest ideals, and as a vital strategic ally in an important part of the world....Every year we provide more security assistance to Israel than to any other nation. We consider that aid to be one of the best investments we can make—not only for Israel's security but for ours as well.[80]

In 1986, AIPAC Executive Director Thomas Dine reported at the group's twenty-seventh annual policy conference that relations had never been better between the United States and Israel.[81] Dine said that in the process of this development "a whole new constituency of support for Israel is being built in precisely the area where we are weakest—among government officials in the state, defense and treasury departments, in the CIA, in science, trade, agriculture and other agencies." Israel, Dine added, was now treated by the United States as an "ally, not just a friend, an asset, rather than a liability, a mature and capable partner, not some vassal state." He added that Reagan and Shultz were going to "leave a legacy that will be important to Israel's security for decades to come." Shultz, he said, had vowed to him to "build institutional arrangements so that eight years from now, if there is a secretary of state who is not positive about Israel, he will not be able to overcome the bureaucratic relationship between Israel and the U.S. that we have established."

Later in 1986, former AIPAC staffer Richard B. Straus wrote in *The Washington Post* that "American Middle East policy has shifted so dramatically in favor of Israel" that now it could only be described as "a revolution." He quoted Dine as saying that Shultz was the "architect of the special relationship," which, Dine added, "is a deep, broad-based partnership progressing day-by-day toward a full-fledged diplomatic and military alliance." Straus added:

> State Department Arabists acknowledge that Arab interests hardly get a hearing today in Washington. "We used to have a two-track policy," says one former State Department official. Now only Israel's interests are considered.

While Straus credited Reagan's "gut" support for Israel as a major reason for the change, it was, Straus observed, only after George Shultz finally decided to throw his full weight behind Israel that the "revolution was complete."[82]

Amid such total commitment at the highest levels of the Reagan Administration, the so-called Arabists of the State Department had little opportunity to exercise their expertise. Despite the Saunders Document of 1975, the Palestinians remained ignored and even shunned by Shultz. Meanwhile Israel continued to do all it could to deny the Palestinians their claims to inalienable rights. On 6 August 1986, the Knesset passed an amendment to the Prevention of Terrorism law prohibiting contact between Israelis and any person holding an executive position in "an organization that the Israeli government had declared a terrorist organization." These included the Palestine Liberation Organization and thirteen other Palestinian groups.[83]

By 1987, AIPAC Executive Director Dine reported that the U.S.-Israeli relationship was even closer and that

> there is wide agreement that Ronald Reagan is among the best friends of Israel ever to sit in the oval office, and that George Shultz has been a friend beyond words as Secretary of State....These stalwarts have truly transformed U.S. policy over the past five years, raising the relationship to a new level.[84]

Dine said that despite a year in which there was the Pollard spy scandal, Israel's entanglement in the Iran/Contra scandal, Israel's selling of weapons to South Africa, speculation about Israel's nuclear policy and leadership confusion in Israel, "We have had one of the best years on record in terms of concrete legislation, in the strategic relationship between our country and Israel, and in the gains scored by our cause in the results of the 1986 elections."[85]

Dine noted that from 1983, when Israeli sales of goods and services to the Department of Defense equalled $9 million, such sales had reached in 1986 $205 million. As for Congress, Dine reported "a year of extraordinary achievements....I refer you to our just published 1986 Legislative Report which consumes over sixty fact-filled pages. It is not an understatement to say the achievements have been spectacular."

Dine listed AIPAC's goals for the coming year as 1) assuring no cuts in Israel's $3 billion grant-aid; 2) "look to Congress for other areas of assistance beyond foreign aid—especially in terms of defense cooperation...and to fight against various 'Buy American' amendments which restrict such bilateral defense cooperation;" and 3) "continue to oppose those transfers [of arms] to nations that oppose peace with Israel" and enact a law strengthening Congress' role in arms sales by making such sales conditional upon majorities in each House; currently sales are made if either House supports by a vote of one-third plus one (enough to sustain a veto)." He concluded by asserting that "what strengthens Israel equally strengthens America." After the meeting, *The New York Times* reported that AIPAC

> has become a major force in shaping United States policy in the Middle East....the organization has gained power to influence a presidential candidate's choice of staff, to block practically any arms sale to an Arab country and to serve as a catalyst for intimate military relations between the Pentagon and the Israeli army. Its leading officials are consulted by State Department and White House policy markers, by senators and generals.[86]

The *Times* article concluded that AIPAC "has become the envy of competing lobbyists and the bane of Middle East specialists who would like to strengthen ties with pro-Western Arabs." By the beginning of 1988, former CIA analyst Kathleen Christison observed that

> the Reagan years have witnessed a marked change in the lobby's influence on policy-making. If in past administrations it was thought to have a major limiting impact on policy formulation, the magnitude of its influence today is so great that it can no longer be considered merely a constraint on policy.[87]

Under Reagan, AIPAC had become a partner in policy-making. Christison quoted former Carter Administration National Security Council Middle East analyst William Quandt as saying:

> We would sometimes go to the Israelis in advance of some action and ask them not to make trouble, but we never went to AIPAC. The Reagan Administration has elevated AIPAC to the level of a player in this game.[88]

* *

No matter how hard the Reagan Administration and Israel tried, the Palestinians could not be ignored forever. This became apparent in 1988 when at the nineteenth meeting of the Palestine National Council, the PLO's parliament, the PLO officially and unequivocally renounced terrorism, accepted UN Security Council resolutions 242 and 338, called for an international peace conference and declared "establishment of the state of Palestine."[89] The PLO had by this action on 15 November fulfilled the conditions set out by Kissinger thirteen years earlier for recognition and negotiations with the United States. Nevertheless, Shultz quarreled that the PLO still had not specifically affirmed Israel's "right" to exist, even though in accepting resolution 242 and calling for a peace conference it implicitly recognized Israel.

Diplomats, both American and foreign, generally considered Shultz's reaction petty—aimed at humiliating Arafat by denying him a visa, even though the PLO leader had been officially invited to attend the current UN General Assembly session in New York and even though it was a violation of America's 1947 Headquarters Agreement with the United Nations to deny a visa to an official UN guest.[90]

In retaliation, the General Assembly took the unprecedented step of moving to Geneva for an extraordinary session, where Arafat was the featured speaker on 13 December 1988. Although he again condemned terrorism and pleaded for peace, he made no mention of Israel and the State Department again insisted that he had failed to address U.S. conditions "clearly, squarely, without ambiguity."[91] The next day Arafat declared at a Geneva press conference:

> It was clear that we mean...the right of all parties concerned in the Middle East conflict to exist in peace and security, and, as I have mentioned, including the state of Palestine, Israel and other neighbors, according to the resolutions 242 and 338. As for terrorism, I renounced it yesterday in no uncertain terms, and yet, I repeat for the record...that we totally and absolutely renounce all forms of terrorism, including individual, group and state terrorism.[92]

Given America's estrangement from the world community over the Palestinian issue, Shultz finally conceded. He called a press conference in the State Department that same evening and noted the conciliatory nature of Arafat's remarks, adding:

> As a result, the United States is prepared for a substantive dialogue with PLO representatives....Nothing here may be taken to imply an acceptance or recognition by the United States of an independent Palestinian state. The position of the U.S. is that the status of the West Bank and Gaza cannot be determined by unilateral acts of either side, but only through a process of negotiations.[93]

In response to a reporter's question, Shultz said: "It's obvious that if you're going to get to a peaceful settlement in the Middle East you have to include Palestinians in the process from the beginning and at the end."[94]

The Reagan Administration allowed talks with the PLO to go ahead in Tunisia, starting 15 December. A week later Pope John Paul II received Arafat in the Vatican, saying that Arabs and Jews had "an identical, fundamental right to their own homelands."[95] By the first week of 1989, about seventy countries had recognized the new state of Palestine, but not the United States.[96] In fact, Shultz had seen to it that the U.S.-PLO talks were so narrowly restricted that no progress was reported by the end of the Reagan Administration five weeks later. The talks continued desultorily under Bush Administration (1989–1993), but mounting pressure by Israel on Congress finally caused Bush on 20 June 1990 to suspend them, nominally because of the PLO's refusal to condemn a terrorist attack that had resulted in no injuries to Israelis.[97]

* *

George Bush's Secretary of State, James A. Baker III, was one of the shrewder and more evenhanded secretaries in dealing with the conflict. His achievements were significant in the overall region. He doggedly pursued a peace process at the cost of significant amounts of his time, and he put on notice both Israelis and Arabs that to gain peace they had to limit their ambitions. It was Baker who finally, for the first time, managed to get Palestinian representatives accepted in the peace process at Madrid in 1991, albeit under the guise of belonging to the Jordanian delegation. Nonetheless, under Bush and Baker, Palestinians gained a direct voice in their own future, side-by-side with other Arabs and Israelis.

Moreover, Baker and President Bush played an important role in unseating extremist Prime Minister Yitzhak Shamir and ending fifteen years of Likud rule, which was violently anti-Palestinian. Bush and Baker pressured Shamir to end his ambitious settlement program, and Baker openly urged Israel to "reach out to the Palestinians as neighbors who deserve political rights."[98] In May 1992, the administration openly expressed reaffirmation of UN resolution 194's refugee formula calling for repatriation or resettlement and compensation, goading Shamir to widen the growing split between the two countries when he responded: "It will never happen in any way, shape or form. There is only a Jewish right of return to the land of Israel."[99] The next month, on 23 June 1992, the hard-line prime minister was defeated at the polls, in no small measure because of the Bush Administration.

However, in the end, Baker was unable to convince Israel to recognize the Palestinians as a people before Bush was voted out of office in 1992, nor was Bush ever strong enough to extend the right of self-determination and a homeland to the Palestinians.

It was only during the Clinton Administration, inaugurated in January 1993, that Baker's Madrid process culminated with Israel finally recognizing the Palestinians for the first time. At the 13 September 1993 ceremony on the White House lawn presided over by President Clinton, Prime Minister Yitzhak Rabin of Israel and PLO Chairman Yasser Arafat shook hands and signed the Declaration of Principles on Interim Self-Government Arrangements that recognized "their mutual legitimacy and political rights." In a letter of mutual recognition signed three days earlier, Rabin had written to Arafat that Israel undertakes "to recognize the PLO as the representative of the Palestinian people...."[100] After a century of struggle and denial, Israel at last had recognized that there were Palestinians and that they represented a distinct people. The United States followed Israel's lead and also finally and officially recognized the PLO as the Palestinians' representative.

Astoundingly, less than two months later, on 8 December 1993, the Clinton

Administration, the most pro-Israel ever, declined to support in the UN General Assembly reaffirmation of UN resolution 194. This was the first time the United States had failed to support the resolution. It had supported the original resolution that endorsed refugee rights when it was passed in 1949 and the forty subsequent reiterations of it.[101] The Clinton Administration claimed that the 13 September Israeli-PLO accords made previous resolutions "obsolete and anachronistic" and that it did not serve the peace process to discuss them or reiterate them.[102]

Thus, once again, the Palestinians were left in limbo. On the one hand, Secretary of State Warren Christopher went out of his way to meet occasionally with Arafat, treating him as a sovereign leader. But on the other the administration continued to oppose in the United Nations all previous resolutions establishing the legal framework of the Palestinian cause.

6 | JERUSALEM
From Corpus Separatum *to Israel's Capital, 1947–1995*

"[The US agrees with] the [UN] resolution of December 11, 1948, [that] states that Jerusalem should be accorded special and separate treatment from the rest of Palestine and should be placed under effective United Nations control."
Acting Secretary of State Robert A. Lovett, 1949[1]

"[Israel has] made no commitment to halt or reduce construction in East Jerusalem [and] has affirmed its intention to continue settlement construction in a 100 square mile surrounding area termed 'Greater Jerusalem.'"
State Department report, 1993[2]

THE UNITED STATES' ORIGINAL POLICY PILLAR on Jerusalem assumed that it would be an international city. From 1947 to 1967 Washington supported neither Arab nor Jewish control of the city that was revered by Christians, Jews and Muslims alike. It insisted that the only practical and fair status of the city was to place it under United Nations supervision with limited autonomy for Arab and Jewish districts. In the meantime, however, Washington and the world community quietly acquiesced in the city's division between Israel and Jordan, accepting the hard reality that neither the Arabs nor the Jews would surrender their claims short of war. The United Nations had no troops, and no member country, certainly not the United States, was willing to volunteer any to internationalize Jerusalem against the wishes of its bitterly competing citizens.

After Israel's capture of the whole city in 1967, Washington dropped its support of internationalization. It threw the problem back to the Arabs and Jews, saying it was up to them to determine Jerusalem's status between themselves. Until that unlikely event, however, the United States refused to recognize either Arab or Jewish claims that Jerusalem was their capital. Thus the United States and most other nations kept their embassies in Tel Aviv, where the Jewish state had first been proclaimed and which to this day is considered by most countries Israel's official capital. To emphasize its recognition, but not its acceptance, of both Arab and Jewish claims, Washington maintains two consulates in Jerusalem, one in the western section that has been part of Israel since 1948 and the other in predominantly Palestinian East Jerusalem.

* *

Refusal by Washington to recognize Jerusalem as Israel's capital was by no means as capricious a policy as Israel and its supporters often contended. The State Department's reasoning rested on the terms of the original partition plan for Palestine adopted by the United Nations in 1947. This designated Jerusalem a *corpus separatum* with its own government under a six-member UN Trusteeship Council. The council would have had authority to appoint a governor to exercise wide powers over all aspects of life in the city.[3] The governor was not to be a citizen of either the Arab or the Jewish state.[4] Jerusalem's borders were defined as "the present municipality...plus the surrounding villages and towns, the most eastern of which shall be Abu Dis; the most southern, Bethlehem; the most western, Ein Karem (including also the built up area of Motsa); and the most northern Shu'fat...."

A "special international regime" was established for Jerusalem and surrounding areas, in which there were 105,000 Palestinians and 100,000 Jews. Within Jerusalem's old municipal limits, the Jews formed a majority with 100,000, while the Palestinians totaled 60,000. The remaining 45,000 Palestinians lived outside the municipal boundaries but within the larger metropolitan area created by the international regime.[5]

Inside the old municipal boundaries of East Jerusalem was the ancient Old City, an area of about one and a half square miles with stone walls forming an irregular square of nearly 1,000 by 1,000 yards. About 1,700 Jews and 20,000 mostly Muslim Arabs lived in the Old City, where the vast majority of property was privately owned by Palestinians or belonged to Muslim and Christian institutions.[6] There were thirty-six sites holy to Christians, Jews or Muslims within the municipality, thirty-four of them inside the Old City.[7]

Beyond the walls of the Old City, but still within the municipality, lived about 40,000 Palestinians, some 10,000 in the eastern part and about 30,000, mainly Christians, in West Jerusalem, the new or modern part of the city where the vast majority of the city's Jews lived. Although forming the majority in "new" Jerusalem, the Jews owned only about 26 percent of the property there, with the Arabs owning 40 percent and non-Arab Christians 14 percent, the remainder being public property. In the Jerusalem subdistrict as a whole, Palestinians owned 84 percent of the land and the Jews 2 percent, the rest being public property.[8] The Palestinian property in the western part of the city included a number of comfortable residential quarters such as Katamon, Talbiya, Upper Baka, Lower Baka, the "Greek" and "German" colonies, Mamilla, and Sheikh Badr.[9]

Immediately following the withdrawal of British troops from Palestine and the declaration of the establishment of Israel on 14 May, the Jews captured Jewish western Jerusalem, driving out all the Palestinian inhabitants and gaining a fortune in real estate, including 10,000 homes, many of them fully furnished.[10] Fighting between the Arab and Jewish communities turned Jerusalem into a war zone, destroying any chance for the UN council to perform its work in the city. It adjourned sine die on 17 May, never to return.[11]

It was amid such chaos and uncertainty that UN Mediator Count Folke Bernadotte caused consternation on 28 June 1948 when he abandoned *corpus separatum* and instead proposed giving Jerusalem to Transjordan. Under Bernadotte's proposal, the Jews would get municipal autonomy, and a special arrangement would be made for the protection of the Holy Places. Bernadotte's reasoning was that Jerusalem was surrounded by UN-designated Arab territory and, in any event, the city was "never intended to be part of the Jewish state" under the partition plan and therefore the Jewish state would be "unaffected."[12] Israel's UN delegate, Abba Eban, complained that "the effrontery of his proposal left us breathless....It was very much as though the surgeon went away with most of the patient's vital organs."[13]

With the United States opposing and Israel firmly refusing to consider Bernadotte's proposal, it faded away but not before causing fury among Jews. Their anger undoubtedly contributed to the decision by Jewish Stern Gang terrorists to assassinate Bernadotte, which they did on 17 September 1948 in Jerusalem.[14] Ironically, by that time Bernadotte himself had abandoned his proposal and returned to internationalization of Jerusalem in his final proposal submitted only the day before his assassination.

Bernadotte's final plan for Jerusalem found complete acceptance by the United States since it essentially echoed the original partition plan.[15] A major difference was its stronger endorsement than the resolution for local autonomy. The partition plan called merely for "wide powers of local government and administration." Bernadotte's final proposal said:

> The City of Jerusalem, which should be understood as covering the area defined in the resolution of the General Assembly of 29 November, should be treated separately and should be placed under effective United Nations control with maximum feasible local autonomy for its Arab and Jewish communities, with full safeguards for the protection of the Holy Places and sites and free access to them, and for religious freedom.[16]

While the outside powers accepted Bernadotte's formulation, the two parties directly involved rejected it. The nascent state of Israel was particularly upset because as Jewish gains on the battlefield increased so too had the desire to control Jerusalem. As early as 11 July 1948, the Consul General in Jerusalem, John J. Macdonald, reported to the State Department that an

> increasing demand for incorporation new Jerusalem within state of Israel now apparent here. Immediately following May 14 projected international status for Jerusalem was accepted by Jewish officials and people but...[a] noticeable shift in attitude occurred which will probably be

> accentuated with resumption fighting....Jews justify claim to Jerusalem
> by pointing to failure of United Nations take effective action protect
> city or establish government....Apparent Christian indifference to plight
> of holy city often mentioned and authorities appear willing take any
> military action necessary regardless possible destruction old city.[17]

In fact, the Jews attempted to capture the Old City, but with repeated failures. Jordanian troops remained in charge of the Old City at the time of the 1949 truce, thus leaving Jerusalem divided with about 60,000 Palestinians in the eastern side of the city and its environs and around 100,000 Jews in the west.[18] Because of their effective control of parts of Jerusalem, both Jordan and Israel opposed the United Nations' international regime for the Holy City.

Thus, after the fighting Jerusalem remained divided by barricades and barbed wire in separate Palestinian and Israeli areas for the next nineteen years. Only a single crossing point connected Eastern and Western Jerusalem at the Mandelbaum Gate. The crossing was open only to diplomats, foreigners and occasional Christian pilgrims. Each side accused the other of desecrating holy places under their control, and both were guilty of it.[19]

* *

From this division of Jerusalem onward, Israel inexorably tightened its official grip on the western section. As early as 2 August 1948, Israeli leader David Ben Gurion, acting as minister of defense, issued Proclamation No. 12 declaring that West Jerusalem was occupied territory and subject to Israeli law.[20] The new Israeli law essentially rejected UN claims that Jerusalem was an international city and made Jewish control of West Jerusalem a fait accompli.[21] Then on 20 December 1948, the Israeli Cabinet secretly decided to begin to move "government institutions" to Jerusalem from Tel Aviv.[22] Eleven days later the Israeli Jerusalem Municipal Council was established and the military Government of Jerusalem was disbanded, meaning Jerusalem was now under Israeli civil control.[23] The Knesset, Israel's parliament, held its first session in Jerusalem on 14 February 1949.

To protest this creeping absorption of West Jerusalem, the representatives of the United States, Britain and France did not attend the inauguration of Israel's parliament.[24] It was the first time Western nations sought by concrete action to deter Israel's claim to Jerusalem. But it proved, as would later actions, unsuccessful.

The United Nations also sought to deter Israel by twice refusing it admittance to the world body. Israel finally gained admission on 11 May 1949, in part on the basis of assurances by Israeli Representative Abba Eban about Israel's benign attitude toward Jerusalem. He assured the General Assembly that Israel's actions in the city had not been taken in order to create new political facts but to help Jerusalem recover from the ravages of war.[25] The preamble of the resolution admitting Israel to the world body specifically referred to its adherence of the UN

Charter and the partition plan, which called for internationalization of Jerusalem.[26]

In reality, Israel up to this point still had not spelled out its ambitions toward Jerusalem and, in fact, deliberately had indicated it intended no claim to Jerusalem.[27] Even the holding of the first Knesset in Jerusalem in February 1949 had been explained away by Ambassador Eban as being based solely on "an historical motive which had nothing whatever to do with the future status of Jerusalem."[28] Eban over the months continued to imply that Israel's position remained flexible and was not aimed at claiming Jerusalem as its own.

Yet, at the same time the international community suspected Israel was tightening its grip on Jerusalem as a prelude to claiming it a Jewish city. *The New York Times* noted in a September 1949 story from Lausanne, Switzerland, where peace talks were being held, that there was a feeling among commissioners of the Palestine Conciliation Commission that "the Israel government was seeking to get itself so entrenched in Jerusalem that internationalization would become overwhelmingly difficult."[29]

Meanwhile, the United States was beginning to waver and weaken in its support of full internationalization. This came about as a result of recognizing the reality on the ground—meaning Israel's possession of West Jerusalem and Jordan's control of the Old City—and succumbing to fierce political pressures from Israel's American supporters.

By the summer of 1949, the State Department concluded that the original concept of a *corpus separatum* was unworkable. The new U.S. policy was defined by the State Department as one that considered Jerusalem as a single, undivided and international city for which details of its governance still had to be worked out. Internally, the justification for the U.S. change was spelled out in a State Department memorandum concluding "that it [*corpus separatum*] was unrealistic as it could not be implemented by the United Nations against the wishes of Israel and Jordan without the use of substantial forces."[30]

Washington signaled its change on 20 August 1949 when it shepherded through the UN's Palestine Conciliation Commission a proposal calling for a limited form of internationalization of Jerusalem. Under the PCC proposal, both sides would be denied designating Jerusalem as their capital, the city would be demilitarized into autonomous Arab and Jewish zones with the authority of a UN Commissioner being confined generally to international matters and jurisdiction over the Holy Places. The major changes in this new plan were expanding the terms of autonomy to the Arab and Jewish communities and thereby constraining UN rule in the city. The practical result of these changes was to accept, if not overtly endorse, Israel's control of West Jerusalem and Jordan's control of East Jerusalem.[31]

However, the Jewish American community opposed even this limited form of internationalization. Jewish leaders denounced it as "the unworkable and morally indefensible" plan and the community mobilized a "Save Jerusalem" campaign. As Israeli scholar Yosse Feintuch reported: "Together with the American Zionist organizations, leaders of all branches of Judaism, inspired and encouraged by the grassroots support of their faithful, organized a strenuous political endeavor aimed at convincing the United States government to 'reject any plan which would sever the new city of Jerusalem from Israel.'"[32]

The issue became so heated that it was injected into the 1948 senatorial contest between Democrat Herbert H. Lehman and Republican John Foster Dulles in New York. The daily *Jewish Morning Journal* demanded the candidates declare their position on the PCC's Jerusalem proposal since "a state such as New York where there are approximately two and half million Jews [is]...entitled to hear how the candidates feel about Jerusalem." Lehman responded by announcing he favored "the territorial inclusion of the New City of Jerusalem in the State of Israel." Dulles declined to respond, saying he could not repudiate the PCC proposal during an election campaign since such "action would be interpreted as influenced by a desire for political advantage."[33] For the rest of his distinguished career, Dulles would be plagued with suspicions and open charges that he was anti-Semitic.[34]

Meanwhile, with U.S. policy now diluted, with Jewish Americans actively campaigning against any form of internationalization, and with Israel showing every sign that it planned to claim Jerusalem as its capital—although in public it continued to remain ambiguous about its plans—the international community became increasingly concerned. Pope Pius XII already had issued an encyclical, "Redemptoris Nostri" (Of Our Redeemer), urging the internationalization of Jerusalem.[35] Following Pius' lead, Catholic countries, particularly in Latin America, demanded during the summer and fall of 1949 that the partition plan's concept of a *corpus separatum* be honored. This powerful group was joined by Muslim countries as well as by the Soviet Union and its Communist clients. As a result, there existed by the autumn of 1949 a worldwide group of Catholic, Communist and Muslim countries all supporting internationalization. Pressures were so great that a new vote on the issue was scheduled in the General Assembly for December.

In preparation for the General Assembly discussion, Israel on 15 November submitted a thirty-six page memorandum to the United Nations detailing its opposition to internationalization of Jerusalem—but not yet going so far as publicly to declare its intentions to annex West Jerusalem. The memo asserted that "there is not the slightest shred of evidence" that internationalization could work. It added that Israel could never accept the "administrative or judicial intrusions in the secular life of Jerusalem...."[36] Nevertheless, the United States stuck by its policy. Secretary of State Acheson wrote to President Truman:

> The United States objective at this session of the General Assembly is to obtain approval of an international regime for the Jerusalem area which (a) will adequately recognize the status of Jerusalem as the center of three great world religions and will provide for the necessary protection of and access to the Holy Places under United Nations supervision; (b) will contribute to peace and stability in the area; (c) will be workable; and (d) will take into account the interests of the principle communities in Jerusalem and the views of Israel and Jordan.[37]

It was not until 5 December, four days before the UN vote, that Prime

Minister David Ben Gurion publicly declared for the first time Israel's claim to the city:

> We regard it as our duty to declare that Jewish Jerusalem is an organic and inseparate part of the State of Israel, as it is an inseparable part of the history of Israel, of the faith of Israel, and of the very soul of our people. Jerusalem is the heart of hearts of the State of Israel....We declare that Israel will not give up Jerusalem of its own free will just as throughout thousands of years it has not surrendered its faith, its national identity, and its hope to return to Jerusalem and Zion despite persecutions which have no parallel in history.[38]

To Ambassador James G. McDonald, Ben Gurion bitterly declared: "Christianity still cannot accept nor tolerate fact that Jewish state now exists and that its traditional capital is Jerusalem." He added: "It would take an army to get Jews out of Jerusalem; and the only army I see willing to occupy Jerusalem is Russia's" [39]

The General Assembly reacted on 9 December by passing a resolution reaffirming Jerusalem as a *corpus separatum*. The vote was 38 to 14 with 7 abstentions; the United States was among those who voted against, basing its decision on the contention that full internationalization was unworkable.[40] In reaction to the new UN resolution, Ben Gurion two days later declared: "Jerusalem is an inseparable part of Israel and her eternal capital. No UN vote can alter this historic fact."[41] On 13 December, Ben Gurion urged the Knesset to move from Tel Aviv to Jerusalem. On 16 December, he moved the prime minister's office to Jerusalem and on 20 December he held a Cabinet meeting in the city.[42] Ben Gurion fixed the beginning of the New Year of 1950 as the date for the transfer of all government offices to Jerusalem with the exception of the foreign and defense ministries and the national police headquarters, which remained in Tel Aviv.[43]

Acheson formally protested these moves in a message 20 December to Israel's Foreign Ministry:

> As a friendly govt which has followed with interest and sympathy course of Israel's development, US Govt desires to inform Israeli Govt that it considers particularly unfortunate any step or course of action on part of Israel likely to prejudice or complicate settlement of Jerusalem questions....[44]

On the same day the UN Trusteeship Council asked Israel to remove its government offices from Jerusalem. The vote was 7–0–7 with the United States, Britain and the Soviet Union among those who abstained.[45] The United States and Britain explained their abstentions on grounds they were not sure the council legally was empowered to take such action since the partition plan and subsequent UN resolutions did not specifically prohibit Israel from establishing its capital at Jerusalem.[46]

In the face of such wavering in Washington, Israel on 31 December formally informed the council it would not remove the government from Jerusalem and questioned the council's right to make such a request. The Israeli statement noted its measures to move offices to Jerusalem were taken with "full and complete authority" by the Israeli government, adding: "These measures mark the continuation of a process begun long ago as part of an effort to restore Jerusalem to its traditional place in the life of the country."[47] Israel's open defiance culminated on 23 January 1950 when the Knesset passed a proclamation declaring Jerusalem as Israel's capital from the time of Israel's creation and expressing its "wish that the construction of the seat of the government and the Knesset in Jerusalem be proceeded with speedily."[48]

Anticipating the Israeli move, the State Department on 4 January 1950 imposed a boycott on U.S. officials doing business in Jerusalem. In a cable to Ambassador McDonald, Secretary of State Acheson ordered him not to "conduct official business in Jerusalem with Israeli Central Government officials who may move there" and to "restrict to an absolute minimum" unofficial visits to Jerusalem.[49] This order continued the boycott begun in 1949 at the opening of Israel's first Knesset in Jerusalem.

The boycott lasted until 14 February 1951. It was ended because Israeli officials insisted on doing business in Jerusalem with the result that the U.S. Embassy in Tel Aviv, some forty miles away, found it "increasingly difficult [in] efficiently carrying out routine business with Israel Government agencies." Since the administration was under constant pressure from Israel's friends to align its policy closer to Israel's, Acheson bowed to the politically expedient and practical complaints from the Tel Aviv embassy and decreed that U.S. diplomats could "proceed Jerusalem as necessary [to] carry on official business with Israel Government officials." In addition, the diplomats were authorized to "visit Jerusalem for unofficial purposes often as desired."[50]

Meanwhile, not to be outdone by Israel, Jordan on 24 April 1950 officially annexed East Jerusalem and the lands of the West Bank of the Jordan River not controlled by Israeli troops.[51] Although the United States did not officially accept Jordan's annexation of Jerusalem any more than it did Israel's, the reality on the ground was that Israel and Jordan were planted firmly in Jerusalem. Neither the United States nor the United Nations was willing to reverse the situation by force. Moreover, support for a *corpus separatum* received a heavy blow on 17 April 1950 when the Soviet Union announced it no longer agreed with the idea.

The General Assembly failed to act on the matter in 1950 and in 1951 did not even discuss the Jerusalem issue, signalling the international community's disillusionment with the problem. After 1952, the Jerusalem issue was not discussed in the United Nations for the next fifteen years.[52]

Yet, the United States tried one more time to take action, although hardly forceful, to protest Israel's annexation of West Jerusalem. It came during the early years of the Eisenhower Administration when John Foster Dulles was secretary of state. Still smarting from charges of anti-Semitism that had resulted from his bruising senatorial campaign against Herbert Lehman in 1949 and especially from demands by Jewish Americans who had insisted he declare his opposition to the internationalization of Jerusalem, Dulles was not sympathetic to the de facto division of Jerusalem. In 1953, as the official directly in charge of U.S. policy on the Holy City, Dulles personally visited Jerusalem in May On his return, he reported that he had found Jerusalem

> divided into armed camps split between Israel and the Arab nation of Jordan. The atmosphere there is heavy with hate. As I gazed on the Mount of Olives, I felt anew that Jerusalem is, above all, the holy place of the Christian, Muslim and Jewish faiths. That's been repeatedly emphasized by the United Nations, and that fact does not necessarily exclude some political status in Jerusalem for Israel and Jordan. But the world religious community has claims in Jerusalem which take precedence over the political claims of any particular state.[53]

In other words, Dulles still clung in 1953 to U.S. policy that considered some vague limited form of internationalization for Jerusalem and opposed both Israeli and Jordanian annexation of the city. His resolve was tested by Israel on 13 July when the Israeli Foreign Ministry moved from Tel Aviv to Jerusalem despite worldwide opposition. In retaliation, the United States denounced the move and joined with Britain and other countries, including the Soviet Union, in boycotting all functions in Jerusalem and refusing to visit the Foreign Ministry.[54]

But, like the Truman Administration's boycott three years earlier, the sheer impracticality of not having direct access to Israeli officials except through a small liaison office in Tel Aviv began taking its toll. Moreover, U.S. supporters of Israel displayed common cause in backing Israel's Jerusalem policy and applied domestic political pressure on the Eisenhower Administration. At the end of 1953 Israel took an action that brought the issue to a head. It decreed that foreign envoys would have to present their papers of accreditation to the president in Jerusalem. Under such pressures, the boycott began weakening and finally ended when a new ambassador was chosen by Washington in the fall of 1954. On 12 November 1954, Ambassador Edward Lawson was allowed to present his credentials in Jerusalem, effectively ending the boycott.[55]

Despite this second failure at trying to reverse Israel's claim to Jerusalem by a boycott, the State Department stood firm in refusing to recognize Jerusalem as Israel's capital and therefore continued to maintain its embassy in Tel Aviv. U.S. policy remained, in the words of an internal memo, "to keep the Jerusalem question an open one and to prevent its being settled solely through the processes of attrition and fait accompli."[56] Thus, when Israel opened its new Knesset building in Jerusalem on 30 August 1966, no U.S. diplomats attended although a group of Congressmen did.[57] Similarly, the United States boycotted Israel's Independence Day military parades in Jerusalem, including the one in May 1967, less than a month before the 1967 war.[58] Israel never returned its Foreign Ministry to Tel Aviv.

In the interim, between 1953 and 1967, there was a tendency in Washington to try to ignore the issue of Jerusalem because it was recognized as intractable and so inflammatory in domestic political terms. Thus, in his policy statement on 24 February 1956 before the Senate Foreign Relations Committee, Dulles did not mention Jerusalem as one of the core issues of the conflict. These he identified as "the plight of the refugees, the pall of fear that hangs over the Arab and Israeli people alike and the lack of fixed boundaries between Israel and its Arab neighbors" as the "three principal aspects" of the conflict.[59] By dropping in public Jerusalem as a core issue, Dulles bowed to the reality of Israel's determination as well as the domestic political pressures that accompanied it. Nonetheless, U.S. policy quietly remained that Jerusalem was "a single, undivided and international city even though this status never had come into actual being."[60]

* *

No serious actions were taken about the status of Jerusalem until Israel's sudden military occupation of Arab East Jerusalem, including the storied Old City, in 1967. On 7 June, the third day of the war, Israeli troops took over the Old City, after less than sixty hours of fighting.[61] Within a half hour, Shlomo Goren, the chief Ashkenazi rabbi of the Israel Defense Forces, arrived before the Western (Wailing) Wall at the head of a small of followers, carrying a Torah and blowing a shofar. Declared Goren: "I, General Shlomo Goren, chief rabbi of the Israel Defense Forces, have come to this place never to leave again."[62] Defense Minister Moshe Dayan also arrived, saying: "We have united Jerusalem, the divided capital of Israel. We have returned to the holiest of our holy places, never to part from it again."[63]

In the predawn darkness of 11 June—the day after the end of the war— Israeli soldiers ordered Palestinians living in the ancient Maghrabi Quarter of the Old City of Jerusalem next to the Western Wall of the Temple Mount/Haram al-Sharif out of their homes on three hours' notice. Then Israeli bulldozers crushed two mosques and the Palestinians's homes, leaving 135 families with 650 members homeless. It was the first confiscation of Palestinian property following the war.[64]

Confiscation of the Maghrabi area in front of the Western Wall realized one of Zionism's earliest dreams. Ownership of the area clearly was established as belonging to the Abu Maydan *waqf*, public Muslim trust, dating back 800 years to the days of Saladin. As early as 1918, Zionists attempted to rehouse the Arab residents so that the area could be cleared for Jewish worshipers. British military Governor Ronald Storrs sought to negotiate the deal but found opposition within the Muslim community so great that he abandoned the effort.[65] Muslims for centuries had allowed Jews access to the wall for worship, but as Storrs noted of the scene after World War I, "the Jewish right is no more than a right of way and of station, and involves no title, expressed or implied of ownership, either of the surface of the Wall or of the pavement in front of it."[66]

A week after destroying the Maghrabi Quarter, Israeli soldiers on 18 June 1967 began ordering Palestinians to leave the old Jewish Quarter, where they had been living since the expulsion of the Jews during the fighting in 1948. At first the expulsions of the Palestinians were only a few hundred but over the years they totaled the entire Palestinian population of the quarter, about 6,500 persons. Jews began moving into the quarter as early as October 1967.[67]

Despite Israel's actions in Jerusalem, President Lyndon B. Johnson suddenly and dramatically weakened U.S. policy. In a major speech on 19 June announcing the "five great principles of peace," Johnson confined his remarks about Jerusalem to a simple formula: "[T]here must be adequate recognition of the special interest of three great religions in the Holy Places of Jerusalem."[68]

Johnson's failure to cite traditional policy regarding Jerusalem left U.S. policy in shambles. There was no detailed plan to replace it. As Lucius D. Battle, then the assistant secretary of state in charge of the region, recalled, the State Department's concentration at the time was on protecting the Holy Places but there was not any serious effort made to work out those intricate details.[69] As fast-moving post-war events overwhelmed officials, the main emphasis was on fashioning a UN Security Council resolution embracing a comprehensive peace formula. The practical effect of this was for Washington to treat Jerusalem as just another aspect of the overall Arab-Israeli conflict. As a result, the details of America's new Jerusalem policy only began to emerge out of the wreckage of the old policy in the months ahead as Washington reacted to events in as pragmatic way as politics allowed.

The policy that finally came into being was one that greatly pleased Israel and its U.S. supporters. Henceforth the United States no longer would support internationalization of the whole city or consider Jerusalem a separate entity deserving recognition as a major and distinct problem. Instead, the United States would support the idea that Jerusalem should remain an undivided city and that the city's future was up to the parties themselves, thus relieving Washington of direct responsibility except for the Holy Places. However, U.S. policy continued to regard Israel's claim to West Jerusalem as its capital a violation of UN resolutions, and it considered Arab East Jerusalem as territory under Israeli military occupation. As a result, the U.S. Embassy remained in Tel Aviv.

Johnson's new policy apparently was strongly influenced by Arthur Goldberg, the U.S. ambassador to the United Nations and an ardent Zionist. Because Secretary of State Dean Rusk at this time was bogged down in the Vietnam quagmire, as was Johnson himself, daily action was at the United Nations. Thus, the Jerusalem problem became the province of the U.S. UN delegation under Goldberg.[70] His cooperation with the Israeli mission was so close that Arabs accused the American delegation of being an extension of Israel's foreign ministry.[71] Lucius Battle recalled: "Arthur certainly worked intimately with the Israelis."[72]

Goldberg had warned Johnson before his 19 June speech that it would be wise to ignore Jerusalem because it was "inconceivable that Jerusalem would ever be divided again."[73] Johnson received similar advice from other supporters of Israel, and quickly saw that dropping any reference to Jerusalem's political status was a way to gain support from a grateful Jewish community at a time when he was under mounting domestic criticism for his Vietnam policies. Among those who helped Johnson write his "Five Principles of Peace" speech were two close friends and strong supporters of Israel, Arthur and Mathilde Krim.[74]

Johnson won praise from Israel and its supporters for his pro-Israel tilt. Abraham Feinberg, a New York Jewish fund-raiser and confidante of Johnson, called the White House after the 19 June speech to report that the Jewish community was delighted. According to a memorandum to the president: "Mr. Feinberg said he had visited with Israelis and Jewish leaders all over the country and they are high in their appreciation."[75] A poll in Israel showed Johnson was more popular there than even the war's two heroes, Moshe Dayan and Yitzhak Rabin.[76]

Israel reacted to this latest shift in U.S. policy by claiming all of Jerusalem as its capital. On 28 June, less than three weeks after the 1967 war, Israel expanded significantly the city limits and effectively annexed all of Jerusalem.[77] The new boundaries more than doubled Jerusalem's size by extending the city limits northward 9 miles and southward 10 miles, increasing Jerusalem's municipal limits from 25 square miles to over 62 square miles.[78] Jordan's East Jerusalem at the time had measured less than four square miles.[79] Jerusalem's new boundaries were carefully laid out to ensure, as Jewish Deputy Mayor Meron Benvenisti later reported, "an overwhelming Jewish majority" within the new boundaries.[80] Areas densely populated by Palestinians were omitted while the land abutting Arab villages was incorporated into the enlarged city.[81] The result was that the new city limits of Jerusalem now contained 197,000 Jews and 68,000 Palestinians.[82]

The next day, on 29 June, Israeli troops forcefully removed the barriers that had separated the Palestinian and Israeli parts of the city since 1948. Sniper nests were destroyed, walls blown up, check points dismantled and barbed wire and land mines removed. For the first time in nearly two decades Arabs and Jews faced each other over open spaces.[83] Israeli Foreign Minister Abba Eban, in words reminiscent of his assurances in 1949, denied to the United Nations that these actions meant Israel was actually annexing Arab Jerusalem. But that was the practical effect and that was how the State Department and most of the rest of the world regarded it.[84]

A special report to the UN Secretary-General by Ambassador Ernesto Thalmann of Switzerland reported that

> it was made clear beyond any doubt that Israel was taking every step to place under its sovereignty those parts of the city which were not controlled by Israel before June 1967....The Israeli authorities stated unequivocally that the process of integration was irreversible and not negotiable.[85]

The United States issued two statements in June 1967 containing muted warnings to Israel not to change the status of Jerusalem. Neither statement called Jerusalem an international city, condemned Israel nor explicitly demanded that it surrender Arab East Jerusalem. Instead, Israel was reminded that "the hasty administrative action taken today [28 June] cannot be regarded as determining the future of the Holy Places or the status of Jerusalem in relation to them....The United States has never recognized such unilateral actions by any of the states in the area as governing the international status of Jerusalem."[86]

The United Nations also weakened its previous policy. On 4 July, the UN General Assembly called on Israel to rescind all measures already taken to change the status of Jerusalem and to "desist forthwith" from taking any further actions that would change the city's status; the vote was 99–0–20, with the United States abstaining.[87] Significantly, the resolution made no mention of previous UN policy calling Jerusalem a *corpus separatum* nor did it refer to the status quo ante of Jordan's rule of East Jerusalem. The Assembly repeated its criticism on 14 July, this time deploring Israel's refusal to abide by the Assembly's resolution of 4 July; the vote was 99–0–18, with the United States again abstaining.[88] Once again, as on 4 July, the resolution made no mention of previous UN policy calling Jerusalem a *corpus separatum* nor did it refer to the status quo ante.

This retreat by the world body from the original partition plan of 1947 culminated in the passage of Security Council Resolution 242 on 22 November 1967. The resolution did not even mention Jerusalem. Nonetheless, U.S. policy and the United Nations continued to demand that the status of Jerusalem not be changed unilaterally. However, now there was an important difference. The United Nations began citing the articles of the Fourth Geneva Convention instead of the authority of the United Nations' own partition plan as the basis for opposing changes in the status of Jerusalem, a rationale that continued into the 1990s. This spelled the final retreat from *corpus separatum*.

Regardless of the words of the United States and the United Nations, Israel routinely ignored them. When it moved its police headquarters to Arab East Jerusalem in mid-1969, replacing an Arab hospital, both the United States and the United Nations protested. U.S. Ambassador to the United Nations Charles W. Yost on 1 July publicly criticized Israel's action, noting that the United States believed "the part of Jerusalem that came under the control of Israel in the June war, like other areas occupied by Israel, is occupied territory and hence subject to the provisions of international law governing the rights and obligations of an occupying power."

However, he made no mention about its status as an international city and he emphasized that Jerusalem should be treated within the context of the whole Arab-Israeli conflict.[89] Yost's remarks were a dramatic, if tacit, demonstration that Jerusalem was no longer considered by Washington as deserving "special and separate treatment." It had become just one more aspect of the broader conflict.

Yost's words had no effect on Israel. The police headquarters remained in East Jerusalem and Washington took no action to force Israel to move it.

* *

The first detailed public description of the new U.S. policy that emerged from President Johnson's abandonment of internationalization was not spelled out until December 1969. On 9 December Secretary of State William Rogers proposed that Israel withdraw from nearly all of the occupied territory and that the Arabs enter peace negotiations. Concerning Jerusalem, he described a policy that followed the Johnson Administration's lead in completely abandoning any form of internationalization. However, the new policy maintained that neither party should take any unilateral action to change Jerusalem's status, and it called for a joint Israeli-Jordanian role in the civic and other affairs of Jerusalem. Moreover, Rogers publicly and forcefully rejected Israel's claim to the whole city:

> We have made clear repeatedly in the past two-and-a-half years that we cannot accept unilateral actions by any party to decide the final status of the city. We believe its status can be determined only through the agreement of the parties concerned, which in practical terms means primarily the governments of Israel and Jordan, taking into account the interests of other countries in the area and the international community. Specifically, we believe Jerusalem should be a unified city within which there would no longer be restrictions on the movement of persons and goods. There should be open access to the unified city for persons of all faiths and nationalities. Arrangements for the administration of the unified city should take into account the interests of all of its inhabitants and of the Jewish, Islamic and Christian communities. And there should be roles for both Israel and Jordan in the civic, economic and religious life of the city.[90]

Israel firmly rejected the Rogers Peace Plan, as it became known, charging that it was an attempt by the superpowers to impose a settlement. It continued to treat Jerusalem as its capital.[91]

Israel's continuing defiance finally provoked the UN Security Council to condemn strongly the Jewish state on 25 September 1971 with U.S. support. [92] More important, perhaps, it caused the United States to issue its most detailed policy statement on Israel's occupation of Jerusalem and other Arab territories. In explanation of his vote that same day, U.S. Ambassador George Bush said that "In our view, the ultimate status of Jerusalem should be determined through negotiation and agreement between the governments of Israel and Jordan in the context of an overall peace settlement, taking into account the interests of its inhabitants, of the international religious communities who hold it sacred and of other countries in the area." After detailing the remarks made by Yost in July 1969 and Rogers five months later, Bush added:

> We regret Israel's failure to acknowledge its obligations under the Fourth Geneva Convention as well as its actions which are contrary to the letter and spirit of this Convention. We are distressed that the actions of Israel in the occupied portion of Jerusalem give rise to understandable concern that the eventual disposition of the occupied section of Jerusalem may be prejudiced. The Report of the Secretary General on the Work of the Organization, 1970-71, reflects the concern of many governments over changes in the face of this city. We have on a number of occasions discussed this matter with the Government of Israel, stressing the need to take more fully into account the sensitivities and con-

cerns of others. Unfortunately, the response of the Government of Israel has been disappointing.[93]

Ambassador Bush noted that an "Israeli occupation policy made up of unilaterally determined practices cannot help promote a just and lasting peace any more than that cause was served by the status quo in Jerusalem prior to June 1967 which, I want to make clear, we did not like and we do not advocate re-establishing....But we have supported this resolution out of the belief that it was time to reiterate our concern that nothing be done in Jerusalem that can prejudice an ultimate and peaceful solution."

The next day the Israeli cabinet formally rejected the resolution and ruled that the government would not negotiate on it or earlier resolutions on Jerusalem.[94] An Israeli statement said: "Israel's policy with regard to Jerusalem remains unchanged."[95]

By the latter part of 1971, the criticism by the Jewish community of Rogers and his plan grew louder as the presidential campaign began to take shape. Columnists Evans and Novak reported that Jewish Americans were becoming so restive that there was concern among Nixon's political advisers that "the American Jewish community will not be very forthcoming in 1972 campaign cash for Mr. Nixon."[96] Nixon's enthusiasm for Rogers' efforts steadily cooled as the election year neared.[97] Nixon later complained in his memoirs:

> One of the main problems I faced...was the unyielding and shortsighted pro-Israeli attitude in large and influential segments of the American Jewish community, Congress, the media and in intellectual and cultural circles. In the quarter century since the end of World War II this attitude had become so deeply ingrained that many saw the corollary of not being pro-Israel as being anti-Israeli, or even anti-Semitic. I tried unsuccessfully to convince them that this was not the case.[98]

It was not until 1976 during the Ford Administration that Washington again spoke forcefully about Jerusalem. On 23 March U.S. Ambassador to the United Nations William W. Scranton declared in the Security Council during a debate on Palestine that Israel's claim to all of Jerusalem was void:

> The United States position on the status of Jerusalem has been stated here on numerous occasions since the Arab portion of that city was occupied by Israel in 1967....[T]he future of Jerusalem will be determined only through the instruments and processes of negotiation, agreement and accommodation. Unilateral attempts to predetermine the future have no standing.[99]

The speech brought an official protest from Israel and charges that U.S. policy was tilting toward the Arab position.[100] These angry remarks may help explain why the United States, despite Scranton's bold words, two days later, on 25 March, vetoed a resolution deploring Israel's changing the status of Jerusalem and calling on Israel to stop establishing settlements on Arab land; the vote was 14 to 1.[101] At the time, President Gerald Ford was in the midst of an uphill fight for election on his own. He believed he needed support and contributions from the Jewish community. After the November election, and Ford's defeat, the United States reversed field once again and on 11 November joined in a UN Security Council consensus statement declaring "invalid" Israel's absorption of Arab East Jerusalem.[102]

* *

The Carter Administration's record on Jerusalem in the United Nations reflected more Jimmy Carter's concern with domestic politics than any solid policy on Jerusalem. While Washington voted with the majority in the General Assembly on 18 December 1978 strongly to deplore Israel's failure to acknowledge the applicability of the Fourth Geneva Convention to the territories occupied since 1967, "including Jerusalem," the resolution had more to do with the Geneva Accords than with the specific status of Jerusalem.[103] Hereafter, Carter followed the dictates of domestic politics. For instance, the next year, on 22 March 1979, the United States abstained in the Security Council on a resolution saying Israeli settlements on Arab land, including Arab East Jerusalem, had no legal status and "constitute a serious obstruction in achieving a comprehensive, just and lasting peace in the Middle East."[104]

The explanation of the U.S. abstention may be found in the timing of the resolution. It came just five days before the signing of the Egypt-Israel peace agreement, an accomplishment that President Jimmy Carter did not want marred or delayed by a UN vote. Similarly, Carter was preparing to run for re-election and he was seeking friends in the Jewish community. Thus, the United States abstained again in another Security Council resolution, passed 20 July 1979, urging Israel "to cease, on an urgent basis, the establishment, construction and planning of settlements in the Arab territories occupied since 1967, including Jerusalem."[105]

The influence of politics on Carter's Jerusalem policy became even more pronounced in 1980 as the presidential campaign heated up. On 1 March the United States joined in the passage by the Security Council of resolution 465 condemning Israel's settlements as illegal, "including Jerusalem," and demanding that Israel cease building new settlements and dismantle existing ones.[106] The reaction in the Jewish community and Israel was immediate and vociferous. Democratic political operatives quickly perceived that the vote would harm Carter's chances in the approaching primaries in New York and Illinois. Thus Carter two days later, on 3 March, announced that the U.S. vote had been a mistake, the result of an error in communications between the White House and the United Nations. The United States really had meant to abstain, he declared. The explanation was widely doubted and European and Arab nations heaped scorn on the beleaguered president.[107]

Carter displayed similar political concerns four months later when on 20 June the Security Council declared "null and void" Israel's changing of the status of Jerusalem; the vote was 14–0–1, with the United States abstaining.[108] A month later, on 29 July, the Carter Administration placed the United States among only seven nations that voted against a General Assembly resolution demanding that Israel withdraw from the territories occupied in 1967, including Arab East Jerusalem, and that it refrain from changing the status of Jerusalem.[109]

Israel responded the next day, on 30 July, by formally and publicly annexing all of Jerusalem. The Knesset declared that "Jerusalem united in its entirety is the capital of Israel." By designating the ordinance a "basic law," Israel's Knesset gave it quasi-constitutional rank.[110] The annexation was a landmark in the long struggle by Israel against the world community's opposition to all of Jerusalem being an Israeli controlled city. Although the annexation provoked an immediate international uproar, Israel refused to retreat.[111]

Even this bold flouting of U.S. policy and international law was not enough to overcome Carter's concern to gain favor among Israel's supporters in the final months of a bruising presidential campaign. When the Security Council strongly censured Israel on 20 August for annexing Jerusalem, the United States abstained. All fourteen other members supported the censure.[112]

* *

Despite his pro-Israeli record, Carter was roundly defeated in 1980 by Ronald Reagan, a man far more supportive of Israel. However, not even Reagan was ready to concede to Israel and its American supporters what they wanted most—moving the U.S. Embassy to Jerusalem. This would amount to the final victory, a public endorsement by the United States of Israel's claim to the whole city. It also would be tantamount to a declaration of war to the Islamic world, where Muslims revere Jerusalem as their third most holy city after Mecca and Medina.

Nonetheless, relocating the embassy to Jerusalem has been one of the top goals of the influential AIPAC, the American Israel Public Affairs Committee. The campaign gathered steam in the mid-1980s during the Reagan Administration and remains a priority goal.[113] To this end, bills have been introduced repeatedly in the House and Senate. For instance, in late 1983 one bill demanded the move to Jerusalem and was only killed after considerable effort by the White House.[114] The House Foreign Affairs subcommittee on international operations and on Europe and the Middle East passed on 2 October 1984 a nonbinding resolution saying it was a sense of Congress that the embassy should be moved to Jerusalem "at the earliest possible date." [115]

This position was officially endorsed in the Democratic national platform in 1984: "The Democratic Party recognizes and supports the established status of Jerusalem as the capital of Israel. As a symbol of this stand, the US Embassy should be moved from Tel Aviv to Jerusalem."[116] Democratic presidential candidates Gary Hart and Walter Mondale both vowed in the 1984 presidential campaign that they would move the embassy if elected. In 1988 Democratic presidential candidate Michael Dukakis also indicated his willingness to move the embassy to Jerusalem, as did Bill Clinton in 1992, adding that he recognized Jerusalem as "the eternal capital of Israel."[117] The 1992 Democratic platform said Jerusalem was Israel's capital, though it stopped short of calling for moving the embassy there.

In 1988, Republican Senator Jesse Helms of North Carolina added an amendment to the Department of State Appropriations Act calling for the construction of two separate diplomatic facilities in Israel, one in Tel Aviv and one in Jerusalem "or the West Bank."[118] The amendment said that each facility should be able to serve as an embassy or consulate but "shall not be denominated as the United States Embassy or Consulate until after construction of both facilities has begun, and construction of one facility has been completed, or is near completion...." In his remarks on the Senate floor, Helms made clear the purpose of his amendment was to bring about the move of the embassy to Jerusalem. He said: "Many of us here in the Senate—I venture to say most of us here—believe that Israel has a right to choose its own capital, and that the United States should locate its Embassy accordingly."[119]

On the last full day of Reagan's presidency, the administration signed with Israel a 99-year lease and land purchase agreement to carry out the amendment.[120] The agreement covered fourteen acres in West Jerusalem. In October 1994, Israel zoned the plot for "diplomatic purposes," although no construction had yet occurred. But there was a rub. The land may not have been Israel's to lease. Two prominent Palestinian families, the Khalidis and Nashashibis, claimed the property belonged to a *waqf*, an Islamic trust, and had been illegally seized by Israel. If construction does go ahead, Washington could find itself under intense criticism not only for moving its embassy to Jerusalem but for building the embassy on disputed land.[121]

The Bush Administration displayed considerably more courage than Congress or the Reagan Administration in its Jerusalem policy. Despite political pressures, it strongly stood by policy that called Arab East Jerusalem occupied territory. President Bush said on 3 March 1990 at a press conference in Palm Springs, California: "My position is that the foreign policy of the United States says we do not believe there should be new settlements in the West Bank or in East Jerusalem." He added that is "our strongly held view."[122]

The statement touched off a political storm in the United States and Israel because Bush's implication was clear: East Jerusalem, like the West Bank, was occupied territory. Israeli Prime Minister Yitzhak Shamir responded by declaring that Jerusalem "is part of Israel and it will never be divided again."[123] The uproar was so great that White House Chief of Staff John Sununu had to declare publicly on 7 March that Bush's remark did not represent any change in U.S. policy. He said the policy remained that "the United States supports a united Jerusalem whose final status should be determined by negotiations."[124]

* *

In perspective, it is clear that while U.S. policy has wavered and weakened, Israeli policy had remained steady and determined. This was starkly illustrated by the fact that Israel has continued to make significant changes in Jerusalem's status despite repeated Security Council resolutions ordering it to desist. Jewish housing continued to go up in and around the city and Jews increasingly moved into Palestinian areas, sometimes after Palestinians have been forcibly evicted.

In 1990, militant Jews belonging to Ateret Cohanim (Crown of the Priests) and associated with the Temple Mount Faithful, began moving into the Christian Quarter of the Old City. Overnight on 12 April some 150 heavily armed Jews occupied the vacant St. John's Hospice. The complex was within a block of the Holy Sepulcher, said to be the site of Christ's burial. They were the first Jews to try to settle in the Christian section since Israel captured the Old City in 1967 and their presence touched off a melee. Hundreds of Christian clerics protested and Israeli police responded with tear gas, felling Greek Orthodox Patriarch Diodoros I. The Jews said they intended to remain in the four-building, 72-room complex to re-establish a Jewish presence that they said had existed in 1920.[125]

After denying for two weeks any involvement in the takeover, the care-taker government of Yitzhak Shamir admitted on 22 April that it had helped to obtain lease of the property.[126] The admission brought international condemnation. State Department spokesperson Margaret Tutwiler said the takeover of the hospice was "an insensitive and provocative action....and the admission by the Israeli Housing Ministry that it subsidized the settlers' action is deeply disturbing."[127] Israel responded with a statement saying: "It is the right of Jews to live everywhere, and to purchase or rent property in all parts of the Land of Israel, and especially in Jerusalem."[128]

As if to emphasize the point, hundreds of militant Jews, including some members of the Knesset, stormed Palestinian homes in Silwan in Arab East Jerusalem in the pre-dawn darkness of 9 October 1991, evicted the Palestinian inhabitants and occupied at least a half-dozen of the homes. Police removed the Jews from all but one home, where the Palestinian family was dispossessed and the Jews were allowed to remain.[129] A report leaked to the Israeli press said the Silwan take-over was only part of a master plan spearheaded by Ateret Cohanim for massive Jewish colonization outside the walls of the Old City. The plan pinpointed twenty-two locations in and around the Arab neighborhoods of Sheikh Jarrah, Wadi Joz, the American Colony, Damascus Gate, Jabal Muqabbar and Silwan for construction of 4,000 housing units exclusively for Jews. The report said the proposal had been approved by Ariel Sharon's housing ministry.[130]

While Sharon was too wily a politician to admit publicly the details of such a plan, he did reveal to the Knesset, in his capacity as housing minister, on 28 August 1991 that he had plans for expanding what he called "Greater Jerusalem" to the western heights of the Jordan Valley with a population of a million Jews. Sharon's plan would link up Jerusalem with the largest Jewish settlement on the West Bank, Maale Adumim, three miles to the east, and Maale Adumim would expand eastward to the ridges overlooking Jericho in the Jordan Valley, establishing a line of hilltop Jewish construction that would cut the West Bank in two between Jerusalem and Jericho. Sharon said: "We have set for ourselves a goal of guaranteeing that in Jerusalem, the capital of the Jews and the eternal capital of Israel, there will be a Jewish majority."[131]

The outline for accomplishing this goal was already in place in 1991. Two circles of Jewish construction surrounded Jerusalem: an inner circle comprising major housing developments in Arab East Jerusalem, and an outer circle in the West Bank anchored at such Jewish settlements as Givat Zeev in the north and, going eastward and then southward, Abir Yaacov, Adam, Almon, Maale Adumim and, going southwestward and then northward, Tekoa, Efrat, Gush Etzion and Betar. In rough outline, the metropolitan area extended northward above Ramallah, eastward almost to Jericho and southward nearly to Hebron.[132]

At the beginning of 1992, the Jewish population of "Greater Jerusalem" totaled 523,000, including 350,000 in Jewish West Jerusalem, 140,000 in Arab East Jerusalem and 33,000 in surrounding settlements in the West Bank bounded by Ramallah in the north, Hebron in the south and the hills overlooking Jericho in the east. Palestinian population in the same area was 205,000, including 55,000 in the West Bank and 150,000 in Arab East Jerusalem.[133]

Construction of some 10,000 housing units restricted for Jewish use continued in Arab East Jerusalem under the new Labor government of Yitzhak Rabin, who marked the twenty-sixth anniversary of the occupation of East Jerusalem by declaring: "Jerusalem will forever remain the united capital of Israel."[134] In its annual report to Congress on Israeli settlements, the State Department in April 1993 reported without comment that Israel has "made no commitment to halt or reduce construction in East Jerusalem [and] has affirmed its intention to continue settlement construction in a 100 square mile surrounding area termed 'Greater Jerusalem.'"[135]

Under the Clinton Administration Israel's settlements in East Jerusalem for the first time went ahead with the open, if tacit, approval of Washington. This became obvious in the course of a session of the House Foreign Affairs subcommittee on the Middle East on 9 March 1993. Assistant Secretary of State for Near Eastern and South Asian Affairs Edward Djerejian was asked about construction of Jewish housing in the occupied territories, including East Jerusalem. He replied: "There is some allowance for—I wouldn't use the word 'expansion' but certainly continuing some activity—construction activities in existing settlement. And that's basically in terms of...natural growth and basic, immediate needs in those settlements."[136]

This was another major retreat in U.S. policy. Basically, it meant that America was now helping finance construction of Jewish housing in occupied parts of Arab Jerusalem. About all that was left to give up was Washington's traditional opposition to Israel's claim to Jerusalem as its capital. Given the devolving trajectory of American policy over the past four and a half decades, that significant concession may not be far ahead.

With the sweep of congressional elections in November 1994 by the Republicans, the impetus for moving the embassy gained a powerful new voice. New House Speaker Newt Gingrich was quick to announce that he was a supporter of the transfer, saying on 15 January 1995: "I strongly favor moving the American Embassy. I think it is absurd for us to single out Israel as a country where we define what we think the capital should be. It's the right of Israel to define its capital, and we as an ally should in fact be responsive. So if it comes to the floor this year I would be very supportive of it."[137]

Gingrich, clearly ignorant of the tortured history of the struggle over Jerusalem and his country's own position on the legalities of the issue, could hardly have been more wrong in asserting that it was Israel's choice when it came to naming Jerusalem as its capital. But then, when it came to Jerusalem, right or wrong seldom played a role.

This was emphasized once again in the spring of 1995. By then, 93 Senators were on record supporting a letter to the Secretary of State urging him to move the embassy to Jerusalem by May 1999. The implied threat was that if he did not act, the Senate would pass legislation mandating the move.

7 | SETTLEMENTS
The Geneva Convention
and Israel's Occupation, 1967–1995

"Clearly...substantial resettlement of the Israeli civilian population in occupied territories, including East Jerusalem, is illegal under the [Geneva] convention ....Indeed, the presence of these settlements is seen by my government as an obstacle to [peace]."
> U.S. Ambassador to the United Nations
> William W. Scranton, 1976[1]

"I think [settlements are] a complicating factor."
> Assistant Secretary of State Robert H. Pelletreau, 1994[2]

FROM THE START of Israel's 1967 occupation of Arab lands the United States opposed the establishment of Jewish settlements in the territories. This pillar of U.S. policy was based on the legal bedrock provided by the Fourth Geneva Convention Relative to the Protection of Civilian Persons in Time of War, adopted in 1949 and signed by Israel in 1951. Paragraph 6 of the convention's Article 49 states: "The occupying power shall not deport or transfer parts of its own civilian population into the territory it occupies." It was this clear and forthright international accord that provided the basis for the universal opposition that greeted Israel when it began establishing Jewish settlements in the occupied territories in the immediate aftermath of the war, a process that has continued without pause despite U.S. and world condemnation.

Israel started the 1967 war on 5 June and won it by the end of 10 June, leaving it in military occupation of Jordan's West Bank, including Arab East Jerusalem; Syria's Golan Heights; Egypt's Sinai Peninsula, and the Gaza Strip with its teeming refugees.[3] As discussed in chapter 6, Israel on 11 June, one day after the end of the fighting, began the process of colonizing the Arab territories by razing the Maghrabi Quarter of the Old City of Jerusalem.[4] On 15 July Israel quietly established its first settlement in occupied territory. It was Kibbutz Merom Hagolan near Quneitra on Syria's Golan Heights.[5]

These steps marked the beginning of a steady program to place Jewish settlements in all of the occupied territories. By the beginning of 1968, Israel had cautiously established pioneering settlements in every one of the occupied territories. It had expropriated 838 acres for new settlements, expelled hundreds of Arabs from the Jewish Quarter in the Old City of Jerusalem, razed or partly destroyed Palestinian refugee towns at Tiflig and near Jericho as well as 144 homes in Gaza and secretly embarked on a major plan for building four large settlements in Arab Jerusalem.[6]

* *

In retrospect, what was plain about the beginning of Israel's settlement policy was that it was based on a premeditated and pragmatic plan specifically aimed at testing whether Israel could resist successfully international pressure. Israel had every reason to believe that if the past was any guide, it would be successful. As early as 8 June 1967 former prime minister Ben Gurion had warned: "Members of this generation who were inhabitants of the Old City [of Jerusalem], of Hebron, and the Etzion region should be among those returning to those areas to mark the continuity of Jewish [settlement] in those areas, before the beginning of political pressures to make Israel leave these."[7]

Ben Gurion had reason to know about international pressure. He had experienced the wrath of President Eisenhower, the only president who had ever acted forcefully to curtail Israel's territorial ambitions. It occurred in 1953 when he withheld U.S. aid to force Israel to halt a water diversion scheme from the Jordan river that infringed on Arab rights. After a month, Israel caved in and aid was resumed.[8] The second time was Eisenhower's demand that Israel surrender its conquests in the 1956 Suez crisis. He persevered over David Ben Gurion, mainly by threatening another cut in U.S. aid and by going public on the injustice of the Israeli land-grab. In the end, Israel withdrew its forces from all of Egypt's northern Sinai, including the Gaza Strip.[9]

But now in Eisenhower's place was Lyndon B. Johnson, the most pro-Israel president up to that time. U.S. policy was as compliant toward Israel as in Truman's day. Under Truman the United States had made no serious effort to oppose Israel's confiscation and settlement of Palestinian villages during the 1948 war. Nor had it particularly objected in the early 1950s when Israel drove thousands of Bedouin out of the Negev and destroyed two Christian towns in the Upper Galilee, Iqrit and Bir Am. Again, during the 1950s, even Eisenhower had not taken strong action against Israel's take-over of demilitarized zones it shared with Egypt and Syria in violation of the armistices. With this background still fresh, Israel adopted a settlement strategy that had two distinct parts: absorption of all of Jerusalem and the establishment of settlements on all of the occupied territories.

Israel's ambitions toward Jerusalem were the more urgent and it moved with great rapidity to secure the entire city for itself. It did that within eighteen days of the end of fighting. By then Israel was evicting Palestinians from the Old City, had redesigned the City of Jerusalem so that its population was overwhelmingly Jewish and had laid legal claim to the entire city as Israel's eternal capital. Although these actions brought protests from the United States and two separate UN General Assembly resolutions criticizing Israel, they elicited from Washington no actions similar to Eisenhower's strong stance. As a result the Labor government of Prime Minister Levi Eshkol ignored the outcries and instead turned its attention to settling the rest of the occupied territories.

It was not until 24 September that Eshkol made the first public acknowledgment that Israel had plans to establish settlements in the newly occupied territories.[10] Although he had declared in public at the start of the war that Israel sought no territory, Eshkol now said Israel had limited ambitions. It would rebuild settlements in the Etzion bloc, an area of four settlements that had been lost to Jordanian forces in the 1948 war, and he revealed plans were being discussed to reestablish Beit Haarava, also lost in 1948, on the northwest shore of the Dead Sea.[11]

Prior to 1948, there had been only seven Jewish settlements in the newly occupied lands of the West Bank and the Gaza Strip; Jewish land ownership had been at most 1 percent and the total Jewish population 5,000, including East Jerusalem.[12] Despite these statistics, the implication of Eshkol's remarks was that Israel merely was reclaiming settlements where Jews had lived before Israel's founding. In reality it had already established Kibbutz Merom Hagolan on Syria's Golan Heights where no modern Jewish settlement had existed before.[13]

Eshkol's claim to Arab territory brought a mild public rebuke from the United States, charging that Eshkol's announcement broke Israel's earlier promise that it would not retain any territory.[14] However, Washington took no action and Israel continued on its settlement program and as a result the process of establishing Jewish settlements where none had been before continued cautiously. Levi Eshkol, of course, was not acting in a vacuum. He faced increasingly powerful forces within Israel to retain the land that Zionism promised to immigrant Jews. As early as 21 September—three days before his public announcement that Israel planned to establish some settlements—there emerged a far-right group known as the Land of Israel Movement. Its slogan was "Not an inch" and its founding manifesto said:

> The whole of Eretz Israel[15] is now in the hands of the Jewish people, and just as we are not allowed to give up the State of Israel, so we are ordered to keep what we received there from its hands: the land of Israel....Our present borders guarantee security and peace and open up unprecedented vistas of national material and spiritual consolidation. Within these boundaries, equality and freedom, the fundamental tenets of the state of Israel, shall be shared by all citizens without discrimination.[16]

Supporters of the Land of Israel Movement embraced the range of political parties, including Eshkol's ruling Labor Party and, especially, Menachem Begin's opposition Herut party.[17] Its emergence had a major political impact that neither Eshkol nor the State Department could ignore. While the movement did not last as an organized force beyond 1973, its emergence gave impetus to the even more activist Gush Emunim, which supplanted it.[18]

If Washington had acted during this period with the same determination and clarity of purpose as had the Eisenhower Administration, the chances are high that it would have blunted the militant settler movement. Instead, Washington's reaction was only tepid words and no serious measures. This provided the opportunity for Israeli settlers to argue that if the United States was not ready to act to impose its own policies, why should Israel? Why should Israel be more holy than America? It was a cogent argument that was to be voiced time after time over the following decades to justify Israel's building of exclusive Jewish settlements.

* *

Although the United States publicly indicated as early as three days after the 1967 war that it believed the Fourth Geneva Convention applied to Israel's administration of the occupied territories, it took four years for Washington to announce in specific words that Israel was violating the convention. On 25 September 1971 U.S. Ambassador to the United Nations George Bush became the first American official since the 1967 war unequivocally to apply the Geneva Convention to Israel's conduct in the occupied territories during a Security Council debate: "We regret Israel's failure to acknowledge its obligations under the Fourth Geneva Convention as well as its actions which are contrary to the letter and spirit of this convention."[19]

However, it was not until 23 March 1976 that the United States finally condemned settlements as being both illegal and an obstacle to peace. The strong announcement came in response to a surge in settlement activity by the Labor government under the prod of hard-line settlers. By the time of the 1976 U.S. declaration there were about sixty-eight settlements in the territories, not counting Jerusalem: twenty-seven in the West Bank, including seventeen in the Jordan Valley; twenty-three on the Golan Heights, and eighteen in the Gaza Strip/Sinai. Total investment by Israel in the settlements was estimated at $500 million.[20] U.S. Ambassador to the United Nations William W. Scranton spelled out U.S. policy by condemning Israel's claim to Jerusalem and then told the Security Council:

> Next, I turn to the question of Israeli settlements in the occupied territories. Again, my government believes that international law sets the appropriate standards. An occupier must maintain the occupied areas as intact and unaltered as possible, without interfering with the customary life of the area, and any changes must be necessitated by the immediate needs of the occupation and be consistent with international law. The Fourth Geneva Convention speaks directly to the issue of population transfer in Article 49....Clearly then substantial resettlement of the Israeli civilian population in occupied territories, including East Jerusalem, is illegal under the convention and cannot be considered to have prejudged the outcome of future negotiations between the parties or the location of the borders of states of the Middle East. Indeed, the pres-

ence of these settlements is seen by my government as an obstacle to
the success of the negotiations for a just and final peace between Israel
and its neighbors.[21]

Despite those spirited words, the Ford Administration two days later turned
around and vetoed a Security Council resolution deploring Israel's changing the
status of Jerusalem and calling on Israel to stop establishing settlements on Arab
land. The vote was 14 to 1.[22] At the time President Gerald Ford was already deep
in the presidential race to be held in November and apparently believed that a vote
in favor of the resolution would damage his electoral prospects among Jewish
voters.

It took until 22 March 1979—twelve years after Israel's settlement campaign began—before the Security Council finally addressed the matter with a stern
resolution. It found the Geneva Accords applied to the Arab territories under Israel's
occupation, "including Jerusalem." Furthermore, the resolution stated that the settlements were therefore illegal and a "serious obstruction" to peace. The vote was 12-
0-3, with the United States abstaining although President Jimmy Carter earlier had
personally declared them illegal.[23]

In one sense the U.S. abstention was meaningless since by 1979 the UN
action was too late to influence events. The resolution was passed just before a
United Nations commission created to study Israel's settlement policy issued a
strong report documenting the vigor of Israel's settlement program. It reported
that there were currently 133 Jewish settlements in the occupied territories and
nearly 100,000 settlers, adding:

> The commission found evidence that the Israeli Government is engaged
> in a willful, systematic and large-scale process of establishing settle-
> ments in the occupied territories for which it should bear full responsi-
> bility.[24]

The dramatic increase in settlements was attributable to the coming to
power of ultranationalist Menachem Begin in mid-1977. Although Begin and his
Herut (Freedom) party had persevered as the major political opposition from the
beginning of Israel, he never had enjoyed wide popularity. This began changing in
the wake of the 1973 war and a general rise of unrest with the Labor Party, especially its cautious policy toward settlements. The number of settlements Labor had
established was relatively modest up to 1974, numbering under twenty outside of
Jerusalem.[25]

Begin's upward political trajectory coincided in the winter of 1974 with
the founding of Gush Emunim (Bloc of the Faithful).[26] The leader was extremist
Rabbi Moshe Levinger, who in 1968 had spearheaded the founding of the controversial and unauthorized Kiryat Arba settlement at Hebron in defiance of the Labor government. Kiryat Arba became the center of settler extremism, resulting in
many violent attacks against Hebron's Palestinians.[27]

Begin's popularity began a notable rise when he sided with the settlers
against the Labor government over the issue of establishing settlements amid the

heavily Palestinian population in the northern half of Palestine. Up to 1975, the Labor government of Yitzhak Rabin had prohibited settlements there. But on 30 November the settlers successfully defied the government by establishing Elon Moreh south of Nablus. Gush Emunim leader Levinger left no doubt about the group's aim: "This is the beginning of settlement in Samaria.[28] One more settlement, and another, and all of Samaria will be ours!"[29] Thus Elon Moreh became the symbol of the struggle between the settlers and Menachem Begin on the one hand, against moderates and the cautious Labor government on the other.

Two years later, on 17 May 1977, Begin came to power with 33.4 percent of the vote.[30] Among his first actions was to travel to Elon Moreh and declare: "There will be many more Elon Morehs." [31] He was true to his word.

At the time, there were about 50,000 Jews living in Arab East Jerusalem and about 7,000 in forty-five settlements in the West Bank and in an additional forty-five in the rest of the occupied territory.[32] When he left office six years later, there were 112 on the West Bank, five in the Gaza Strip and the Golan Heights and Jerusalem officially had been annexed. The number of Jewish settlers had increased from 3,000 to more than 40,000, with an additional 100,000 in East Jerusalem. Despite occasional pro forma criticisms of them, the Reagan Administration essentially accepted the settlers and their settlements as a fact of life.[33]

This distribution essentially established the central points for Jewish settlement throughout the territories. Begin's Likud successor, Yitzhak Shamir—like Begin a former leader of Jewish terrorists during pre-state days—then pursued an active program over the next decade that was substantially to thicken and expand these focal points. In terms of new settlements Shamir's accomplishments were fairly modest. Where he exceeded even Begin was in expanding settlements to accommodate the movement of Jews into the territories.[34] When Shamir finally left office in mid-1992, there were some 245,000 Jews in some 250 settlements, including Arab East Jerusalem.[35]

* *

President Jimmy Carter came to power the same year as Menachem Begin. But while Begin dreamed of Jewish settlements, Carter had a vision of finding a solution to the Arab-Israeli conflict based on UN resolution 242's formula of trading land for peace. To Carter's mind, peace meant Israeli withdrawal and that meant Israel should not establish settlements in the territories. Carter and Begin thus were diametrically opposed in their views on settlements, as quickly became clear after they held their first meeting 19–20 July 1977 in the White House.

During their meeting, Carter told Begin that under resolution 242 Israel would have to withdraw on all three fronts and "I then explained to the Prime Minister how serious an obstacle to peace were the Israeli settlements being established within the occupied territories." Despite that advice, Begin returned to Israel and in less than a week the cabinet defiantly conferred legal status on three more settlements.[36] When Washington objected by saying it was "deeply disappointed" and the move created "an obstacle to the peacemaking process," Tel Aviv pointed out that these were not new settlements and that Prime Minister Begin in the meeting days earlier with President Carter had said nothing about not legalizing settlements already in existence.[37]

Carter responded by becoming the first president to label in public the settlements as illegal. He said at a press conference on 28 July: "The matter of settlements in the occupied territories has always been characterized by our government, by me and my predecessors, as an illegal action."[38] Actually Carter was the first and only president ever to defy the Israeli lobby and declare himself that settlements were illegal.

The experience left Carter "extremely annoyed" with Begin, an emotion that was to grow more intense.[39] For his part, Begin was less than impressed by the negotiating talents of the new president. After the White House sessions, Begin privately told his aides that he planned to go ahead establishing settlements despite Carter's opposition. The Americans, he said, would be angry for six months but then they would acquiesce.[40] He was also heard to describe Carter as a "cream puff."[41]

Relations between America and Israel quickly soured. A series of private and public quarrels ensued. On 17 August Israel announced it officially had approved three more settlements.[42] Carter responded the next day with a letter bluntly stating his opposition to new settlements: "These illegal, unilateral acts in territory presently under Israeli occupation create obstacles to constructive negotiations." Then he added a threat: "...the repetition of these acts will make it difficult for the President not to reaffirm publicly the U.S. position regarding 1967 borders with minor modifications."[43]

Less than two weeks later, Agriculture Minister Ariel Sharon unveiled an ambitious plan called "A Vision of Israel at Century's End," which envisioned the settlement of two million Jews in the occupied territories by 2000.[44] There currently were 57,000 Jews in the occupied territories, plus 50,000 in Jerusalem. The others were in more than forty-five settlements in the West Bank, Golan Heights and the Gaza Strip.[45] In addition, plans already existed for forty-nine more settlements in the next five years. Sharon promised to establish even more settlements. Said Sharon: "Make no mistake about it. This government will establish many new settlements. That's what it was elected to do and that's what it will do."[46]

With the typical confusion in which Israel's policies left Washington, Foreign Minister Moshe Dayan then personally promised Carter at a meeting in mid-September that only six new settlements would be established during the next year. He added that they would be inside military camps. However, at the start of 1978 Israel announced it was establishing four new settlements in the Sinai.[47] When Carter challenged Begin about settlements outside military bases, the Israeli leader replied that the promise extended only to the end of 1977—not for a whole year starting in September 1977. Observed analyst William Quandt: "As much as anything else, this response helped convince Carter that Begin was not always a man of his word."[48]

But Begin would not stop. On 23 January ground was broken for a new Jewish settlement at Shiloh on the West Bank. President Carter declared publicly: "I am confident that Prime Minister Begin will honor the commitment personally made to me and thus will not permit this settlement to go forward."[49] Begin denied any such commitment and the settlement was completed, albeit under the guise that it was an archeological site. Said Foreign Minister Dayan: "The policy of all the Israeli governments in the future, like that of their predecessors, will be to continue establishing settlements in the West Bank."[50]

Secretary of State Cyrus Vance responded on 10 February by declaring that the Carter Administration considered Israel's settlements in the occupied territory "contrary to international law and that therefore they should not exist."[51] Two days later Israel issued a communique declaring that settlements in the occupied territories were "legal, legitimate and necessary."[52]

By now confusion was rampant. On 27 February, the Jewish Agency called for establishment of forty-nine new settlements by 1992. It reported there were currently 6,500 settlers in seventy-six settlements in the occupied territories.[53] The day before, the Israeli cabinet had voted to make no change in the country's settlement policy, in effect affirming Begin's expansionist policy.[54] At a White House meeting in March Begin flatly told Carter that he was "not willing to stop the construction of new settlements or the expansion of existing settlements...[or] to acknowledge that UN resolution 242 applies to the West Bank-Gaza area."[55]

Carter retaliated by ordering the State Department legal adviser to make a public report on the legal status of settlements. On 21 April 1978, Herbert Hansell asserted that the 1949 Fourth Geneva Convention Relative to the Protection of Civilian Persons in Time of War applied to all the occupied territories under Paragraph 6 of Article 49. Hansell's opinion effectively rebutted all of Israel's arguments that the Geneva Accords did not apply to settlements. Hansell's conclusion:

> While Israel may undertake, in the occupied territories, actions necessary to meet its military needs and to provide for orderly government during the occupation, for the reasons indicated above the establishment of the civilian settlements in those territories is inconsistent with international law.[56]

Israel ignored the report and continued to argue that the accords did not apply.

Although the Carter Administration proved itself consistent in speaking out against settlements, it was not consistent in its votes in the United Nations. Of the seven resolutions critical of settlements that were passed during Carter's four-year term, the administration supported only three, one in the Security Council and two in the General Assembly.[57] It abstained in the four other cases, twice in the Security Council and twice in the General Assembly.[58]

The single affirmative vote in the Security Council involved the embarrassing episode in which Carter retreated under withering criticism by Israel's supporters for supporting a resolution that said settlements were illegal, "including Jerusalem."[59] Carter claimed there had been miscommunications and that the vote should have been an abstention.[60] This extraordinary turnabout on 3 March 1980 came because Carter recognized that the vote would harm his chances in the approaching presidential primaries in New York and Illinois.[61]

By the time Carter left office, Israel formally had annexed Jerusalem as its "eternal capital." It had at least eighty-nine settlements on the West Bank, thirty in the Gaza Strip and northern Sinai and twenty-eight on the Golan Heights.[62]

* *

Jimmy Carter's ringing declaration that settlements were illegal lasted only until the end of his term. Less than a month after he assumed office, Ronald Reagan declared on 2 February 1981: "I disagreed when the previous administration referred to them as illegal—they're not illegal." He added, however, that Israel's "rush" to establish settlements was "maybe...unnecessarily provocative."[63] This odd formulation, which implied that the settlements were legal but did not explicitly say so, left the United States without a coherent policy toward settlements. David A. Korn, who was the State Department's director for Israel and Arab-Israeli affairs at the time, recalled:

> For more than a year afterward, the United States remained mute on Israeli settlements. American silence was all the signal Mr. Begin's Likud government needed to initiate an accelerated settlements program. By September 1982, the administration realized what damage it had done to its Middle East peace efforts and the formula "settlements are an obstacle to peace" became standard State Department rhetoric.[64]

The Bush Administration barely had occupied the White House before Israel announced on 15 March 1989 the establishment of a new settlement near Ramallah in the occupied West Bank, adding that it was the first of seven more to come.[65] Unlike all presidents before, Bush was intimately familiar with the settlement issue because of his tenure in the 1970s as ambassador to the United Nations and his eight years as vice president. He strongly opposed settlements, but he had no illusions about Israel's unbending attitude toward them, especially under a Likud government headed by Yitzhak Shamir. In his inaugural speech Shamir had pledged to continue the "holy work" of establishing settlements.[66]

The stark contrast between the views of Bush and Shamir was signalled on 22 May 1989 when Secretary of State James A. Baker III appeared before the annual meeting of Israel's powerful American lobby AIPAC, the American-Israel Public Affairs Committee, and sternly warned Israel:

> For Israel, now is the time to lay aside, once and for all, the unrealistic vision of a greater Israel. Israeli interests in the West Bank and Gaza, security and otherwise, can be accommodated on a settlement based on resolution 242. Foreswear annexation. Stop settlement activity.[67]

Despite Baker's words, settlement activity increased dramatically toward the end of 1989 when a flood of Jews from the Soviet Union began to arrive in

Israel in the waning days of the Cold War. By the beginning of 1990 they were landing in Israel at the rate of 1,000 a week.[68] On 14 January 1990 Shamir took the opportunity to respond to Baker. He said the number of Soviet immigrants was expected to increase and as a result "we need the Land of Israel and a big and strong state of Israel. We will need a lot of room to absorb everyone, and every immigrant will go where he wants."[69] A spokesman for Shamir later whispered to the media that the prime minister supported settling in any part of Palestine and would not be unhappy to see Soviet Jews move to the occupied territories.[70]

On 1 March, Secretary of State Baker had made an historic declaration. He said the administration would consider guaranteeing a loan to build housing for the new Soviet immigrants—but only if the money was not used in the territories. This was a truly memorable declaration since it was the first time any administration since Eisenhower's had linked U.S. aid to making Israel conform with U.S. policy.

However, the linkage was not to Israel's $3 billion annual official aid but to a separate request it had made for $400 million in loan guarantees. Baker told the House Appropriations Subcommittee on Foreign Aid that the administration was sympathetic to the request but that Washington wanted to be sure that "guarantees provided will not simply supplant other money that is then used to support settlements in the occupied territories."[71]

Despite Baker's concerns, the House and Senate quickly approved the measure. However, the administration refused to act on the loan guarantee until it received specific assurances from Israel about its usage. Political pressure from Israel's friends mounted for the administration to release the funds and, finally, on 3 October Baker said it was ready to do so. He explained that he had received the proper assurances from Israel not to use the money in the territories.[72] But within four days Prime Minister Shamir publicly said the agreement did not cover Arab East Jerusalem and that Israel would go ahead with construction of a new Jewish settlement between the Mount of Olives and Mount Scopus in East Jerusalem.[73]

Baker retaliated by continuing to withhold the funds. (They were not finally released until 20 February 1991.[74]) Baker and Bush further showed their displeasure on 12 October 1990 by having the United States join in a unanimous United Nations Security Council resolution condemning Israel for "acts of violence" against Palestinians during a confrontation 8 October at the Haram al-Sharif in Jerusalem in which seventeen Palestinians were killed.[75]

In early 1991 Israel began letting it be known that it wanted the United States to guarantee a total of $10 billion in loans over a five-year period to house Soviet immigrants. The Bush Administration succeeded in getting Israel to delay its formal request until September, giving Washington time to build the case that there should be linkage between U.S. aid and settlements. But even with this enormous aid request pending, Shamir refused to delay or stop establishing new settlements. Instead, Israel embarked on an unprecedented settlement campaign. More Israeli housing units were scheduled for construction during fiscal 1991 (March 1991–March 1992) than during all of the 1967–1984 period.[76] By spring 1991 *The*

Washington Post's Jackson Diehl was reporting that Israel was involved in "the biggest settlement construction program ever launched."[77]

By September 1991 there were about 225,000 Jewish settlers living in the territories: 120,000 in Arab East Jerusalem, 90,000 in the West Bank, 12,000 in the Golan Heights and 3,000 in the Gaza Strip.[78] Plans for an even more massive program already were being considered by the Shamir government.[79]

Israel set 6 September 1991 as the day it would make formal its application for $10 billion in loan guarantees. Bush wanted it to wait for another four months because the peace process finally was showing encouraging signs. Shamir refused. On the eve of the date, Bush and Baker swung into action. However, their personal entreaties to Shamir and Israel's U.S. lobby, AIPAC, fell on deaf ears. Not even appeals based on the fact that the historic Madrid peace conference was about to take place deterred Israel.[80] Shamir lodged the formal request on 6 September.

An angered President Bush responded by calling reporters to the Oval Office on the same day and, in effect, declared war on Shamir. Still basking from the lightning victory over Iraq, Bush publicly appealed to Congress to delay action on the request for 120 days.[81] Shamir's response was to declare on 8 September that the United States had a "moral obligation" to give Israel the guarantee.[82]

The fight was now joined. On 12 September some 1,000 Jewish Americans descended on Washington from at least thirty-five states to personally lobby with lawmakers as part of an organized pro-guarantee effort.[83] That same day Bush called a news conference to threaten that he would veto any congressional effort to grant the guarantees to Israel any time short of his request for a 120-day delay. Bush said: "I'm going to stand for what I believe here....And I'm asking the American people to support me in this request."[84]

Israeli Prime Minister Yitzhak Shamir shrugged off Bush's threat of a veto, saying: "We don't see any reason to change our position."[85] It took until 2 October before the Senate finally agreed to Bush's request and delayed the matter for four months.[86] It had been one of the bitterest public confrontations between an administration and Israel and its supporters. Although Bush won, he would pay dearly for it in the presidential campaign. *The New York Times* reported that Bush's Democratic opponent, Bill Clinton, received 60 percent of his campaign funding from Jewish sources and that he gained 80 percent of the Jewish vote.[87]

* *

A breakthrough in the peace process occurred on 18 October 1991 when the Soviet Union restored diplomatic relations with Israel, as Tel Aviv long had sought. In return, on 20 October, Israel accepted a joint Moscow-Washington invitation to attend an international peace conference in Madrid on 30 October.[88] It was the first time Palestinians actually would represent themselves, although under the umbrella of the Jordanian delegation. But to assure an accurate presentation of his expansionist policies, Shamir himself decided to represent Israel, saying: "Everybody knows what I represent."[89] Just what he represented was later explained by Shamir himself. After his electoral defeat as Israel's leader and the elapse of nearly a year of fruitless negotiations between Israel and its Palestinian and Arab partners in the Madrid peace process, Shamir admitted:

> I would have conducted the autonomy negotiations for ten years, and in the meantime we would have reached half a million souls in Judea and Samaria [the West Bank]....Without such a basis there would be nothing to stop the establishment of a Palestinian state.[90]

Despite Shamir's later admission about the futility of the Madrid peace process, hard-liners within his coalition remained adamantly opposed to the talks. Two factions deserted Shamir's coalition on 19 January 1992, forcing the government to face new elections in the summer.[91] Shamir responded the next day by taking an even harder stance on settlements. Symbolically starting his re-election campaign in the West Bank settlement of Betar Illit, Shamir declared:

> No force in the world will stop this construction. We say to ourselves, and to the Gentiles of the world and to the next generations, here will be our homeland, here will be our home, forever and ever....We will build, and I hope very much that we will also obtain guarantees.[92]

President Bush reportedly "went ballistic" when he heard Shamir's remarks.[93] However, no public comment came from the White House. Instead, with a wiliness born of a lifetime in politics, Bush launched a subtle campaign to demonstrate to Israel's supporters how tough it could get if Shamir continued his obstructive ways. Suddenly a series of negative reports and even more negative public comments began appearing in the media. On 14 February a report by the General Accounting Office revealed that Israel's pledges to restrict new housing within Israel in return for the $400 million loan guarantee in 1991 had been violated. Much of the money actually had been spent in the occupied territories.[94]

A month later came a damaging leak that there was "overwhelming" evidence of Israel's cheating on written promises not to re-export U.S. weapons technology to Third World countries, including China and South Africa, both on America's embargo list.[95] Unnamed U.S. officials added there was well founded suspicion Israel also was selling secrets of America's vaunted Patriot anti-missile missile to China.[96] Instead of denying or not commenting on the leaks, the State Department inspector general charged on 1 April that Israel was engaged in a "systematic and growing pattern" of selling secret U.S. technology in violation of U.S. law.[97]

Finally, on 8 May the State Department released a study showing that Jewish settlements in the occupied territories had increased by 25 percent over the past year. The building activity was so great that it outpaced Israel's efforts to entice residents to the new housing units. The report said about 245,000 settlers resided in around 250 settlements in the West Bank, Gaza, Golan Heights and East Jerusalem, making the number of Jewish settlers equal to 13 percent of the occupied population.[98]

In the meantime, the Bush Administration also pursued public diplomacy on a parallel track. Baker strongly defended linkage between guarantees and settlements in February during appearances before congressional committees on the Hill. The next month, on 17 March, Bush turned down a proposed compromise on the guarantees offered by Senate leaders on the grounds that there were too many loopholes in the proposal. In April, Bush ignored a 99 to 1 vote in the Senate expressing a non-binding sense of the Senate "that the United States Government should support appropriate loan guarantees to Israel for refugee absorption."

By such maneuvers, Bush managed to retain high support for his hard-line against Israel. In the end he won: Shamir lost the 23 June elections, thereby ending fifteen stormy and expansionistic years of rule by his Likud bloc. The Labor party headed by Yitzhak Rabin won forty-four seats against Likud's thirty-two in the 120-seat Knesset and assumed power on 13 July 1992.[99]

Bush Administration officials openly welcomed Rabin's victory and Shamir's loss. They predicted there would be an improvement in relations with the United States and that Bush now would approve Israel's pending request for $10 billion in loan guarantees.[100] The predictions were correct. But the implied euphoria was not. In the final analysis it was Bush, not Rabin, who capitulated and the historic attempt to link settlements to aid was essentially abandoned.

* *

Yitzhak Rabin was hailed by U.S. officials and the media as a leader with whom the United States could work. However, George Bush was in the waning days of a presidential campaign in which he was waging a losing battle for his political life. Rabin, on the other hand, had a strong constituency committed to settlements. Both men were confronted with the necessity to save face among their domestic constituencies.

Rabin as prime minister two decades earlier had proved to be a supporter of settlements. But he differed from the ultranationalists by believing they should not be placed among heavy concentrations of Palestinians, where they caused needless friction. Thus Rabin made a distinction between what he called "political" and "strategic" settlements. He identified the strategic settlements as those that Labor had founded in the first decade after the 1967 war along the sparsely populated frontiers with Syria and Jordan. Jerusalem was a separate case. He considered it, as did Likud, Israel's capital and therefore Israel's right to settlement was beyond question.

Bush, on the other hand, could not be seen as backing down on an issue that had become the centerpiece of his administration's policy and which directly had led to the deteriorating relations with Israel over the past three years. Yet, Bush's mantel as the hero of the Gulf war long since had fallen. By the time Rabin officially took office it was clear that something dramatic had to be done to save Bush's faltering re-election bid. In this atmosphere of political desperation the president invited Rabin to the Bush summer retreat at Kennebunkport and struck a deal on 11 August that allowed both sides to claim victory. Only Rabin's claim was true.

In return for Bush approving Israel's request for $10 billion in loan guarantees, Rabin promised to halt "political" settlements. But he added that Israel would continue "security" settlements and he left no doubt that settlements would continue in Arab East Jerusalem. Rabin also let it be known that he intended to go ahead with completion of some 11,000 housing units already under construction.[101] This was some improvement over Likud's program but hardly anything that approached compliance with traditional U.S. policy opposing all settlements. In fact, it was merely a return to the consistent settlement policy the Labor Party had carried out between 1967 and 1977.

The Rabin government continued to expand settlements, and in the process it practically doomed the 1993 peace accord with the Palestinians. As *New York Times* columnist Thomas L. Friedman wrote in early 1995:

> [Rabin's] government has increased settlements in the West Bank by ten percent in two years. That's crazy. It undermines Mr. Arafat's credibility and leaves Palestinians feeling they are being duped. It's time for Mr. Rabin to draw them a line where Israel stops and they start.[102]

By allowing the growth of settlements on Palestinian land in the midst of peace talks, the historic attempt to link U.S. aid to U.S. policy was lost—and perhaps even the peace process itself. Yet, the administration and Israel hailed the Bush-Rabin accord a breakthrough and an important concession by Israel. The impression was left that Israel actually was stopping all settlement activity, when in fact it had made no such pledge.[103] A compliant media fell in with the euphoric mood and acted as though Bush had won a major victory. Congress likewise was impressed. On 1 October 1992, it approved the loan guarantees, to be used over five years. As an added fillip to Israel, Congress reserved to itself the right to override any presidential suspension of the guarantees should Israel use them outside of its pre-5 June 1967 frontiers.[104] This last provision was a needless one, since Bush already had indicated that he would overlook completion of some 11,000 units in the West Bank and all new construction in occupied sections of Jerusalem as well as establishment of "security" settlements on the Golan Heights and along Israel's frontiers.

Passage of the loan guarantees was Israel's greatest victory in its decades-long struggle to gain U.S. approval for settlements. While no public announcement was made about the president's position on how the loan guarantees could be used, Israel made obvious by its actions that for the first time Washington was acquiescing in employing U.S.-guaranteed funds to build and expand settlements.

Washington tried to put a gloss on the change by insisting that if Israel did use any of the funds in the territories the amount would be deducted from the next year's $2 billion increment. This gave the appearance that Washington was standing fast in its opposition to settlements. But it was only an appearance. The reality was that if the only penalty Israel paid for violating U.S. policy was a deduction in future guarantees than it was no penalty at all. It was obvious that there was a limit to how much Israel profitably could spend in the territories before they were overbuilt. Indeed, in early June 1993 a symposium was held under the theme of "What Do You Do with $10 Billion?" The guarantees had put Israel in the position of having all the money it needed to do with as it liked.[105]

The bottom line implicit in the penalty arrangement was the clear understanding that the United States agreed that Israel could go ahead with settlement activity as long as it was willing to pay what amounted to a very modest price. Indeed, when the Clinton Administration on 5 October 1993 recommended to Congress that the $2 billion in loan guarantees for Israel in fiscal 1994, which began 1 October, be cut by $437 million—the price it put on Israel's use of the loans in the territories—there was barely a peep out of Israel.[106] One reason was that Israel had almost certainly spent far more than that sum in the territories during fiscal 1993. Another was that there already was afoot a scheme to have the president annul the penalty or find some other way to grant it to Israel as additional aid.[107]

The underlying reality was that a significant erosion of U.S. policy had occurred. For the first time the United States implicitly was allowing use of funds backed by U.S. guarantees for Israeli settlements in the occupied territories. It was only a half-step from that to approving use of direct U.S. aid funds, a step that may not be too far distant. That appears to be the direction being followed by President Bill Clinton. During the 1993 session of the United Nations, the U.S. delegation refused to condemn Israel's settlement activity because it was "unproductive to debate the legalities of the issue."[108]

Clinton's administration also has already further watered down the U.S. description of settlements. Under Clinton, there were neither illegal nor obstacles to peace. They became a "complicating factor." That was the way they were described on 1 March 1994 by Assistant Secretary of State for Near East Affairs Robert H. Pelletreau before the Europe and Middle East subcommittee of the House Foreign Affairs Committee. Asked what effect Jewish settlements had on the peace process, he replied: "Well, I think it's a complicating factor, sir."[109] He repeated the phrase on 14 June 1994 before the same committee.[110]

To characterize settlements as a "complicating factor" is a long step toward total desertion of a basic U.S. policy that had stood since 1967.

8 | ARMS

How Israel became a
Regional Superpower, 1947–1995

"The United States, as a matter of policy, has never been a major supplier of arms for Israel and doesn't intend to be, nor to any other country in the area."
President Dwight D. Eisenhower, 1960[1]

"We will [support Israel] by further reinforcing our commitment to maintaining Israel's qualitative military edge."
President Bill Clinton, 1993[2]

AMERICA'S POLICY ON PROVIDING WEAPONS to Israel and the Middle East will not be part of the final status talks. Yet, an understanding of that policy is necessary to grasp how the Middle East has become what it is today. Israel now occupies the position of the superpower of the Middle East solely because of changing U.S. arms policy. Its military strength is supreme and without parallel in the Arab world.

It is this foundation of massive military power that gives Israel a decided advantage as the master of the region. Israel's dominance is an ever-present and brooding factor that influences every subject of the talks. How U.S. policy allowed this growth of Israeli military power is thus a significant component to the negotiations, and of considerable importance in understanding the current Middle East.

* *

America's original policy on arms was to embargo sales to both Arabs and Jews. A "rigorous" embargo went into effect on 14 November 1947, although many weapons, including airplanes, illegally were smuggled by American supporters to the emergent Israeli state.[3] The embargo remained in place throughout the fighting of 1948 and beyond, despite considerable pressure from Israel's supporters to sell weapons to the Jewish state. A plank in the 1948 Democratic Party platform favored "revision of the arms embargo to accord the State of Israel the right of self-defense" but failed to move Washington.[4] Reinforcing the embargo were two calls by the United Nations on 29 May and 15 July 1948 for all nations to refrain from shipping arms to the region.[5]

The steadfastness of the Truman Administration on the arms issue had less to do with the Arab-Israeli conflict than the Soviet Union. The Cold War had dawned and become Washington's major concern. Keeping the Russian bear out of the Middle East was one of Washington's strategic concerns. Soviet communism was on the move in 1948. Communists had just seized the government of Czechoslovakia. Scandinavia seemed imperiled. Moscow had "invited" Finland to sign a mutual assistance pact and Norway feared it was about to receive a similar "invitation." Four-power rule in Germany was at the point of disintegration, the final collapse of the wartime alliance between East and West. Elections were approaching in Italy, where it was feared the communists might win. Communist guerrillas were threatening the government in Greece. In Asia, Chiang Kai-shek's China was besieged by communist troops and near collapse. Korea was divided with communist forces firmly in control of the north. A National Security Council study observed: "Today Stalin has come close to achieving what Hitler attempted in vain. The Soviet world extends from the Elbe River and the Adriatic on the west to Manchuria on the east, and embraces one fifth of the land surface of the world."[6]

Before the Palestine problem grew acute after the end of World War II, the Middle East had been "virtually clean" of Soviet influence, in the words of one British general.[7] But since 1945 Soviet influence had made some modest gains in Israel because of Moscow's support of partition, its quick recognition of the Jewish state as a fellow socialist country, its decision to allow Soviet Jews to emigrate to Israel and its secret supply to Israel of weapons via Czechoslovakia.[8] A mid-1948 report to Secretary of State George C. Marshall from Ambassador to the United Nations Philip C. Jessup observed:

> [I]t is not apparent that communism has any substantial following among the [Arab] masses. On the other hand, there are apparently a substantial number of Communists in the Irgun, the Stern Gang and other dissident [Jewish] groups. Beyond that, the Soviet Union, through its support of partition and prompt recognition of Israel, must be considered as having a substantial influence with the PGI [Provisional Government of Israel]. The communist influence is, of course, capable of substantial expansion through whatever diplomatic and other missions the Soviet Government may establish in Israel.[9]

At the time, it was not clear whether Israel, with its population mainly from Eastern Europe, would align itself with Moscow or Washington. Indeed, the Israelis themselves were not sure. Both superpowers had resources Israel needed. The Soviet Union had the people in terms of a large Jewish minority and the weapons Israel wanted. In the first three years after World War II the Soviet Union had allowed 200,000 Jews who had fled eastward for safety in the Soviet Union to emigrate to the West and Palestine while Czechoslovakia provided Israel with all the Messerschmitts and Spitfires that formed its new air force, as well as other weapons.[10] The United States had the money. Israel's total exports in 1949 were only $40 million whereas contributions from generous Jewish Americans accounted for $100 million.[11]

Israel's solution was to adopt a policy called *ee-hizdahut*, "non-identification."[12] *New York Times* correspondent Anne O'Hare McCormick reported from Jerusalem in early 1949 that "It is true that Israel cherishes the ideal of remaining 'neutral' between the United States and the Soviet Union, constantly referred to as 'our two powerful friends,' but there is no evidence whatever of any strong leaning toward communism."[13] Israeli Foreign Minister Moshe Sharett explained that "Israel will in no case become identified with one of the great blocs of the world as against the other."[14]

In forming his first government, which was confirmed by the Knesset on 10 March 1949, Prime Minister David Ben Gurion vowed to pursue "a foreign policy aimed at achieving friendship and cooperation with the United States and the Soviet Union."[15] However, he also noted that the Soviet Union was a "great and growing world power, controlling a number of states not hostile to us....and in it and its satellites lives the second part of the Jewish people."[16] In 1950 Ben Gurion said:

> Our security is entirely dependent on immigration. We cannot give up so easily on hundreds of thousands of Jews. There is still immigration from Poland, Czechoslovakia, Bulgaria. If there is any chance of bringing Jews from the East, and especially from Romania, we must not abandon them.[17]

The policy of neutrality lasted until the early 1950s, when Israel sided with the United States in Korea and began to look to Washington as a possible source of arms.[18] By then, however, the United States had joined with Britain and France in an official declaration against arms sales to the region. On 5 May 1950, the three countries issued the Tripartite Declaration expressing "their opposition to the development of an arms race between the Arab states and Israel." The three countries said they would use the Declaration's principles to consider any arms requests and they would sell arms only to Middle Eastern countries that certified they intended no act of aggression.[19]

Despite such high sentiments, France soon secretly broke the treaty. Seeing Israel as a natural ally against Arab nationalists opposing its claim to Algeria, Paris in the early 1950s began making covert arms sales to Israel. By the beginning of 1955, shortly after the Algerian rebellion erupted into open warfare, the sales increased to include such major items as jet warplanes, battle tanks and heavy artillery.[20]

Israel's strength led it into a more aggressive policy against its Arab neighbors, particularly Egypt. On 28 February 1955, it launched a heavy raid in the Gaza Strip against an Egyptian military outpost. Thirty-six Egyptian soldiers and two civilians were killed, making it the largest incident between Egypt and Israel since the 1948 war. The death toll sent such a shock through Egypt that Gamal Abdul Nasser, the young colonel who had taken power in 1952, began a desperate search for arms. The incident started the region on the path to war, which erupted in 1956.[21]

With America, Britain and France officially pledged to an arms embargo and other European nations refusing to deal with Egypt, Nasser had only one source. On 27 September 1955, he announced to a stunned world that Czechoslovakia had agreed to provide Egypt with all the major weapons systems that France already was providing Israel, including bombers, jet warplanes, tanks and artillery. Instantly, Nasser became a hero throughout the Arab world—and so too did the Soviet Union, the nation everybody knew was behind the deal.

The sudden success of the Soviet Union caused Secretary of State John Foster Dulles to complain that

> we are in the present jam because the past Administration had always dealt with the area from a political standpoint and had tried to meet the wishes of the Zionists in this country and that had created a basic antagonism with the Arabs. That was what the Russians were now capitalizing on.[22]

Despite nearly a decade of effort by Washington and London to keep Moscow out of the region, the Czech arms deal marked the Soviet Union's emergence as a full-blown major player in the Middle East. Henceforth, Cold War rivalry would pit Washington and Moscow on opposite sides, confusing what at heart remained the Palestinian-Israeli conflict with what increasingly became to be perceived as the Arab-Israeli conflict within a Cold War context. For Israel, the arms deal marked the moment it decided to provoke a war with Egypt, which it successfully did the next year in secret collusion with Britain and France.[23] For the region, it made a Cold War-motivated arms race inevitable.

* *

With Israel secretly receiving weapons from France, the United States continued over the next seven years its embargo on arms sales. As late as 17 February 1960, President Dwight D. Eisenhower declared that the United States had no intention of becoming a major arms supplier to the Middle East, saying: "The United States, as a matter of policy, has never been a major supplier of arms for Israel and doesn't intend to be, nor to any other country in the area."[24] However, only two years later President John F. Kennedy breached this traditional policy. On 26 September 1962 the State Department announced the sale of an unspecified number of Hawk antiaircraft missiles to Israel. Considerable emphasis was placed on the fact that these were defensive weapons.[25] As usual, any such presidential decision had a major political dimension, and the president and his aides went out of their way to curry favor in the Jewish American community by privately notifying some Jewish leaders before making the public announcement.[26]

Kennedy's breaking of the arms embargo was Israel's greatest achievement in its relations with the United States up to that time. There could be little doubt that the dam, once breached, would unleash more weapons. Indeed, before the decade was out Israel had received the latest in American warplanes and other offensive weapons. From the early 1960s on, Israel with increasing success sought to define the conflict in Cold War terms: Israel and the United States against the Arabs and the Soviet Union, even though there was almost no sympathy for Communism in the Arab world. Egyptian Foreign Minister Mahmoud Riad observed: "With the total alignment of the U.S. to Israel we were left no other choice but to turn totally to the Soviet Union."[27]

Parallel with its quest for American weapons, Israel pursued in secret a program to obtain a nuclear arsenal. This effort did not go undetected in Washington. In late 1960, an American U-2 spy plane established that Dimona was a 24,000-kilowatt nuclear facility, despite Israeli claims at first that it was a textile plant. When confronted with the evidence, Israel vowed that Dimona was dedicated to peaceful research and that no weapons would be produced there. Publicly, Washington accepted that position. But informed American officials strongly suspected Israel was embarked on a major nuclear weapons program. In a secret session at the beginning of 1961 of the Senate Foreign Relations Committee, Senator Bourke Hickenlooper said:

> I think the Israelis have just lied to us like horse thieves on this thing. They have completely distorted, misrepresented, and falsified the facts in the past. I think it is very serious, for things that we have done for them to have them perform in this manner in connection with this very definite production reactor facility [meaning it was specifically designed to produce plutonium] which they have been secretly building, and which they have consistently, and with a completely straight face, denied to us they were building.[28]

It was in part an effort to smoke out Israel's nuclear intentions that caused Kennedy to lift the embargo on conventional weapons. The month before the Hawk missile announcement, Kennedy had sent Myer Feldman, the White House liaison with the Jewish community, to Israel to dangle the Hawk missiles as bait for getting Israel's cooperation on two items: a secret peace proposal then being pursued known as the Johnson Plan and Washington's concern about Israel's nuclear intentions.[29] In return for American weapons, Israel reluctantly agreed to allow American scientists limited inspection of Dimona, the installation in the Negev Desert suspected of housing a bomb facility.[30]

American scientists were allowed closely supervised inspections between 1962 and 1969, but the visits were halted when the scientists reported they were so constrained by Israeli authorities that they could not certify there were no bombs being made at Dimona. In fact, reported journalist Seymour Hersh, the Israelis had built a false control room in Dimona to mislead the inspectors.[31]

In reality, the Kennedy Administration's strategy was flawed by a certain naivete. As John Hadden, the former head of the Tel Aviv CIA station, observed:

"The Israelis were way ahead of us. They saw that if we were going to offer them arms to go easy on the bomb, once they had it we were going to send them a lot more, for fear that they would use it."[32] The diplomatic parallel to this was related by Henry Kissinger a decade later: "I ask [Prime Minister Yitzhak] Rabin to make concessions, and he says he can't because Israel is too weak. So I give him arms, and he says he doesn't need to make concessions because Israel is strong."[33]

* *

Israel's efforts to attain a nuclear capability were as old as the state. In 1948, the year Israel was founded, the Defense Ministry set up the Research and Planning Branch to explore uranium resources in the Negev Desert. In 1952, Israel established its Atomic Energy Commission under the Israeli Defense Ministry. The next year it signed a nuclear cooperation agreement with France covering heavy water and uranium production. Although the details were secret the agreement was believed to have provided Israel with a large (24-megawatt) reactor capable of producing one or two bombs' worth of plutonium a year in the form of spent fuel. Construction of the reactor at Dimona began in the late 1950s.[34]

France also provided Israel with blueprints for a reprocessing plant for turning spent fuel into weapons' grade plutonium. It later withdrew its help in protest of Israel's launching of the 1967 war, as revealed by Charles de Gaulle. The French president wrote in his memoirs: "...French cooperation in the construction of a factory near Beersheva [Dimona] for the transformation of uranium into plutonium—from which, one fine day, atomic bombs might emerge—was brought to an end."[35]

By 1968, the CIA was convinced Israel had produced nuclear weapons, or was capable of doing so, and informed President Lyndon Johnson. His response was to order the CIA not to inform any other members of the administration, including Defense Secretary Robert McNamara and Secretary of State Dean Rusk.[36] As for Johnson, he made no known use at all of the information.

In September 1974, the CIA concluded in a secret five-page report that "We believe that Israel already has produced nuclear weapons." It said its conclusion was "based on Israeli acquisition of large quantities of uranium, partly by clandestine means." Other reasons cited by the report supporting belief of Israel's production of nuclear weapons included "the ambiguous nature of Israeli efforts in the field of uranium enrichment, and Israel's large investment in a costly missile system designed to accommodate nuclear warheads."[37]

In February 1976, an unnamed CIA official revealed at a rare CIA briefing that Israel had ten to twenty nuclear bombs "ready and available for use."[38] In 1980, the former head of France's Atomic Energy Commission, Francis Perrin, said: "We are sure the Israelis have nuclear bombs....They have sufficient facilities to produce one or two bombs a year."[39] On 5 October 1986, *The Sunday Times* of London, quoting a disaffected worker at Dimona, Mordechai Vanunu, reported that Israel had "at least 100 and as many as 200 nuclear weapons." It said Israel had been producing the weapons for twenty years and that it now was a leading nuclear power.

Israel's official position over the years has been expressed by a tantalizingly vague formulation: Israel will not be "the first to introduce nuclear weapons into the Middle East." But on 2 December 1974, Israeli President Ephraim Katzir, a biophysicist and former chief scientific adviser to the defense ministry, said: "It has always been our intention to develop the nuclear potential. We now have that potential."[40] Similar revealing remarks were echoed seven years later on 24 June 1981, by former defense and foreign minister Moshe Dayan who said:

> We don't have any atomic bomb now. But we have the capacity, we can do that in a short time. We are not going to be the first ones to introduce nuclear weapons into the Middle East, but we do have the capacity to produce nuclear weapons, and if the Arabs are willing to introduce nuclear weapons into the Middle East, then Israel should not be too late in having nuclear weapons too.[41]

Through all the twists and turns and revelations, the United States has posed as the champion of non-proliferation. Yet it has never taken any action against Israel, which has not signed the Non-Proliferation Treaty or accepted IAEA (International Atomic Energy Agency) safeguards.[42] Israel's refusal to sign the NPT became an acute problem in 1995 when the United States sought extension of the twenty-five-year-old treaty. Egypt and other Arab nations, which had signed the treaty, demanded that Israel join them.[43] Israel refused. Only heavy U.S. pressure on other nations finally won extension of the treaty.

One immediate result in the 1960s of Washington's failure to take any strong action against Israel's nuclear program was to provoke Arab mistrust and push Arab states into closer arms ties with the Soviet Union. Soviet aid to Egypt had already become so generous in the early part of the 1960s that there was criticism in the Eastern Bloc that communist nations were being shortchanged in order that Moscow could help a noncommunist nation that gave no shrift to domestic communists. There were even rumors that this generous policy toward Egypt may have contributed to Nikita Khrushchev's fall in 1964.[44]

Yet, Moscow's contributions to the Arabs continued to grow, and, after the 1967 war, reached enormous levels as the Soviet Union sent weapons to resupply its defeated clients in Egypt and Syria. Political scientist Alvin Z. Rubinstein concluded about Moscow's postwar resupply operation:

> The magnitude of the Soviet commitment was unprecedented, surpassing in both quantity and quality the aid given to North Vietnam and exceeding the rate at which aid had hitherto been given to allied or friendly countries....The military assistance programs tightened the political links between Moscow and Cairo; they strengthened the Nasser regime and gave Nasserite elements in the Arab world a new lease on life; they expanded the Soviet presence in Egypt and enhanced the USSR's status as a major Mediterranean power; and they raised the ante in open challenge to two decades of American domination.[45]

In return, the Soviet Union received more than just a symbolic presence in Egypt and the Middle East. The first postwar rewards came in January 1968 when Nasser formally granted the Soviet navy support facilities for maintenance, repair and provisioning of its ships at Mersa Matruh, Port Said and Alexandria on the Mediterranean.[46] Three months later Soviet Tu-16 reconnaissance aircraft were given permission to use Egyptian airport facilities at Cairo West so they could fly surveillance flights over the U.S. Sixth Fleet and Israel.[47]

Thus, Moscow finally regained, and increased, the infrastructure in the eastern Mediterranean it had been seeking since Albania denied it a naval base at Vlone in 1961.[48] With the Egyptian bases, Russia's naval strength in the region grew significantly. From 750 ship-days in 1963 the Soviet navy logged 1,624 ship days in just the first half of 1970.[49] The number of Soviet ships patrolling the Mediterranean following the 1967 war ranged between forty to seventy, hitting a high of seventy-one in September 1969, including 34 surface ships and 19 submarines.[50] By late 1969, a Soviet N-Class nuclear-powered submarine visited Alexandria, the first time such a vessel anchored in a foreign port. In addition, it was suspected that in 1970 Libya granted Moscow the right to use harbors at Tripoli and Tobruk, thus extending Soviet facilities to the west as well as the east of the Mediterranean.[51]

By 1970 the CIA and the Pentagon reported in separate studies:

> The Soviet Mediterranean Squadron is now sufficiently powerful in conventional as well as nuclear armament to threaten the Sixth Fleet and other NATO naval units. Submarines and surface ships armed with antiship cruise missiles are a significant threat to our surface ships— including aircraft carriers, and the torpedo attack submarines continue to pose a threat to allied naval forces. In fact, the Sixth Fleet is faced with the highest density of deployed Soviet submarines anywhere in the world.[52] ....the Soviets can hope to undermine the southern flank of NATO, erode American influence in the region, and create serious economic problems for West Europe—and for U.S. interests—by turning radical and possibly other Arab states against the West, the U.S. and its investments in Middle East oil.[53]

* *

The overlay of the Cold War on top of the local nature of the conflict completely distorted reality—to Israel's advantage. The distortion of the nature of the conflict justified sending massive amounts of military equipment to Israel. Not unexpectedly, Israeli leaders actively advocated the Cold War perception. For instance, Prime Minister Golda Meir forcefully argued this view in a 1970 meeting with Nixon in the White House. "Mrs. Meir said that Israel's problems were not caused primarily by the Arabs," Nixon noted in his memoirs. "They were the direct result of the Soviet presence and Soviet military equipment."[54]

The Cold War connection was embraced by Secretary of State Henry

Kissinger. He believed that tiny Israel could be an ally worthy of abundant economic and military aid as a result of the Black September civil war in Jordan between Palestinians and King Hussein's army in 1970. At one point in the tense struggle, Nixon and Kissinger sought an air strike by Israel against Syrian forces in northern Jordan.[55] Although Syrian withdrawal made the attack unnecessary, the incident was later claimed by Kissinger to show that Israel could be useful to the United States. According to Israeli Ambassador Yitzhak Rabin, Kissinger said:

> The President will never forget Israel's role in preventing the deterioration in Jordan and in blocking the attempt to overturn the regime there. He said that the United States is fortunate in having an ally like Israel in the Middle East. These events will be taken into account in all future developments.[56]

In fact, Kissinger's version is a distortion of the reality. From the start of the crisis to its end, Nixon and Kissinger treated the civil war in Jordan mainly as a confrontation with the Soviet Union, and at its end Kissinger even bragged that Russia had "backed off."[57] But what Moscow backed off from was not clear to critics. The Soviet Union never took a strong stance during the crisis.[58] At no time did Moscow issue public threats. Instead it exhibited a cautious attitude and confined itself to warning against outside intervention, which of course applied as much to the Arab countries as it did to Israel and the United States.[59]

Diplomat Talcott W. Seelye, a career foreign service officer who headed the State Department's special task force during the crisis, completely disagreed, as did others, with the Nixon-Kissinger assertion that the United States had somehow backed down the Soviet Union. "Moscow's involvement in fomenting the crisis did not exist to the best of our knowledge," he said. "In fact, we had reliable intelligence reports indicating that the Soviets sought to restrain Syria—which conceivably might have contributed to Assad's decision to withhold his air force from helping the invading tanks." Seelye added: "The White House contention that we stood the Soviets down is pure nonsense."[60]

Nonetheless, from this time onward Israel increasingly was seen as a U.S. ally worthy of massive support. The first evidence of the magnitude of America's appreciation came three months later, on 22 December, when Washington signed a far-reaching Master Defense Development Data Exchange Agreement that provided for the greatest transfer of technology to Israel ever undertaken to that time.[61] The United States agreed to give advanced technology to Israel so it could produce American weapons at home, meaning Israel would have formalized access to American technology.[62] Transfer of the technology was provided by the release of what was known as technical data packages, the entire complex of blueprints, plans and types of materials required actually to construct new weapons. More than 120 such packages were given to Israel over the next eight years.[63]

Nixon also pledged an additional twelve F-4s and twenty A-4s for delivery in the first half of 1971.[64] These new warplanes were part of a large package of supplemental new support totalling $500 million for Israel that officially was approved on 11 January 1971. It allowed the purchase by Israel of a vast array of heavy weapons, including M-60 tanks, 105mm gun tanks, M-109 self-propelled 155mm howitzers, M-107 self-propelled 175mm guns, M-113 armored personnel carriers, Ch-53 Sikorsky helicopters and Hawk surface-to-air missiles.[65] This aid came on top of a special $90 million grant provided in October.[66]

The extraordinary aid package signalled the emergence of the new and close relationship that was now well underway between the two countries. It also helped lull Israel into believing that it was now so strong that it had no need to negotiate with its Arab neighbors who were demanding return of their land captured in 1967. This feeling of false security was shared by Kissinger. He supported Israel's intransigence, arguing in Cold War terms that it proved to the Arabs that the door to a deal was through Washington and not Moscow: "...our objectives were served if the status quo was maintained until either the Soviets modified their stand or moderate Arab states turned to us for a solution based on progress through attainable stages."[67]

The problem with this strategy was that it underestimated Egyptian and Syrian determination to regain their land. Egyptian President Anwar Sadat warned with increasing shrillness through 1971, 1972 and on into 1973 that war would come if Israel did not return Egypt's Sinai Peninsula and Syria's Golan Heights. But Kissinger and the Israelis dismissed him as a clown, as did the U.S. media.[68] Kissinger, along with such high administration officials as Treasury Secretary George P. Shultz, also discounted unusual rumbles that began emerging from Saudi Arabia in the spring of 1973. The word was that the Arabs would impose an oil boycott if Washington failed to become more evenhanded in its Middle East policy.[69]

These were strategic errors and they contributed directly to the war that broke out on 6 October 1973 with coordinated attacks by Egypt and Syria against Israeli troops stationed on occupied territory. No fighting actually took place on Israeli territory, but the shock of the attacks often made it seem in the U.S. media that Israel itself was under siege. Demands instantly arose for a massive supply effort by the United States to Israel. President Nixon at the time already was deeply involved in the spreading Watergate scandal and much of the pressure from the Israeli lobby focused on Kissinger.

By 12 October, Israeli Ambassador Simcha Dinitz bluntly warned Kissinger that "if a massive American airlift to Israel does not start immediately then I'll know that the United States is reneging on its promises and its policy, and we will have to draw very serious conclusions from all this." Kissinger's biographers, Bernard and Marvin Kalb, observed of this remark: "Dinitz did not have to translate his message. Kissinger quickly understood that the Israelis would soon 'go public' and that an upsurge of pro-Israeli sentiment could have a disastrous impact upon an already weakened administration."[70]

That same day, U.S. oilmen sent a joint memorandum to President Nixon expressing their alarm at the dangerous possibility of steep oil production cuts and price rises if the U.S. continued its protective policies toward Israel.[71] Nonetheless, Nixon and Kissinger ignored the warning and openly launched a huge air operation to supply Israel on 13 October.[72] In retaliation, the Arab oil states began raising prices on 16 October. When a delegation of Arab foreign ministers met with Kissinger the next day to warn him about a boycott, he once again dismissed the threat.[73] That brought to Washington on 18 October a personal emissary from Saudi Arabia's King Faisal to deliver a clear message: unless Israel returned to the 1967 lines and the United States stopped its arms supply to Israel, an embargo would be placed on all oil shipments to the United States.[74] Despite this latest warning, Kissinger concluded that first a way must be found for Washington "to gain a little more time for Israel's offensive...." and he thus made no effort to appease the Arabs.[75]

Nixon, meanwhile, chose the very next day to appease Israel's clamoring supporters by requesting from Congress $2.2 billion in emergency aid for Israel, an act that infuriated the Arabs.[76] Saudi Arabia responded the next day by imposing a total oil boycott against the United States, an economic Jihad, in retaliation for its unlimited support of Israel. Abu Dhabi, Algeria, Bahrain, Kuwait and Qatar quickly followed suit, causing an economic earthquake that was felt around the world.[77]

The boycott struck a stupendous blow against the United States and the global economy, bringing about the greatest peaceful transfer of wealth in history and basic changes in the way people lived around the world. Kissinger estimated the direct costs to the United States were $3 billion and the indirect, mainly from higher prices of oil, $10 billion to $15 billion. He added: "It increased our unemployment and contributed to the deepest recession we have had in the post war period."[78]

This was a high price to pay for a country that was supposed to enhance U.S. interests. But an even graver event loomed before the fighting finally stopped. On 24 October, the possibility of a nuclear confrontation between the Soviet Union and the United States suddenly appeared. Kissinger on that day ordered a worldwide alert of all U.S. military forces, including nuclear units. It turned out Kissinger was mainly trying to frighten the Soviets, which he sufficiently did, into not taking too forceful actions against the Israelis, and the crisis quickly passed.[79]

On that note of terror the 1973 war ended. Israel retained its Arab territory occupied since 1967 and, paradoxically, relations between Israel and the United States were closer than ever. Even though the costs to the United States had been enormous and the war had been mainly one of retaining captured territory more than of national defense, Israel was now regarded in Washington as a firm Cold War ally. Together they had stood against the Arabs and the Soviets. Israel's Cold War credentials earned during Black September in 1970 were confirmed and enhanced.

Increasingly generous aid packages became routine in the years that followed. U.S. aid rose from $93.6 million in fiscal 1970 to $2,646.3 million in 1974. In another decade it settled at an annual $3 billion and continued at that level for more than a decade, all of it in grants that did not have to be repaid.[80] The $3 billion figure covered only the official economic and military aid granted Israel.

But far larger figures were involved, including special arrangements on loans, favorable depreciation allowances and such deals as giving Israel its funds early so that it could earn interest payments.

In 1992, Democratic Senator Robert C. Byrd of West Virginia detailed for the first time on the Senate floor the array of aid and special benefits Israel had received from the United States from 1949 to 1991. He said the total equalled $53 billion. Since the 1979 Egyptian-Israeli peace treaty, the amount totaled $40.1 billion. Byrd noted that "we have poured foreign aid into Israel for decades at rates and terms given to no other nation on earth....Beyond the massive economic and military aid, however, in our so-called strategic relations with Israel, we have served as a protector almost in the same sense as the Government of the United States would protect one of our 50 states." He then listed the varied special arrangements granted Israel:

> Additionally, items of assistance or special treatment that were contained in fiscal years 1991 and 1992 legislation are: Continued participation in the American Schools and Hospitals Grant Program, representing $2.7 million for 1991; $7 million for Arab-Israeli cooperative programs, of which approximately half is spent in Israel; $42 million for joint research and development on the Arrow antitactical ballistic missile follow-on program. This amount increased to $60 million in the fiscal year 1992 Defense Appropriations Act; also, authority to use up to $475 million of its military aid in Israel instead of spending it in the United States. Although the President has the authority to allow countries to engage in non-United States procurement in certain limited cases, Israel is the only country that receives specific legislative authority and a designated dollar amount for such procurement; moreover, priority over every other country, except Turkey, to receive excess defense articles; additionally a major new petroleum reserve of 4.5 million barrels, worth $180 million, which is available for Israel's use in the case of an emergency; furthermore, $15 million to improve military facilities at the Israeli port of Haifa in 1991 and another $2 million in 1992 to study the costs of further improving the facilities to allow for full-scale maintenance and support of an aircraft carrier battle group; in addition thereto, specific inclusion in the Overseas Workload Program, allowing Israel to bid on contracts for the repair, maintenance, or overhaul of United States equipment overseas; and additionally $1 million in investment insurance in Israel, provided by the Overseas Private Investment Corporation.
>
> Other, earlier legislative initiatives that provide continuing benefits to Israel include:
>
> Immediate transfer each year of the $1.2 billion Economic Support fund grant and the $1.89 billion military assistance grant. Thus, our grants to Israel are turned into interest bearing assets for Israel while our own budget deficit is increased, resulting in higher interest charges to us. This immediate transfer created approximately $86 million in interest income for Israel in fiscal year 1991. Such an arrangement has

been in place for the Economic Support Fund since 1982 and was extended to military aid in fiscal year 1991 and applies to no other country; moreover, debt restructuring that took place in the late 1980s allowed Israel to lower interest payments by an estimated $150 million annually; additionally, the fair pricing initiative within the Foreign Military Sales Program that allows Israel to avoid certain administrative fees normally charged on foreign military sales. This benefit saved Israel an estimated $60 million in 1991....

Since 1984, Israel has been allowed to use a portion of its foreign military financing credits for procurement of Israeli-made military items. Unlike other countries that receive United States military assistance, Israel does not have to spend all of those funds to purchase United States equipment. In 1991, of a $1.8 billion military assistance grant, we allowed Israel to use $475 million to buy the output of its own defense industry instead of American-made products. Moreover, Israel was allowed to spend an additional $150 million of the 1991 grant for its own research and development in the United States. We also have provided $126 million in funding for the development of the Arrow antimissile defense system in Israel, with another $60 million appropriated for the Arrow follow-on in fiscal year 1992, and the prospect of several hundred million more dollars in the future....[81]

* *

It was during the Reagan Administration that the informal relationship between the United States and Israel turned into a formal alliance. Secretary of State Alexander M. Haig believed against the evidence of a quarter-century that America could form an alliance of Israelis and Arabs aimed at opposing communism in the region. As he explained to the House Foreign Affairs Committee on 18 March 1981, shortly before his first official trip to the area:

> We feel it is fundamentally important to begin to develop a consensus of strategic concerns throughout the region among Arab and Jew and to be sure that the overriding dangers of Soviet inroads into this area are not overlooked.[82]

While in the Middle East Haig discovered, like John Foster Dulles nearly three decades earlier, that the Arabs had no interest in cooperating with Israel in a "strategic consensus" against the Soviet Union. Although they did not like the Soviet Union, they feared and disliked Israel more. Thus spurned, Haig turned totally to Israel as America's ally. At his urgings, the United States on 30 November 1981, signed the historic Memorandum of Understanding on Strategic Cooperation with Israel.[83] Israeli Defense Minister Ariel Sharon hailed the agreement as "quite important" because "it tightened bilateral security ties and recognized in formal language the mutually important nature of the relationship."[84]

Such partisanship towards Israel caused the United States difficulties not only with the Arab world in general but in its policy toward friendly and vital countries like Saudi Arabia as well. In the midst of the negotiations on the strategic alliance, the Reagan Administration found itself embroiled in a fierce struggle with Israel's supporters on arms sales to Saudi Arabia, including five AWACS (airborne warning and control system airplanes). AIPAC, the American Israel Public Affairs Committee, waged what was later called "among the most intense [lobby efforts] ever experienced by Congress."[85] The campaign became so intense that on 1 October President Reagan, in an unusual public criticism of Israel, complained at a press conference that "it is not the business of other countries to make American foreign policy."[86]

Nonetheless, the House voted 301 to 111 against the sale on 14 October and it was only heavy pressure from Reagan that finally got the sale through the Senate on 28 October with a vote of 48 to 52.[87] While the administration won the battle, Israel and the American Jewish lobby had made a potent point: if the administration bucked Israel's wishes, it would have to pay dearly in time, effort and, ultimately, political prestige. For legislators, its message was grim. As Professor Cheryl A. Rubenberg noted:

> ...thereafter how a senator voted on this issue became the most important factor in the [Jewish] lobby's determination of an individual's 'friendship' toward Israel. Those who were labeled 'unfriendly' faced serious problems at reelection.[88]

Reagan understood this message well. He vowed on 22 February 1982 that his administration would maintain Israel's "qualitative edge" over the military power of all other countries in the Middle East.[89] The commitment was repeated in the Republican Party national platform adopted on 21 August 1984 and in every GOP platform since. Democratic President Bill Clinton repeated the pledge shortly after coming to power in 1993.[90]

In late 1983 Reagan took another step to strengthen even more America's ties with Israel. On 29 October Reagan signed top secret National Security Decision Directive 111, which redefined U.S. goals in the Middle East and reaffirmed strategic cooperation with Israel against Soviet moves in the region. The policy was opposed by Defense Secretary Caspar Weinberger and the Central Intelligence Agency, but it had the strong backing of Secretary of State Shultz. Weinberger warned against neglecting friendly ties with Arab states and of allowing the United States to become a "hostage of Israeli policy," a concern that some critics remembered in 1986 when the Iran/Contra scandal was revealed.[91] In return for its cooperation, Israel was pledged massive aid and intimate access to American national security officials.[92]

Later in 1983, the Reagan Administration turned all military aid to Israel and Egypt into non-repayable grants instead of loans. Israel as America's largest recipient of U.S. arms aid was the biggest gainer with $1.4 billion slated for the next fiscal year followed by Egypt with $1.1 billion.[93] (In fiscal 1985, Congress turned all economic aid as well into grants.[94] Since that time neither Israel nor

Egypt has had to repay any U.S. aid.)

These massive benefits for Israel did not gain for Reagan the freedom he sought in dealing with the Arabs. In 1984, Reagan again sought to sell weapons to Saudi Arabia, as well as Jordan, and appealed directly to the Jewish community by going before the Young Leadership Conference of the United Jewish Appeal:

> First, we must deter the Soviet threat....Second, we must prevent a widening of the conflict in the Persian Gulf....Third, we seek to go on promoting peace between Israel and her Arab neighbors....Since the security of Jordan is critical to the security of the entire region, it is in America's strategic interest—and I believe in Israel's strategic inter-est—for us to help meet Jordan's legitimate needs for defense against the growing power of Syria and Iran.[95]

Congressional opposition to the sales, spurred on by AIPAC, was so strong, however, that the administration decided on 20 March to drop its request. In re-turn, it worked out a deal with AIPAC: the lobby would encourage Congress to drop pending bills ordering the move of the U.S. embassy from Tel Aviv to Jerusa-lem.[96]

* *

Reagan's failure to sell weapons to the Arabs in 1984 contained a signifi-cant message: The U.S.-Israeli relationship had been turned totally upside down. The trajectory went from 1947 when Washington refused to sell weapons to Israel to 1984 when Israel was able to prevent U.S. sales to the Arabs. This bizarre occur-rence affected negatively America's strategic interests. It also had a considerable impact on its economy. A dramatic example came in 1985 when Saudi Arabia turned to Britain to purchase warplanes instead of the United States in order to escape congressional interference. The cash deal was worth at least $7 billion— some observers estimated nearly three times that amount—making it the largest arms sale in history.[97] Loss of the sale was a major blow to U.S. workers and industry. The Chamber of Commerce conservatively estimated that every $1 bil-lion deal lost to foreign countries equaled the loss of at least 20,000 American jobs.

Israel used its influence not only to deny weapons to the Arabs but to gain more military equipment for itself. Thus, in 1990 the Bush Administration was forced by Congress to reduce a pending arms deal with Saudi Arabia worth $21 billion in cash down to $7.3 billion. At the same time AIPAC negotiated with the administration major new U.S. non-repayable grants to Israel worth around $1 billion in exchange for dropping its opposition to the pared-down Saudi package.[98]

The upward trend of U.S. transfers of its treasury and technology to Israel accelerated under President Clinton. He promised Israeli Prime Minister Yitzhak Rabin at the White House on 21 November 1994 continued high levels of military and economic aid and enhanced technological support. A major new item offered was the sale of two supercomputers, a request that had been denied since 1987 because the computers can be used in the development of hydrogen bombs and advanced missiles. Clinton also agreed to continue financing Israel's Arrow anti-missile missile program "in principle" for several more years.[99]

Total costs of the Arrow by 1994 had been around $500 million, with the United States paying $483 million and donating a wealth of free technology. The United States long had suspected Israel was selling such advanced technology illegally to third countries, thus denying profits and jobs to Americans.[100] Israel denied the allegations. Nevertheless, suspicions lingered among some U.S. officials about Israel's handling of secret U.S. technology.[101]

Obviously, the U.S. supply of weapons to Israel had become an extremely complex and sensitive issue, fraught with consequences of potentially significant detriment to the interests of both countries. But, as of 1995, the only changes in sight were an increasingly generous supply of U.S. aid, technology and weapons to Israel. President Clinton was publicly committed to strengthening the Jewish state into the undefined future, leaving American interests subject to an uncertain fate.

9 | CONCLUSION

"A passionate attachment of one nation for another produces a variety of evils."
President George Washington, 1796[1]

"I think it's important for everyone to understand that the United States regards its friendship and the strength of its relationship with Israel as key and unshakable."
Secretary of State George P. Shultz, 1988[2]

AMERICA'S UNIQUELY CLOSE RELATIONSHIP with Israel has caused unintended strains and contradictions in U.S. foreign policy. At times, it has confused friends and aided enemies, distorted U.S. goals, and left Americans unsure about their own country's policies.

There have always been unanticipated consequences of the passionate attachment between the two countries. Washington's toleration of Israel's nuclear arsenal is an example. While an argument might be made that Israel deserves to belong to the Nuclear Club, the United States has never tried making a case for it in public. Instead, its quiet toleration has cast doubt on the sincerity of the U.S. approach to the whole issue of global non-proliferation. The underlying contradiction in Washington's position was vividly demonstrated in 1981 by two legislators, Democratic Representatives Stephen J. Solarz and Jonathan B. Bingham, both of New York. After being privately briefed by Under Secretary of State James L. Buckley and others on 8 December 1981, they dropped an amendment to ban U.S. aid to countries manufacturing nuclear weapons, admitting they were afraid it would affect Israel. Solarz explained:

> We didn't want to find ourselves in a position where we had inadvertently and gratuitously created a situation that might lead to a cutoff of aid for Israel. They left us with the impression that such a requirement might well trigger a finding by the administration that Israel has manufactured a bomb.[3]

Such confessions of favoritism do not go unnoticed in the rest of the world, nor do they enhance America's image as a country whose foreign policy is based on the historic ideals it professes.

The contradictions are even starker at the United Nations. There the United States arguably damaged the effectiveness of the world institution by its uncritical support of Israel. In this pursuit the United States abstained or voted against resolutions expressing some of its most cherished policies such as self-determination and inalienable human rights, and against the spirit of such international covenants as the UN Charter and the Fourth Geneva Convention. In its pursuit to shield Israel, the United States cast its veto twenty-nine separate times in the Security Council between 1972 and 1990, an unprecedented exercise of its veto power. The irony was that the United States was tolerating Israel's evolving apartheid policies against the Palestinians while at the same time United Nations pressure, with the support of the United States, was successfully achieving the dismantling of apartheid in South Africa. This bias brought contempt from other nations who were not slow to recognize the distance between Washington's words and its acts when it came to Israel.

Such contradictions between official U.S. policy and its practices toward Israel were especially evident in Washington's consistent refusal to apply the kind of pressure it possessed to temper Israel's harsh occupation policies against the Palestinians, or to halt Israel's establishment of settlements in violation of the Geneva Convention or terminate Israel's military occupation of Arab land. To America's enemies, and some of its friends as well, the United States was not only guilty of condoning Israel's expansion and occupation but of directly sharing in its transgressions against the Palestinians by its generous awards of aid that helped finance internationally condemned practices.

The costs of supporting Israel have not stopped with violations of America's own ideals. They have extended to trespassing America's own direct interests. A dramatic example was the 1973 war. No fighting took place in Israel itself and the Jewish state fought mainly to retain the Arab territory it occupied in violation of the UN Charter and America's own policy against acquiring territory by force. However, that did not stop Washington from giving Israel unprecedented diplomatic and financial aid. The result was the United States, and the rest of the world, suffered the consequences of a disastrous oil boycott and, briefly, the terrors of what appeared to be a nuclear confrontation with the Soviet Union.

A similar dire cost accrued to the United States in Lebanon after Israel's invasion of 1982. Because America was perceived as Israel's ally, Shia Muslim guerrillas launched deadly attacks against the U.S. embassy in Beirut and Marines stationed at Beirut International Airport, claiming nearly 300 American lives in 1983 alone. The Muslim guerrillas then launched a kidnapping and terror campaign aimed at driving all Americans out of the land where they had friendly relations and prospered for a century, a campaign that was essentially completed in 1988 when nearly all Americans were gone. Even as late as 1995 Americans were still prohibited from traveling to Lebanon.

Economically, Israel has been the most expensive ally the United States has ever had. From 1949 through 1995, Israel has received more than $65 billion, about 13 percent of all U.S. economic and military aid given during that period. Since the 1979 Egyptian-Israeli peace treaty, the amount totaled $40.1 billion, equal to 21.5 percent of all U.S. aid, including all multilateral as well as all bilateral aid.[5] From 1985 onward, all the money has been in outright grants that do not have to be repaid. These figures do not include a variety of special arrangements routinely granted Israel, including large transfers of surplus military equipment, subsidies for Israel's foreign aid program, early lump-sum payments of aid and refinancing of its debt.[6] By contrast, the much heralded U.S. Marshall Plan to rebuild Western Europe after World War II cost some $12 billion.[7]

The economic costs of supporting Israel have not been confined to direct aid. Israeli opposition to the sale of U.S. weapons to Saudi Arabia and some other Arab states denied American workers and industry lucrative contracts, as the loss of the $7 billion warplane deal with Saudi Arabia in 1985 proved.[8] Moreover, Israel had not been hesitant in profiting from its access to advanced U.S. technology by learning from it—and perhaps even pirating it—and thus becoming a major exporter of high-tech weapons in direct competition with U.S. firms.[9]

Obviously, such costs strongly suggest that current U.S. policy needs major adjustment.

* *

With the Cold War over and Israelis and Arabs undergoing basic changes in their relationships, it is an appropriate time for the United States to take a new look at its policies.

Israel at this point in its history is in a position to begin paying its debt to the past. It can do this without jeopardizing its security or its growing economy. Israel is now the region's superpower. It is the strongest nation, economically and militarily, among its immediate neighbors.

Moreover, for the first time it is poised to become an accepted member of the Middle East, as it has already become an acknowledged member of the world community. It is no longer a pariah among nations. Its enemies are now its friends, or they are weak and in disarray, like Iraq. Israel faces no serious threat to its security. As of 1995, Israel had formal diplomatic relations with nearly 150 countries and its relations among Arab states were spreading.[10]

Along with international and Arab acceptance of the Jewish state has come prosperity. Israelis are now enjoying a lifestyle far beyond that of many people of the world. Per capita income for Israelis reached $14,000 in 1994, placing Israel among the top ten nations.[11]

As Israeli journalist Sever Plutzker wrote in 1994: "Israel has never had it so good."[12] Resolving the compensation issue would add to the momentum of peace and give tangible proof to the Palestinians that peace has its rewards.

A first step could be to work for a solution of the refugee problem, or at least that element of it that admits to some kind of solution. The most obvious area to jump-start the process is to begin paying generous compensation to Palestinians for their property lost during nearly a half-century of Israeli conquest and confiscation. But for real peace to come much more will have to be done, especially in Washington. To convince Israeli extremists that the moderates have the right approach, Washington would have to take a strong stance on such remaining issues as boundaries, settlements and Jerusalem. They comprise the heart of the final status negotiations and must be resolved before peace can get a chance.

Yet at no time in the history of the conflict has the United States had an administration less likely to take the kind of tough positions that Israel's moderates need to make compromises than the administration of President Bill Clinton.

The Clinton Administration appears to have abandoned completely all previous policy pillars and is now involved in attempting to rewrite the past. There was in 1995 an active effort by Washington in the United Nations to soften or eliminate past resolutions that were critical of Israel or supportive of the Palestinians. The campaign is especially pertinent to final status negotiations because the targeted resolutions are those touching upon the issues that will be involved in those talks.[13]

These resolutions formed the legal framework of such basic Palestinian rights as self-determination, the right to struggle, the rights of refugees and even the right to be considered a separate people. Another group of resolutions under U.S. assault involved those critical of Israeli practices such as establishing settlements in the occupied territories, imposing communal punishment, claiming all of Jerusalem and violating the Fourth Geneva Convention.

The dimensions of how thoroughly the Clinton Administration wanted to rewrite the record were contained in a letter to UN members sent 8 August 1994 by U.S. Ambassador to the United Nations Madeleine K. Albright. Citing the diplomatic accords achieved between Israel and the Palestine Liberation Organization and Israel and Jordan during the previous ten months, Albright suggested that the General Assembly adapt itself to "today's realities" and "consolidate," "improve" and "eliminate" what she called "contentious resolutions that accentuate political differences without promoting solutions." Recommended for elimination was the landmark resolution of 1970 extending the right of self-determination to Palestinians. Albright added:

> We also believe that resolution language referring to "final status" issues should be dropped, since these issues are now under negotiation by the parties themselves. These include refugees, settlements, territorial sovereignty and the status of Jerusalem.[14]

These were the essence of the conflict. For the United Nations to soften or revoke these resolutions would amount to what Jordanian journalist Mahmoud Rimawi called "an attempted assault on the past and theft of the collective memory."[15] The Arab League, the Palestine Liberation Organization and Egypt announced they would oppose the U.S. campaign, but that did not deter Washington from pressing ahead.[16]

The ultimate aim of the Clinton Administration strategy was to eradicate the past and turn the Israel-Palestinian conflict into a strictly local affair. That would have been a fair approach prior to 1947. But when the United Nations directly imposed itself by favoring partition of Palestine, the Israeli-Palestinian conflict ceased to be a local matter and became an international burden. Yet, if Washington prevails it would mean that Israel would shed five decades of UN condemnation of its behavior while the Palestinians would lose their hard-gained legal framework within the international community affirming their rights and peoplehood.

It was not likely the Palestinians would accept such a thorough rewriting of history. They more likely would be forced by their own nationalists and Islamic fundamentalists to abandon the peace process or to boycott the final status talks, once again plunging the region into crisis.

Thus, as the peace process hesitantly unfolded in the last half of the last decade of the twentieth century, war and peace still remained in balance. Much depended on the final status negotiations. If they failed to take place no one could be optimistic that peace will out or that Israel will long remain secure.

APPENDIX I

*Memorandum by the Director of the Office of Near Eastern and African Affairs (Henderson)
to the Secretary of State, with two annexes, Washington, D.C., August 24, 1945.*

[WASHINGTON], AUGUST 24, 1945.

Mr. Secretary: I venture to bring to your attention the attached memoranda relating to the problem of Palestine which have been prepared in the Division of Near Eastern Affairs of the Department. This problem is likely to assume an acute form during the next few months and may be brought to your attention by the British during your stay in London. The strong internal and international reaction to the President's comments on the subject of Palestine during a recent press conference serves to give an indication of the delicacy and importance of this problem.

No solution of the Palestine problem can be found which would be completely satisfactory to both the Arabs and the Jews. Many plans for the future of Palestine have been advanced. Some are so impractical that they deserve no consideration whatsoever. The attached memoranda present a summary of four plans for the possible settlement of the Palestine question and a summary of observations upon them. The four plans are as follows:

1. Palestine: Status as a Jewish Commonwealth.
2. Palestine: An Independent Arab State.
3. Proposed Plan for the Partition of Palestine Under the Trusteeship System.
4. Proposed Trusteeship Agreement for Palestine.

We are aware that Palestine has become a problem in American internal politics as well as one in the field of foreign relations. The President and his political advisers are in a much better position than we to evaluate the domestic political factors involved and, therefore, we do not presume to give advice in this regard.

We feel, however, that we would be derelict in our responsibility if we should fail to inform you that in our considered opinion the active support by the Government of the United States of a policy favoring the setting up of a Jewish State in Palestine would be contrary to the policy which the United States has always followed of respecting the wishes of a large majority of the local inhabitants with respect to their form of government. Furthermore, it would have a strongly adverse effect upon American interests throughout the Near and Middle East. We believe it would be almost inevitable that the long-established American cultural, educational and religious institutions in the Near East would be placed in a difficult position and might be forced to suspend their activities; that American trade would probably be boycotted; that American economic interests, including our oil concessions in Saudi Arabia and in other Arab countries would be jeopardized. At the present time the United States has a moral prestige in the Near and Middle East unequaled by that of any

189

other great power. We would lost that prestige and would be likely for many years to be considered as a betrayer of the high principles which we ourselves have enunciated during the period of the war.

On the other hand, for the United States to support the recognition of Palestine as an independent Arab State would almost inevitably mean that we would be endeavoring to assist in setting up a regime which would fail to give to the large Jewish minority in Palestine the just an equitable treatment to which that minority is entitled. Encouraged by announcements made by governmental authorities and private persons and organizations in the United States and Great Britain during the last twenty-five years, tens of thousands of ardent Jewish nationalists have immigrated into Palestine and have been devoting their lives unselfishly, in the face of tremendous hardship and frequently of physical danger, to the task of laying an economic and political basis for a Jewish homeland. It is almost certain that these settlers would encounter difficulties from any Arab Government which might be set up in Palestine, regardless of the safeguards which we might endeavor to erect. Furthermore, as a result of past policies of this Government with regard to a Jewish National Home, a large amount of Jewish-American capital has been invested in Palestine, and it would possibly not be secure in an Arab State.

The proposed plan for partition under the trustee system also has serious defects. A technical Royal Commission sent to Palestine by the British Government in 1938[1] in order to attempt to devise a practical plan of partition found that there were almost unsurmountable obstacles to this kind of solution of the Palestine problem.

Plan No. 4 for the proposed trustee agreement for Palestine would not satisfy either the Arabs or the Zionists since it is in the nature of a compromise. Nevertheless, our present opinion is that some kind of a solution similar to this plan, which has been prepared by members of the Division of Near Eastern Affairs, in close cooperation with other interested Division of the Department, after months of research and study, would be preferable to the other plans suggested herein from an international point of view. Our support of a plan of this nature might subject us to considerable criticism among the more extreme Arab nationalists. It would not, however, stir such acute resentment as would be aroused by our support of the plan for the establishment of a Jewish State in Palestine. Similarly our support of such a compromise plan would give rise to protests on the part of the Zionist organizations in the United States and of some of their friends and political allies. We are inclined to believe, however, that the more moderate Arabs and Jews would be likely to regard the adoption of a plan of this character as being equitable a solution as any that could be found in the circumstances.

In our opinion it is important that Great Britain, the United States, the Soviet Union, and, if possible, France should endeavor to reach an agreement among themselves with regard to the future of Palestine and, after having done so, consult with the Jews and with the Arabs before putting their plan into effect. Otherwise, there is a danger that one or more of these great Powers might endeavor to pass on to the other Powers the responsibility for the decision made, with the result that both Arabs and Jews might have grounds to hope that with a sufficient amount of agitation of their part the decision could be reversed. Such a situation would almost inevitably lead to years of political instability in Palestine and in the Near East. Moreover, Palestine is a problem of world-wide importance and should in our judgment be dealt with by the five major Powers.

The detailed plans of which the enclosures are summaries are in the possession of the Division of Near Eastern Affairs. The Division has been studying and living with the difficult Palestine problem for many years and would be glad to make available to you or to anyone whom you might care to designate such information and specialized knowledge as it has been able to acquire.

LOY W. HENDERSON

[annex 1]

[Washington], August 24, 1945.

Four Proposed Plans for a Palestine Settlement

1.   NE has drafted four different plans for a settlement of the Palestine problem. These plans are based upon extensive research work done by members of NE and of the now defunct Division of Territorial Studies extending over a period of almost three years.

Two of these plans are designed to meet respectively the Zionists' demand for a Jewish State and the Arabs' demand for an Arab State. The third plan is based on partition, and the fourth is a compromise plan.

Each of the four plans is accompanied by observations in regard to the implications inherent in the implementation of each plan.

2.   *Plan No. One—Palestine: Status as a Jewish Commonwealth.*

This plan proposes that the Biltmore Program[2] of the Zionists be carried out by placing Palestine temporarily under the trusteeship system with Great Britain as the administering authority. The proposed trusteeship agreements set forth as the principal and special objective the creation of those conditions, including unrestricted Jewish immigration and land purchases, which will lead to the creation of a Jewish majority and the early recognition of Palestine as an independent, democratic Jewish commonwealth.

The plan provides for an interim trustee government with wide powers given to a Jewish agency in order to enable the government with the aid of a Jewish agency to undertake those economic and political measures which would lead to the creation of an independent Jewish commonwealth.

3.   *Plan No. Two—Palestine: An Independent Arab State.*

This plan proposes that the demands of the Arabs for an independent Arab Palestinian State be met after a transitional period under the present Mandatory Power. During the transitional period, the Arabs of Palestine shall draft a constitution for submission to the General Assembly by the United Nations. Provision is made for a Bill of Rights and adequate protection of the Jewish minority. Immigration would be controlled by the local government, but would based on the principle of economic need and economic absorptive capacity without discrimination on the basis of race, religion or nationality.

4.   *Plan No. Three—Proposed Plan for the Partition of Palestine Under the Trusteeship System.*

This plan proposes that Palestine be partitioned into three political entities each under trusteeship, with Great Britain as the administering authority for each of the three trusteeship territories. Trusteeship territory *A* would consist of an area including Haifa and Jerusalem, the undeveloped areas of the Jordan Valley and the Negeb, and such territory as would provide for the safeguarding of the sacred shrines and the protection of the main lines of communication. Trusteeship territory *B* would be a Jewish State, and Trusteeship territory *C* would be an Arab State. The Trusteeship Council would appoint a technical commission to decide upon the actual boundaries of the three trusteeship territories.

5.   *Plan No. Four—Proposed Trusteeship Agreement for Palestine.*
This plan proposes that Palestine as a Holy Land sacred to Christians, Jews and Moslems be given a special status as an international territory under the trusteeship system with Great Britain as the administering authority. It proposes that the Arabs and Jews of Palestine be recognized as national communities with the right to organize communal governments having jurisdiction over all those rural districts, villages, towns and cities where the Arabs and Jews respectively are in the majority, with the exception of Haifa, Jerusalem, the undeveloped areas of the Jordan Valley and the Negeb. It makes provision for future immigration without restrictions as to race, religion or nationality, for the regulation of land transfers on an equitable basis for both Arabs and Jews, and for the economic development of the undeveloped areas of the Jordan Valley and the Negeb.

[annex 2]

[Washington], August 24, 1945.

Observations on Four Proposed Plans for Palestine

1.   *Plan No. One—Palestine: Status as a Jewish Commonwealth.*
This plan, which would fulfill Zionist demands, would certainly provoke widespread discontent among all Arabs and Moslems, would result in civil war in Palestine and diplomatic if not armed intervention in more than one Arab State. This plan would be profoundly injurious to American cultural, religious and commercial interests in all the Arab and Moslem countries of the Near East, and it would probably result in the cancellation of the important American oil concession in Saudi Arabia. United States endorsement of this plan would be a serious blow to American prestige throughout the Near East.

On the other hand, this plan would fulfill the promises made to the Zionists in the relevant planks of the 1944 platforms of the Democratic and Republican parties and endorsed by the Presidential candidates of both parties. It would be applauded by the American Zionist organizations.

2.   *Plan No. Two—Palestine: An Independent Arab State.*
This plan, which would fulfill Arab demands, would certainly provoke widespread discontent among all Zionists and most Jews, would result in civil war in Palestine and diplomatic if not armed intervention by the Arab States. The probable armed resistance to this plan by Palestinian Jews would necessitate the maintenance of large armed forces in Palestine for a considerable period of time. The support of this plan by the United States would have very serious political repercussions in American domestic politics.

On the other hand, the Arabs throughout the Near East would be greatly pleased with this solution, and United States support of it would increase American influence and prestige in all Near Eastern countries.

3.   *Plan No. Three—Proposed Plan for the Partition of Palestine Under the Trusteeship System.*

This plan is based on the assumption that a unitary Palestine is not possible because of irreconcilable antagonisms between Arabs and Jews. The partition of Palestine would not meet the demands of either the Arabs or the Zionists. It is doubtful whether the Arabs would give their approval willingly to this settlement; there are, however, some indications that some of the Zionist leaders might assent to the partition of Palestine as the only way out of an impossible impasse.

If this settlement were imposed by the unanimous backing of the three great Powers, the United Kingdom, the Union of Socialist Soviet Republics and the United States, the Arab States might feel compelled to acquiesce without offering armed resistance. It would be likely to arouse widespread discontent in the Arab and Moslem worlds which would be somewhat unfavorable to American interests.

4.   *Plan No. Four—Proposed Trusteeship Agreement for Palestine.*

This plan is clearly a compromise solution which would meet with disapproval of both Arabs and Zionists. It presents some intricate problems of administration and will require international financial assistance in order to carry out economic development projects which are part of the general plan.

On the other hand, this plan would not be likely to provoke widespread discontent in Arab States resulting in violence and armed intervention, nor be likely to result in reprisals against the United States injurious to American interests. This plan would probably receive considerable support from non-Zionist Jewish groups who may be expected to look upon it as a reasonable compromise solution.

---

1. See British Cmd. 5854, (1938): *Palestine Partition Commission Report* (The Woodhead Report).

2. An "extraordinary Conference" of American Zionists, attended by such leaders of international Zionism as Dr. Chaim Weizmann and David Ben-Gurion, met at New York City's Biltmore Hotel in May 1942, and on May 11, 1942, formulated its views in a number of resolutions which became known as the Biltmore Program. The closing paragraph of the resolutions stated: "The Conference urges that the gates of Palestine be opened; that the Jewish Agency be vested with control of immigration into Palestine and with the necessary authority for upbuilding the country, including the development of its unoccupied and uncultivated lands; and that Palestine be established as a Jewish Commonwealth integrated in the structure of the new democratic world."

APPENDIX II

President Truman to the King of Saudi Arabia (Abdul Aziz Ibn Saud), US Urgent, NIACT, Washington, D.C., October 25, 1946.

US Urgent   NIACT   Washington, October 25, 1946.[1]

Your Majesty: I have just received the letter with regard to Palestine which Your Majesty was good enough to transmit to me through the Saudi Arabian Legation under date of October 15, 1946, and have given careful consideration to the views expressed therein.

I am particularly appreciative of the frank manner in which you expressed yourself in your letter. Your frankness is entirely in keeping with the friendly relations which have long existed between our two countries, and with the personal friendship between your Majesty and my distinguished predecessor; a friendship which I hope to retain and strengthen. It is precisely the cordial relations between our countries and Your Majesty's own friendly attitude which encourages me to invite your attention to some of the considerations which have prompted my Government to follow the course it has been pursuing with respect to the matter of Palestine and of the displaced Jews in Europe.

I feel certain that Your Majesty will readily agree that the tragic situation of the surviving victims of Nazi persecution in Europe presents a problem of such magnitude and poignancy that it cannot be ignored by people of good will or humanitarian instincts. This problem is worldwide. It seems to me that all of us have a common responsibility for working out a solution which would permit those unfortunates who must leave Europe to find new homes where they may dwell in peace and security.

Among the survivors in the displaced persons centers in Europe are numbers of Jews, whose plight is particularly tragic in as much as they represent the pitiful remnants of millions who were deliberately elected by the Nazi leaders for annihilation. Many of these persons look to Palestine as a haven where they hope among people of the own faith to find refuge, to begin to lead peaceful and useful lives, and to assist in the further development of the Jewish National Home.

The Government and people of the United States have given support to the concept of a Jewish National Home in Palestine ever since the termination of the first World War, which resulted in the freeing of a large area of the Near East, including Palestine, and the establishment of a number of independent states which are now members of the United Nations. The United States, which contributed its blood and resources to the winning of that war, could not divest itself of a certain responsibility for the manner in which the freed territories were disposed of, or for the fate of the peoples liberated at that time. It took the position, to which it still adheres, that these peoples should be prepared for self-government and also that a national home for the Jewish people should be established in Palestine. I am happy to note that most of the liberated peoples are now citizens of independent countries. The Jewish National Home, however, has not as yet been fully developed.

It is only natural, therefore, that my Government should favor at this time the entry into Palestine of considerable numbers of displaced Jews in Europe, not only that they may find shelter there, but also that they may contribute their talents and energies to the upbuilding of the Jewish National Home.

It was entirely in keeping with the traditional policies of this Government that over a year ago I began to correspond with the Prime Minister of Great Britain in an effort to expedite the solving of the urgent problem of the Jewish survivors in the displaced persons camps by the transfer of a substantial number of them to Palestine. It was my belief, to which I still adhere, and which is widely shared by the people of this country, that noting would contribute more effectively to the alleviation of the plight of these Jewish survivors than the authorization of the immediate entry of at least 100,000 of them to Palestine. No decision with respect to this proposal has been reached, but my Government is still hopeful that it may be possible to proceed along the lines which I outlined to the Prime Minister.

At the same time there should, of course, be a concerted effort to open the gates of other lands, including the United States, to those unfortunate persons, who are now entering upon their second winter of homelessness subsequent to the termination of hostilities. I, for my part, have made it known that I am prepared to ask the Congress of the United States, whose cooperation must be enlisted under our Constitution, for special legislation admitting to this country additional numbers of these persons, over and above the immigration quotas fixed by our laws. My Government, moreover, has been actively exploring, in conjunction with other governments, the possibilities of settlement in different countries outside Europe for those displaced persons who are obliged to emigrate from that continent. In this connection it has been most heartening to us to note the statements of various Arab leaders as to the willingness of their countries to share in this humanitarian project by taking a certain number of these persons into their own hands.

I sincerely believe that it will prove possible to arrive at a satisfactory settlement of the refugee problem along the lines which I have mentioned above.

With regard to the possibility envisaged by Your Majesty that force and violence may be used by Jews in aggressive schemes against the neighboring Arab countries, I can assure you that this Government stands opposed to aggression of any kind or to the employment of terrorism for political purposes. I may add, moreover, that I am convinced that responsible Jewish leaders do not contemplate a policy of aggression against Arab countries adjacent to Palestine.

I cannot agree with Your Majesty that my statement of Oct 4 is in any way inconsistent with the position taken in the statement issued on my behalf on Aug 16. In the latter statement the hope was expressed that as a result of the proposed conversations between the British Government and the Jewish and Arab representatives a fair solution of the problem of Palestine could be found and immediate steps could be taken to alleviate the situation of the displaced Jews in Europe. Unfortunately, these hopes have not been realized. The conversations between the British Government and the Arab representatives have, I understand, been adjourned until December without a solution having been found for the problem of Palestine or without any steps having been taken to alleviate the situation of the displaced Jews in Europe.

In this situation it seemed incumbent upon me to state as frankly as possible the urgency of the matter and my views both as to the direction in which a solution based on reason and good will might be reached and the immediate steps which should be taken. This I did in my statement of October 4.

I am at a loss to understand why Your Majesty seems to feel that this statement was in contradiction to previous promises or statements made by this Government. It may be well to recall here that in the past this Government, in outlining its attitude on Palestine has given assurances that it would not take any action which might prove hostile to the Arab people, and also that in its view there should be no decision with respect to the basic situation in Palestine without prior consultation with both Arabs and Jews.

I do not consider that my urging of the admittance of a considerable number of displaced Jews into Palestine or my statements with regard to the solution of the problem of Palestine in any sense represent an action hostile to the Arab people. My feelings with regard to the Arabs when I made these statements were, and are at the present time, of the most friendly character. I deplore any kind of conflict between Arabs and Jews, and am convinced that if both peoples approach the problems before them in a spirit of conciliation and moderation these problems can be solved to the lasting benefit of all concerned.

I furthermore do not feel that my statements in any way represent a failure on the part of this Government to live up to its assurance that in its view there should be no decision with respect to the basic situation in Palestine without consultation with both Arabs and Jews. During the current year there have been a number of consultations with both Arabs and Jews.

Mindful of the great interest which your country, as well as my own, has in the settlement of the various matters which I have set forth above, I take this opportunity to express my earnest hope that Your Majesty, who occupies a position of such eminence in the Arab world, will use the great influence which you possess to assist in the finding in the immediate future of a just and lasting solution. I am anxious to do all that I can to aid in the matter and I can assure Your Majesty that the Government and the people of the United States are continuing to be solicitous of the interests and welfare of the Arabs upon whose historic friendship they place great value.

I also take this occasion to convey to Your Majesty my warm personal greetings and my best wishes for the continued health and welfare of Your Majesty and your people.

Very sincerely yours,
HARRY S. TRUMAN

---

1. Sent to the Legation in Jidda as Department's telegram 266, with the instruction: "Please transmit urgently through appropriate channels following message from President to King in reply to King's message of Oct 15 on Palestine and confirm immediately by telegram receipt of message and hour of delivery. Message will be made public here in near future since King's letter was made public by Saudi Arabian Govt."

In telegram 322, October 28, 1946, from Jidda, the Minister reported that the President's message had been delivered to the King by the Legation's interpreter, Mohammed Effendi, presumably on the evening of October 26. According to the interpreter, the King was extremely vexed, observing that the President had expressed an obviously hostile point of view and that his communication was not based on logical grounds. The King stated further that the United States had nothing to do with the Palestine question, a matter which should be settled by the British, who had enticed American involvement in order to prejudice Saudi Arabian friendship with the United States. He concluded that if the United States desired to preserve its relations with the Arabs, it should give up its interest in the Palestine question.

APPENDIX III

The King of Saudi Arabia (Abdul Aziz Ibn Saud) to President Truman, Undated but received in Washington on November 2, 1946.[1]

[Translation]

Your Excellency:

I have received with deep appreciation, your message of October 25, 1946 which you sent to me through the American Legation.

I value Your Excellency's friendship and that of the American people to me personally, to my country and to the rest of the Arab countries. In appreciation of the humanitarian spirit which you have shown, I have not objected to any humanitarian assistance which Your Excellency or the United States may give to the displaced Jews, provided that such assistance is not designed to condemn a people living peacefully in their land. But the Zionist Jews have used this humanitarian appeal as an excuse for attaining their own ends of aggression against Palestine:—these aims being to conquer Palestine and by achieving a majority to make it Jewish, to establish a Jewish state in it, to expel it original inhabitants, to use Palestine as a base for aggression against the neighboring Arab states, and to fulfill (other aspects of) their aggressive programs.

The humanitarian and democratic principles on which the foundations of life in the United States have been built are incompatible with enforcement on a peaceful people, living securely in their country, of foreign elements to conquer and expel the native people from their country. In the attainment of their objectives these foreign elements have confused world opinion by appealing to the principles of humanity and mercy while at the same time resorting to force.

When the first World War was declared not more than 50,000 Jews lived in Palestine. The Arabs took up the fight on the side of Great Britain, its ally the United States and the other Allies. With the Allies, they fought in support of Arab rights and in support of the principles enunciated by President Wilson—particularly the right of self-determination. Nevertheless Great Britain adopted the Balfour Declaration and in its might embarked upon a policy of admitting Jews into Palestine, in spite of the desires of its preponderantly Arab population and in contradiction to all democratic and human principles. The Arabs protested and rebelled, but they were ever faced with a greater force than they could muster until they were obliged to acquiesce against their wishes.

When this last World War commenced the forces of the enemy were combined and directed against Great Britain. Great Britain stood alone and demonstrated a power and steadfastness which have won for her the admiration of the whole world. Her faith and courage did truly save the world from a grave danger. In those dark days the enemies of Great Britain promised the Arabs to do away with Zionism. Sensing the gravity of England's position at that time, I stood firm by her. I advised al the Arabs to remain quiet and assured them that Britain and her Allies would never betray those principles of humanity and democracy which they entered the war to uphold. The Arabs heeded my counsel and gave whatever assistance to Great Britain and her Allies they could, until victory was attained.

And now in the name of humanity it is proposed to force on the Arab majority of Palestine a people alien to them, to make these new people the majority, thereby rendering the existing majority a minority. Your Excellency will agree with me in the belief that no people on earth would willingly admit into their country a foreign group desiring to become a majority and to establish its rule over that country. And the United States itself will not permit the admission into the United States of that number of Jews which it has proposed for entry into Palestine, as such a measure would be contrary to its laws established for its protection and the safeguarding of its interests.

In you message, Your Excellency mentioned that the United States stands opposed to all forms of aggression or intimidation for the attainment of political objectives, if such measures have been applied by the Jews. You also expressed your conviction that responsible Jewish leaders do not contemplate the pursuit of an antagonistic policy toward the neighboring Arab states. In this connection I would call Your Excellency's attention to the fact that it was the british Government which made the Balfour Declaration, and transported the Jewish immigrants into Palestine under the protection of its bayonets. It was the British Government which gave and still gives shelter to their leaders and accords them its benevolent kindness and care. In spite of all this the British forces in Palestine are being seared by Zionist fire day and night, and the Jewish leaders have been unable to prevent these terroristic attacks. If, therefore, the British Government (the benefactor of the Jews) with all the means at its disposal is unable to prevent the terrorism of the Jews, how can the Arabs feel safe with or trust the Jews either now or in the future!

I believe that after reviewing all the facts Your Excellency will agree with me that the Arabs of Palestine, who form today the majority in their country, can never feel secure after the admission of the Jews into their midst nor can they feel assured about the future of the neighboring states.

Your Excellency also mentioned that you were unable to understand my feeling that your last declaration was inconsistent with previous promises and declarations made by the Government of the United States. Your Excellency also mentioned the assurances which I had received that the United States would not undertake any action modifying the basic situation in Palestine without consulting the two parties. I am confident that Your Excellency does neither intend to break a promise which you have made, nor desire to embark on an act of aggression against the Arabs. For these reasons I take the liberty to express to Your Excellency quite frankly that by an act which renders the Arab majority of Palestine a minority, the basic situation would be changed. This is the fundamental basis of the whole problem. For the principles of democracy dictate that when a majority exists in a country, the government of that country shall be by the majority, and not the minority. And should the Arabs forego the right conferred upon them by their numerical superiority, they would inevitably have to forego their privilege of their own form of government. What change can be considered more fundamental! And would the American people acquiesce in the admission into the United States of foreign elements in sufficient numbers to bring about a new majority? Would such an act be considered consonant with the principles of humanity and democracy?

I am confident that Your Excellency does not intend to antagonize the Arabs, but desires their good and welfare. I also believe that the American people will not agree to acts which are contrary to democratic and human principles. Relying on your desire for frankness and candidness in our relations I am prepared to do my best to remove all sources of misunderstanding by explaining the facts not only for the sake of truth and justice but also to strengthen the bonds of friendship between Your Excellency, the American people and myself.

I trust that Your Excellency will rest assured that my desire to defend the Arabs and their interests is no less than my desire to defend the reputation of the United States, throughout the Moslem and Arab worlds, and the entire world as well. Therefore you will find me extremely eager to persist in my efforts to convince Your Excellency and the American people of the democratic and human principles involved, which the United Nations, Your Excellency and the American people all seek to implement. for this reason I trust that Your Excellency will review the present situation in an effort to find a just solution of the problem—a solution which will ensure life for those displaced persons without threatening a peaceful people living securely in their country.

Kindly accept our salutations.
ABDUL-AZIZ

---

1. Transmitted to the Secretary of State by the Saudi Arabian Chargé in his note of November 2, 1946, asking that the message be communicated to President Truman.

APPENDIX IV

Memorandum by the Chief of the Division of Near Eastern Affairs (Merriam) to the Director of the Office of Near Eastern and African Affairs (Henderson), Top Secret, Washington, D.C., December 27, 1946.[1]

Top Secret   [Washington,] December 27, 1946.

Subject: United States Policy Regarding Palestine

The Palestine question and the related question of the future of the Jewish DP's form an open sore, the infection from which tends to spread rather then to become localized. Moreover, the almost world-wide feeling of insecurity felt by Jews, results in something like a cosmic Jewish urge with respect to Palestine. But the development of our Palestine policy up to this time in regard to these questions and pressures, however well-intentioned, has not contributed anything concrete to their solution, and seems unlikely to do so in its present form. Not only is our Palestine policy of no real assistance to the Jews (whatever it may afford them in the way of moral encouragement), it keep us constantly on the edge of embroilment with the British and the Arabs. Therefore, it is desirable to reconsider our policy in order to see whether it cannot be improved.

The main defects appear to be these:

1. We advocate and press for the admission of 100,000 Jewish DP's into Palestine. By doing so we have pleased the Jews. But they now probably realize that it is unlikely that we are going either to force these Jews upon Palestine by direct action, or to exert decisive pressure upon the British to do so. Since the British remain adamant against all Jewish immigration save for a trickle (1,500 a month), in the absence of an overall solution for Palestine, most Jews have now completely rationalized illegal Jewish immigration into Palestine, which they assert is as legal, or as justified, as the Boston Tea Party. This is a situation from which no good can be expected.

Moreover, the 100,000 figure has lost meaning. Originally, at the time of the Harrison report, this was the approximate number of Jews in DP camps in the American and British zones in Europe for whom the Jewish Agency requested certificates in June 1945. The number is now probably over 250,000, which is certainly too many for Palestine over a short period of time, even neglecting political consideration. An examination of the DP and political situations as a whole might indicate more or less than 100,000 but there is no longer, in the absence of a re-assessment, any persuasive reason to rest on a particular figure.

2. Our position on a political settlement for Palestine is qualified and to some extent indefinite. While it has given some satisfaction to the more moderate "viable state" Zionists, it does not go as far as they would like. It is definitely out of line with the Biltmore program which envisages a Jewish state in all of Palestine, and even more our of line with the Revisionist program which includes Transjordan. Therefore, our policy is only moder-

ately satisfactory to the Zionists.

3. Our policy, while not meeting the demands of the Zionists, is disliked and feared by the Arabs; it already handicaps and may eventually jeopardize our political and other interests in the Arab world.

It seems true to say that our policy has gradually taken form, though it is still somewhat indefinite, as the result of the pressures that have been applied to us from various directions. We go as far as we can to please the Zionists and other Jews without making the Arabs and the British too angry.

The main point which it is desired to make in this memorandum is that our policy, as it stands, is one of expediency, not one of principle. Time after time we have been maneuvered into acceptance of more or less specific propositions: 100,000 immigrants; a compromise between the Goldmann and British Government schemes, and we have then had the task—not always easy—of finding principles to justify them.

In the formulation of any policy which is really worth while, the procedure must be the exact opposite. We ought to proceed from principle to the specific, not vice versa. Operating a policy of expediency is an uncomfortable and dangerous business which we ought to get out of with all speed possible.

What should our Palestine policy, based on principle, be? First let the main premises be stated. These seem to be:

(1) Palestine is an A Mandate. As such, it was to be prepared for independence. Were it not for the complication of the Jewish National Home, it would be independent today, as all the other A mandates have become. Arabs and Jews live there and must, sooner or later, come to some sort of a political agreement based on a minimum of mutual confidence and give-and-take, if they are to govern Palestine.

(2) The Jewish National Home was and is a new concept, undefined. The British statesmen who worked out the Balfour Declaration thought that the Jewish National Home would probably develop into a Jewish state, but they underestimated or misjudged the Arab reaction (Balfour did not realize that Arabs lived in Palestine).

(3) The Jews could run Palestine if it were full of Jews; the Arabs if it were full of Arabs.

(4) The Jewish DP problem, as well as the almost universal Jewish feeling of insecurity, presses powerfully and perhaps irresistibly upon Palestine in both the human and political sense.

(5) The reception accorded by Arabs, Jews, or both, to the report of the Anglo-American Committee of Inquiry, to the Grady Mission plan—indeed, to all schemes and plans proposed by third parties—strongly indicates that no third-party plan has any chance of success, unless imposed and maintained by force.

The foregoing, taken together with the consideration mentioned earlier, plus certain general consideration which are in all of our minds, appears to lead to a set of principles which could appropriately constitute our Palestine policy:

The following is an attempt to state them:

(1) The mandate (or trusteeship) for Palestine should be replaced as soon as possible by independence. The form which Palestinian independence takes should be decided by free agreement between interested Arabs and Jews within and without Palestine, and must conform to United Nations principles. Questions relating to representation of Arabs and Jews for the purpose of the negotiations should be decided by the General As-

sembly of the United Nations after considering the recommendation of the Trusteeship Council, which will be formulated after hearings. The area of the Holy Places should be placed under a trusteeship administered by the British Government. Immigration and land ownership policies will be determined by the political entity or entities created as the result of the Arab-Jewish negotiations, subject to guarantees agreed upon between Arabs and Jews and approved by the general Assembly of UN on the recommendation of the Trusteeship Council.

(2)   The United States will support any political arrangement for Palestine agreed to as the result of the negotiations between Arabs and Jews and approved by the United nations.

(3)   Until the security system of the United Nations is able to provide, directly or indirectly, for the general security of the Near Eastern area, and possibly by virtue and under the authority of that system when in operation, Great Britain should have control, under trusteeship, of an adequate area or adequate areas and facilities in Palestine for the purpose of providing regional security, such areas and facilities to be demarcated and specified by the Security Council on the recommendation of the Military Staff Committee (?).

(4)   Pending agreement between Arabs and Jews on the future of Palestine, the existing mandate should be replaced by a trusteeship under the United Nations, administered by Great Britain. Detailed immigration and land settlement policy should be determined by the General Assembly of the United Nations after considering the recommendations of the Trusteeship Council, which will consider the views and claims of those interested, including the recommendations of the Intergovernmental Committee on Refugees and the International Refugee Organization.

The foregoing is merely in the nature of a suggestion. The important thing is for us to adopt a policy of principle and general procedure which will be approved as fair and reasonable by the general public in this and other countries, and to break away from a policy of attempting to thread a way between the specific projects and plans of the contending pressure groups. A policy of principle and procedure would also be a move in the direction of getting world responsibility and handling for the world problems, which the Palestine and Jewish problems are.

The reasoning in the memorandum is capable to development at various points and can be expanded, if you think it of sufficient interest, along such lines as you may desire. Also, if you think it worthwhile, an estimate can be made as to the probable reactions of the Arabs and Jews to the suggested modification of our policy, and, more fundamental, an assessment can be made of what there would be in it for both Arabs and Jews.

GORDON P. MERRIAM

---

1. Transmitted by Mr. Henderson to Mr. Acheson with an undated memorandum which stated: "I feel that you should read the attached memo from Mr. Merriam, Chief of the Near Eastern Division. Of course, we have practically been forced by political pressure and sentiment in the U.S. in direction of the 'viable Jewish state'. I must confess that when I view our policy in light of principles avowed by us I become uneasy." The files do not disclose the reaction of Mr. Acheson.

APPENDIX V

The Director of the Office of Near Eastern and African Affairs (Henderson) to the Secretary of State [Partition], Top Secret, Washington, D.C., September 22, 1947.

TOP SECRET   [WASHINGTON], SEPTEMBER 22, 1947.

DEAR MR. SECRETARY: I went to New York on September 15 with General Hilldring at the request of Mr. Lovett to present our views as to what you might say in you speech of September 17 with regard to Palestine. I had just returned from Greece and was not really prepared to enter into a full discussion as to the attitude which we should assume with regard to the UNSCOP report. I am afraid, therefore, that I did not give the views of my office, which are also those of nearly every member of the Foreign Service or of the Department who has worked to any appreciable extent on Near Eastern problems, in the manner in which they should have been presented.

The attitude which we assume towards the Palestine problem during the proceedings of this Special Session may have far-reaching effects upon our relations with the peoples of the Near East and with Moslems everywhere. It may greatly influence the extent of success or of failure of some of our efforts to promote world stability and to prevent further Soviet penetration into important areas free as yet from Soviet domination. I consider, therefore, that it is my duty briefly to point out some of the considerations which cause the overwhelmingly majority of non-Jewish Americans who are intimately acquainted with the situation in the Near East to believe that it would not be in the national interests of the United States for it to advocate any kind of a plan at this time for the partitioning of Palestine of for the setting up of a Jewish State in Palestine.

CERTAIN CONSIDERATIONS AGAINST ADVOCACY BY THE U.S. OF THE MAJORITY PLAN

1. *An advocacy on our part of any plan providing for the partitioning of Palestine or the establishment in Palestine of a Jewish state would be certain to undermine our relations with the Arab, and to a lesser extent with the Moslem, world at a time when the Western World needs the friendship and cooperation of the Arabs and other Moslems.*

Without at least a degree of Arab cooperation we shall encounter numerous difficulties in connection with any support which we may give to the efforts of the British to find bases which will enable Great Britain to remain as a stabilizing power in the Eastern Mediterranean. We shall need the confidence and cooperation of the Arabs in the near future if we are to achieve any success in forestalling violent Arab nationalists uprisings against the French in Tunisia, Algeria and Morocco. the resources and geographical position of the Arab countries are of such a character that those countries are necessarily factors of importance in the international economic field. Arab friendship is essential if we are to have their cooperation in the carrying out of some of our vital economic programs. During the next few years we are planning to draw heavily on the resources of the area, not only for our use, but for the reconstruction of Europe. Furthermore, we are intending to make important use of the communications facilities in the area. Already, partly as a result of our policies regarding Palestine, the attitude of the Arab Governments towards American firms has changed sharply and their demands on the firms are becoming more and more truculent and extravagant. Loss of confidence in the sense of justness and in the impartiality of the United States has been accompanied during the last two years in the Arab world by a growing suspicion of our overall motives and by increasing doubts as to our national integrity. Although the Arabs have in general no use for Communism, they feel so emotional with regard to the problem of Palestine that if an attempt should actually be made to set up a Jewish State in Palestine in pursuance of decisions supported by us, they may consider the United States as their foremost enemy and enter into at least temporary cooperation with the Soviet Union against us just as we cooperated with the Russians during the war years against common enemies.

If we press for a Jewish state, we shall undoubtedly weaken the position of the moderate Arabs who are friends of the western world and strengthen that of the fanatical extremists. Just last week, for instance, one of the moderate Arab leaders was slain in Palestine by followers of the fanatical Mufti.

2. *If we advocate a plan providing for partitioning and the setting up of a Jewish State, we shall certainly be expected to make major contributions in force, materials and money to the implementation of such a plan if it is adopted.*

We are under tremendous pressure at the present time to advocate such a plan. If we do, and if the plan is adopted, we shall be under still greater pressure to contribute to its implementation. We shall be lacking in courage and consistency, it will be argued, if after a plan supported by us has been adopted we do not do our part in carrying it out. Furthermore, we shall be expected to bear the main burden of implementation. We have shown more interest in the Palestine problem than any other great Power, except Great Britain, and Great Britain is beginning to weary of the Palestine burden. Furthermore, the execution of a partition plan such as that in the majority report will be a task lasting over a period of many years. Differences arising from attempts to carry out such a plan will arise to plague every session of the General Assembly. As one of the sponsors for the execution of the plan, we shall be the target for bitter attacks by both Arabs and Jews.

3. *Any plan for partitioning Palestine would be unworkable.*

Of all the previous committees which have ever studied the Palestine problem, only the Royal (Peel) Commission 1937 recommended partition as a solution.

The Partition (Woodhead) Commission set up in 1938 to carry out the Peel proposals was unable to devise a practicable plan for partition, so the Peel recommendations fell to the ground. The Anglo-American Committee of Inquiry, composed of six prominent Britishers and six well-known Americans, stated in their report of April 20, 1946:

"Partition has an appeal at first sight as giving a prospect of early independence and self-government to Jews and Arabs, but in our view no

partition would have any chance unless it was basically acceptable to
Jews and Arabs, and there is no sign of that today. We are accordingly
unable to recommend partition as a solution."

If complete partition would be unsuccessful unless acceptable to Jews and Arabs,
how much chance of success in the face of fierce Arab opposition has the UNSCOP majority plan which provides for an economic union of the two states—a union which cannot
possibly succeed without Arab-Jewish friendship and cooperation? Irrigation ditches, rail-
ways, roads, telephone and telegraph lines, etc. must pass through both states. These facilities cannot function if the population of one state is hostile to that of the other. If political
partition providing for the incorporation of 400,000 Arabs in a Jewish State is forced on the
population of Palestine, this hostility will exist and will increase.

4. *The UNSCOP majority Plan is not only unworkable; if adopted, it would
guarantee that the Palestine problem would be permanent and still more complicated in the
future.*

Some of the reasons for the unworkability of the Majority Plan are:
(*a*) It is not possible for the two states to have political individuality and economic unity if the population of one or both of these states objects to such a partnership and
refuses to cooperate;
(*b*) In case economic unity is found to be unworkable, it would not be possible to
have complete economic individuality since the terrain of the country and the nature of the
communications are such that the two states are inextricably meshed economically.
(*c*) In spite of the arguments advanced to the contrary in the report, an Arab state
of the type envisaged would not be viable even if subsidized by receiving half of the rev-
enues derived from the customs and other services;
(*d*) The cost of policing, in view of both extreme Arab and Jewish irredentism,
would be more than the combined national budget could bear.

5. *The Majority Plan does not dispose once and for all of the Palestine problem
because:*

(*a*) It provides for an economic union to be presided over by a Joint Economic
Board, the members of which shall consist of three representatives of each of the two States
and the foreign members appointed by the Economic and Social Council. An organ of the
United Nations must, therefore, indefinitely act as an economic umpire between these two
States. Will representatives of the Great Powers serve on this Board? If so, will an American
serve? In case important Jewish interests are involved, is the American Government to be
put under constant internal political pressure to order its representative to side with the
Jewish States? Is the Soviet Union or a Soviet satellite to be represented by one of the three
members? If so, what kind of a role would such a representative be likely to play?
(*b*) The majority Plan provides that if either of the two states should fail to take
the steps suggested in the plan, including the calling of a constituent assembly, the setting
up of a provisional government, the making of a Declaration, etc., that fact will be communicated to the United Nations for such action by the General Assembly as may be deemed
proper.
It is likely that the Arab State will not take the steps suggested and that, therefore,

the whole Palestine problem will be back on the doorstep of the General Assembly at least within two years.

We are convinced that no plan can be found which will completely dispose of the Palestine problem so far as the United Nations is concerned at this session. I have stressed the fact that the majority plan does not rid us of this problem merely because there has been some thinking in the Department to the effect that if it is adopted, we can finally wash our hands of this disagreeable matter.

6.   *The proposals contained in the UNSCOP plan are not only not based on any principles of an international character, the maintenance of which would be in the interests of the United States, but they are in definite contravention to various principles laid down in the Charter as well as to principles on which American concepts of Government are based.*

These proposals, for instance, ignore such principles as self-determination and majority rule. They recognize the principle of a theocratic racial state and even go so far in several instances as to discriminate on grounds of religion and race against persons outside of Palestine. We have hitherto always held that in our foreign relations American citizens, regardless of race of religion, are entitled to uniform treatment. The stress on whether persons are Jews or non-Jews is certain to strengthen feelings among both Jews and Gentiles in the United States and elsewhere that Jewish citizens are not the same as other citizens.

The United States is undoubtedly honor bound to take steps to make sure that the Jews in Palestine are not discriminated against and that they participate on at least an equal basis with other peoples in the Government of Palestine. We are under no obligations to the Jews to set up a Jewish State. The Balfour Declaration and the Mandate provided not for a Jewish State, but for a Jewish national home. Neither the United States nor the British Government has ever interpreted the term "Jewish national Home" to be a Jewish national state.

7.   *Tactics which the United States should pursue in the handling of the Palestine problem before the present session of the General Assembly.*

In our opinion, there is no ready solution of the Palestine problem to which both Jews and Arabs would acquiesce to such an extent as to render it workable. Any kind of an imposed solution opposed by the majority of either the Arabs or the Jews is bound to result in failure, involving much loss of property and bloodshed and loss of prestige to the supporters and executors of the plan, as well as to the whole United Nations. If a solutions is found which is workable, it will, we believe, be evolved only after long and protracted discussions during the course of which the moderate Jews and moderate Arabs would find common ground. If we at the beginning take wither the Arab or the Jewish side of the controversy, it will be extremely difficult for either the moderate Arabs or the moderate Jews to get together.

Our Government has already states that we give serious weight to the majority proposals. On an early occasion, we should repeat this statement, making it clear at the same time that our minds are by no means closed and that we shall also give due weight to the views of other nations and particularly of the interested parties.

During the debates regarding the merits of the various plans, we should not play too active a role. We should create the respect of all fair-minded persons by being, so far as possible, strictly impartial. We should concentrate our efforts primarily on working out agreements of all parties with regard to as many points as possible. It seems to us that there is a possibility that the moderates in both camps might be led to acquiesce in a sufficient number of points to enable the setting up of a trusteeship for a period of years which would be instructed to function in such a neutral manner as not to favor either partition or a single state. At the conclusion of this term of years, there could be a plebiscite on the question of partition, in the light of which the General Assembly could make its final decision on this fateful question. Any kind of a temporary arrangement should probably provide for immediate Jewish immigration of at least 100,000 persons.

It may be impossible even to work out a delayed solution such as that outlined above. If so, the Palestine problem will probably become even more of a world problem than at the present time.

It is realized that the tactics outlined above are not likely to appeal to those of us who prefer to approach all problems with energy and decisiveness. There are times, however, when energy and decisiveness are not appropriate.

APPENDIX VI

Memorandum by the Director of the Office of Near Eastern and African Affairs (Henderson) to the Under Secretary of State (Lovett) [Partition], Top Secret, Washington, D.C., November 24, 1947.

TOP SECRET   [WASHINGTON,] NOVEMBER 24, 1947.

Attached hereto is a copy of a personal telegram which I have just received from Hamdi Al Pachachi, who was Prime Minister of Iraq during the last year that I was United States Minister to that country. I trust that you will read this telegram in full, since, in my opinion, it represents fairly the feelings of the Arab world with regard to the United States and Palestine.

I feel it again to be my duty to point out that it seems to me and all the members of the Office acquainted with the Middle East that the policy which we are following in New York at the present time is contrary to the interests of the United States and will eventually involve us in international difficulties of so grave a character that the reaction throughout the world, as well as in this country, will be very strong.

We ar committed to the idea that the security of the Middle East is vital to the United States. We also agree that unless the British continue to remain a force in the Middle East, the security of the Middle East will be gravely endangered. It is impossible for the British to remain a force in the Middle East unless they retain the friendship of the Arab world. By our Palestine policy, we are not only forfeiting the friendship of the Arab world, but we are incurring long-term Arab hostility towards us. What is important is that the Arabs are losing confidence in the integrity of the United States and the sincerity of our many pronouncements that our foreign policies are based on the principles of the Charter of the United Nations. In Mr. Johnson's speech of Saturday,the British were castigated before the whole world for not agreeing to suggestions of the Subcommittee which, if followed, would certainly have ruined British relations with the Arab world and would probably have resulted in the British being forced to withdraw from the whole Middle East. It is extremely unfortunate that we should be criticizing the British for following the only kind of policy which, it seems to me, they can follow if they are to remain in the Middle East. I am afraid that the reactions in London to criticisms of this kind will not help us in our efforts to prevail upon Mr. Bevin not to withdraw the remaining British troops from Greece.

I wonder if the President realizes that the plan which we are supporting for Palestine leaves no force other than local law enforcement organizations for preserving order in Palestine. It is quite clear that there will be wide-scale violence in that country, both from the Jewish and the Arab sides with which the local authorities will not be able to cope. It is my understanding that Mr. Johnson, on Saturday, indicated before the Subcommittee that if the situation in Palestine should develop into a menace to peace, the matter would naturally come before the Security Council and that the United States, along with the other four

Great Powers, would be prepared to share responsibility for removing the menace. Our plan envisages apparently the despatch of American, Soviet and perhaps other troops to Palestine in order to preserve law and order. It seems to me that we ought to think twice before we support any plan which would result in American troops going to Palestine. The fact that Soviet troops under our plan would be introduced into the heart of the Middle East is even more serious. I know that you have so many problems facing you that you cannot keep informed regarding the details of all of them, and I am sending you this memorandum in order to make sure that you realize the direction in which we are headed.[1]

Loy W. Henderson

---

1. Mr. Armour noted, in a marginal notation on November 24: "I entirely agree with the above memorandum." In an undated marginal notation, Mr. Lovett stated: "I read this [memorandum] to the President at the 12:30 meeting today. I explained that the Dept thought the situation was serious that he should know of the probable attempts to get us committed militarily. We are continuing to refuse."

      The memorandum, except for the first paragraph and the last sentence, was transmitted to Messrs. Johnson, Hilldring and Rusk at Mr. Henderson's request and with Mr. Lovett's approval in telegram Gadel 31, November 24, to New York.

APPENDIX VII

Report by the Policy Planning Staff on the Position of the United States with Respect to Palestine, Top Secret, Washington, D.C., January 19, 1948.

TOP SECRET   [WASHINGTON,] JANUARY 19, 1948.

The Problem:

1.   To assess and appraise the position of the U.S. with respect to Palestine, taking into consideration the security interests of the U.S. in the Mediterranean and Near East areas, and in the light of the recommendation of the General Assembly of the United Nations regarding the partition of Palestine.

Analysis

2.   Palestine occupies a geographic position of great strategic significance to the U.S. It is important for the control of the eastern end of the Mediterranean and the Suez Canal. It is an outlet for the oil of the Middle East; which, in turn, is important to U.S. security. Finally, it is the center of a number of major political cross-currents; and events in Palestine cannot help being reflected in a number of directions. For these reasons, and particularly in view of the Soviet pressure against the periphery of that area, and Soviet infiltration into the area, it is important that political, economic, and social stability be maintained there.

Because of the present irreconcilable differences between Arabs and Jews in Palestine, great danger exists that the area may become the source of serious unrest and instability which could be readily exploited by the USSR unless a workable solution can be developed.

3.   The UN General Assembly on November 29, 1947, recommended the partition of Palestine into separate Arab and Jewish sovereign states, substantially as proposed by the majority report of the UN Special Committee on Palestine. The partition plan provides for an economic union of the two states, administered by a Joint Economic Board, and for the city of Jerusalem to be placed under international trusteeship. The mandate for Palestine would be terminated by August 1, 1948 and the newly created states and special regime for Jerusalem would come into existence by October 1, 1948. Provision was made for a five-member UN Commission to take over progressively the administration of Palestine and to establish Provisional Councils in each new state.

4.   The boundaries of the proposed new Arab and Jewish states do not satisfy Zionist aspirations from either the political or the economic viewpoint, and the whole plan of partition with economic union is totally unacceptable to the Arabs. Although frequent reference has been made to "sacrifices" accepted in the interest of compromise, the partition plan was strongly supported by the Jewish Agency for Palestine and by various Zionist organizations favoring the establishment of a sovereign Jewish political state in Palestine. It

did not, however, have the support of the Irgun, the Revisionists or the Stern gang (the so-called leftist groups), whose influence among the Jews of Palestine appears to be increasing.

5.   The Arabs of Palestine and the Arab states have uniformly and consistently maintained their unequivocal opposition to any form of partition. The Arabs of Palestine have indicated their determination not to establish a separate government in the Arab area of Palestine designated by the UN, and to boycott all activities of the UN Commission charged with the transfer of authority from the British to the new Arab and Jewish states. Even if partition were economically feasible, the Arab attitude alone renders it improbable that any economic union could be effected between the two new states.

The General Assembly, in adopting the recommendation for partition, left unanswered certain questions regarding the legality of the plan as well as the means for its implementation. Nor did the General Assembly, in the circumstances prevailing at the time, have an opportunity to explore the last minute announcement by the Arab States on November 29 of their willingness to accept the principle of a Federal State in Palestine[1] which they had previously opposed. There was no indication of any real effort by the UN toward conciliation between the Jews and the Arabs.

6.   The U.S. and USSR played leading roles in bringing about a vote favorable to partition. Without U.S. leadership and the pressures which developed during UN consideration of the question, the necessary two-thirds majority in the General Assembly could not have been obtained. From this there has grown a belief that the United States has a heavy responsibility for seeing that partition works. It has been shown that various unauthorized U.S. nationals and organizations, including members of Congress, notably in the closing days of the Assembly, brought pressure to bear on various foreign delegates and their respective home governments to induce them to support the U.S. attitude on the Palestine question. Evidence to this effect is attached under Tab A.[2]

7.   The decision of the U.S. Government to support the UN Special Committee's majority plan was based primarily on the view, expressed to the GA by Secretary Marshall on September 18 [17], 1947, that "great weight" should be accorded the majority opinion of a UN Committee.[3]

8.   Strong nationalistic and religious feelings were aroused throughout the Arab world as a result of the UN recommendation on Palestine. Widespread rioting has followed. In Palestine, the outbreaks have consisted of armed clashes between Arabs and Jews; in certain of the Arab states, there have been attacks on Jewish quarters and demonstrations directed primarily against the U.S. These manifestations of popular feeling have not so far represented organized Arab resistance to partition, although a "jihad" (holy war) against the Jews of Palestine has been proclaimed by Moslem leaders in most of the Arab states and has been joined by Christian leaders in Syria.

9.   As British forces are progressively withdrawn from Palestine and as steps are taken with a view to implementing the UN decision, organized large scale opposition by the Arabs is to be expected. Irregular military units are now being organized in Iraq, Syria, Egypt, Transjordan and Saudi Arabia to fight in Palestine. There are strong indications that at an appropriate moment at least some of these units will move into the Arab portion of Palestine as defined by the UN. That these forces will come into violent conflict with the Haganah or other Jewish military bodies operating from the Jewish state is probable.

10.   In order to protect themselves and to secure the establishment of a Jewish state, Zionist representatives will seek armed support from the U.S., for without substantial external assistance the proposed Jewish state cannot be established or exist. This may take the form of an attempt (a) to obtain money, arms and volunteers in the U.S. and/or (b) to

induce the U.S. Government to assist in organizing an international armed force under the UN to enforce partition.

11. The UN decision did not provide for outside armed forces to impose the partition scheme, either in maintaining law and order in the two new states or in affording protection to the five-member UN Commission which is to implement the decision. The UN Commission is almost certain to meet with armed Arab opposition in seeking to discharge its functions. Palestine police authorities have declined to assume responsibility for its safety outside of Tel-Aviv. There can be no assurance that in the present and foreseeable circumstances, local security forces will be able to maintain law and order; rather may their failure to do so be confidently predicted.

12. The U.S. has suspended authorization for the export of arms, ammunition and other war material intended for use in Palestine or in neighboring countries. [4] If we resist pressure by the Zionists to alter this position, the question then arises whether we should send troops to Palestine as part of an international force under the UN. It may be assumed that the Soviet Union would, in certain circumstances, be prepared to contribute troops to such an international force. If the USSR should do so, it would be awkward for the U.S. to decline to take similar action. If Soviet troops are sent to Palestine, further opportunities would be provided for the exercise of Russian influence in the whole Near Eastern area.

13. U.S. support of partition has already brought about loss of U.S. prestige and disillusionment among the Arabs and other neighboring peoples as to U.S. objectives and ideals. U.S. support of the principles of self-determination was a basic factor in the creation of the Arab states out of the Ottoman Empire after World War I. U.S. officials, missionaries, and educational institutions in the Near East have built successfully on this foundation, and U.S. businessmen have reaped the benefit of the widespread belief that the U.S. had no political motives in the area inimical to Arab welfare.

14. The position of Saudi Arabia in the Palestine question is of particular importance. King Ibn Saud values the friendship between his country and the U.S. and recognizes the significant financial aid to Saudi Arabia derived from oil royalties. He is reluctant to sever political and economic ties with the U.S. Nevertheless, he is under strong pressure from other Arab states to break with the U.S. Prince Faisal, his son and Foreign Minister, departed for Saudi Arabia from the UN General Assembly in a bitterly anti-American mood and may give strength to a faction of less moderate elements which will force the King's hand. Important U.S. oil concessions and air base rights will be at stake in the event that an actively hostile Government should come into power in Saudi Arabia.

15. In view of the evident determination of the Arabs to resist partition with all the means at their disposal, it may be anticipated that, if an attempt is made to carry out the UN decision (with of without U.S. assistance), the more moderate and intellectual leader of the Arab states, most of whom have ties with the west, will be swept out of power by irresponsible elements. Leaders such as Azzam Pasha, Secretary General of the Arab League, would be displaced by extremists such as the Grand Mufti of Jerusalem. Hatred of the Zionists or of those identified with Zionism might be extended to include all westerners in direct proportion to the latter's support of Zionist armies in general and of partition in particular.

16. Any assistance the U.S. might give to the enforcement of partition would result in deep-seated antagonism for the U.S. in many sections of the Moslem world over a period of many years and would lay us open to one or more of the following consequences:

(*a*) Suspension or cancellation of valuable U.S. air base rights and commercial concessions, cessation of U.S. oil pipeline construction, and drastic curtailment of U.S. trade with that area.

(*b*) Loss of our present access to the air, military and naval facilities enjoyed by the British in the area, with attendant repercussions on our overall strategic position in the Middle East and Mediterranean.

(*c*) Closing or boycotting of U.S. educational, religious and philanthropic institutions in the Near East, such as the American University at Beirut established in 1866 and the American University at Cairo.

(*d*) Possible deaths, injuries and damages arising from acts of violence against individual U.S. citizens and interests established in the area. Official assurances of the Arab Governments to afford protection to U.S. interests could not be relied on because of the intensity of popular feeling.

(*e*) A serious threat to the success of the Marshall Plan. the present oil production of the Middle East fields is approximately 800,000 barrels a day. To meet Marshall Plan requirements, production must be raised to about 2,000,000 barrels a day, since no oil for Europe for this purpose could be provided from the U.S., from Venezuela, or from the Far East. Before the current disturbances, U.S. oil companies had made plans for the required development in the Middle East, with which it will be impossible to proceed if the present situation continues.

17.   The USSR stands to gain by the partition plan if it should be implemented by force because of the opportunity thus afforded to the Russians to assist in "maintaining order" in Palestine. If Soviet forces should be introduced into Palestine for the purpose of implementing partition, Communist agents would have an excellent base from which to extend their subversive activities, to disseminate propaganda, and to attempt to replace the present Arab government by "democratic peoples' governments". The presence of Soviet forces in Palestine would constitute an outflanking of our positions in Greece, Turkey and Iran, and a potential threat to the stability of the entire Eastern Mediterranean area.

18.   It is not certain, however, that the USSR would choose to send its forces into Palestine. To do so would be to place those forces in an exposed position, far from a base of supply, and without suitable lines of communication. Rather than risk the enmity of the Arab world by such action, the Soviet Union might prefer to have U.S. forces bear the brunt of enforcement and incur the odium of the local population and Moslems everywhere as a result.

19.   Other choices are open to the USSR besides the furnishing of troops. Evidence is accumulating that the USSR may be covertly or indirectly supplying arms not only to the Jews but to the Arabs, thus aggravating the friction in the Near East. From the Soviet viewpoint, it might be preferable to exploit in this manner the explosive character of the situation created by partition rather than to enter the area in a military sense.

Whether or not Soviet forces should assist in implementing partition, the UN decision is favorable to Soviet objectives of sowing dissention and discord in non-communist countries. The partition of Palestine might afford the USSR a pretext on the basis of "self-determination of minorities" to encourage the partition of areas in Iraq, Iran, Turkey and Greece, with a view to setting up separate [Kurdish?] Azerbaijani, Armenian and Macedonian states enjoying the support of the USSR.

All in all, there is no way of telling in exactly what manner the USSR will attempt to turn partition to its advantage. It must be assumed, however, that Moscow will actively endeavor to find some means of exploiting the opportunity.

20.   Various other factors would enter into the situation if an attempt is made to enforce the UN recommendation. The foregoing is intended merely to suggest the principle elements in the problem. So numerous would be the ramifications of mounting Arab ill will, of opening the door to Soviet political or military penetration, and of generally chaotic conditions in Palestine and neighboring countries that the whole structure of peace and security in the Near East and Mediterranean would be directly or indirectly affected with results impossible to predict at this stage in detail but certainly injurious to U.S. interests.

Conclusions

21.   As a result of U.S. sponsorship of UN action leading to the recommendation to partition Palestine, U.S. prestige in the Moslem world has suffered a sever blow and U.S. strategic interests in the Mediterranean and Near East have been seriously prejudiced. Our vital interests in those areas will continue to be adversely affected to the extent that we continue to support partition.

22.   The original U.S. premise in supporting the partition of Palestine was founded on the belief that, with certain modifications in the majority proposals of the UN Special Committee on Palestine, a just and workable plan could be devised *immediately* which would receive broad international support, *provided always that there was cooperation between the parties concerned.* A study of the present plan raises serious doubts as to its workability because of the artificial and arbitrary political subdivision of a complicated economic area. Events have demonstrated that the Arab inhabitants of Palestine will not cooperate even to endeavor to make the partition plan work. Therefore, one of the major premises on which we originally supported partition have proved invalid.

23.   The United States should not send armed forces to Palestine, either on a volunteer or contingent basis, for the following reasons: (*a*) This would represent a political or military commitment of which the dimensions, both in time and space, cannot be calculated or foreseen and which might carry us into action of a major character, out of all proportion to the foreign policy objectives involved; and (*b*) to do so would invite the possibility of the movement of Soviet armed forces to the strategic Near Eastern and Mediterranean area. For similar reasons, the U.S. should oppose the sending of armed forces of any nationality to Palestine.

24.   While the governments in Arab countries have partially succeeded in restraining demonstrations against Jews within their borders, in the case of open conflict major massacres of Jews in Moslem countries would seem to be inevitable, despite efforts of the governments of those countries to control popular feeling. Moreover, a basis would be provided for anti-Jewish agitation in other parts of the world. The process of assimilation or integration of the individual Jew in the life of the country of which he is a citizen, which has been strongly advocated by World Jewry in the past, would be made more difficult and he would be singled out for attack as an alien political factor. In the U.S., the position of Jews would be gravely undermined as it become evident to the public that in supporting Jewish state in Palestine we were in fact supporting the extreme objectives of political Zionism, to the detriment of overall U.S. security interests.

25.   Unless an effort is made to retrieve the situation, the prestige of the UN itself will be at stake because of the notoriety and resentment attendant upon the activities of U.S. pressure groups, including members of Congress, who sought to impose U.S. views as to partition on foreign delegations. Furthermore, the probable abstention by the Arab states from active participation in many UN activities may further weaken the effectiveness

of the UN and the U.S. position within the UN, as has Soviet abstention in certain other activities.

26.   The U.S. Government should face the fact that the partition of Palestine cannot be implemented without the use of force, and that the U.S. would inevitably be called upon to supply a substantial portion of the money, troops and arms for this purpose. The British have made it cleat that they would not accept any role in the enforcement of partition. No other nation except Russia could be expected to participate in such implementation to any appreciable extent.

26a.   It must be concluded that the partition of Palestine will not be possible of attainment without outside assistance on a substantial scale. If the U.S. is determined to see the successful establishment of a Jewish state in Palestine (either as proposed or as may be geographically modified because of Arab noncooperation in the proposed economic union), the U.S. must be prepared to grant economic assistance, together with aid to the Jewish authorities through the supply of arms, ammunition and implements of war. Ultimately the U.S. might have to support the Jewish authorities by the use of naval units and military forces. It should be clearly recognized that such assistance given to the Jewish state, but withheld from the Arabs and the Arab States, would in Arab eyes be a virtual declaration of war by the U.S. against the Arab world. It is improbable that the Jewish state would survive over any considerable period of time in the fact of the combined assistance which would be forthcoming for the Arabs in Palestine from the Arab States, and in lesser measure from their Moslem neighbors. The preparations now being made for intensive guerrilla warfare by the approximately 400,000 Arabs resident in the proposed new Jewish state are alone giving rise to serious doubts as to whether the Jewish people in Palestine could themselves control the situation.

Recommendations

27.   We should take no further initiative in implementing or aiding partition.

28.   We should oppose sending armed forces into Palestine by the UN or any member thereof for the purpose of implementing partition. We should also oppose the recruitment of volunteers for this purpose.

29.   We should maintain and enforce our embargo on arms to Palestine and neighboring countries.

30.   We should endeavor as far as possible to spread responsibility for the future handling of this question, and to divest ourselves of the imputation of international leadership in the search for a solution to this problem.

31.   When and if the march of events has conclusively demonstrated that the effort to carry out the partition plan as prescribed by the UN General Assembly offers no reasonable prospect for success without the use of outside armed force, we should then take the position that we have been obliged to conclude that it is impracticable and undesirable for the international community to attempt to enforce any form of partition in the absence of agreement between the parties, and that the matter should go back to the UN General Assembly.

32.   Thereafter, our position in the UN should be that we would cooperate loyally in working out and implementing any proposals designed (a) to encourage pacific settlement between the Palestine Arabs and Palestine Jews or (b) to investigate the possibilities of any other suggested solution such as a federal state of trusteeship, which would not require outside armed force for implementation.

33.   We should oppose referring to the International Court the question of the

UN recommendation on Palestine on the grounds that the fundamental issue, i.e., whether the two communities involved will cooperate to make the partition plan effective, is not a proper question for the Court.[5]

1. See telegram 1274, December 1, 1947, from New York, *Foreign Relations*, 1947, vol. v, p. 1293.

2. Not printed; for documentation on the subject of these pressures, see *ibid.*, pp. 99 ff.

3. See statement by the Secretary of State, *ibid.*, p. 1151.

4. See telegram Telmar 42, December 6,1947, to London, *Foreign Relations*, 1947, vol. v, p. 1300.

5. According to *The Forrestal Diaries*, edited by Walter Millis (New York, The Viking Press, 1951), p. 360. Mr. Lovett showed PPS/19 to Secretary of Defense Forrestal on January 21. The latter was said to have expressed the view that the United States was not committed to support the partition plan which was unworkable without the use of force; that it was against American interest to supply arms to the Jews while embargoing arms to the Arabs or to accept unilateral responsibility for carrying out the partition plan; and that the United States should attempt to have the plan withdrawn as soon as possible.

APPENDIX VIII

Report by the Policy Planning Staff, Review of Current Trends, U.S. Foreign Policy, Top Secret, Washington, D.C., February 24, 1948.

TOP SECRET   [WASHINGTON,] FEBRUARY 24, 1948.

[Extracts]

Review of Current Trends
U.S. Foreign Policy

....

V. PALESTINE AND THE MIDDLE EAST

The Staff views on Palestine have been made known in a separate paper. I do not intend to recapitulate them here. But there are tow background considerations of determining importance, both for the Palestine question and for our whole position in the Middle East, which I should like to emphasize at this time.

1. *The British Strategic Position in the Middle East*
   We have decided in this Government that the security of the Middle East is vital to our own security. We have also decided that it would not be desirable or advantageous for us to attempt to duplicate or to take over the strategic facilities now held by the British in that area. We have recognized that these facilities would be at our effective disposal anyway, in the event of war, and that to attempt to get them transferred, in the formal sense, from the British to ourselves would only raise a host of new and unnecessary problems, and would probably be generally unsuccessful.

   This means that we must do what we can to support the maintenance of the British of their strategic position in that area. This does *not mean* that we must support them in every individual instance. It does *not mean* that we must back them up in cases where they have got themselves into a false position or where we would thereby be undertaking extravagant political commitments. It *does mean* that any policy on our part which tends to strain British relations with the Arab world and to whittle down the British position in the Arab countries is only a policy directed against ourselves and against the immediate strategic interests of our country.

2. *The Direction of Our Own Policy*
   the pressures to which this Government is now subjected are ones which impel us toward a position where we would shoulder major responsibility for the maintenance, and

even the expansion, of a jewish state in Palestine. To the extent that we move in this direction, we will be operating directly counter to our major security interests in that area. For this reason, our policy in the Palestine issue should be dominated by the determination to avoid being impelled along this path.

We are now heavily and unfortunately involved in this Palestine question. We will apparently have to make certain further concession to our past commitments and to domestic pressures.

These concessions will be dangerous ones; but they will not necessarily be catastrophic if we are thoroughly conscious of what we are doing, and if we alt our general course toward the avoidance of the possibility of the responsibility I have referred to. If we do not lat our course in that direction but drift along the lines of least resistance in the existing vortex of cross currents, our entire policy in the Middle Eastern area will unquestionably be carried in the direction of confusion, ineffectiveness, and grievous involvement in a situation to which there cannot be—from our standpoint—any happy ending.

I think it should be state that if this Government is carried to a point in the Palestine controversy where it is required to send U.S. forces to Palestine in any manner whatsoever, or to agree either to the international recruitment of volunteers or the sending of small nation forces which would include those of Soviet satellites, then in my opinion, the whole structure of strategic and political planning which we have been building up for the Mediterranean and Middle Eastern areas would have to be reexamined and probably modified or replaced by something else. For this would then mean that we had consented to be guided, in a highly important question affecting those areas, not by national interest but by other considerations. If we tried, in the face of this fact, to continue with policy in adjacent areas motivated solely by national interest, we would be faced with a duality of purpose which would surely lead in the end to a dissipation and confusion of effort. We cannot operate with one objective in one area, and with a conflicting one next door.

If, therefore, we decide that we are obligated by past commitments of U.N. decision or any other consideration to take a leading part in the enforcement in Palestine of any arrangement opposed by the great majority of the inhabitants of the Middle Eastern area, we must be prepared to face the implications of this act by revising our general policy in that part of the world. And since the Middle East is vital to the present security concepts on which this Government is basing itself in its worldwide military and political planning, this would further mean a review of our entire military and political policy.

....

X. CONCLUSIONS

....

In the Mediterranean and Middle East, we have a situation where a vigorous and collective national effort, utilizing both our political and military resources, could probably prevent the area from falling under Soviet influence and preserve it as a highly important factor in our world strategic position. But we are deeply involved, in that same area, in a situation which has no direct relation to our national security, and where the motives of our involvement lie solely in past commitments of dubious wisdom and in our attachment to the U.N. itself. If we do not effect a fairly radical reversal of the trend of our policy to date, we will end up either in the position of being ourselves militarily responsible for the protection of the Jewish population in Palestine against the declared hostility of the Arab world, or of sharing that responsibility with the Russians and thus assisting at their installation as one of the military powers in the area. In either case, the clarity and efficiency of a sound national policy for that area will be shattered.

APPENDIX IX

Draft Memorandum by the Director of the Office of United Nations Affairs (Rusk) to the Under Secretary of State (Lovett) [Jewish aggression], Secret, Washington, D.C., May 4, 1948.

SECRET   [WASHINGTON,] MAY 4, 1948

Subject: Future Course of Events in Palestine

The refusal of the Jewish Agency last night to agree to our proposal for on-the-spot truce negotiations in Palestine on the grounds that they could not accept the "moral obligation" to undertake such conversations rather clearly reveals the intention of the Jews to go steadily ahead with the Jewish separate state by force of arms. While it is possible that Arab acceptance of our proposal might place the Jewish Agency in such a position vis-à-vis public opinion that it would have to go through the motions of looking for a truce, it seems clear that in the light of the Jewish military superiority which now obtains in Palestine, the Jewish Agency will prefer to round out its State after May 15 and rely on its armed strength to defend that state from Arab counterattack.

Military operations after May 15 will probably be undertaken by the Haganah with the assistance of the Jewish terrorist organizations Irgun and Stern. Copies of Consul General Wasson's excellent reports, as set forth in his telegram 530 of May 3, are attached, and provide the estimate of the British General Officer Commanding as to the probable course of military events after British withdrawal on May 15.

If these predictions come true we shall find ourselves in the UN confronted by a very anomalous situation. The Jews will be the actual aggressors against the Arabs. However, the Jews will claim that they are merely defending the boundaries of a state which were traced by the UN and approved, at least in principle, by two-thirds of the UN membership. The question which will confront the SC in scarcely ten days' time will be whether Jewish armed attack on Arab communities in Palestine is legitimate of whether it constitutes such a threat to international peace and security as to call for coercive measures by the Security Council.

The situation may be made more difficult and less clear-cut if, as is probable, Arab armies from outside Palestine cross the frontier to aid their disorganized and demoralized brethren who will be the objects of Jewish attack. In the event of such Arab outside aid the Jews will come running to the Security Council with the claim that their state is the object of armed aggression and will use every means to obscure the fact that it is their own armed aggression against the Arabs inside Palestine which is the cause of Arab counterattack.

There will be a decided effort, given this eventuality, that the United States will be called upon by elements inside this country to support Security Council action against the

Arab states. To take such action would seem to me to be morally indefensible while, from the aspect of our relations with the Middle East and of our broad security aspects in that region, it would be almost fatal to pit forces of the United States and possibly Russia against the governments of the Arab world.

Given this almost intolerable situation, the wisest course of action might be for the United States and Great Britain, with the assistance of France, to undertake immediate diplomatic action seeking to work out a *modus vivendi* between Abdullah of Transjordan and the Jewish Agency. This *modus vivendi* would call for, in effect, a *de facto* partition of Palestine along the lines traced by Sir Arthur Creech Jones in his remark to Ambassador Parodi on May 2, as indicated on Page 3 of USUN's telegram [549], May 2, which has been drawn to your attention.

In effect, Abdullah would cut across Palestine from Transjordan to the sea at Jaffa, would give Ibn Saud a port at Aqaba and appease the Syrians by some territorial adjustment in the northern part, leaving the Jews a coastal state running from Tel Aviv to Haifa. If some *modus vivendi* along these lines could be worked out peaceably, the United nations could give its blessing to the deal.

APPENDIX X

Memorandum of Conversation by Secretary of State [Recognition of Israel], Top Secret, Washington, D.C., May 12, 1948.

TOP SECRET   [WASHINGTON,] MAY 12, 1948

Participants: The President
The Secretary of State
The Under Secretary of State
Messrs. Clark Clifford, David Niles,
      Matthew Connelly—The White House
Fraser Wilkins (NE)—State Dept.
Robert McClintock (UNA)—State Dept.

The President said that he had called the meeting because he was seriously concerned as to what might happen in Palestine after May 15.

Mr. Lovett gave a lengthy exposition of recent events bearing on the Palestine problem. He recalled that on the preceding Saturday, May 8, the Political Representative of the Jewish Agency, Mr. Moshe Shertok, had called upon the Secretary and himself, accompanied by Dr. Epstein. Mr. Shertok had related that the British Minister for Colonial Affairs, Sir Arthur Creech Jones, had told him that Abdullah, the King of Transjordan, might enter the Arab portions of Palestine but that there need be no fear that Abdullah's forces, centered upon the British subsidized and officered Arab Legion, would seek to penetrate Jewish areas of Palestine. Furthermore, Mr. Shertok told the Secretary that a message, a week delayed in transmission, had been received from the Jewish Agency in Palestine, recounting overtures by a Colonel Goldy, an officer of the Arab Legion, suggesting that a deal could be worked out between Abdullah and the Jewish Agency whereby the King would take over the Arab portion of Palestine and leave the Jews in possession of their state in the remainder of that country.

Mr. Lovett said that this intelligence had obviously caused an abrupt shift in the position of the Jewish Agency. Only a week before, the Jewish Agency had officially communicated to the Security Council its charges that Arab armies were invading Palestine. Likewise, only a week before, Mr. Shertok and other representatives of the Jewish Agency had seemed seriously interested in proposed articles of truce. Now, however, their attitude had shifted and they seemed confident, on the basis of recent military successes and the prospect of a "behind the barn" deal with Abdullah, that they could establish their sovereign state without any necessity for a truce with the Arabs of Palestine.

I intervened at this juncture to recall what I had told Mr. Shertok on May 8. I had stresses that it was extremely dangerous to base long-range policy on temporary military success. There was no doubt but that the Jewish army had gained such temporary success but there was no assurance whatever that in the long-range the tide might not turn against them. I told Mr. Shertok that they were taking a gamble. If the tide did turn adversely and they came running to us for help they should be placed clearly on notice now that there was no warrant to expect help from the United States, which had warned them of the grave risk which they were running.

Later during the conversation a telephone call was received from General Carter [1] stating that a UP press despatch from Tel Aviv reported that following two interviews with me by Mr. Shertok the latter had flown to Tel Aviv bearing a personal message from me to Mr. Ben Gurion, who was styled in the press despatch as the forthcoming President of the Jewish State. The despatch likewise was reported as saying that Shertok had informed me of the intention of the Jewish Agency to establish a sovereign state of May 16.

I directed, with the President's concurrence, that no comment be made on this press story. In actual fact, no message had been sent to Mr. Ben Gurion, and I did not even know that such a person existed. Furthermore, Shertok had not told me of any intention to establish a Jewish State of May 16.

Resuming his summary of the situation, Mr. Lovett read a telegram just received from New York City, indicating that, while the United Kingdom Government was prepared to support our draft resolution, it desired that the United States give further consideration to the possibility of a commission being appointed by the General Assembly to deal with the administration of Palestine, this commission to be made up of Belgium, France and the United States.

It was generally agreed that the British had played a lamentable, if not altogether duplicitous, role in the Palestine situation and that their last-minute approaches and indications of a change in heart could have no effect upon our policy.

The President then invited Mr. Clark Clifford to make a statement. Mr. Clifford said that he had three main suggestions to offer, base upon consultation with colleagues of the White House staff.

Mr. Clifford said that he objected to the first article of our draft resolution which would place the General Assembly on record as reaffirming support of the efforts of the Security Council to secure a truce in Palestine. He said this reference was unrealistic since there had been no truce and probably would not be one. He said that on march 24, Mr. Rusk at a White House conference had estimated that a truce could be negotiated within two weeks but this goal was still not in sight. Instead, the actual partition of Palestine had taken place "without the use of outside force".

Mr. Clifford's second point was strongly to urge the Palestine to give prompt recognition to the Jewish State after the termination of the mandate on May 15. He said such a move should be taken quickly before the Soviet Union recognized the Jewish State. It would have distinct value in restoring the President's position for support of the partition of Palestine.

Mr. Clifford's third point was that the President, at his press conference on the following day, May 13, should make a statement of his intention to recognize the Jewish State, once the provision for democratic government outlined in the resolution of November 29, had been complied with, which he assumed would be the case. The proposed statement would conclude: "I have asked the Secretary of State to have the Representatives of the United States in the United Nations take up this subject in the United Nations with a view toward obtaining early recognition of a Jewish State by the other members of the United Nations".

The rebuttal was made by Mr. Lovett. With regard to Mr. Clifford's reference to the article on truce, Mr. Lovett pointed out that the Security Council was still seized of this matter under its resolutions of April 1, April 17 and April 23. The United States in fact was a member of the Security Council's Truce Commission on Palestine. Surely the United States could not by its unilateral act get the Security Council to drop this matter and it would be most unbecoming, in light of our activities to secure a truce.

On the question of premature recognition, Mr. Lovett said that it would be highly injurious to the United Nations to announce the recognition of the Jewish State even before it had come into existence and while the General Assembly , which had been called into special session at the request of the United States, was still considering the question of the future government of Palestine. Furthermore, said Mr. Lovett, such a move would be injurious to the prestige of the President. It was a very transparent attempt to win the Jewish vote but, in Mr. Lovett's opinion, it would lose more votes than it would gain. Finally, to recognize the Jewish State prematurely would be buying a pig in a poke. How did we know what kind of Jewish State would be set up? At this stage Mr. Lovett read excerpts from a file in intelligence telegrams and reports regarding Soviet activity in sending Jews and Communist agents from Black Sea areas to Palestine.

Mr. Lovett also failed to see any particular urgency in the United States rushing to recognize the Jewish State prior to possible Soviet recognition.

I remarked to the President that, speaking objectively, I could not help but think that the suggestions made by Mr. Clifford were wrong. I though that to adopt these suggestions would have precisely the opposite effect from that intended by Mr. Clifford. The transparent dodge to win a few votes would not in fact achieve this purpose. The great dignity of the office of the President would be seriously diminished. The counsel offered by Mr. Clifford was based on domestic political considerations, while the problem which confronted us was international. I said bluntly that if the President were to follow Mr. Clifford's advice and if in the elections I were to vote, I would vote against the President.

Mr. Lovett and I told the President that naturally after May 16 we would take another look at the situation in Palestine in light of the facts as they existed. Clearly the question of recognition would have to be gone into very carefully. A paper presenting the legal aspects of the problem had been prepared in the Department and would be promptly sent to Mr. Clifford.

The President initialed the draft resolution and the underlying position paper of May 11, and terminated the interview by saying that he was fully aware of the difficulties and danger in the situation, to say nothing of the political risks involved which he, himself, would run.

---

1. Marshall S. Carter, Special Assistant to the Secretary of State.

APPENDIX XI

The British Embassy to the Department of State [invoking Article 39 of the UN Charter], Secret, May 22, 1948.

SECRET

SUMMARY OF A TELEGRAM FROM THE FOREIGN OFFICE REPORTING A CONVERSATION ON PALESTINE BETWEEN MR. BEVIN AND THE UNITED STATES AMBASSADOR IN LONDON ON THE 22ND MAY

On the 21st May, I sent a message to Mr. Douglas that I should like to see him on the morning of the 22nd May to discuss further the question of Palestine, and, in particular, our grave concern at the increasing divergences of American and British policy on this question.

2.   In the course of a long talk with Mr. Douglas this morning (22nd May), I said that we had made great progress with the United States over the questions of ERP, the Brussels Treaty and security measures for Europe. We were perturbed at the possible consequences of a continued drift apart. I said that changes in United States policy and some if the initiatives taken had left us bewildered and frustrated. Although His Majesty's Government had not felt able to agree to certain of the United States proposals, they had brought heavy and successful pressure to bear on the Arab Governments to withhold action until the 15th May in spite of constant Jewish provocation. On the 14th May, we had been insistently urging the Arab States to agree to the United States truce proposals. But the immediate *de facto* recognition of the Jewish State by the United States Government had cut the ground from under the efforts which we were making, not entirely unsuccessfully, with the Arabs on the basis of these United States proposals.

3.   United States recognition of the provisional Jewish Government was followed by the sudden introduction into the Security Council of the United States resolution proposing action under Article 39. If we agreed to the American proposal, we should be opening the door to Soviet intervention in the Middle East, and since no other powers were, so far as we knew, prepared to participate in consequential action, the result must be to discredit still further the United Nations.

4.   I felt strongly that the implications of the present situation and of any remedial action in the United Nations designed to meet it needed to be very fully and carefully thought out. Palestine was a question of deep concern to the countries of the Middle East, to Pakistan and to other countries with Moslem inhabitants. American policy was antagonising these nations and making them feel that considerations of justice and fair dealing were being subordinated to electoral pressure from the Zionists in New York. All the facts unfavourable to the Arabs were being emphasised and none of the facts unfavourable to the Jews. Take the case of Jerusalem, the High Commissioner had succeeded in securing the agreement of both parties to a cease-fire for eight days and the agreement of the Arabs to a truce. The Jews had refused a truce and had then proceeded to break the cease-fire. That was

the reason why fighting was now taking place in Jerusalem, and who could justly blame the Arabs? The Jews had occupied Jaffa and Acre, both of them Arab cities, as well as a large part of Western Galilee. These facts were overlooked or concealed. His Majesty's Government were trying to hold on to the balance even to prevent international action which would be as unjust as it would be unwise. But for this they were being abused and threatened.

5.   I made it plain to Mr. Douglas that His Majesty's Government would not abandon the line which they believed to be right. But I was genuinely concerned at where all this was leading. The attitude of the whole Moslem world, and American and British interests in the Middle East, were at stake. I appealed for measured discussion between us of all the issues involved before matters proceeded further.

6.   Mr. Douglas said that he fully agreed that it was most important that we should discuss and weigh together the whole range of political and strategic questions involved before either of us took further action, and said that he would inform his Government of my views.

7.   We have therefore agreed to supply Mr. Douglas with an appreciation of the position in relation to defence and of likely developments arising from the Palestine situation throughout the Middle East, India and Burma. He will discuss this with his Government, and it has also been arranged that he should meet myself, the Prime Minister, the Secretary of State for Commonwealth Relations, the Minister of Defence and the Chiefs of Staff here on this matter on the 25th May.

8.   I earnestly trust the United States Government will respond to our plea, and will suspend any further attempt to invoke Article 39 of the Charter or to raise their arms embargo pending the proposed joint review of the whole situation.

Washington, 24th May 1948.

APPENDIX XII

Memorandum by the Department of State to President Truman [Refugees], Secret, Washington, D.C. [Undated but drafted August 19, 1948].

SECRET   WASHINGTON, [UNDATED].

Subject: Relief of Arab and Jewish Refugees in the Near East.

As the result of the recent fighting in Palestine, approximately 330,000 Arab inhabitants of that country residing in areas now under occupation by the Provisional Government of Israel or the military forces of Israel precipitately fled from their homes and are now scattered either in the Arab portions of Palestine or in neighboring countries, including Syria, Transjordan and Egypt. There are likewise approximately 7,000 Jewish refugees who require assistance. The plight of the Arabs, however, is much more grave. They are destitute of any belongings, are without adequate shelter, medical supplies, sanitation and food. Their average daily ration, made up exclusively of bread, is only 600 calories. Only the rainy season commences and winter sets in, tragedy on the largest scale will be inevitable unless relief is forthcoming.

Thus far the Provisional Government of Israel has refused to admit the Arab refugees to their former homes, which have in some cases been destroyed by fighting and in others preempted by Jewish immigrants. The Israeli Foreign Minister has officially stated that his government will not permit the return of the refugees except in conjunction with a general peace settlement and under conditions which will not threaten either the economic stability or the internal security of Israel.

The United Nations Mediator, Count Bernadotte, on August 16, requested the Government of the United States to assist the 330,000 destitute Arab refugees and 7,000 Jewish refugees by donating and diverting to him at Beirut 2500 tons of wheat, 100 tons of canned meat, 50 tons of cheese, 50 tons of butter and 20 tons of DDT. He has further requested that 10 percent of these items be diverted immediately from United States seaborne supplies or in the nearest ports and that the remaining 90 percent be furnished within three months at the latest, except for the full amount of DDT which is required immediately.

In the absence of public United States funds authorized to meet the request of Count Bernadotte, the Department of State has turned to private American agencies, such as the Near East Foundation, the American Red Cross, and the Church World Service Committee, all of which have already contributed toward the relief of Arab and Jewish refugees in the Near East. In addition, the American-Arabian Oil Company has offered $100,000 to the Mediator for relief purposes. The American Red Cross has offered to furnish the 20 tons of DDT requested, and a telegram has been sent to the Chairman of the Red Cross, who is now in Stockholm, asking authorization to furnish $300,000 of needed supplies for the Mediator's purposes as outlined in his telegram.

Although Count Bernadotte's immediate requirements of the United States do not total more than $414,000, without adding the cost of transportation, his present request is but the first of many measures which will have to be taken if the Arab and Jewish refugees remain separated from their homes and without means of livelihood. It is estimated that if they continue as at present the total relief need will run between $2 and $4 million a month to keep them from starvation and epidemic disease.

The Department of State recommends:

1. That the Department continue its efforts to secure immediate donations from American private relief organizations.

2. That the Department be authorized to approach other agencies of this government with a view to assuming some share of the international burden of relief for refugees in the Near East.

3. That, as part of this government's diplomatic participation in securing a peaceful settlement of the Palestine problem, it urge upon the Provisional Government of Israel and other government concerned the need for repatriating Arab and Jewish refugees under conditions which will not imperil the internal security of the receiving states.

APPENDIX XIII

The Secretary of State to the Special Representative of the United States in Israel (McDonald) [Refugees], Top Secret, US Urgent, Washington, D.C., September 1, 1948.

TOP SECRET US URGENT   WASHINGTON, SEPTEMBER 1, 1948—6 P.M.

For McDonald. I have carefully considered your No. 70, Aug. 24, and have discussed it with the President.

Re section 1, urtel, it would appear that PGI [Provisional Government of Israel] may be making several issues out of an integral problem, professing its desire for immediate peace negotiations but maintaining its disinclination to carry out ceratin essential preliminary steps which you cite as "partial measures", including maintenance of truce, demilitarization of Jerusalem, and alleviation of Arab refugee problem.

The maintenance of truce is indispensable to successful peace negotiations. We do not, as member of UN, intend to see solution of Palestine problem by force or arms and accordingly if there is any sincere desire for peace negotiations on either side, they must be carried out while strict truce is maintained.

As for demilitarization of Jerusalem, this was in response to Security Council resolution of July 15, which reflected worldwide concern for fate of his holy city and determination of international community that sacred shrines of Jerusalem should not further be desecrated by conflict.

Arab refugee problem is one which, as you quote PGI as saying, did develop from recent war in Palestine but which also began before outbreak of Arab-Israeli hostilities. A significant portion of Arab refugees fled from their homes owing to Jewish occupation of Haifa on April 21–22 and to Jewish armed attack against Jaffa April 25. You will recall statements made by Jewish authorities in Palestine promising safeguards for Arab minority in areas under Jewish control. Arab refugee problem is one involving life or death of some 300,000 people. The leaders of Israel would make a grave miscalculation if they thought callous treatment of this tragic issue could pass unnoticed by world opinion. Furthermore, hatred of Arabs for Israel engendered by refugee problem would be a great obstacle to those peace negotiations you say PGI immediately desires.

In the light of the foregoing I do not concur in your conclusion that "Jewish emphasis on peace negotiations now is sounder than present US and UN emphasis on truce and demilitarization and refugees".

Nevertheless, this govt has for months past been seeking possible bases for a settlement which, if not agreed to, might be acquiesced in, and has made several efforts to bring about negotiated settlement. Some efforts failed because of Arabs, some because of Jews. When you state that Jewish emphasis on peace negotiations now is sound, do you mean that PGI has any assurance that there is any Arab govt with which it can negotiate? Please telegraph on this point.

Provided Arab govts as a group can be induced to participate in peace conversations with Israel, which at the moment seems most improbable, or provided that PGI can initiate private peace talks with one Arab govt such as Transjordan, which seems more within limit of possibility, we feel that PGI would be wise in not insisting on too much. We had reluctantly derived impression from recent developments that PGI desired to obtain all that was recommended in GA Resolution on November 29, 1947 (and for which they formally accepted by public proclamation in requests for recognition) plus such additional territory as is now under military occupation by Israeli forces, including the rich area of western Galilee and a portion of Jerusalem. We are aware of the problem presented by Extremists and internal political complications presented thereby. However, we would appreciate some indication of the true intentions of PGI in respect to their territorial claims.

For your own info, the US feels that the new State of Israel should have boundaries which will make it more homogeneous and well integrated than the hourglass frontiers drawn on the map of the November 29 Resolution. Perhaps some solution can be worked out as part of any settlement with Transjordan which would materially simplify boundary problem. Specifically, it would appear to us that Israel might expand into the rich area of Galilee, which it now holds in military occupation, in return for relinquishing a large portion of the Negev to Transjordan. This would leave the new State with materially improved frontiers and considerably enriched in terms of natural resources by acquisition of Galilee in return for the desert Negev.

Since Jerusalem is such a bone of contention between Arabs and Jews and is focal center of Christian interest in Palestine, we believe that it should form international enclave along lines recommended by GA resolution of Nov. 29, 1947, or by Trusteeship Council in its meetings in April and May, 1948. Any other arrangement satisfactory to both Jews and Arabs would, however, be acceptable to us, provided guarantees were given for access to and safety of holy places.

Please discuss foregoing suggestions with Ben Gurion and Shertok, making clear that although tentative and in the nature of "trying on for size" they are offered in an earnest desire of this govt to assist Israel to become a permanent factor for economic development and maintenance of peace in Middle East.

You should make clear to Shertok and Ben Gurion that we feel that demands in excess of foregoing suggestions would prejudice the possibility of a permanent peace in Palestine.

If authorities of PGI show any constructive response to these suggestions US is willing to present them to Mediator, in its role as member of SC Truce Commission, as being proposals which commend themselves to very serious consideration, and will take similar line with UK which can be expected to exert considerable pressure on Arab govts.

Adverting to concluding paragraph of reference telegram you should make very clear to Israeli leaders that this govt in Security Council will be zealous in advocating that Council apply measures, if necessary, under Chapter VII or Charter, to restrain resort to arms, whether by Arabs or by Israel. Leaders of PGI should be quick to see that non-military sanctions voted by SC as, for example, a ban on any financial transactions with aggressor state or modification of arms embargo, would have immediate consequences in such a state as Israel. In fact we are hopeful that wise counsels in Israel will perceive that new state cannot exist except by acceptance of international community and that PGI, of all new govts, should be most responsive to this fact.

We believe that leaders of Israel stand at moment of greatest opportunity for showing true statesmanship and thus to establish their republic on impregnable moral basis which will lead to sound political and economic development. US stands ready to give Israel its assistance to this end.

MARSHALL

APPENDIX XIV

The Acting Secretary of State to Mr. Mark F. Ethridge, signed Robert A. Lovett [U.S. policy], Top Secret, Washington, D.C., January 19, 1949.

TOP SECRET   WASHINGTON, JANUARY 19, 1949.

Sir: Before you depart for Palestine to assume your duties as the American representative on the Palestine Conciliation Commission, I am setting forth the following basic positions for your guidance:

A) A final settlement on all questions outstanding between the parties in Palestine should be achieved by negotiation as set forth in the General Assembly resolution on December 11, 1948. You should do everything possible as a member of the Conciliation Commission to assist the parties to reach an agreement by this means. You should consult the Department periodically during the course of these negotiations.

B) If it becomes necessary during the course of the negotiations for you to express the views of this Government, you should bear in mind that American policy is based on the following premises:

1. No modifications should be made in the boundaries of the State of Israel as established by the General Assembly resolution of November 29, 1947, without the full consent of the State of Israel.

2. If Israel desires additions to its territory as defined under the November 29 resolution, i.e., areas allotted by the General Assembly to the Arabs such as western Galilee and Jaffa, now under Israeli occupation, Israel should make territorial concessions elsewhere, i.e., the southern Negev. Israel is not entitled to keep both the Negev and western Galilee and Jaffa. If there is no agreement between the parties, the Israelis should relinquish western Galilee and Jaffa and the Arabs should relinquish the Israeli portion of the Negev.

3. If Israel desires to retain western Galilee and Jaffa, the southern border of Israel should not be drawn further south than the thirty-first parallel within the territory allotted to Israel under the resolution of November 29.

4. *Status of Jerusalem*—The resolution of December 11 states that the Jerusalem area should be accorded special and separate treatment from the rest of Palestine and should be placed under effective United Nations control. This could be accomplished by appointing a United Nations Commissioner for Jerusalem and by establishing the machinery to enable him to supervise the administration of the area, to guaran-

tee free access to the city and the Holy Places, and to insure adequate protection of the latter. The effective administration of the area of Jerusalem should be left to Arabs and Jews, the delineation of the parts of the area to be administered by each party to be determined by agreement.

It is not unlikely that Israel may call for a land corridor to connect the State of Israel with Jerusalem. Agreement to such a demand would not be in accord with the November 29 resolution, which provided only for freedom of access to Jerusalem; moreover, since such a corridor would bisect the territory which the November 29 resolution allotted to the Arabs, it would create a geographical anomaly. In the event, however, that the creation of such a land corridor appears to be essential to a final settlement, Israel should be prepared to make territorial concessions to the Arabs elsewhere.

5.   *The Port of Haifa*—The State of Israel should give assurances of free access for the interested Arab countries to the port of Haifa. The Arab countries in turn should undertake to place no obstacle in the way of oil deliveries by pipeline to the Haifa refinery. The products of the refinery should continue to be distributed on the basis of the historical pattern.

6.   *Lydda airport*—The airport of Lydda should be open to international air traffic without restrictions, and the interested Arab countries should be assured of access to its facilities.

7.   *Palestinian refugees*—You should be guided by the provisions of the General Assembly resolution of December 11 concerning refugees.

8.   *Disposition of Arab Palestine*—US favors incorporation of greater part of Arab Palestine in Transjordan. the remainder might be divided among other Arab states as seems desirable.

C) If negotiations, either directly between the parties or through the Commission, should fail, you will be authorized to join with the other members of the Commission in an effort to persuade the parties to agree upon frontiers between Israel and Arab Palestine as set forth in paragraph (3) above. At the same time, the United States Government will concert with the British Government to attempt to induce the parties to reach agreement on this basis.

Very truly yours,
ROBERT A. LOVETT

APPENDIX XV

Policy Paper Prepared in the Department of State, Palestine Refugees, Secret, Washington, D.C., March 15, 1949, [Excerpts].

[WASHINGTON,] MARCH 15, 1949.

PALESTINIAN REFUGEES
[EXCERPTS]

THE PROBLEM

The problem is to determine the nature and extent of United States interest in the question of some 725,000 Arab refugees from the palestine hostilities, and in the light of the findings, to make recommendations concerning United States policy towards the long-range disposition of this question.

DISCUSSION

(1) *Background:* As a result of hostilities in Palestine preceding and following the termination of the British Mandate and establishment of the State of Israel on May 15, 1948, almost the entire Arab population of Palestine fled or was expelled from the area under Jewish occupation. These Arabs, now estimated at 725,000, took refuge in Arab-controlled areas of Palestine and in the neighboring Arab states. The present distribution of the refugees is approximately the following:

Lebanon:	100,000–105,000 an addition of 10–10.5% to the normal population	
Syria:	85,000–100,000 an addition of 3.5–4% to the normal population	
Transjordan:	85,000 an addition of 21% to the normal population	
Iraq:	5,000 an addition of 0.1% to the normal population	
Egypt:	8,000–10,000 an addition of 0.04–0.05% to the normal population	
Palestine		
	North	230,000 areas under Egyptian, Iraqi, and Transjord
	South	225,000 anian military occupation

No accurate statistical breakdown of the refugees exists. However, the International Children's Emergency Fund considers 425,000 or 58% of the refugees eligible for assistance under its program: this group consists of infants, young children, pregnant women, and nursing mothers. Approximately 15% of the refugees are aged, sick, and infirm. It would appear that the able-bodied men and women amount to a maximum of 25 percent of the total, or 180,000.

The condition of these refugees, dependent upon their own slender resources and upon those of the neighboring states, rapidly became acute. Since the Government of Israel refused to permit repatriation of Arab refugees into israeli territory while a state of war existed, and since relief assistance enlisted by the United Nations Mediator for Palestine in August was wholly inadequate to meet a problem of this magnitude, the Mediator referred the problem to the General Assembly in September, with a renewed appeal for assistance. This appeal was reiterated by the Acting Mediator in a report to the United Nations on October 18, 1948, in which he made recommendations for the establishment of a United Nations relief program for assistance to the refugees.

(2) *Action taken up to present.*

In response to the Mediator's initial request in August for emergency supplies, the Department's only resource, in the absence of authorized public funds, was to appeal to American voluntary agencies. As a result of this action, funds and supplies exceeding $1,500,000 have been contributed by American voluntary sources as of March 1, 1949.

On November 19, 1948, the General Assembly unanimously passed a joint US-UK-Belgian-Dutch resolution calling for a United Nations program for the relief of Palestinian refugees. This resolution declared that a sum of $32,000,000 would be required for a nine months' program, to be raised by voluntary contribution, and authorized an immediate advance of $5,000,000 from the UN working capital fund.

This Government granted a leave of absence to Stanton Griffis, American Ambassador to Egypt, to enable him to accept the appointment as Director of United Nations Relief for Palestine Refugees.

On December 7, President Truman announced his intention of recommending to the Congress that the United States contribute 50 percent of the amount called for in the United Nations resolution, or $16,000,000. The authorizing legislation for this appropriation has been passed by the Senate, and is now pending in the House of Representatives.

The General Assembly resolution of December 11, 1948, establishing a Conciliation Commission for Palestine resolves "that the refugees wishing to return to their homes and live at peace with their neighbors should be permitted to do so at the earliest practicable date, and that compensation should be paid for the property of those choosing not to return and for loss of or damage to property which, under principles of international law or in equity, should be made good by the Governments or authorities responsible". A machinery for implementing these objectives is provided by the resolution, which "instructs the Conciliation Commission to facilitate the repatriation, resettlement and economic and social rehabilitation of the refugees and the payment of compensation, and to maintain close relations with the Director of the United Nations Relief for Palestine Refugees and, through him, with the appropriate organs and agencies of the United Nations," We strongly supported the resolution of December 11, and have instructed the American member of the Conciliation Commission to be guided, with respect to the refugee question, by its terms.

With respect to the attitude of the Israeli Government towards the question of repatriation, we have undertaken and are undertaking action on the diplomatic level in two respects: (1) with the underlying purpose of safeguarding Arab absentee property interests in Israel against application of the Israeli ordinance of December 12, 1948 authorizing sale of such property, we are urging Israel not to take unilateral action which would prejudice achievement of an agreed settlement on the return of refugees to their homes and return of property to refugee owners; (2) we are urging Israel to implement the purposes of the December 11 resolution, as a means of facilitating political settlement of the Palestine problem and preparing the way for a *modus vivendi* with the Arab states.

If Israel indicates agreement in principle with the December 11 resolution, or expresses its willingness to cooperate in resolving the refugee question, we also contemplate making representations to the Arab states, with a view to their adoption of a more realistic attitude towards the question of accepting a share of the refugees on a permanent basis and with a view to stimulating them to make constructive plans to this end.

(3)   *Assumptions that can be made with respect to the problem.*

Failure to liquidate or materially reduce the magnitude of the Arab refugee problem would have important consequences. The Arab states presently represent a highly vulnerable area for Soviet exploitation, and the presence of over 700,000 destitute, idle refugees provides the likeliest channel for such exploitation. In addition, their continued presence will further undermine the weakened economy of the Arab states, and may well provide the motivation for the overthrow of certain of the Arab Governments. Moreover, failure to liquidate the problem would adversely affect the possibility of a permanent settlement in Palestine, and would create a permanent source of friction between Israel and the Arab states.

Conversely, speedy action looking to the equitable solution of the refugee problem would further the restoration of peace and security and contribute to the stabilization of the Near East. It would prevent the exploitation of the refugee problem by foreign interests inimical to the best interests of the peoples of the Near East.

In view of the stated position of Israel towards the question of repatriation, and the large-scale preemption of Arab lands and housing by Jewish immigrants, who are entering Israel at the rate of 25,000 monthly, it would be wholly unrealistic to expect Israel to agree to the repatriation of all those so desiring. Although the Jews originally accepted the partition resolution of November 29, 1947, under which the Arab population of the Jewish state would have numbered 500,000, it is doubtful that the State of Israel would now permit more than a small number of refugees to return to Israel. If Israel could be persuaded to accept any substantial number, it is probable that it would request financial assistance in carrying out their repatriation.

It is reasonable to assume that as many as 600,000 refugees will have to be permanently settled in the Arab states. The Arab states, however, will be unable to accomplish the resettlement of this number without adverse economic and political repercussions, unless material assistance is forthcoming.

It can also be assumed that any machinery and resources which are placed at the disposal of the Conciliation Commission to implement its task will be inadequate to deal with a resettlement problem of this magnitude. Moreover, the resources of the United Nations and its specialized agencies are presently inadequate to handle this problem and, to judge from the response of the member states to the appeal for funds to implement the November 19 resolution establishing a relief program, the member states would not be willing to contribute the material resources required to carry out a mass resettlement program if such action were proposed in the United Nations.

Finally, it can be assumed that Great Britain is the only major foreign power whose degree of interest in the liquidation of the refugee question is sufficient to insure any significant participation in its solution. (Attention should be called in this respect to Great Britain's close treaty relations with Egypt and Iraq, and to her special position with respect to Transjordan, the latter two of which would probably be heavily involved in any mass resettlement program.)

(4)   *United States interests and policy in the Near East.*

The Near Eastern area, which consists of Israel and the Arab states, is an area of vital strategic importance, a communications center, and a major source of petroleum. As such, it is an area of special concern to all the great powers and to certain lesser powers. During recent years our chief objective in the Near East was to prevent inherent rivalries and conflicting interests in that area from developing into conditions which might lead to a third world war, and objective dictated by our primary interest in safeguarding the security of the United States.

Because of the special significance of Palestine, the conflicting interests and aspirations of the Near East as a whole have had a primary focus in that country and, during the past year, found expression in open hostilities. Prior to the outbreak of hostilities, this Government took a leading part in seeking a solution to the Palestine problem which would be acceptable to the interested parties. Since the failure of these attempts, we have been active in supporting measures designed to end the conflict, and to achieve a permanent settlement of the Palestine problem. These efforts, carried on within the framework of the United Nations, have been governed by out desire to support in the Near East the principles of the United Nations, and to put an end to the threat to international security and to American strategic interests in the Near East which the present situation represents.

In conjunction with our efforts to achieve the permanent settlement of Arab-Jewish differences with respect to Palestine, we are striving to promote the establishment of cooperative relationships between Israel and the Arab states, as a condition to the stabilization and peaceful development of the area.

On a regional basis, it is out policy to assist the Near Eastern countries in maintaining their independence, to strengthen their orientation towards the West, and to discourage any tendencies towards the development of authoritarian and unrepresentative forms of government. Such efforts are designed both to minimize the debilitating effects of internal discontent, and to strengthen the determination of these states to resist external pressures and intervention.

(5)   *Effect of the refugee problem upon United States interests and policy.*

From the political point of view, the stabilization of the Near East is a major objective of American foreign policy. The refugee problem, therefore, as a focal point for continued unrest within the Arab states, a source of continuing friction between Israel and the Arabs, and a likely channel for Soviet exploitation, is directly related to our national interests.

From the strategic point of view, the Joint Chiefs of Staff, on September 22, 1948, with specific reference to the Arab refugee question, characterized the Near Eastern area as an area of critical strategic importance, and emphasized the necessity, from a military standpoint, of maintaining the Arab world oriented towards the United States and the United Kingdom. They therefore recommended that, as a measure to strengthen our military position, the United States should make provision for generous assistance to the Arab refugees from Palestine. The Secretary of Defense on January 25, 1949, characterized the presence of the refugees in the Near East as a serious threat to the political, economic and social stability of this region, and a serious danger to the health and welfare of the peoples of the Arab states and Israel.

Our present policy with respect to Palestinian refugees, as set forth in the Secretary's Policy Problem Book, if the following:

We should use our best efforts, through the Conciliation Commission and through diplomatic channels, to insure the implementation of the General Assembly resolution of December 11, 1948;

We should endeavor to persuade Israel to accept the return of those refugees who so desire, in the interests of justice and as an evidence of its desire to establish amicable relations with the Arab world;

We should furnish advice and guidance to the governments of the Arab states in the task of absorbing into their economic and social structures those refugees who do not wish to return to Israel.

(6) *Attitudes of UN, individual governments, and refugees themselves toward the problem.*

(a) *Attitude of the UN.*

Count Bernadotte, the slain Palestine Mediator, very early established the principle of UN responsibility for the Palestine refugees. In Conclusion (G) of his report, dated September 16, in Part Three (Assistance to Refugees), he said:

"So long as large numbers of the refugees remain in distress, I believe that responsibility for their relief should be assumed by the United Nations in conjunction with the neighboring Arab States, the Provisional Government of Israel, the specialized agencies, and also all the voluntary bodies or organizations of a humanitarian and non-political nature."

However, at the Third Session of the General Assembly in Paris, the United States Delegation was careful to insist in conversations with other Delegations that there was no *legal* responsibility for refugee relief devolving upon the United Nations. The United States Delegation succeeded in eliminating from the United Kingdom draft of the Preamble of the resolution before the Third Committee providing for an emergency relief program, a paragraph which would have established United Nations responsibility for this problem. The issue was placed before the Third Committee and the Assembly on its own merits as a question involving humanitarian as well as political elements which would have to be met on an *ad hoc* basis without establishing a precedent for similar United Nations action in other cases.

Nevertheless, in the eyes of the refugees themselves and to an even greater extent in the view of the Arab Governments, there is a United Nations responsibility for the care of the refugees only slightly less than an imagined United States responsibility, since the Arab Governments are prone to insist that Israel would not have come into existence with United States support and, had there been no Israel, there would have been no refugees.

Subsequent to the passage of the resolution, the UN in the field, under the directorship of Ambassador Stanton Griffis, has undertaken primary responsibility for the emergency phase of refugee relief. These is no doubt that the Secretary General, Mr. Trygve Lie, feels convinced that the United Nations must continue to show effective leadership in meeting this problem. However, in essence, the continuing participation of the United Nations in dealing with the interim and long-range phases of the matter will depend on the attitudes of the Governments who compose the United Nations.

(b) *Attitudes of Governments.*

It was significant that when the Palestine refugee problem was considered by

Committee 3 in Paris last autumn, support was more verbal than valuable in tangible terms. Mr. Mayhew of the British Delegation, at the very commencement of the session, insisted that the Third Committee should immediately devise measures to meet the refugee problem. When asked, however, what measures the United Kingdom had in mind or even if its delegation had a draft resolution, Mr. Mayhew confessed that they had neither ideas not the embodiment of ideas in resolution form. The British attitude seemed to be one of viewing with great alarm, but most of the spade work in developing the resolution which was finally adopted by the Assembly was done by the United States Delegation. It is probable, however, that it was due to British influence that the Netherlands and Belgium associated themselves with the United Kingdom, and the United States, in jointly sponsoring a resolution. Unfortunately, however, the interest of these governments in contributing to the refugee relief in more tangible terms than sponsorship of a resolution has not proved to be very great. Although the Belgian Government has contributed approximately one-half million dollars, the Dutch have given nothing, while the French contribution still awaits Parliamentary approval. The British contribution totals one million pounds.

The response of other governments has been even less enthusiastic. In fact, the great brunt of relief expenditures has been borne, perforce, by the Arab States, on whom these refugees are quartered. Dr. Bayard Dodge estimates that from the time the first refugees escaped from Haifa and Jaffa in the spring of 1948, to December 1 in that year, the Arab Governments contributed $11 million in cash or kind to their sustenance. This sum, in light of the very slender budgets of most of these Governments, is relatively enormous. [1]

The conclusion seems inescapable, therefore, that even though the United Nations should formulate a program for the interim and long-range relief periods, its constituent Governments cannot be relied upon for very effective contributions with the possible exception of the United Kingdom.

The United Kingdom has definitely indicated its mounting concern at the refugee problem, realizing as it does how the presence of 700,000 demoralized and hungry people can threaten the entire stability of the strategic Middle East in which the United Kingdom has a vital interest. Thus, the British Foreign Secretary on March 2 spoke to Ambassador Douglas in London of the depth of his concern regarding the plight of the Arab refugees. Mr. Bevin felt that this was a problem of alarming proportions which "deserves the utmost efforts of the United States and United Kingdom as well as the United Nations", to say nothing of being a political problem of the first magnitude for the reestablishment of peace in the Middle East (London telegram 787, March 3).

* * * *

(c) Attitude of the Refugees Themselves.

All reports from the field—i.e., those of Dr. Bayard Dodge and Mr. Colin Bell of the Friends Service Committee, recently returned from Gaza, and of Mr. St. Aubin, the Field Director in the Near East of the American Red Cross, plus reports from United States Missions in that area—confirm that the great bulk of the refugees wish to return to their homes and cling to the illusion that it will be possible to do so.

The danger point will come when the refugees realize that it will be impossible for the majority to return home. It is true that Mr. Stanton Griffis in Cairo's airgram A-254, March 1, expresses the opinion that, once peace is restored, large numbers of refugees will infiltrate across the Israeli border and return to their former abode. Nevertheless, the Representatives of the Provisional Government of Israel have very clearly indicated that Israel has no intention of taking back more than a portion of the refugees. The Israeli Representative in Washington, Mr. Eliahu Elath, told Mr. Mark Ethridge that he though that maybe the Christian Arabs might be permitted to return but the Moslem Arabs would be an intractable element who could not assimilate in Israel. Furthermore, Israeli authorities have followed a systematic program of destroying Arab houses in such cities as Haifa and in village communities in order to rebuild modern habitations for the influx of Jewish immigrants from DP camps in Europe. There are, thus, in many instances, literally no houses for the refugees to return to. In other cases incoming Jewish immigrants have occupied Arab dwellings and will most certainly not relinquish them in favor of the refugees. Accordingly, it seems certain that the majority of these unfortunate people will soon be confronted with the fact that they will not be able to return home. Unless some alternative is prepared and some hope offered them of an improved life in the future, it is certain that the political, to say nothing of the social, repercussions of this discovery will be very great.

If a proper program can be devised and implemented promptly, it is to be anticipated that the refugees will cooperate in carrying out the program, especially since they will in any case have no alternative. These people, for the most part, have long been inured to hardship and to life on a subsistence level. Although they have a very natural desire to return to their local fig tree and vine, to use Ambassador Griffis' phrase, it should be possible, if they had a reasonable prospect of acquiring some other fig tree and vine elsewhere, to maintain their morale and to put tools in their hands for their own salvation. The danger will be, if through lack of a proper program of adequate funds, they find themselves, on one hand, cut off from a hope of return to their former homes and, on the other hand, bereft of hope in establishing a new life for themselves elsewhere. If this should transpire it seems almost a foregone conclusion that the ensuing conditions of unrest and despair would provide a most fertile hotbed for the implantation of Communism, and we should in that moment expect to see in the vitally important strategic Middle East a reproduction of the present debacle in China.

(d) Attitude of the Arab states.

It is the present policy of the Arab states to insist upon the repatriation of all the Palestinian refugees, and none of the Arab states with the exception of Transjordan contemplates the permanent settlement of any refugees within its own territory. It can be assumed that the most vigorous efforts will have to be exerted by the Conciliation Commission and by interested governments if the Arab states are to be persuaded to adopt a more realistic and cooperative attitude towards this question. Moreover, it can be assumed that their active cooperation could only be obtained under the following circumstances:

(1) they would require evidence that substantial material assistance would be forthcoming from outside sources to aid in solving the refugee problem;

(2) they would require assurances that such aid would be of material benefit to their countries and populations, as well as to the refugees themselves;

(3) they would require assurances that the administration of such aid would involve no derogation of sovereignty; and

(4) they would require evidence that Israel was prepared to cooperate effectively in the liquidation of the refugee problem.

(7) United States Public Attitude Toward the Problem.

The American public, generally is unaware of the Palestine refugee problem, since it has not been hammered away at by the press or radio. Aside from the *New York Times* and the *Herald Tribune*, which have done more faithful reporting than any other papers, there has been very little coverage of the problem. With the exception of a Sunday feature article by Max Boyd, the wire service stories, if filed, have not been used. Editorial comment is still more sparse. Freda Kirchwey in *Nation*, and few editorials in *America* (Catholic), and editorialized article in the *New Leader* and one editorial each in the *Baltimore Sun* and the *Des Moines Register* nearly exhausts the list. Most of the news articles and editorials have had a friendly slant, except for the *New York Post*, which was violently opposed to helping the Arabs. While some of the articles have addressed themselves to the question of the nature of the settlement as regards repatriation or resettlement, none of them have raised the question of continuing aid. Consequently one may conclude that, barring any dramatic developments which would arouse prejudices or create new issues, a continuing but not spectacular aid program would probably be supported by the enlightened few, and would no, in all likelihood, run into strong opposition.

* * * *

RECOMMENDATIONS

The following objectives are recommended as a basis for planning with respect to the problem, subject to change as the plan develops:

(1) To stimulate the adoption of plans to expedite the transfer of the problem from its present unproductive relief basis to a basis for a definitive settlement;

(2) To persuade Israel to accept the principle of repatriation of an agreed number or category of refugees, with provision by Israel for appropriate safeguards of civil and religious rights and on condition that those repatriated desire to live at peace within Israel and to extend full allegiance thereto;

(3) To persuade Israel to initiate the gradual repatriation of an agreed number or category as soon as possible;

(4) To urge the Israeli Government to make equitable compensation for the property and assets of those refugees who do not desire to return and of those whose property and assets have been expropriated or otherwise disposed of by the State of Israel;

(5) To provide for the permanent settlement in Arab Palestine in the near future of as large a number of the refugees as appears economically practicable;

(6) Under the assumption that Arab Palestine, or at least a large portion thereof, will be allotted to Transjordan in the final peace settlement, to undertake concerted planning with the British Government with a view to the early integration of a large portion of the refugee population into the economic and political structure of the expanded state as a whole;

(7) To examine the developmental resources common to Israel and the expanded state of Transjordan, with special reference to their water resources, with a view to stimulating cooperative economic development projects, where feasible, for the mutual benefit of both states;

(8) If the repatriation of substantial number of refugees becomes feasible, to give special consideration to those areas having the greatest relative concentrations of refugees, particularly Lebanon, which is undergoing serious economic pressures and facing potential political pressures, and the Gaza area of southwestern Palestine, with its limited developmental potentialities;

(9) With respect to those refugees who cannot be assimilated in Israel or the expanded state of Transjordan, to examine the potentialities for permanent resettlement elsewhere in the Near East, bearing in mind the capabilities of northeastern Syria and northern Iraq, where basic manpower shortages and large cultivable areas exist;

(10) Where feasible, in the resettlement of refugees, to plan on utilization of projects which will contribute to the long-range development of the productive capacity and economic potential of the area, as contrasted with short-term projects which might be without ultimate benefit to the countries involved.

---

1. The total direct relief offered the Arab refugees by the Israeli Government to date consists of 500 cases of oranges.

APPENDIX XVI

The Minister in Lebanon (Pinkerton) to the Secretary of State [Ethridge on Arabs and Israel], Top Secret, NIACT, Beirut, March 28, 1949.

TOP SECRET NIACT BEIRUT, MARCH 28, 1949—5 P.M. URGENT

For the Secretary (and at his discretion for the President) from Ethridge. Talks with Arabs governments over past week have only confirmed what I previously reported to Department; That if Jews would only make conciliatory gesture on refugee problem PCC could get on with its work of trying to get peace. Failure of Jews to do so has prejudiced whole cause of peaceful settlement in this part of world.

As we anticipated Commission has been confronted by insistent demand from Arabs that Jews evidence good faith and willingness to abide by GA resolution December 11 before negotiations were entered. They argued since Jews have constantly flouted UN resolution there was noting for the Arabs to gain by entering negotiations under UN auspices. They have maintained that only when Jews show respect for UN or until other guarantees of fulfillment are forthcoming will they be willing to enter peace talks.

Arab attitude toward refugee problem proceeds from two or three reasons. One is that they recognize presence of 700,000 or 800,000 homeless idle people as political weapon against Jews. They feel they can summon world opinion even if some refugees die in meantime. They frankly say, moreover, that when Israel comes up for confirmation in GA they intend to fight her and are trying to get their friends to fight her on ground she cannot pretend to be peace-loving as long as her aggression continues and on ground that, since she is defying UN resolution and directives, as in the Akaba incident and on refugee problem, it is mockery to admit her as nation willing and able to undertake obligations of charter. It has been intimated to me that government "friendly to Arabs" might even suggest the GA direct SYG to send telegram to PCC asking whether the countries involved under December 11 resolution had accepted resolution in principle and were assisting in implementing it. If such a move is made and not defeated in GA I might be in very embarrassing position of having to join fellow commissioners in reporting that Israeli Government has not accepted resolution in principle and refuses implement it.

Second reason for Arab position is fear of domestic repercussions on refugee problem. Since Egypt and Saudi Arabia have no refugees (Egypt has reportedly sent all of hers into Gaza strip) and Iraq has only about 4,000, figure of 800,000 constitutes about one-tenth population remaining Arab states. Since they generally more advanced than other Arabs they constitute potential core of dangerous agitators offering a threat to existence of Arab government. They also create, so Arab leaders have told me, core of irredentist movement that will plague all Arab states and provide basis for continual agitation to point that there will be no possibility of having anything more than armistice in Middle East.

In private conversations both Saudi Arabian and Egyptian have told me that if

242

Israel would take token number of refugees back as preliminary gesture, peace talks could move along. Frightened Transjordanians desperately want peace talks but are also extremely sensitive to idea of "running out" on other Arab states. I am convinced they will talk peace, particularly boundary lines, when they have signed their armistice, but it is likely that on refugee problem they will continue to maintain Arab line. I am more than ever of opinion that if Jews are not deliberately stalling peace negotiations until they can consolidate their position and grab off more land as they seem to be doing in triangle, they are being most short-sighted and making it difficult for themselves ever to have peaceful relations with their neighbors.

Although Commission is making bricks without straw and with, I fear, too little support from home, it is going on with its work. We are staying in beirut until Arab governments have agreed to further "exchange of views" with Commission in some neutral city where Jews will also be present. In their present mood the Arabs will not even talk about peace conference. We will have to try to ease them into it. In meantime, Commission intends, when it leaves Beirut, to go back to Tel Aviv for talks with [Ben-] Gurion. Jews told us they were ready for direct negotiations, but again refugee problem is not one that can be negotiated directly between Israel and another government, since all Arab governments except Yemen involved.

Although we feel we must go back to Tel Aviv it will do us little good unless Israel Government is pressured by USG to make concession which it could easily make without prejudicing its position in peace negotiations and without revealing its final hand. It is pure rubbish for Shertok to say he cannot do so; Israeli Government already knows how many it will take back and under what conditions. If it had any respect for UN and any desire to live by its ordinances it could make PCC's job easier and shorter and make its own position vis-à-vis the Arabs much more secure than it will ever be if it continues to allow refugee problem to be source agitation in every Arab country and refugees a ready prey to agitators who already working among them.

My own position is most unhappy. It is bad enough to realize UN prestige in this part world already gone, but worse than that is realization that US prestige constantly declining and feeling toward US increasingly despairing. Since we gave Israel birth we are blamed for her belligerence and her arrogance and for cold-bloodedness of her attitude toward refugees. Of course everybody expects US to pass miracle but none is needed in this case. All that is needed is effective pressure directed toward making Israel realize that her own interests and ours are also being jeopardized in this strategic area by her intransigence. So far as we are aware, Israel has not replied to approach made in Deptel 144 March 9. Firm reiteration of policy enunciated in GA by Jessup on territorial questions and insistence that Israel abide by resolution as to refugees would, I am convinced, clear atmosphere and bring quick peace which Israel needs as badly as Arabs. If Dept intends to do anything along that line, it should be done before PCC goes to Tel Aviv.

I am frankly asking for help. If we do not help out I can see no good result from the work of this Commission. What I can see is an abortion of justice and humanity to which I do not want to be midwife; complete destruction of all faith in an international organization and creation of a very dangerous flame against US in this part of world. [Ethridge.]

PINKERTON

APPENDIX XVII

Mr. Mark F. Ethridge to the Secretary of State [Ethridge on Israel's policy], Secret, April 13, 1949, [Excerpts].

SECRET   JERUSALEM, APRIL 13, 1949—1 P.M.

For the Secretary from Ethridge. Two days after Commission's talk with Ben-Gurion last week Lipschitz, one of three Israeli members of Jerusalem Committee set up in Foreign Office, called me and urgently asked to see me. Obvious his primary purpose was to arrange meetings here for Comay who seems to be second man at Foreign Office during Sharett's absence. Comay came to Jerusalem and talked with Halderman and Yenissey, Turkish member of Jerusalem Committee. Afterwards he had three-hour talk with me, during course of which he disclosed Israel's position on almost all matters under PCC consideration. Following is summary of Israeli views on primary questions:

Jerusalem: Comay said that Ben-Gurion had been angered by Yalcin's observation that Commission was bound by its terms of reference and question of full internationalization was not therefore debatable. Ben-Gurion had reacted more strongly than had been intended and had therefore over-stated Israel's position. Intent of Ben-Gurion's statement was that if Commission felt bound to propose full international regime in letter and spirit of resolution, Israel would be compelled to oppose in GA. It was not Ben-Gurion's intention to deny possibility of acceptable solution within resolution. He desired to correct PCC report which was sent to Lake Success and would write the Commission letter correcting impression left upon Commission. Comay's main point was that Commission should strive to achieve plan acceptable to parties concerned, namely Israel, Transjordan (or other adjacent state) and UN. If Committee were to proceed without reference to states immediately concerned, product of its work would probably be unacceptable and would not contribute to solution of problem. he considered it possible to achieve plan which would be acceptable to all concerned. he was convinced that UN would accept plan containing more limited form of internationalization than might have been contemplated when resolution was adopted last December, provided plan were acceptable to parties concerned. Ben-Gurion, basis of his own extensive experience with UN here is convinced that GA would not only accept such plan, but would be extremely pleased to achieve settlement of problem.

Comay advised "month of masterly inactivity" while Transjordan and Israel try to work out through special committee agreement on Jerusalem. He thought there would be no difficulty about Jewish-Arab lines in Jerusalem since Israel would be willing to compensate for Arab expropriated property inside city. What Israel had proposed to Transjordan, in informal talks that seem to be going on now, is division of city into three zones: Jewish, Arab and international (Old City). Dayan told me later that Transjordan had shown reluctance to discuss any matters other then these strictly within armistice terms although

Transjordan had previously evidenced willingness to effect opening of Bethlehem and Scopus roads and to deal with other technical matters preliminary to any peace settlement.

Comment: Ben-Gurion's strong reaction in which he virtually announced that Jerusalem would be capital of Israel did in fact create strong reaction in Commission. As reported previously, French and Turkish delegations refused to allow their members of Jerusalem Committee to meet formally with Comay for further explanations of Israeli position. For US Del I said that whether other members met or not I would instruct Halderman to do so and to explore with both sides and all parties concerned fullest possible area of agreement. Commission finally agreed that Halderman should represent Jerusalem Committee in talks with Comay and convey information to Commission. I told Comay that I did not of course consider that he had so far helped us toward a solution and I hoped he would continue his talks with Halderman and give us his full views. He promised to do so "a little later". I am sure what he has in mind is trying to work out a deal with Transjordan and present the Commission with written agreement, achieved perhaps in manner of Tulkarm agreement. Nevertheless, I am willing to consider any agreement that can be made between them although I am afraid it will give my French colleague apoplexy.

Comay has so far not even discussed anything substantive on Jerusalem. it is obvious from French plan previously reported that French will press for full internationalization including international force, special courts, distinct citizenship and special currency for Jerusalem. I consider that impossible and fantastic. I am afraid, however, that Turks will swallow it and that we may come to situation where there will be two reports to GA although I will do all I can to prevent it. Turkish attitude is not based so much upon any consuming passion for protection of holy places as upon distinct pro-Arab bias and upon, I fear, growing desire to put Israel in defensive position whenever possible perhaps a personal reaction to Israel's refusal to give at any point. My own position, I feel, accords with Department's and with my Contel 192, March 7.

* * * *

Refugees: Comay's position on refugees was pretty much as has been reported with few additions. He said that at low point there were about 70,000 Arabs in Israel-held territory but number has increased to about 130,000 through infiltration and through taking over of new territory, such as Tulkarm and in Beersheba area. Israel did not feel, therefore, that it could take many more. he asked if Commission had any figure in mind. I told him Commission had not discussed figure because it stuck to principle of resolution but that my own feeling was that since Israel had once accepted state with 400,000 Arabs in it she should be prepared to take back at least 250,000 refugees and compensate others. He said it was completely impossible, that Israel was deterred at moment from reducing her immigration quota of Jews only by sentiment and political dynamite. On any practical basis, he added, immigration would certainly have to be cut because adequate employment, housing and services were not being provided for those who are coming in and Israel could not possibly double her burden in next two years. Later in conversation he said that it was probable that total number of Arabs in Israeli territory might reach 200,000 eventually through infiltration and "our taking a token number". Aside from economic burden, Israel determined not to have any fifth column inside its lines particularly if faced by stronger Arab state backed by major power.

Comment: It is obvious that Israel has not changed position on refugee problem whatever. Israeli Cabinet yesterday considered memorandum of suggestions from Commission as to steps that might be taken now to mitigate plight of refugees and also proposal of statement by Ben-Gurion clarifying Israeli position and mollifying Arab sentiment. No word has come from that meeting. Israel does not intend to take back one refugee more than she is forced to take and she does not intend to compensate any directly if she can avoid it. Ben-Gurion and Comay have both argued that refugees are inevitable result of war and no state in modern history has been expected to repatriate them. Both cite Baltic states and Turkey. They contend also that number greatly exaggerated and they can prove it. Israel refuses to accept any responsibility whatever for creation of refugees. I flatly told Ben-Gurion and Comay that while Commission was no tribunal to judge truth of contentions, I could not for moment accept that statement in face of Jaffa, Deir Yassin, Haifa and all reports that come to us from refugee organizations that new refugees are being created every day by repression and terrorism such as now being reported from Haifa. I have repeatedly pointed out political weakness and brutality of their position on refugees but it has made little impression. They are aware that world sentiment is being roused to some extent by plight of Arab refugees but they contend they are being subject to calumnies and vicious propaganda. I have answered that they are master propagandists of world and that if Arabs had tenth the genius at it they would rouse public opinion to where it would engulf Israel in wave of indignation, particularly in view of fact that world has so greatly helped Israel to come into being. They don't admit that world has helped. Comay told me that but for US intervention at wrong time (apparently with proposal for second truce) Israel would be in Jordan. "And," he added, "she needs space".

Territorial Settlements: Comay said that there will be little difficulty with Lebanon or Syria and "only minor local adjustments of border on a give-and-take basis to increase out security" will be suggested. He thought either Lebanon or Egypt might be first to sign peace agreement. Israel, he said, has no territorial claims on Egypt and he did not think Egypt would make any on Israel. Settlement of Gaza strip, he thought, would be between Transjordan and Egypt rather than between Israel and Egypt.

As to Transjordan, Comay said that Abdullah had advanced idea of port on mediterranean with corridor across Negeb but Israel had no intention of giving up Negeb or allowing it to be cut in half. He felt that something could be worked out to give Transjordan guaranteed access to some port, either Gaza or one further north. Any arrangement with Transjordan would depend upon the position of Arab Palestine. he repeated that if Arab Palestine were to fall to Transjordan, which he considered inevitable, a "new situation" would arise in which Israel would have to give greater consideration to her security. That would involve not giving up any territory in Samaria but of getting more by going to the Samarian foothills. Tulkarm, for instance, would sooner or later have to become Jewish. It would also increase security, importance of Western Galilee which Israel intended to hold in any case.

Comay did not feel that Abdullah would have any great reluctance to give up more of Arab Palestine because, he argued, "He is getting a bonus out of the war by additional territory and more population". Comay insisted that Israel would not sign any peace treaty with Transjordan that envisioned extension of British-Transjordan treaty to Arab Palestine. He said there has been mention of federation of Transjordan and Arab Palestine.

Comay thought that in southern Arab bulge, the armistice lines would pretty well hold.

Comment: Israel's position as to Gaza strip is, I believe, that she does not want it with 330,000 Arabs in it, 230,000 of them refugees, particularly since she has back country upon which they have been living. She is probably content at the moment to let it wither.

That is also true as to Tulkarm. Palestine Arabs with whom I have talked say that armistice clause not only created thousands of new refugees in that they will eventually be driven out of villages that were given up but that it was the death sentence of Tulkarm, which has lived on rich land that Abdullah surrendered. palestine Arabs are bitter with Abdullah, Britain and US. They contend that our inactivity amounted to pressure upon Abdullah to sign.

It is obvious from Comay's statement of Israel's territorial claims that she is in direct contravention of US policy. When I told Comay that he was certainly aware that President and Secretary had only recently reaffirmed to Sharret US views on territorial settlement he replied, "yes, but we hope to change Washington's mind".

General Comment: In spite of all Department has done since January, Israel has stiffened rather than modified her position. Armistice talks have emphasized Arab weakness because, as Bunche told me, Israel gave at no point and Arabs gave at every point where concession was necessary. Israel intends to exploit that weakness to the maximum.

Again it seems to me that Israeli position has brought into question whole US policy as to Palestine. One matter of concern is that unfair arrangements sponsored by UN and approved by US would have serious repercussions in Middle East and tend to discredit US, besides providing good basis for exploitation by unfriendly powers.

ETHRIDGE

APPENDIX XVIII

Memorandum by the Acting Secretary of State to the President [State Department complaint about Israel], Top Secret, Washington, D.C., May 27, 1949.

TOP SECRET   WASHINGTON, MAY 27, 1949.

Subject: Representation to Israeli Government on Territorial Settlement in Palestine and Question of Palestinian Refugees.

1. *Israeli Position toward Final Settlement*

Mr. Mark Ethridge, United States Representative on the Palestine Conciliation Commission, reports in a telegram dated may 20 (Tab A) that Israel has now put forth its full territorial demands upon the Arab States. Under authorization from the Israeli Foreign Minister, the Israeli representative at Lausanne has stated as follows: (1) While Israel makes no demands upon Lebanon at present, it would later like a portion of southeastern Lebanon considered necessary to Israeli development plans. The Israeli delegate said Israel would be willing to compensate Lebanon for this territory, but he did not specify in what way this would be done; (2) Israel desires to acquire from Egypt the Egyptian occupied Gaza strip, allotted to the Arabs under the partition resolution of November 29, 1947; (3) Israel makes no demands upon Syria at present, but will accept the international frontier with the proviso, also to be applied to Lebanon, that if either state desires to open negotiations in the future for border rectification, this may be done; (4) Israel will make further demands upon Transjordan for territory in Arab Palestine considered necessary to Israel development plans. Israel has in mind giving Abdullah a few villages in return; (5) Israel will retain occupied areas such as Western Galilee and Jaffa, Lydda and Ramle allotted to the Arabs under the partition plan; (6) Israel will relinquish none of the Negev. The Israeli delegate subsequently, however, indicated to Mr. Ethridge the possibility that Israel might make some compensation in the Negev in return for the Gaza strip.

The Israeli delegate further stated that Israel will do nothing more concerning the Arab refugees at the present time.

2. *United States Position*

In the interest of achieving an equitable territorial settlement for Palestine, this Government has consistently supported the position that Israel should offer territorial compensation for any territorial acquisition which it expects to obtain beyond the boundaries allotted to Israel in the resolution of November 29,1947. Moreover, since the General Assembly resolution of December 11, 1948 calls for the repatriation of those refugees desiring to return to their homes and live at peace, and in view of the impossibility of resettling the total number of refugees in the Arab States within a reasonable period of time and at a reasonable cost, this Government has recently made representations to the Israeli Government urging its agreement to repatriation of a substantial number of refugees and the immediate commencement of repatriation of some portion thereof. Despite the emphasis upon repatriation in the resolution of December 11, we have urged upon the Arabs the necessity for their agreement to the resettlement in the Arab States of a substantial portion of the refugees, in view of the fact that the return to their homes of all the refugees desiring to go back would be difficult because of the continuing arrival in Israel of large numbers of European displaced persons.

Our representations on these two questions have thus far met with no success with the Israeli Government. Israeli officials have in fact informed our representatives in Palestine that they intend to bring about a change in the position of the United States Government on the above points, through means available to them in the United States. There are also indications that the Israelis are prepared to use the implied threat of force to obtain the additional territory which they desire in Palestine.

3. *Efforts of the Palestine Conciliation Commission*

The Conciliation Commission has vigorously endeavored to persuade the Israelis and the Arabs to withdraw from their extreme positions concerning a final Palestine settlement. With respect to refugees, the Commission has succeeded in persuading the Arabs to give up their pervious insistence upon repatriation as a prerequisite to negotiations on other outstanding issues, and in persuading certain of the Arab States to give favorable consideration to resettlement of a portion of the refugees. The Commission has failed to obtain any concessions from the Israelis on a territorial settlement or the refugee question. It is now the considered opinion of Mr. Ethridge that the conference at Lausanne is likely to break up when the Arabs learn of the present Israeli position toward a final settlement and that there will exist no possibility of peace on any basis heretofore envisioned by the United States Government unless Israel modifies its demands. Mr. Ethridge believes that such modification is unlikely.

4. *United States Interest*

The United States interest in the security and stability of the Near East has been a principle motivation of our efforts, both in the United Nations and on the diplomatic level, to urge both parties to the Palestine dispute to take measures leading to a sound and equitable peace. The strategic interests of the United States demand early termination of the present conditions of instability and mutual suspicion, which provide such a favorable atmosphere for Soviet penetration and exploitation of the Near East. The present instability will certainly continue if the Lausanne talks break down as a result of the new Israeli position, which is susceptible of interpretation by the Arabs as confirming their constant fears of Israeli territorial expansionism. Failure of the Israelis to modify their present demands will inevitably aggravate Arab distrust of Israel and bring about renewed Arab charges that the United States remains passive no matter how unreasonable the demands of Israel. The Department of State is firmly convinced that the Israelis as well as the Arabs must therefore be prepared to make some concessions, and that, if Israel will modify its present demands, a solution can be achieved which will be both advantageous to Israel and acceptable to the Arabs.

5. *Recommendations*

(*a*) The Department believes that the time has come to make a basic decision concerning our attitude toward Israel. The United States has given generous support to the foundation of the Jewish State, since we believed in the justice of this aspiration. We are convinced that there is no reason why the Jews and the Arabs cannot live together in peace in the Near East, providing they each adopt a reasonable attitude toward the other.

In the light of all the foregoing, the Department considers that it is now essential to inform the Israeli Government forcefully that, if it continues to reject the friendly advice which this Government has offered solely in the interest of a genuine peace in the Near East, this Government will be forced with regret to revise its attitude toward Israel. There is attached a draft note to the israeli Government for your consideration (Tab B). This note has been discussed with Mr. Ethridge, who believes that it would strengthen his hand at Lausanne and strongly recommends that it be sent.

(b) If the Israeli Government does not respond favorably to this proposed representation, it will be necessary to take measures designed to convince Israel of the importance to this Government of a revision of Israel's present policy. Such measures, in addition to a generally negative attitude in the future toward Israel, might include (1) refusing the request of the Israeli Government for United States technical advisers and for the training of Israeli officials in the United States; (2) withholding approval of the $49,000,000 as yet unallocated of the $100,000,000 earmarked by the Export-Import Bank for loan to Israel.

(c) Although the Department of State is convinced of the necessity of carrying out this plan of action in the light of our national interest in the field of foreign policy and strongly recommends that you approve this suggested course, the matter involved other important considerations, since the proposed course of action would arouse strong opposition in American Jewish circles. It is therefore suggested that you may wish to ask your advisers to give careful consideration to the possible implications of the above procedure.

The Department hopes that it will receive your reply on a most urgent basis if this Government is to achieve a modification of the Israeli attitude in time to save the Lausanne meeting. Mr. Ethridge informed the Department by telephone on May 23 that he does not believe the meeting can last much longer than a week under the present circumstances. Dr. Bunche and General Riley concur.

JAMES E. WEBB

APPENDIX XIX

The Acting Secretary of State to the Embassy in Israel [U.S. complaints to Israel], Top Secret, Priority, NIACT, Washington, D.C.. May 28, 1949.

TOP SECRET   PRIORITY WASHINGTON, MAY 28, 1949—11 A.M. NIACT

Pres desires you deliver following not classified secret immediately to Ben-Gurion.

"Excellency: I have the honor to inform Your Excellency that the Pres of the US has instructed me to inform the Govt of Israel as fols:

The Govt of the US is seriously disturbed by the attitude of Israel with respect to a territorial settlement in Palestine and to the question of Palestinian refugees,as set forth by the representatives of Israel and Lausanne in public and private meetings. According to Dr. Eytan, the Israeli Govt will do nothing further about Palestinian refugees at the present time, although it has under consideration certain urgent measure of limited character. In connection with territorial matters, the position taken by Dr. Eytan apparently contemplated not only the retention of all territory now held under military occupation by Israel, which is clearly in excess of the partition boundaries of Nov 29, 1947, but possibly an additional acquisition of further territory within Palestine.

As a mem of the UN PCC and as a nation which has consistently striven to give practical effect to the principles of the UN, the US Govt has recently made a number of representations to the Israeli Govt, concerning the repatriation of refugees who fled from the conflict in Palestine. These representations were in conformity with the principles set forth in the resolution of the GA of Dec 11, 1948, and urged the acceptance of the principle of substantial repatriation and the immediate beginnings of repatriation on a reasonable scale which would be well within the numbers to be agreed in a final settlement. The US Govt conceded that a final settlement of the refugee problem must await a definite peace settlement. These representations, as well as those made concurrently to the Arab States concerning the resettlement outside of Palestine of a substantial portion of Palestine refugees, were made in the firm conviction that they pointed the way to a lasting peace in the area.

In the interests of a just and equitable solution of territorial questions the US Govt, in the UN and as a mem of the PCC, has supported the position that Israel should be expected to offer territorial compensation for any territorial acquisition which it expects to effect beyond the boundaries set forth in the res of the GA of Nov 29, 1947. The Govt of Israel has been well aware of this position and of the view of the US Govt that it is based upon elementary principles of fairness and equity.

The US Govt is deeply concerned to learn from Dr. Eytan's statements that the suggestions both on refugees and on territorial questions which have been made by it for the sole purpose of advancing prospects of peace have made so little impression upon the Govt of Israel.

The US attitude of sympathy and support for Israel has arisen out of broad American interest and principles, particularly out of its support for the UN and its desire to achieve peace and security in the Near East on a realistic basis. The US Govt and people have given generous support to the creation of Israel because they have been convinced of the justice of this aspiration. The US Govt does not, however, regard the present attitude of the Israeli Govt as being consistent with the principles upon which US support has been based. The US Govt is gravely concerned lest Israel now endanger the possibility of arriving at a solution of the Palestine problem in such a way as to contribute to the establishment of sound and friendly relations between Israel and its neighbors.

The Govt of Israel should entertain no doubt whatever that the US Govt relies upon it to take responsible and positive action concerning Palestine refugees and that, far from supporting excessive Israeli claims to further territory within Palestine, the US Govt believes that it is necessary for Israel to offer territorial compensation for territory which it expects to acquire beyond the boundaries of the Nov 29, 1947 res of the GA.

The Govt of Israel must be aware that the attitude which it has thus far assumed at Lausanne must inevitably lead to a rupture in those conversations. The US Govt must state in candor that it considers that the Govt of Israel must provide a basis for a continuation of such talks under the auspices of the PCC and that a rupture arising out of the rigid attitude of the Govt of Israel would place a heavy responsibility upon the Govt and people.

If the Govt of Israel continues to reject the basic principles set forth by the res of the GA of Dec 11, 1948 and the friendly advice offered by the US Govt for the sole purpose of facilitating a genuine peace in Palestine, the US Govt will regretfully be forced to the conclusion that a revision of its attitude toward Israel has become unavoidable."

Please report time of delivery niact in order that Department may furnish copy to Elath.[1]

---

1. A marginal notation states that this telegram was "cleared with the White House 5/27/49."

Mr. Satterthwaite, on May 30, handed to the Israeli Chargé Uriel Heyd, the text of the United States note to the Israeli Government. The latter made no comment after reading the note. Mr. Satterthwaite "made no comment other than to emphasize the fact that the note had been delivered under the instructions of the President." (Memorandum of conversation by Mr. Satterthwaite, 867N.01/5-3049.)

Israeli Ambassador Elath called on Acting Secretary Webb on May 31 just prior to his departure for a visit to Israel. The prime subject of their discussion was the United States notes. Mr. Webb records that "With strong emotion in his voice the Ambassador said he prayed to God that the United States Government would not underestimate Israeli determination to preserve the security of Israel at all costs. It would be a tragic thing, he said, if the friendly relations between our two countries should be altered because the United States Government insisted on a course of action which would threaten Israeli security. he expressed the fervent hope that this would not come to pass.

"I said that I was sure the Israeli Government realized that the United States Government would not send such a note without prior and careful consideration of all the aspects involved. I referred to the friendly relations between our two countries, and to the United States desire to see these relations continue, and I said that it was out of the deep friendship of the United States of Israel that we had made the recommendations which we believed would lead to a lasting peace in the Near East. I reiterated that what was necessary was a sincere desire by all the parties to bring about a genuine peace." (Memorandum of conversation, 501.BB Palestine/5-3149.)

APPENDIX XX

The Ambassador in France (Bruce) to the Secretary of State, From Ethridge, USDel at Lausanne commenting separately on Israel note, Top Secret, Paris, June 12, 1949.

TOP SECRET   PARIS, JUNE 12, 1949—1 P.M.

From Ethridge. USDel at Lausanne commenting separately on Israel note.

(1) If there is to be any assessment of blame for stalemate at Lausanne, Israel must accept primary responsibility. Commission members, particularly US Rep, have consistently pointed out to Prime Minister, Foreign Minister, and Israeli delegation that key to peace is some Israeli concessions of refugees. USDel prepared memo months ago of minor concessions which could be made without prejudice to Israel's final position, pointing out that such concessions would lay the basis for successful talks at Lausanne. Israel has made minor concessions with reservations, but has steadfastly refused to make important ones and has refused to indicate either publicly or privately how many refugees she is willing to take back and under what conditions. Israel's refusal to abide by the GA assembly resolution, providing those refugees who desire to return to their homes, etc., has been the primary factor in the stalemate. Israel has failed even to stipulate under what conditions refugees wishing to return might return; she has given no definition of what she regards as peaceful co-existence of Arabs and Jews in Israel and she consistently returns to the idea that her security would be endangered; that she can not bear the economic burden and that she has no responsibility for refugees because of Arab attacks upon her. I have never accepted the latter viewpoint. Aside from her general responsibility for refugees, she has particular responsibility for those who have been driven out by terrorism, repression and forcible ejection.

(2) The statement, "the Government of Israel is at a loss to understand the reference in the note to the alleged contemplation by Mr. Eytan of 'an additional acquisition of further [territory] within Palestine'" is a falsehood. Also the statement that the GA [*Gaza?*] proposal was first advanced by me. As previously reported it was first advanced by Ben Gurion and so reported to the Department at the time. In appearing before the general committee Sassoon and Lifschitz presented Israel's claim for more of Arab Palestine and used the Hayes (TVA) project map to justify proposed new boundaries with Arab Palestine. It was made clear that the proposed canal must be all inside Israel, which would mean that further territory, including Tulkarm and the northwest corner of the Triangle, must go to Israel. In addition members of Israeli delegation have told me that their demand for withdrawal of Arab troops was designed to establish bargaining position with Abdullah so that Arab Palestine could be further divided. Comay said, "we will point out to Abdullah that he is getting a bonus out of the war." Ben Gurion told me (see telegram re Tiberias talk; do not have reference here) Israel wanted the entire western shore of the Dead Sea. Sharret told the

commission in his first meeting that strip from Haifa to Tel Aviv must be widened back to Samarian Hills for security reasons. Under threats Israel took over Tulkarm area villages. By force she has taken over new territory in Jerusalem.

(3) I leave to the Department whether Israel's admission to UN sanctified what she is doing. Personally, I do not see how the argument can be accepted. Israel was state created upon an ethical concept and should rest upon an ethical base. her attitude toward refugees is morally reprehensible and politically short-sighted. She has no security that does not rest in friendliness with her neighbors. She has no security that does not rest upon the basis of peace in the Middle East. Her position as conqueror demanding more does not make for peace. It makes for more trouble.

(4) As to Gaza strip: I have felt since it was first mentioned that it could be a basis for settlement of refugee problem to extent of Israel's responsibility and also a basis for territorial settlement. I have pointed out consistently that it is a good proposal providing it is accompanied by a *quid pro quo:* some part of the Negev. I have also pointed out that a concession in the Negev is more than a satisfaction of strategic concepts; it is a major point in Arab thinking. One thing that will make for eternal friction in the Middle East is to drive the wedge into the Arab world.

There never has been a time in the life of the commission when a generous and far-sighted attitude on the part of the Jews would not have unlocked peace. Perhaps they are too close to the siege of Jerusalem to see it now. As an advocate of the new state I hope they come on to it eventually. Otherwise there will be no peace in the Middle East, no security for Israel and possibility of lifting the economic blockade with which she must remain a remittance-man nation.[1]

Repeated Bern 37 for USDel Lausanne.

ETHRIDGE.

---

1. Acting Secretary Webb met with President Truman on June 13. His memorandum of conversation stated: "The President read the enclosed telegram from Ethridge, No. 2413, with great interest, and was particularly impressed by the last paragraph."

APPENDIX XXI

The Consul at Jerusalem (Burdett) to the Secretary of State [Israel's ambitions], Secret, Jerusalem, July 6, 1949.

SECRET   JERUSALEM, JULY 6, 1949.

The following general observations, admittedly of a speculative nature, are respectfully submitted regarding the current situation in Palestine:

1—The favorable opportunity for settlement of the present phase of the Palestine problem existing at the time of the signature of the first armistice agreement has now passed. Willingness on the part of the Arabs to end, at least for the time being, the fight over Palestine has been replaced by a general hardening of attitude and reaffirmation of their early conviction that it is impossible to do business with the Jews. The turning point and one of the principle causes of this change was the harsh terms exacted by Israel in the "Triangle." Thus Israel has missed an opportunity to start on the long and difficult road towards achieving at least a working relationship with the Arabs upon which her future depends.

2—Arab efforts are now turning to relatively long range plans for the time when it will be possible to resume the war against Israel. Recognition of their past weaknesses and readiness to actually work for that future date rather than rely on talk is growing. The Arab Legion program for training Palestinians has met with good response and recruits are now drilling at numerous villages. The Arabs have no immediate intention of resuming hostilities, but the movement is towards a day in the future when a successful war will be possible instead of a day in the future when real cooperation with Israel will be possible. Although Arab disunity is still great, each state is apparently working separately towards the same objective.

3—The immediate desire of the Arab refugees is to return to their original homes regardless of the government in control. Morale is low, they see little hope in the future, and the meagre personal possessions which were salvaged have been expended. The Palestinians consider themselves the victims not only of the UN and Israel but of the failure of the other Arab States to live up to their boasts.

4—Despondency, misery, lack of hope and faith, and destruction of former standards of values, make the refugees an ideal field for the growth of communism. Having lost everything, the rosy, although vacuous, pictures of a Communist society are a strong temptation.

5—Recent reports of US pressure on Israel have raised to a high pitch Arab expectations that Israel will be forced to conform to the often stated US policy both with respect to territories and refugees. Non-fulfillment of these hopes will bring a correspondingly bitter reaction.

6—The State of Israel has no intention of allowing the return of any appreciable number of refugees except, perhaps, in return for additional territory. By this date there is much truth in the Israel contention that their return is physically impossible. Arab houses and villages, including those in areas not given Israel by the partition decision, have been occupied to a large extent by new immigrants. Others have been deliberately destroyed. There is practically no room left. Arab quarters in Jerusalem, until recently a military zone, are now almost full and new immigrants are pouring in steadily.

7—Despite Israel's declarations, the state is financially unable to pay compensation for Arab property taken over. Great difficulty is experienced even in financing current Jewish immigration and settlement. barring outside loans or gifts, the funds are not on hand.

8—The UN and particularly the US thus find themselves in the position of indirectly supporting and financing Jewish immigration and settlement. By feeding and settling Arab refugees deprived of property and means of livelihood, the UN and US are enabling Israel to use the same property and means of livelihood for new immigrants.

9—Failure of the UN in the past to protect the rights and interests of the Palestinian Arabs by forcing Israel to comply with the various UN Resolutions is largely responsible for the present situation. The policies which Israel has been permitted to follow have placed her in a position where a reversal is almost impossible.

10—The State of Israel has no intention of consenting to any reduction in territory now held except for minor rectifications with full compensation. Israel conducted the armistice negotiations with the intent that the boundaries fixed should be minimum frontiers of the new state and not temporary armistice lines.

11—Israel has three additional immediate demands. If it proves impossible to satisfy them by negotiation, the employment of force is not unlikely. These are: withdrawal of Syrian forces to the former Palestine boundary; elimination of the Latrun salient; free access to, and additional territory on, Mount Scopus.

12—Israel eventually intends to obtain all of Palestine, but barring unexpected opportunities or internal crises will accomplish this objective gradually and without the use of force in the immediate future.

13—Israel is convinced of its ability to "induce" the United States to abandon its present insistence on repatriation of refugees and territorial changes. From experience in the past, officials state confidently "you will change your mind," and the press cites instances of the effectiveness of organized Jewish propaganda in the US.

14—Under the present circumstances the UN and US are confronted with two broad choices:

a—Employ the necessary punitive measures against Israel to force her to consent to a reduction in territory and repatriation of refugees. At this late stage strong measures are required which will have a severe effect of the State of Israel economically and politically.

b—Admit that the US and UN are unable or unwilling to take the required measures, and therefore that US policy on boundaries and refugees cannot be carried out. This will require plans to liquidate the Palestine problem, formed on the premise that the refugees will not return and that no territorial changes will occur.

15—Delay in making the necessary determination will only make it more difficult either to force the necessary reversal on Israel or to develop resettlement plans for the refugees and to conclude at least *de facto* peace treaties.

BURDETT

APPENDIX XXII

Points of Agreement in London Discussion of Arab-Israel Settlement, Top Secret, Alpha, Limited Distribution, London, March 10, 1955.

LONDON, MARCH 10, 1955.

I. General

A. While initiating the project at present is complicated by the still unfinished Johnston negotiations, the ferment in the Arab world created by the Turk-Iraq Pact which may be increased by UK adherence to the Pace and by the Israel attack on Gaza, it is probable that the current year is as favorable a time as is likely to arise in the foreseeable future for an attempt to achieve a settlement in the dispute between the Arab states and Israel.

B. An attempt at an overall settlement will allow us to present a balanced set of proposals which might permit us to dispose of some problems such as boundaries which are resistant to solution in isolation. Indeed, Egyptian Prime Minister Nasser recently stated to Sir Anthony Eden that no solution was to be found in partial settlements.

C. The method which offers the best chance of success and involves the least risk is that the United States and United Kingdom Governments should work out the general terms of a reasonable settlement and then by separate discussion with the parties concerned, and if possible through direct talks between them, attempt to get them to agree to the settlement or to an agreed variation of it.

D. Success of the Johnston Mission would be most helpful in creating a favorable atmosphere for Alpha, but the Alpha inducements, particularly the security guarantee, should not be extended to secure acceptance of the Unified Development Plan alone.

E. The present proposals have been worked out on an ad referendum basis.

II. Method and Timing of the Approach to the Parties

A. The first approach should be made to Egypt, difficult as this may appear at the moment....

B. Two alternatives with respect to the precise timing of the approach are foreseen.

> 1. In the immediate future (but bearing in mind the state of the UK-Iraq treaty negotiations). The argument in favor of this approach is that Egypt has now been aroused by the Gaza incident, is confronted in an acute form with the problem of Israel, and might be willing to make arrangements which would prevent a repetition and further damage to her prestige.
>
> 2. Postponement of the approach for two or three months in the belief that the Gaza raid has so aroused Egyptian hostility to Israel that she would be unwilling to contemplate a settlement with Israel at present.

257

In addition she would not wish to open herself to accusations from Iraq during her present quarrel with that country of following a pro-Israel policy.

The advice of the two ambassadors in Cairo should be sought regarding which course is preferable.

C. Other possibilities are:

1.   If at the end of four or five months the approach to Nasser has not proved feasible, explore the possibilities of an attempt through Jordan.

2.   If none of the above prove possible, publicize some such plan as Alpha as a solution advocated by the Western powers. A variant would be to try to arrange Pakistan-Turkish sponsorship and ostensible authorship.

D. In either event consideration should be given to parallel letters to Sharett from Mr. Dulles and Sir Anthony Eden covering the following points:

1.   Because of the overriding need which must concern all of us, including Israel, we intend to continue with our policy of strengthening the Middle East against outside aggression by working out agreements based on the northern tier approach. Because of the state of Arab feeling toward Israel, not improved since the Gaza raid, it is not possible to consider associating Israel with these area defense arrangements at this time. The first essential is to get these arrangements into shape. When this has been achieved and when the state of Israel's relations with the Arab states permits, we would be prepared to consider discussions with Israel about its role in area defense.

2.   Israel's security problem is receiving our active consideration, but we are not disposed to assume obligations with respect to the security of a border which is continuously marked by border raids and military actions. Therefore, we are giving consideration to steps that could be taken to produce a genuine reduction of tension as a prelude to a security undertaking.

3.   The Israel Government's Gaza raid has obviously set back for some time the possibility of success in this effort.

4.   But we intend to press forward with it and, in view of Israel's need for a security guarantee, we entertain the hope that we may receive more cooperation in the future than we have in the past in our efforts to reduce tensions.

E. In view of the fact that Sir Anthony Eden has already mentioned the problem to Nasser, Ambassador Byroade should broach the matter next probably along the lines of the brief prepared for Sir Anthony. In determining how far he should go Ambassador Byroade would be governed by consultations with Ambassador Stevenson and by Nasser's receptivity.

F. In revealing the proposal to the parties we would not be too specific at first and would not present the plan as a whole. The purpose would be to develop the proposal gradually so that the solution should appear to emerge from the discussions with the parties rather than to have been worked out fully by the UK and US Governments in advance.

G. We should inform the French and Turks in very general terms of our intentions to make some approaches as soon as we are satisfied from contacts with Nasser that progress can be made and thenceforth we should keep both governments informed in a very general way of our discussions with the parties.

H. The UK would outline our intentions to Jordan after headway had been made with Nasser and immediately before the approach to Israel. This is necessary because of the special treaty relationship between the UK and Jordan.[1]

I. We should inform Iraq of our intentions at about the time we inform Israel in order to ensure that she did not make it difficult for Egypt to cooperate by accusing her of following a pro-Israel policy. We should seek an assurance that Iraq would accept whatever Israel's Arab neighbors accept and if necessary we should relay that assurance to Egypt. The Iraqis themselves need not be involved in the negotiations or the settlement.

J. After steps G, H and I above, which we contemplate should not take more than two or three says, the plan would be discussed with Israel. We would indicate that Nasser was prepared to consider a settlement and that from discussions with him we had reached the conclusion that we were justified in putting forward as a basis for discussion a set of ideas which we consider offers prospect of progress toward a settlement. We would state that if Israel is ready to pursue discussions on this basis, we were prepared to continue our efforts. If it should be necessary, we would make clear to Israel the effects of a refusal on her part to cooperate, mentioning particularly that under such circumstances we would be unable to extend the security guarantee she has requested, and that she would have to bear the onus for failure of our efforts to progress toward peace.

K. Mr. Johnston should continue his efforts to secure Israel acceptance of a Unified Development Plan but Alpha need not be delayed until after a possible trip by Johnston to the area in April or May. If Mr. Johnston is unsuccessful the Unified Development Plan should be incorporated as one of the elements of Alpha.

III. Inducements and Psychological Factors

A. The terms of the settlement itself will contain inducements to the parties, but these will probably be insufficient to overcome the Arabs' resistance to any settlement and Israel's reluctance to make the concessions required of her. Outside inducements will therefore be necessary: e.g., military and economic aid, and security guarantees.

B. Since no Arab state is likely to participate in a settlement unless it knows that Egypt is sympathetic, Egyptian cooperation is of first importance in any attempt at a settlement. We shall therefore need to offer inducements to Egypt. However, we could not acquiesce in Nasser's attitude towards the Turk-Iraq Pact as an inducement to him to move towards a Palestine settlement. The following are the main possibilities:

1.   The prestige implied in the fact that we have chosen to consult Nasser first.

2.   The suggestion that if Egypt will take the lead in solving this problem it will eventually strengthen her position as an influential power and enable her to obtain the advantages of cooperation with the West. the solution of the Palestine problem will eliminate a major impediment to such cooperation.

3.   Military assistance, the extent and conditions of which will in any case depend of the state of the relations between Israel and the Arab states.

4.   Prospects of support for Colonel Nasser's domestic plans for the future of Egypt.

5.   Specific offers of economic aid, for example, on the High Aswan Dam project.

6. The offer of a security guarantee.

7. Elimination of the possibility of constant clashes with Israel.

C. Inducements to Israel include:

1. A security guarantee.

2. Elimination of factors creating tension between Israel and her neighbors.

3. Removal of Suez Canal restrictions. Termination of the secondary boycott.

4. Continued US-UK interest in Israel's economic future.

....

6. Military assistance.

7. Brighter prospects for Israel's association in area defense arrangements.

IV. Elements of a Settlement

A. Territorial Adjustments

1. Israel must make concessions. The Arabs will not reconcile themselves to reaching a settlement with an Israel with the present boundaries. However, we cannot expect large transfers of territory. The changes proposed should be such that in presenting them to Israel they can be made to appear as "frontier adjustments" which Sharett has stated Israel would be prepared to make. From the Arab point of view they will reunite village lands. They will be designed to produce a frontier which could last with a minimum of friction.

2. No change is proposed in the border between Israel and Lebanon; it should continue to follow the old international boundary.

....

4. The Jordan frontier should be adjusted so that Arab villages on the jordan side recover a portion of their former lands from which they are separated by the demarcation line, certain Arab villages lying at the border are placed within Jordan and a more rational border is established. All modifications would be in favor of Jordan with the exception of the Latrun salient which would be relinquished to Israel to permit restoration of the old Tel Aviv-Jerusalem Road and eliminate an awkward salient. Israel would give up small areas, generally not containing Israel settlements, along most of the present line....The changes suggested would not affect Israel adversely either militarily or economically and the total area would amount to about __square miles....

....

7. Israel would cede to Egypt and Jordan two small triangles of territory in the southern Negev based respectively on the Egyptian-Israel, and Jordan-Israel frontiers with the apexes meeting on the present or proposed road to Elath. The purpose would be to permit a land connection between Egypt and the rest of the Arab world. International supervision wold be provided at the intersection.

8. Appendix 1 describes the changes in detail.

B. Refugees

1. To prove acceptable to the Arabs the proposals must contain provi-

sion for repatriation of Arab refugees and the payment of compensation. In practice only a small number of refugees probably wish to return to Israel and in general it would not be desirable to increase too
greatly Israel's Arab population.
2.   Israel would be asked to repatriate as Israel citizens up to 75,000
refugees over a five-year period. This could be done through a non-
renewable quota system providing for the admittance of 15,000 yearly
with priority given to refugees from the Gaza strip. persons readmitted
would be settled by the Government of Israel in the same manner as
new Jewish immigrants and UNRWA would provide financial assistance to this end.
3.   The eventual resettlement of all refugees depends upon the general
economic development of the area as well as upon specific UNRWA
projects and freedom of the refugees to move in order to take employment. In the long run the best prospects are provided by the economic
development program under way in Iraq. A very rough forecast of resettlement possibilities is as follows: Syria, 80,000; Lebanon, 40,000;
Iraq, 60,000 (initial increment); Jordan Valley including the Unified
Development Plan, 200,000; Sinai Project, 70,000; Israel, 50,000 (it is
very doubtful that the full 75,000 would want to return); total, 500,000.
4.   Compensation.
        a. Both the Arabs and Israel will advance claims and counter-
        claims which will prove almost impossible to evaluate. these
        will include:on the part of Israel claims for abandoned Jew-
        ish property in Jordan, war damage and Jewish property se-
        questered in the Arab states; on the part of the Arabs, mov-
        able property, tenant's rights and loss of use and rents on prop-
        erty. The most practical approach is first to negotiate with
        Israel a fixed figure which will represent the net amount to be
        paid by Israel for compensation after all claims and counter-
        claims have been taken into account. The suggested figure is
        £100,000,000. This is the PCC estimate, which is understood
        to be conservative, of Arab immovable property abandoned
        in areas of Palestine now held by Israel.
        b. It is important for psychological reasons with respect to
        the Arabs as well as to minimize the financial burden on the
        US and UK that Israel contributions to compensation be as
        large as possible but it [is] recognized that unassisted she is
        unable to finance such a large sum. In view of the time which
        will be consumed in determining individual claims, the diffi-
        culty of providing funds and the low economic absorbative
        [absorptive?] capacity of the area payments should be made
        over a ten-year period. Of the total Israel and world Jewry
        combined should pay 30 per cent and 70 per cent would have
        to be provided by the world community, primarily the US
        and UK, in the form of loans to Israel. Israel should accept
        responsibility for repayment and servicing of the loans.
        c. the funds available for compensation should be distributed

through a quasi-judicial process to persons who are able to establish title to real property. Persons otherwise entitled to compensation would be paid even though repatriated to Israel. To avoid double payment any claims would be reduced by the value of real property or equipment provided to a resettled refugee by UNRWA. Large claimants, estimated at 11,000, should be paid on a deferred basis to reduce dangers of inflation and provisions should be made to encourage maximum investment of the funds in the area. All refugees should receive some payment. This could perhaps be done by dividing the value of common land, to which title is difficult to determine, among refugees with no claims and those with very small claims.

d. A special UN agency should be established to administer the program: UNRWA would make the actual payments.

e. The value of Arab lands returned by Israel to Jordan in the frontier adjustments would be deducted from the compensation total, while the value of land acquired by Israel at Latrun would be added. Payments for property in the demilitarized zones on the Syrian border would be handled separately.

f. Appendix 2 describes in detail the suggested compensation, repatriation and resettlement programs.

C. Jerusalem

1.   The US and UK would inform the parties that they were prepared to sponsor a UN resolution on the lines of the Swedish proposal of 1950 on the supervision of and access to the Holy Places....

2.   Israel would be informed that following agreement upon a settlement and pending the adoption of such a resolution, the US and UK Ambassadors would start to call at the Israeli Foreign Office in Jerusalem,....

3.   Government House would become the seat of the international authority charged with the supervision of the Holy Places and possibly other UN agencies.

4.   Jerusalem would be demilitarized along the lines of plans which are being discussed by the Consuls-General of Britain, France and the USA.

5.   If France is willing to support the present plan she should be invited to participate in the negotiations on Jerusalem and to use her influence with the Vatican. If she does not favor the plan she should not be included and other means of influencing the Vatican and the Catholic States should be sought.

6.   No approach should be made to the Vatican at this time.

D. Communications Arrangements

1.   Israel to offer Jordan free port facilities at Haifa and free access to the port.

2.   Mutual overflight rights for civil aircraft of the parties.

3.   Israel to permit the restoration or construction of telecommunications facilities between the Arab states across her territory.

4.   Some mixed or UN authority to be established to hear complaints on the infringements of communications rights.

E. The Boycott

1.   The Arab states would:

a. remove restrictions on transiting the Suez Canal, including those on Israel vessels,

b. cease the "secondary boycott", defined as attempts to prevent trade between Israel and non-Arab countries, including termination of all pressure on non-Arab firms trading with Israel,

c. abolish the Arab League Boycott offices; repeal all legislation based on the existence of a state of belligerency.

2.   The Arabs states would not be pressed to engage in direct trade with Israel.

V.   The Form of a Settlement and Guarantees to the Parties

A. While treaties of peace between Israel and the Arab states remain our ultimate objective, the state of Arab public opinion does not make it feasible to insist upon such treaties as an immediate objective. We should endeavor to bring about to the maximum extent possible permanent arrangements which would provide the substance, if not the form, of peace. It should be our objective to obtain the termination of the state of belligerency between the countries both to remove the basis for the Suez Canal blockade and the secondary boycott and to justify to the US and UK public and law makers the security guarantees and substantial financial contributions required. The termination of belligerency could be provided for by inserting in the preamble of the revised Armistice Agreements the phrase "recognizing that the state of war (or belligerency) between them has come to an end, the parties, etc."

B. Instrument of Settlement

1.   Permanent frontiers should be established by re-negotiation of the Armistice Agreements. These contain provisions for modification by consent of both parties. The UNTSO should continue to supervise the boundaries as long as necessary. The new frontiers should be noted in any guarantee decided upon.

2.   The whole settlement need not be covered in a single document. Different means should be used for the different components, possibly as follows:

a. *Territorial*. The territorial settlement to be embodied in a revision of the Armistice Agreements (see above).

b. *Jordan Waters*. A separate agreement would be made between the parties on the development of the Jordan Valley and the operation of the unified scheme.

c. *Refugees*. A UN resolution should be passed incorporating the provisions for repatriation, resettlement and compensation previously agreed to and calling upon Israel and the Arab states to comply. The resolution could also provide for the creation of a new agency to handle the mechanics of compensation. Israel and the several Arab states could indicate their intentions to comply by separate letters to the Secretary-General.

d. *Jerusalem*. Arrangements for Jerusalem and the Holy Places would be the subject of a UN resolution.

e. *Communications*. Free ports and transit arrangements would be the subject of direct agreements between the parties.

f. *The Blockade*. The Arab states would dissolve the Arab League Boycott office and repeal domestic legislation based on or presupposing a state of war. This would remove the legal basis for restriction on Suez Canal traffic and the boycott. We would if necessary make it clear to the Arabs that we were not insisting on removal of prohibitions on direct trade with Israel provided these were not based on legislation claiming the existence of a state of belligerency.

C. Security Guarantees

1.   It will be necessary for the US and UK and possibly Turkey and France to guarantee the frontiers to be established between Israel and the Arab states against alteration by force. This could be accomplished by separate treaties between the guaranteeing powers and Israel and the Arab states. The operative clause might read: "The parties to the present treaty will jointly or separately take appropriate measures for the maintenance or restoration of the agreed boundaries."

2.   The Guarantee would not cover other aspects of the settlement; nor would it come into operation in the case of frontier incidents not involving the occupation of territory. Such incidents, however, if they constituted "any threat of an attack by armed force" would bring into operation the commitment of the parties to consult together. The guarantors might inform the Arab states and Israel that they are prepared to discuss the means of implementing the guarantee.

3.   The participating powers might offer one treaty to Israel embodying the guarantee and a separate similar treaty to each Arab state. Should the Arab states be unwilling to sign treaties with the Western Powers, a unilateral guarantee by the Western Powers might be extended to them and the offer of a treaty left open.

4.   In the proposed Treaty with Jordan a special article might be included stating that rights and obligation under the Anglo-Jordan Treaty are not affected.

5.   Draft treaties are attached.

VI.   *The Roles of France, Turkey, and the United Nations*

1.   France should not be included in the planning or negotiations but should be informed of the proposals prior to the approach to Israel. In order to avoid offending her she would not be informed of the project as a complete plan worked out by the US and UK, but its various components would be revealed gradually to her as they are unfolded to the parties. If France were prepared to cooperate, she might be included in the negotiations of Jerusalem. (See IV.C.) The participation of France as a guaranteeing power would be considered in the light of the reaction of the guaranteed states and the general situation at the time.

2.   Turkey would not be included in the planning or in the negotiations but would be informed at the same time and in the same manner as France. The question of Turkey's participation in the guarantee would be considered in the light of the reaction of the guaranteed states and the general situation at the time.

3.   The UN would be involved in the machinery of a settlement, for example, in supervision of the frontier, and UN resolutions would probably be required, for example, in connection with Jerusalem and the refugees. The UN should not be informed of the project until negotiations with the parties are well advanced.

4.   The possibility should be borne in mind that Pakistan might play a useful part in including [*inducing?*] the Arab states to accept the proposals.

VII.   Cost of the Operation

A. As inducements to a resolution of the Arab-Israel problem, it is anticipated that it would be necessary for the United States and the United Kingdom to provide assistance in addition to present and already projected commitments (development assistance, UNRWA relief and rehabilitation, and the unified development of the Jordan Valley). Such new assistance might include:

1.   US-UK participation in the financing of compensation by Israel to the Palestine refugees.

2.   Economic inducements such as substantial grant aid for the High Aswan Dam, etc.

3.   Military aid to the cooperating countries.

VIII.   Conclusions and Agreements of a Subsidiary Nature Are To Be Found in the Minutes

---

1 Reference is to the Anglo-Jordanian Treaty of Alliance, signed at Amman on March 15,

APPENDIX XXIII

Memorandum from the Secretary of State to the Under Secretary of State (Hoover), [U.S. peace proposals], Top Secret, Alpha, Washington, D.C., June 6, 1955.

WASHINGTON, JUNE 6, 1955.

I spent Sunday afternoon sitting on Dick Richard's porch in South Carolina to put down a possible move in the Near East situation. As suggested, this would constitute a memorandum along the lines of the attached which presumably would be transmitted by the US and the UK jointly (although the US could do it alone) to the Governments of Israel and the neighboring Arab States, i.e., Egypt, Jordan, Syria, and Lebanon. It would presumably be made public shortly after transmittal.

The memorandum was dictated purely from memory as I did not have before me any of the Alpha or other relevant papers and no doubt needs a good deal of technical perfecting. However, this will serve to illustrate my idea of a possible approach which we can consider and accept or reject, or accept with modifications as may seem wise.

I would like to have your thoughts on this paper for our meeting on Alpha which I understand has been set up for Wednesday afternoon at 4 p.m.

JFD

ATTACHMENT

Draft Memorandum

I.

The United States and the United Kingdom believe that the time has come to explore the possibilities of promoting conditions of peace and prosperity in Israel and the neighboring Arab countries. In that area the opportunities of the people are tragically shrunken by the aftermath of the hostilities of 1947[1] (?).[2] The large-scale fighting of that year was brought to a close by armistices negotiated under the auspices of the United Nations. But there is no genuine peace and armed clashes are a frequent occurrence. The lines as defined by the armistices are in many respects artificial. They sometimes unnaturally separate homes and villages from their appurtenant gardens and wells. They deny direct land contact from Egypt with other Arab States. Water rights are ill-defined and legal uncertainties under the armistices prevent the maximum development of precious water in those arid lands. Economic relations between Israel and neighboring states are negligible and Israel has only uncertain use of the Suez Canal The Arab refugees, numbering some 600,000(?), are still living in refugee settlements of the most primitive character and their lives depend precari-

ously upon charity. No adequate compensation has been made for the homes and possessions of which the refugees have been deprived in Israel.

Jerusalem, containing the Holy places of three great religions, each of which
teaches love, is a vortex of hatred; and pilgrims from all over the world are denied access to
the places they revere.

But over and above all this there is fear that relations will further deteriorate. The
Arabs fear lest Israel seek violently to expand at their expense. The Israelis fear that the
Arabs will gradually marshal superior forces to be used eventually to drive them into the
sea. This fear hangs like a pall over the Arab and Israeli people. It leads to military preparation which drain the already poor economies of the countries concerned.

The fear on both sides is so great that other countries which would aid both Israel
and the neighboring Arab States find it difficult to do so without attracting the animosity of
those whom they would befriend in a spirit of impartiality. Thus, an area of vast cultural and
strategic value is so weakened by strains and stresses between its component parts that it
could readily fall prey to aggression from without.

Surely it lies within the capacity of the statesmanship, within and without the area
concerned, to better this situation.

The United States and the United Kingdom see possibilities of a happier condition. This condition we outline in the hope that its manifest advantages to all concerned will
come to be appreciated and bring about the concurrent efforts needed for its achievement.

II.

1.   The boundaries as fixed by the armistices should be rectified and as so rectified accepted as permanent. This recommendation would not appreciably alter the useable
area of Israel or impair its strategic or economic assets. It would do away with local causes
of frictions which have no adequate justification.

In addition to local adjustments, Egypt should have sovereignty over a triangular
portion of the Negeb area as is appropriate to assure it direct contact with Saudi Arabia or
with Jordan. This Egyptian triangle would be selected from land without agricultural or
mineral value and presently unsettled. There is ample land in the Negeb which meets these
specifications.

Since, however, Israel should also have contact with the port of __ ,[3] there will
inevitably be a point of Egypt and Israel crossing at the Eastern apex of the Egyptian triangle. There, the sovereignty of one will have to be in terms of an overpass and the sovereignty of the other in terms of an underpass.

2.   The permanent boundaries between Israel and the Arab States should be internationally guaranteed, preferably under United Nations auspices, so that neither the Arabs nor the Israelis need henceforth fear a forcible change of boundary at their expense and
so that both Arabs and Israelis may henceforth devote their efforts to causes more productive than preparations for possible war against each other.

3.   Funds should be provided by Israel to permit the resettlement of the Arab
refugees, chiefly in Arab territory. These funds will represent just compensation by Israel
for the properties of Arabs which have been taken, so far without such compensation.

4.   Resettlement is not merely a question of money but of creating additional
permanent means of livelihood. This, in turn, requires more irrigated land. A first step in
this direction would be the "Johnson" plan which already has been negotiated to a point of
near acceptability to all the parties concerned.

The compensation fund above referred to should be primarily used, and should be supplemented, to make up the funds required to develop additional water for the irrigation of land in those countries which contribute to the solution here envisioned.

5.   The portion of Jerusalem which principally contains the Holy places should be vested in an international body which will be an organ of the United Nations. It will maintain the Holy places and guarantee equal access to pilgrims of Jewish, Moslem and Christian faiths.

6.   The Suez Canal will be open to Israeli flag traffic on the same terms as the traffic of other nations, as called for by the United Nations Security Council Resolution of _____, 1954. [4]

III.

In the event that Israel and any one or more of her Arab neighbors desire to proceed on the basis of the foregoing principles, insofar as applicable to them, the United States and the United Kingdom would be willing to contribute to bring about the acceptance and implementation of these principles. They would:

1.   Lend their good offices to facilitate a direct exchange of views between the parties concerned or an exchange of views through themselves or other acceptable intermediaries.

2.   Join in giving firm guarantees of the new permanent boundaries as against future changes by force.

3.   Advance to the State of Israel funds to assist in making compensation to the refugees for the property taken, and thus facilitate their permanent resettlement.

4.   Make financial advances to Israel and to participating Arab States directly or through the United Nations, so as to permit water development which will increase the arable land of participating nations of the area.

The measures enumerated in Points 2 to 4, inclusive, depend upon parliamentary approvals which would be sought.

IV.

The program here outlined will serve, and will strengthen, each of the Near East nations individually; and the aggregate result will be to end a threat to world peace. The processes will deprive no nation of any rights, since renunciation of force in international relations is already required by the Charter of the United Nations.

The Governments of the United States and the United Kingdom would be pleased to receive in due course any observations from the governments concerned on the point of view set forth in this memorandum.

---

1. Hostilities in Palestine began in May 1948.

2. This and subsequent question marks appear in the source text.

3. Dulles failed to include the port in question.

4. Reference is to the UN Security Council resolution adopted on September 1, 1951.

APPENDIX XXIV

*Letter from the Secretary of State to the President, [Strategy for peace proposal], Top Se-
cret, Alpha, Washington, D.C., August 19, 1955.*

WASHINGTON, AUGUST 19, 1955.

DEAR MR. PRESIDENT: I am sending you separately the "Alpha" statement which I
propose to make with reference to the Near East. This is along the lines we have previously
discussed and is, I understand, concurred in by the UK which will plan to issue a public
statement of concurrence immediately following my own statement.

The section about boundaries we have decided to generalize rather than to touch
on concrete and extremely sensitive subjects such as the access of Egypt to Saudi Arabia
and Jordan through Neguib, the road from Tel Aviv to Jerusalem, and so forth.

We plan, subject to British concurrence expected shortly, to make the statement
in New York before the Council on Foreign Relations next Friday evening.

We have accelerated somewhat the program for a number of reasons. The first is
that momentarily at least Colonel Nasser seems more friendly and more sympathetic to
such a project, although his ambitions in relation to the Neguib are much exaggerated.

The second is that Johnston's project which I had given the right of way now has
taken a bad turn because the Arab States have apparently decided not to deal with him
directly but through the Arab League, and while Johnston is still going out to push on his
project, it now seems less likely that he can carry it through as an independent effort. He has
withdrawn his prior plea to me not to announce this project until he had a further round of
his own.

In the third place, while at the moment there is relative tranquillity, events could
happen in terms of a Soviet-Arab rapprochement so that we would have to back Israel much
more strongly and drop our role of impartiality.

If "Alpha" is to be done at all, it should be done while we can speak as the friend
of both.

As you know, we anticipate that the initial reaction of both sides will be negative.
The Arabs do not really want to have peace with Israel, and Israel does not want to consider
any boundary adjustments. Rather it wants first of all a security treaty with the United
States. I believe, however, that the presentation will come to command a serious hearing
and that at least it represents a positive effort by the United States to deal with this question.
We need to make such an effort before the situation gets involved in 1956 politics.

Both Nixon and Herb Brownell have looked over the statement and think it is
tolerable from a political standpoint.

I expect to have it shown in advance to a few of the Congressional leaders, Republican and Democrat.

The text, which was originally worked out in London, has been cabled back to them so that they can take note of some minor changes which have been made.

I would appreciate knowing whether you authorize me to make the presentation, which, as you will note, contains the statement that "I speak in this matter with the authority of the President."

I would appreciate as early a reply as is practical because we want to have the statement translated into both Yiddish and Arabic and in the hands of all our Near East posts before I speak.

Faithfully yours,
FOSTER

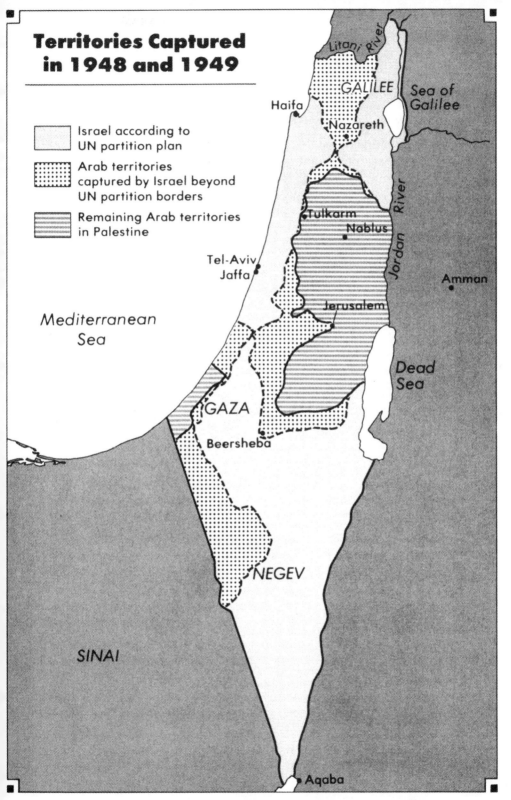

Territories Captured in 1948 and 1949

- Israel according to UN partition plan
- Arab territories captured by Israel beyond UN partition borders
- Remaining Arab territories in Palestine

Litani River

GALILEE

Sea of Galilee

Haifa

Nazareth

Tulkarm

Nablus

Tel-Aviv
Jaffa

Jordan River

Amman

Jerusalem

Mediterranean Sea

Dead Sea

GAZA

Beersheba

NEGEV

SINAI

Aqaba

NOTES

Notes to Preface:

1. The text is in Yehuda Lukacs (ed.), *The Israeli-Palestinian Conflict: A Documentary Record* (New York: Cambridge University Press, 1992), pp. 61–64.

2. Walid Khalidi, "The Palestine Problem: An Overview," *Journal of Palestine Studies* 21, no.1 (Autumn 1991), p. 6. See also Ibrahim Abu-Lughod, "America's Palestine Policy," in *U.S. Policy on Palestine from Wilson to Clinton*, ed. by Michael W. Suleiman (Normal, Ill.: AAUG, 1995).

Notes to Chapter 1: *Zionism*

1. Manuel, *The Realities of American-Palestine Relations*, (Washington, D.C.: Public Affairs Press, 1949), p. 113.

2. John M. Goshko, *Washington Post*, 8 April 1992.

3. Howard M. Sachar, *A History of Israel: From the Rise of Zionism to Our Time* (Tel Aviv: Steimatzky's Agency Ltd., 1976), pp. 44–46.

4. Walid Khalidi (ed.), *From Haven to Conquest: Readings in Zionism and the Palestine Problem until 1948* (Washington, D.C.: Institute for Palestine Studies, 1987), p. xxii.

5. Sachar, p. 40.

6. Peter Grose, *Israel in the Mind of America* (New York: Alfred A. Knopf, 1983), p. 44.

7. Lee O'Brien, *American Jewish Organizations and Israel* (Washington D.C.: Institute for Palestine Studies, 1986), p. 72.

8. Edward Tivnan, *The Lobby: Jewish Political Power and American Foreign Policy* (New York: Simon and Schuster, 1987), pp. 15–16.

9. Grose, p. 226.

10. Lee O'Brien, p. 73.

11. Grose, p. 72.

12. Ibid., p. 45; and Frank E. Manuel, *The Realities of American-Palestine Relations*, pp. 112.

13. Quoted in Irving Howe, *World of Our Fathers* (New York: Harcourt Brace Jovanovich, 1976), p. 204.

14. Manuel, p. 113.

15. Philip Mattar, *The Mufti of Jerusalem: Al-Hajj Amin Al-Husayni and the Palestinian National Movement* (New York: Columbia University Press, 1990), pp. 7, 10.

16. Manuel, pp. 70–73.

17. Ibid., p. 113.

18. Grose, p. 48.

19. Tivnan, p. 16.

20. Bruce Allen Murphy, *The Brandeis/Frankfurter Connection: The Secret Political Activities of Two Supreme Court Justices* (Garden City, N.Y.: Anchor Press/Doubleday & Co., Inc., 1983), pp. 25–26.

21. Yonathan Shapiro, quoted in Lee O'Brien, p. 38.

22. Grose, p. 55.

23. Tivnan, p. 17.

24. Grose, p. 55.

25. In the 18 years between Israel's founding in 1948 and 1976, less than 60,000 Jewish Americans migrated to Israel. Of these, 80 percent returned to the United States, the highest rate of any immigrant group; see Benjamin Beit-Hallahmi, *Original Sins: Reflections on the History of Zionism and Israel* (New York: Olive Branch Press), p. 197.

26. Tivnan, p. 19.

27. Grose, p. 57; and Murphy, p. 56.

28. Grose, p. 64; and Ronald Sanders, *The High Walls of Jerusalem: A History of the Balfour Declaration and the Birth of the British Mandate for Palestine* (New York: Holt, Rinehart and Winston, 1983), pp. 119–20.

29. Grose, p. 63.

30. Ibid., p. 51; and Manuel, p. 163.

31. Lawrence Evans, *United States Policy and the Partition of Turkey, 1914–1924* (Baltimore: Johns Hopkins Press, 1965), p. 43; and Manuel, p. 166.

32. Grose, p. 60.

33. Murphy, p. 57.

34. Ibid.

35. Evans, p. 45.

36. Murphy, p. 58.

37. Ibid.

38. Sanders, *The High Walls of Jerusalem*, p. 585.

39. Ibid., pp. 590–91.

40. Murphy, p. 59.

41. Ibid., p. 60; and Sanders, *The High Walls of Jerusalem*, p. 598.

42. Sanders, *The High Walls of Jerusalem*, p. 598.

43. Ibid., pp. 612–13. The text of the early and the final drafts of the declaration are also in Thomas and Sally V. Mallison, *The Palestine Problem in International Law and World Order* (London: Longman Group Ltd., 1986), pp. 427–29.

44. Mark Tessler, *A History of the Israeli-Palestinian Conflict* (Indianapolis: Indiana University Press, 1994), p. 145.

45. Manuel, p. 172.

46. Ibid., pp. 172–73; and Evans, pp. 47–48.

47. Manuel, p. 175.

48. Ibid., p. 176.

49. Ibid., p. 177.

50. Ibid., p. 278.

51. Ibid., p. 282.

52. Ibid., pp. 281–82.

53. Grose, p. 75.

54. Murphy, p. 247.

55. Lee O'Brien, p. 38.

56. Grose, p. 100.

57. Ibid., p. 94. The following account involving Gibson comes mainly from Grose, pp. 93–95.

58. Grose, p. 139.

59. Ibid., p. 167.

60. Melvin Urofsky, *We Are One! American Jewry and Israel* (Garden City: N.Y.: Anchor Press/Doubleday & Co., Inc., 1978), p. 9.

61. Grose, p. 165.

62. Urofsky, p. 86.

63. Tivnan, p. 23.

64. Urofsky, p. 11.

65. Ibid., p. 37.

66. Manuel, p. 310.

67. Urofsky, pp. 24–25.

68. Grose, p. 171.

69. Urofsky, pp. 27–28.

70. Grose, p. 171.

71. I.L. Kenen, *Israel's Defense Line: Her Friends and Foes in Washington* (Buffalo, N.Y.: Prometheus Books, 1981), p. 14.

72. Urofsky, p. 2.

73. Kenen, p. 14.

74. Among the vast literature documenting the influence of the Jewish lobby, a useful summary is in George W. Ball and Douglas B. Ball, *The Passionate Attachment: America's Involvement with Israel, 1947 to the Present* (New York: W.W. Norton & Co., 1992), pp. 206–13.

75. Grose, pp. 172–73.

76. Urofsky, pp. 33–34.

77. Lee O'Brien, p. 227.

78. Grose, p. 173.

79. Urofsky, pp. 37–38.

80. Ibid., p. 36.

81. Grose, p. 176.

82. Urofsky, pp. 32–33.

83. Ibid., pp. 39–33.

84. Kenen, p. 18.

85. "Memorandum of Conversation by Lieutenant Colonel Harold B. Hoskins," September 27, 1943, *Foreign Relations of the United States* [hereafter *FRUS*] *1943*, pp. 811–14.

86. "President Roosevelt to the King of Saudi Arabia (Abdul Aziz ibn Saud)," Washington, April 5, 1945, *FRUS 1945*, p. 698.

87. "Press Release Issued by the Department of State, October 18, 1945," *FRUS 1945*, pp. 770–71.

88. "Memorandum by the Deputy Director of the Office of Near Eastern and African Affairs (Alling) to the Assistant Secretary of State (Dunn)," Washington, April 6, 1956, *FRUS 1945*, p. 700.

89. Grose, pp. 154–55.

90. "President Roosevelt to the Regent of Iraq (Abdul Ilah)," April 12, 1945; "President Roosevelt to the President of the Syrian Republic," April 12, 1945; and "The Secretary of State to the President of the Lebanese Council of Ministers (Karame)," April 11, 1945, *FRUS 1945*, pp. 703–704.

Notes to Chapter 2: *Partition*

1. William Roger Louis, *The British Empire in the Middle East 1945–1951*, (Oxford: Clarendon Press, 1988) p. 439.

2. David Hoffman, *Washington Post*, 7 September 1988.

3. "The Secretary of State to President Truman," Washington, April 18, 1945, *FRUS 1945*, cited in Harry S. Truman, *Memoirs by Harry S. Truman: Volume II, Years of Trial and Hope* (Garden City, N.J.: Doubleday & Co., 1956), pp. 132–33.

4. Harry S. Truman, *Memoirs by Harry S. Truman: Volume I, Year of Decisions* (Garden City, N.J.: Doubleday & Co., 1956), p. 69.

5. Truman wrote to a friend in 1946: "My only interest is to find some proper way to take care of these displaced persons, not only because they should be taken care of and are in a pitiful plight, but because it is to our own financial interest to have them taken care of because we are feeding most of them...." See Grose, p. 195.

6. Truman, *Years of Trial and Hope*, p. 132.

7. An often repeated quotation attributed to Truman has him saying to a group of U.S. diplomats serving in Arab countries: "I'm sorry, gentlemen, but I have to answer to hundreds of thousands who are anxious for the success of Zionism; I do not have hundreds of thousands of Arabs among my constituents." While there can be no doubt that Truman was indeed motivated by domestic political considerations in his handling of the Palestine problem, it is highly unlikely that he ever made the above statement. In public and private he was always extremely careful to insist that he acted out of reasons of national interest and not for narrow political advantage. He hardly would have made such an admission to diplomats, whom he generally did not like or trust. Moreover, the official record of his comments paraphrases him as saying: "The question was a burning issue in the domestic politics of the United States and that the American Government would try to work out the whole matter on an international plane...." See "Memorandum by the Director of the Office of Near Eastern and African Affairs (Henderson) to the Secretary of State," Annex II, "Replies by the President," Washington, November 13, 1945, *FRUS 1945*, p. 17. This is the exact opposite of the attributed quotation and sounds much closer to Truman's usual comments on the issue. Moreover the only source for the quotation is W.A. Eddy, the ambassador to Saudi Arabia, in his *FDR Meets Ibn Saud*, published in 1954. Eddy in 1948 was hired by ARAMCO to organize an anti-Zionist lobby in Washington; see Michael J. Cohen, *Palestine and the Great Powers 1945–1948* (Princeton, N.J.: Princeton University Press, 1982), p. 51.

8. Robert J. Donovan, *Conflict and Crisis: The Presidency of Harry S. Truman, 1945–1948* (New York: W.W. Norton, 1977), p. 388.

9. Cohen, p. 46.

10. Ibid., p. 49; Grose, p. 219; and Louis, p. 482. Niles' brother, Army Lieutenant Colonel Elliot A. Niles, was identified in an army investigation as responsible for giving classified personnel lists to the Haganah and Irgun for possible recruitment of qualified Americans into the Jewish forces in Palestine; the Neutrality Act prohibited such service. See Stephen Green, *Taking Sides: America's Secret Relations with a Militant Israel* (New York: William Morrow and Co., 1984), pp. 52–54.

11. "Diary Entry for October 21, 1948, by the Secretary of Defense (Forrestal)," *FRUS 1948*, p. 1501. Also see Steven L. Rearden, *History of the Office of the Secretary of Defense: The Formative Years—1947–1950* (Washington, D.C.: Historical office, Office of the Secretary of Defense, 1984), p. 181; and Cohen, p. 46.

12. "Memorandum by the Acting Secretary of State to President Truman," Washington, May 1, 1945, *FRUS 1945*, p. 705.

13. "Memorandum by the Acting Secretary of State to President Truman," Washington, May 14, 1945, *FRUS 1945*, pp. 706–07.

14. "President Truman to the Amir Abdullah of Trans-Jordan," Washington, May 17, 1945; and "President Truman to the President of the Egyptian Council of Ministers (Nokrashy)," Washington, June 4, 1945, *FRUS 1945*, pp. 707, 708–09.

15. "Memorandum by the Acting Secretary of State to President Truman," Washington, June 16, 1945, *FRUS 1945*, p. 709.

16. Donovan, p. 17.

17. "Memorandum by the Director of the Office of Near Eastern and African Affairs (Henderson) to the Secretary of State," Washington, August 24, 1945, *FRUS 1945*, p. 733.

18. Ibid., p. 728.

19. "President Truman to the British Prime Minister (Attlee)," Washington, August 31, 1945, *FRUS 1945*, pp. 737–39.

20. Cohen, p. 57, reports that there were 50,000 DPs in August 1945 but that a year later their number has climbed to 250,000 because the Jewish underground in Europe had been able to smuggle tens of thousands of Jews from eastern Europe westward.

21. William L. Cleveland, *A History of the Modern Middle East* (Boulder: Westview Press, 1994), p. 242.

22. "The Charge in Egypt (Lyon) to the Secretary of State," Cairo, November 11, 1945—6 p.m., *FRUS 1945*, pp. 817–19.

23. "The Charge in Iraq (Moreland) to the Secretary of State," Baghdad, September 28, 1945, *FRUS 1945*, p. 749.

24. "Memorandum by the Chief of the Division of Near Eastern Affairs (Merriam) to the Director of the Office of Near Eastern and African Affairs (Henderson)," Washington, September 26, 1945, *FRUS 1945*, p. 745, fn. 42.

25. "The Secretary of State to Rabbi Stephen S. Wise, at Paris," Paris, August 17, 1946, *FRUS 1946*, p. 686.

26. Louis, p. 422.

27. "The Director of the Office of Near Eastern and African Affairs (Henderson) to the Acting Secretary of State (Acheson)," Washington, October 1, 1945, *FRUS 1945*, pp. 751–53.

28. "Memorandum," Washington, October 2, 1945, *FRUS 1945*, p. 754.

29. Cohen, p. 44.

30. "The British Embassy to the Department of State," Washington, October 19, 1945, *FRUS 1945*, pp. 775–76.

31. Truman, *Years of Trial and Hope*, pp. 141–42.

32. "The Secretary of State to the British Ambassador (Halifax)," Washington, October 24, 1945, *FRUS 1945*, pp. 785–86.

33. Truman, *Years of Trial and Hope*, pp. 144–45.

34. Ibid., pp. 143–44.

35. "The Secretary of State to the Consul General at Jerusalem," Washington, August 18, 1945—5 p.m., *FRUS 1945*, p. 722.

36. "The King of Saudi Arabia (Abdul Aziz ibn Saud) to President Truman," Jidda, October 2, 1945, *FRUS 1945*, pp. 755–76.

37. "Press Release by the Department of State," October 18, 1945, *FRUS 1945*, pp. 770–71.

38. "The Secretary of State to the Charge in Egypt (Lyon)," Washington, December 6, 1945—3 p.m., *FRUS 1945*, p. 837.

39. "The Consul at Jerusalem (Hooper) to the Secretary of State," Jerusalem, November 1, 1945—noon, *FRUS 1945*, p. 805.

40. "The Consul at Jerusalem (Hooper) to the Secretary of State," Jerusalem, November 3, 1945, *FRUS 1945*, pp. 808–10.

41. "The Consul General at Alexandria (Doolittle) to the Secretary of State," Alexandria, November 3, 1945, *FRUS 1945*, p. 808.

42. "The Charge in Egypt (Lyon) to the Secretary of State," Cairo, November 20, 1945—9 a.m., *FRUS 1945*, pp. 828–29.

43. "Memorandum Prepared in the Department of State," Undated, *FRUS 1945*, pp. 841–42.

44. Louis, pp. 418, 423.

45. The British members were Justice of the High Court J.E. Singleton, British chairman; Lord (Robert) Morrison, head of the Labor Party cabinet committee on Palestine; Sir Frederick Leggett, former deputy secretary of the Ministry of Labor and National Services; Wilfrid Crick, an economic adviser to the Midland Bank; Reginald Manningham Buller, a conservative member of parliament, and Richard Crossman, a Labor MP and assistant editor of the *New Statesman*.

46. Louis, p. 421.

47. Quoted in ibid., p. 403. Louis' book has by far the best description of the activities and personalities of the committee.

48. Louis, p. 428.

49. Ibid., pp. 232, 457.

50. Truman, *Years of Trial and Hope*, p. 145.

51. The committee's other eight points concerned such fringe issues as finding alternative homes for Jewish DPs, economic reforms, self–government, education and prevention of violence. Britain's detailed comments on the points are in "The British Prime Minister (Attlee) to President Truman," Personal and Top Secret, London, Undated, *FRUS 1946*, pp. 612–15.

52. Louis, p. 425.

53. Ibid., p. 419.

54. "The Ambassador in the United Kingdom (Harriman) to the Secretary of State," London, May 1, 1946, *FRUS 1946*, pp. 589–90.

55. "The Secretary of State to President Truman," Top Secret, Paris, May 9, 1946—5 p.m., *FRUS 1946*, pp. 601–603.

56. "Memorandum by the Chief of the Division of Near Eastern Affairs (Merriam) to the Under Secretary of State (Acheson)," Washington, May 8, 1946, *FRUS 1946*, pp. 597–99.

57. "The Minister in Syria and Lebanon (Wadsworth) to the Secretary of State," Secret, Urgent, Beirut, May 9, 1946, *FRUS 1946*, pp. 599–601.

58. "The Minister in Egypt (Tuck) to the Secretary of State," Confidential, Cairo, May 3, 1946, *FRUS 1946*, pp. 592–94.

59. "The Charge in Saudi Arabia (Sands) to the Secretary of State," Secret, Urgent, Jidda, May 6, 1946, *FRUS 1946*, p. 595.

60. "Memorandum by the Chief of the Division of Near Eastern Affairs (Merriam) to the Under Secretary of State (Acheson)," Washington, May 8, 1946, *FRUS 1946*, pp. 597–99.

61. "The Secretary of State to President Truman," Top Secret, Paris, May 9, 1946—5 p.m., *FRUS 1946*, pp. 601–603.

62. The Arab Higher Committee, AHC, had been formed in June 1946 with Haj Amin Husseini as its chairman. It was the fourth AHC. The first had been formed by five Palestinian political parties on 26 April 1936 with Husseini as chairman, for purposes of dealing with questions regarding broad Palestinian issues. The first AHC was declared illegal in October 1937 by the British mandatory government and most of its members were deported; Husseini managed to escape to Lebanon and Iraq during World War II, where he helped foment the Rashid Ali revolt. The second AHC was formed in 1942 but quickly dissolved; the third came into being in early 1946, soon to be followed by the reorganization that created the fourth committee; see Issa Nakhleh, *Encyclopedia of the Palestine Problem* (New York: Intercontental Books, 1991), pp. 36–39; and Izzat Tannous, *The Palestinians: A Detailed Documented Eyewitness history of Palestine under British Mandate* (New York: I.G.T. Co., 1988), p. 385. For an excellent biography of Husseini, see Mattar, *The Mufti of Jerusalem*, op cit.

63. "The Consul General at Jerusalem (Pinkerton) to the Secretary of State," Confidential, Jerusalem, May 27, 1946—6 p.m., *FRUS 1946*, p. 615.

64. Louis, pp. 451–63.

65. "President Truman to the British Prime Minister (Attlee)," Secret, Urgent, Washington, June 5, 1946—10 a.m.; and "Memorandum on Matters Regarding Palestine to be Considered Before the London Conference," no date or authorship, *FRUS 1946*, pp. 617–18, 644–45.

66. "The Ambassador in the United Kingdom (Harriman) to the Secretary of State," Top Secret, Urgent, London, July 24, 1946—7 p.m., *FRUS 1946*, pp. 652–67.

67. Louis, p. 435.

68. Nicholas Bethell, *The Palestine Triangle: The Struggle for the Holy Land, 1935–48* (New York: G.P. Putnam's Sons, 1979), p. 263.

69. Louis, p. 435.

70. "Memorandum of Conversation, by the Acting Secretary of State," Secret, Washington, July 30, 1946, *FRUS 1946*, pp. 673–74.

71. "The British Prime Minister (Attlee) to President Truman," Top Secret, London, 9 August, 1946, *FRUS 1946*, pp. 677–78.

72. "The Acting Secretary of State to the Ambassador in the United Kingdom (Harriman)," Top Secret, Urgent, Washington, August 12, 1946, *FRUS 1946*, pp. 679–82.

73. Louis, p. 440.

74. "The Acting Secretary of State to the Ambassador in the United Kingdom (Harriman)," Top Secret, Urgent, Washington, August 12, 1946, *FRUS 1946*, pp. 679–82.

75. Louis, p. 440.

76. "The British Prime Minister (Attlee) to President Truman," Confidential, NIACT, London, Undated, *FRUS 1946*, p. 704, [NIACT stands for night action, meaning the proper official should be immediately informed or an action taken]; and Grose, p. 216.

77. "The British Prime Minister (Attlee) to President Truman," Top Secret, London, 9 August, 1946, *FRUS 1946*, pp. 677–78.

78. "President Truman to the British Prime Minister (Attlee)," Confidential, Urgent, NIACT, Washington, October 3, 1946, *FRUS 1946*, pp. 701–703.

79. Louis, p. 439.

80. "The British Prime Minister (Attlee) to President Truman," Top Secret, Urgent, London, 4 October, 1946—10:35 p.m., *FRUS 1946*, pp. 604–605.

81. "President Truman to the British Prime Minister (Attlee)," Top Secret, U.S. Urgent, Washington, October 10, 1946—4 p.m., *FRUS 1946*, pp. 706–708.

82. "The King of Saudi Arabia (Abdul Aziz Ibn Saud) to President Truman," Undated, *FRUS 1946*, pp. 708–709.

83. Evan M. Wilson, *Decision on Palestine: How the U.S. came to Recognize Israel* (Stanford, Calif.: Hoover Institution Press, 1979), pp. 99–100.

84. "Memorandum by the Chief of the Division of Near Eastern Affairs (Merriam) to the Director of the Office of Near Eastern and African Affairs (Henderson)," Top Secret, Washington, December 27, 1946, *FRUS 1946*, pp. 732–35.

85. "President Truman to the King of Saudi Arabia (Abdul Aziz Ibn Saud)," US Urgent, NIACT, Washington, October 25, 1946, *FRUS 1946*, pp. 714–17.

86. "The King of Saudi Arabia (Abdul Aziz Ibn Saud) to President Truman," Undated but received in Washington on November 2, 1946, *FRUS 1946*, pp. 717–20.

87. Christopher Sykes, *Crossroads to Israel 1917–1948* (Bloomington, Ind.: Indiana University Press, 1973), pp. 305–306.

88. "The Consul General at Basel (Sholes) to the Secretary of State," Secret, Basel, December 30, 1946—7 p.m., *FRUS 1946*, pp. 736–37; and Louis, p. 452.

89. Sykes, p. 307.

90. As an indication of the magnitude of the operation, 69,878 Jews were sent to Palestine as illegal immigrants between 1945 and May 1948 and 51,500 of them were intercepted by the British navy and interned on Cyprus; see Cohen, p. 250.

91. Andrew and Leslie Cockburn, *Dangerous Liaison: The Inside Story of the U.S.–Israeli Covert Relationship* (New York: HarperCollins, 1991), p. 22. Later, a public relations firm hired a young writer, Leon Uris, to write a novel about an illegal immigrant ship entitled *Exodus*. It became a best–seller and then a highly popular movie starring Paul Newman; see Art Stevens, *The Persuasion Explosion* (Washington, DC: Acropolis Books Ltd., 1985), pp. 104–105.

92. Cohen, p. 225.

93. Ibid., p. 223.

94. Ibid., p. 224.

95. Louis, p. 463.

96. Truman, *Years of Trial and Hope*, p. 154; and *New York Times*, 27 February 1947.

97. Sachar, p. 277.

98. Text of UNSCOP's summary report is in Walter Laqueur and Barry Rubin (eds.), *The Israel-Arab Reader* (New York: Penguin Books, 1987), pp. 108–12.

99. Sachar, p. 284.

100. "Position on Palestine," September 15, 1947, 10 a.m., *FRUS 1947*, pp. 1147–51. Also see Wilson, pp. 115–16.

101. "Excerpts From the Minutes of the Sixth Meeting of the United States Delegation to the Second Session of the General Assembly," New York, September 15, 1947, 10 a.m., Top Secret, *FRUS 1947*, pp. 1147–51.

102. "The Director of the Office of Near Eastern and African Affairs (Henderson) to the Secretary of State," Top Secret, Washington, September 22, 1947, *FRUS 1947*, pp. 1153–58. The text is also in Wilson, pp. 117–21.

103. Cohen, p. 287.

104. Ibid., p. 287; and Louis, p. 473.

105. Thomas J. Hamilton, *New York Times*, 3 October 1947.

106. Ibid.

107. Thomas J. Hamilton, *New York Times*, 12 October 1947; text of the statement is in the same issue. Also see Cohen, p. 283.

108. Thomas J. Hamilton, *New York Times*, 11 October 1947.

109. Bethell, pp. 294–95.

110. "Report by the Central Intelligence Agency," Secret, Washington, 28 February 1948, *FRUS 1948*, pp. 666–75. For an interesting analysis of the Irgun's ideology see Israel Shahak, "Yitzhak Shamir's Ideological Heritage," *Middle East International*, No. 338, 18 November 1988.

111. Simha Flapan, *The Birth of Israel: Myths and Realities* (New York: Pantheon books, 1987), p. 32.

112. Thomas J. Hamilton, *New York Times*, 12 October 1947.

113. *New York Times*, 19 October 1947.

114. Ibid.

115. Cohen, p. 284.

116. Janet L. Abu-Lughod, "The Demographic Transformation of Palestine," in *Transformation of Palestine*, 2d ed., edited by Ibrahim Abu-Lughod (Evanston: Northwestern University Press, 1987), p. 153.

117. Cohen, p. 289; and Louis, p. 485.

118. Rearden, p. 181.

119. Cohen, p. 290.

120. "Memorandum by the Director of the Office of Near Eastern and African Affairs (Henderson) to the Under Secretary of State (Lovett)," November 24, 1947, *FRUS 1947*, pp. 1281–82.

121. Wilson, p. 124.

122. Truman, *Years of Trial and Hope*, p. 158.

123. Grose, p. 217.

124. Wilson, p. 127.

125. Grose, p. 151.

126. Wilson, p. 115.

127. William Yale, *The Near East: A Modern History* (Ann Arbor, Mich.: University of Michigan Press, 1958), p. 407.

128. Wilson, p. 115.

129. Louis, p. 485.

130. Sheldon L. Richman, "'Ancient History': U.S. Conduct in the Middle East Since World War II and the Folly of Intervention," Cato Institute, 16 August 1991. An especially good examination of U.S. pressure on other nations is in Cohen, pp. 295–99.

131. Welles, "We Need Not Fail," quoted in Richman. Also see Muhammad Zafrulla Khan, "Thanksgiving Day at Lake Success, November 17, 1947;" Carlos P. Romulo, "The Philippines Changes Its Vote;" and Kermit Roosevelt, "The Partition of Palestine: A Lesson in Pressure Politics," in Khalidi (ed.), *From Haven to Conquest.*

132. Cohen, pp. 298–99. Also see Louis, p. 486.

133. UNGA Resolution 181 (II); the text is in George J. Tomeh (ed.), *United Nations Resolutions on Palestine and the Arab-Israeli Conflict: 1947–1974* (Washington, D.C.: Institute for Palestine Studies, 1975), pp. 4–14.

134. Walid Khalidi, *Before Their Diaspora: A Photographic History of the Palestinians 1876–1948* (Washington, D.C.: Institute for Palestine Studies, 1984), p. 315.

135. Flapan, p. 32; and "Report by the Central Intelligence Agency," Possible Developments in Palestine, Secret, Washington, 28 February 1948, *FRUS 1948*, pp. 666–67. See also Avi Shlaim, *Collusion Across the Jordan: King Abdullah, the Zionist Movement, and the Partition of Palestine* (New York: Columbia University Press, 1988), p. 24.

136. Don Peretz, "The Question of Compensation," *Palestinian Refugees: Their Problem and Future* (Washington, D.C.: The Center for Policy Analysis on Palestine, 1994), p. 16.

137. Michael Palumbo, *The Palestinian Catastrophe: The 1948 Expulsion of a People from their Homeland* (Boston: Faber and Faber, 1987), p. 29.

138. Frank H. Epp, *Whose Land is Palestine?* (Grand Rapids, Mich.: William B. Eerdmans, 1974), p. 184; and Shlaim, *Collusion Across the Jordan*, p. 117.

139. UN Subcommittee Two, "Binationalism not Partition," in Khalidi (ed.), *From Haven to Conquest*, p. 677. This study uses the generally cited number for Arabs in the Jewish state as 407,000 and the Arabs in the Arab state as 725,000, but it was based on figures compiled before the General Assembly decided in late November to award Jaffa to the Arab state. Jaffa had a population of around 75,000. Ben Gurion placed the number of Arabs in the proposed Jewish state at about 350,000; see Flapan, pp. 31–32.

140. Janet L. Abu-Lughod, in Abu-Lughod (ed.), p. 153.

141. *Statistical Handbook of Jewish Palestine* (Jerusalem: Department of Statistics of the Jewish Agency for Palestine, 1947), pp. 36–40, quoted in Nakhleh, p. 4.

142. John Quigley, *Palestine and Israel: A Challenge to Justice* (Durham, N.C.: Duke University Press, 1990), p. 36.

143. Benny Morris, *The Birth of the Palestinian Refugee Problem* (New York: Cambridge University Press, 1987), p. 11. Morris lists Jaffa as a mixed town, but in reality Jews lived in what had become the Tel Aviv suburb and Arabs populated Jaffa City.

144. *Statistical Handbook of Jewish Palestine*, pp. 36–40.

145. Khalidi, *Before Their Diaspora*, pp. 305–306. A formal report listing the numerous reasons to oppose partition, including statistics, maps and reports on Palestine, is in A/AC. 14/32 and Add.I. This was the report of the General Assembly's subcommittee 2 established 23 September 1947 to study alternative proposals to partition. The text is in Khalidi (ed.), *From Haven to Conquest*, pp. 645–702.

146. Wilson, pp. 128–29.

147. *New York Times*, 4 December 1947; and Wilson, pp. 129–30.

148. Sam Pope Brewster, *New York Times*, 1 December 1947.

149. *New York Times*, 9 December 1947.

150. Yossi Feintuch, *U.S. Policy on Jerusalem* (New York: Greenwood Press, 1987), p. 98. See also Michael Brecher, *Decisions in Israel's Foreign Policy* (London: Oxford University Press, 1974), pp. 20–21.

151. Khalidi (ed.), *From Haven to Conquest*, p. lxxix. The text of the plan and Plan Dalet are in a special "1948 Palestine" issue of the *Journal of Palestine Studies* 18, no.1 (Autumn 1988), pp. 20–38.

152. Khalidi, *Before Their Diaspora*, p. 315.

153. *New York Times*, 13 December 1947.

154. Quigley, p. 41. See also Flapan, pp. 90–91.

155. Bethell, p. 352.

156. Tannous, p. 471.

157. "Report by the Policy Planning Staff on Position of the United States With Respect to Palestine," Top Secret, Washington, January 19, 1948, *FRUS 1948*, p. 553.

158. "Memorandum by the Director of the Office of Near Eastern and African Affairs (Henderson) to the Director of the Office of United Nations Affairs (Rusk)," Top Secret, Washington, February 6, 1948, *FRUS 1948*, pp. 600–603.

159. "Memorandum by the Director of the Office of United Nations Affairs (Rusk) to the Under Secretary of State (Lovett)," Top Secret, Washington, February 11, 1948, *FRUS 1948*, pp. 617–19.

Notes to Chapter 3: *Refugees*

1. "The Secretary of State to the Special Representative of the United States in Israel (McDonald)," Top Secret, US Urgent, Washington, September 1, 1948—6 p.m., *FRUS 1948*, pp. 1366–69.

2. Madeleine K. Albright letter to members of the UN General Assembly, 8 August 1994; excerpts are in *Journal of Palestine Studies* 24, no. 2 (Winter 1995), p. 153.

3. Sam Pope Brewer, *New York Times*, 2 March 1948.

4. "The Consul General at Jerusalem (Macatee) to the Secretary of State," Secret, Jerusalem, February 9, 1948, *FRUS 1948*, p. 606.

5. Morris, *Birth of the Palestinian Refugee Problem*, p. 30.

6. Faisal had been spat on and jeered by Jewish mobs while in New York; see Robert Lacey, *The Kingdom* (London: Hutchinson & Co., 1981), p. 289.

7. "Report by the Policy Planning Staff on Position of the United States With Respect to Palestine," Top Secret, Washington, January 19, 1948, *FRUS 1948*, pp. 546–54.

8. "Report by the Policy Planning Staff," Review of Current Trends U.S. Foreign Policy, Top Secret, Washington, February 24, 1948, *FRUS 1948*, pp. 656–57.

9. "Report by the Central Intelligence Agency," Possible Developments in Palestine, Secret, Washington, February 28, 1948, *FRUS 1948*, pp. 666–67.

10. Draft Report Prepared by the Staff of the National Security Council, "The Position of the United States With Respect to Palestine," Top Secret, Washington, February 17, 1948, *FRUS 1948*, pp. 631–32; the quoted section was excised by the editors of *FRUS* and can now be found in the State Department's Declassified Documents.

11. "Editor's Note," *FRUS 1948*, p. 633; also see Donovan, p. 371; and Cohen, p. 348.

12. "The Secretary of Defense (Forrestal) to the Secretary of State," Top Secret, Washington, April 19, 1948, *FRUS 1948*, p. 832.

13. "Memorandum by Mr. Samuel K.C. Kopper of the Office of Near Eastern and African Affairs," The Partition of Palestine and United States Security, Top Secret, Washington, January 27, 1948, *FRUS 1948*, p. 566.

14. "The Department of State to President Truman," Urgent and Top Secret, February 21, 1948, *FRUS 1948*, p. 640.

15. "Draft Memorandum by the Director of the Office of United Nations Affairs (Rusk) to the Under Secretary of State (Lovett)," Top Secret, Washington, February 11, 1948, *FRUS 1948*, p. 618.

16. Truman, *Years of Trial and Hope*, p. 163.

17. "President Truman to the Secretary of State," Top Secret, Urgent, St. Thomas, February 22, 1948—4:55 p.m. EST, *FRUS 1948*, p. 645.

18. Truman, *Years of Trial and Hope*, p. 160.

19. Ibid.

20. *FRUS 1948*, pp. 648–49, fn. 1.

21. However, the Pentagon took a less sanguine view of Israel's future loyalty. It pointed out that there was a possibility that a Jewish state would become an outpost of Soviet communism because the dominant Labor Party "stems from the Soviet Union and its satellite states and has strong bonds of kinship in those regions, and ideologically is much closer to the Soviet Union than to the United States...." See Grose, p. 259.

22. "Memorandum by the President's Special Counsel (Clifford) to President Truman,"

Washington, March 6, 1948; and "Memorandum by the President's Special Counsel (Clifford)," Washington, March 8, 1948, *FRUS 1948*, pp. 687–89, 690–96.

23. Grose, pp. 275–76.

24. "The Consul General at Jerusalem (Macatee) to the Secretary of State," Secret, US Urgent, Jerusalem, March 22, 1948—5 p.m., *FRUS 1948*, p. 753.

25. Grose, pp. 275–76.

26. Truman, *Years of Trial and Hope*, pp. 161–62.

27. Donovan, p. 376.

28. *FRUS 1948*, March 22, 1948, p. 750, fn. 3.

29. "Memorandum by Mr. John C. Ross to the United States Representative at the United Nations (Austin)," Secret, New York, February 12, 1948, *FRUS 1948*, p. 627.

30. Nafez Nazzal, *The Palestinian Exodus from Galilee 1948* (Beirut: Institute for Palestine Studies, 1978), p. 28.

31. Khalidi (ed.), *From Haven to Conquest*, contains a moving firsthand account as well as accounts of attacks on other Palestinian centers, pp. 761–78. Many writers have discussed the massacre, perhaps none better than Eric Silver, *Begin: The Haunted Prophet* (New York: Random House, 1984), pp. 88–96.

32. Numbers of the refugees vary widely, with estimates ranging from 900,000 by Britain to 800,000 by U.S. officials to under 600,000 by Israel. The official United Nations' count was 726,000, which is the number I have used since it is within the range of most estimates even though on the conservative side; see Thomas J. Hamilton, *New York Times*, 19 November 1949, and UN A/6797*, "Report of the special Representative's Mission to the Occupied Territories, 15 Sept. 1967." Demographer Janet L. Abu-Lughod, who had studied the problem carefully, estimated the number at 770,000 to 780,000; see J. Abu-Luhgod, in Abu-Lughod (ed.), p. 161. Palestinian scholar Walid Khalidi also looked closely into the question in his monumental *All That Remains: The Palestinian Villages Occupied and Depopulated by Israel in 1948* (Washington, D.C.: Institute for Palestine Studies, 1991), p. 582, and concluded the number was between 727,000 and 758,300.

33. Donovan, p. 388.

34. "Memorandum of Conversation by Secretary of State," Top Secret, Washington, May 12, 1948, *FRUS 1948*, pp. 972–76.

35. Ibid., pp. 975–76.

36. "Memorandum of Conversations, by the Under Secretary of State (Lovett)," Top Secret, Washington, May 17, *FRUS 1948*, pp. 1005–07. For Clark Clifford's defense, see his memoirs, *Counsel to the President: A Memoir* (New York: Random House, 1991), p. 14.

37. Wilson, p. 145.

38. "Memorandum by the Director of the Policy Planning Staff (Kennan) to the Secretary of State," Top Secret, Washington, May 21, *FRUS 1948*, pp. 1020–21.

39. "Memorandum by the Secretary of State to the Under Secretary of State (Lovett)," Top Secret, Eyes Only, Washington, May 24, *FRUS 1948*, pp. 1036–37.

40. Louis, p. 483.

41. Dean Acheson, *Present at the Creation* (New York: Signet New American Library, 1970), p. 170.

42. Louis, p. 422.

43. A *Newsweek* poll of 50 Washington news correspondents shortly before the election showed not one of them thought Truman could win the election; see Wilson, p. 148.

44. "Draft Memorandum by the Director of the Office of United Nations Affairs (Rusk) to the Under Secretary of State (Lovett)," Secret, Washington, May 4, 1948, *FRUS 1948*, pp. 894–95. A marginal note states that it was drafted by Rusk's aide, Robert M. McClintock, and not sent.

45. Flapan, pp. 195–96. Flapan quotes three studies of manpower and notes that all three credit Israel with more men under arms. The estimates ranged from 21,500 to 23,500 for Arab troops (a pro-Israeli source) and from 25,000 to 65,000 (a British source) for Israelis. In a mid-July study, the Central Intelligence Agency estimated there were 27,000 Arabs troops and irregulars in Palestine and 19,800 near Palestine while Israel had 97,800, including 50,000 settler defense militia; see "Report by the Central Intelligence Agency," Possible Developments From the Palestine Truce, Secret, Washington, July 27, 1948, *FRUS 1948*, p. 1245.

46. Morris, *Birth of the Palestinian Refugee Problem*, pp. 107–109.

47. According to the account of the local Jewish commander who captured Nazareth, Ben Dunkelman, two days after the city's fall he was ordered to force its civilians to evacuate. Dunkelman refused to obey the order and thus spared the Nazarenes the fate that had overtaken so many of their fellow victims. For an account of this intriguing affair, see Kidron, "Truth Whereby Nations Live," in *Blaming the Victims*, edited by Edward W. Said and Christopher Hitchens (New York: Verso, 1988), pp. 85–87. Dunkelman's claim is substantially supported by Morris, *Birth of the Palestinian Refugee Problem*, pp. 201–202.

48. The literature by now on the cause of the flight of the refugees is abundant. Among numerous sources, see Tom Segev, *1949: The First Israelis* (New York: The Free Press, 1986); Morris, *Birth of the Palestinian Refugee Problem*; Kidron, in Said and Hitchens (eds.); Erskine B. Childers, "The Other Exodus," in Khalidi (ed.), *From Haven to Conquest*; Glubb Pasha, *A Soldier with the Arabs* (London: Hodder and Stoughton, 1957); and Nazzal.

49. "The Consul General at Jerusalem (Wasson) to the Secretary of State," Secret, Urgent, NIACT, Jerusalem, May 3, 1948—noon, *FRUS 1948*, pp. 889–91.

50. "The Consul General at Jerusalem (Wasson) to the Secretary of State," Restricted, Jerusalem, May 22, 1948—9 a.m., *FRUS 1948*, p. 1030.

51. "The Charge in Egypt (Patterson) to the Secretary of State," Confidential, Cairo, June 28, 1948—9 a.m., *FRUS 1948*, p. 1155.

52. His appointment was made by Resolution 186 (S–2) (II), which instructed him to "promote a peaceful adjustment of the future of situation in Palestine" and to allowed him to

mediate beyond the terms of the Partition Plan. The text is in Tomeh, pp. 14–15. Bernadotte had been born in 1895 and became a world figure in 1945 when his mediation efforts on behalf of the International Red Cross saved 20,000 persons, including thousands of Jews, from Nazi concentration camps; see Sune O. Persson, *Mediation & Assassination: Count Bernadotte's Mission to Palestine in 1948* (London: Ithaca Press, 1979), pp. 225–29.

53. "The charge in Egypt (Patterson) to the Secretary of State," Secret, Cairo, August 7, 1948—11 a.m., *FRUS 1948*, pp. 1295–96.

54. Sam Pope Brewer, *New York Times*, 15 August 1948.

55. "Memorandum by the Department of State to President Truman," Secret, Washington [Undated but drafted August 19, 1948], *FRUS 1948*, pp. 1324–26.

56. *Official Records of the General Assembly, Third Session, Supplement No. II (A/648), Progress Report of the United Nations Mediator on Palestine*, 16 September 1948.

57. "Progress Report of the United Nations Mediator in Palestine," [Extracts], undated but signed and sent to the UN on 16 September 1948, *FRUS 1948*, pp. 1401–06.

58. UN Doc., A/689, 18 October 1948.

59. "The Secretary of State to the acting Secretary of State," Secret, Priority, Paris, October 14, 1948—10 p.m., *FRUS 1948*, pp. 1477–78.

60. "Memorandum by the Department of State to President Truman," Secret, Washington, October 15, 1948, *FRUS 1948*, pp. 1478–80.

61. "The Acting United States Representative of the United Nations (Jessup) to the Secretary of State," Restricted, New York, July 27, 1948—1:55 p.m., *FRUS 1948*, pp. 1248–49.

62. "The Secretary of State to the Special Representative of the United States in Israel (McDonald)," Top Secret, US Urgent, Washington, September 1, 1948—6 p.m., *FRUS 1948*, pp. 1366–69.

63. "President Chaim Weizmann of Israel to President Truman," Rehovoth, Israel, 24 June 1949, *FRUS 1949*, pp. 1168–73.

64. "The Secretary of State to the Acting Secretary of State," Secret, Priority, Paris, October 16, 1948—1 a.m., *FRUS 1948*, pp. 1481–83.

65. When the draft was finally passed as Resolution 194 on 11 December 1948 the language referring to "pillage" had been removed.

66. Segev, *1949*, p. 70.

67. Morris, *Birth of Palestinian Refugee Problem*, p. 222. See also Palumbo, pp. xii–xiv; Quigley, p. 85; and Nakhleh, p. 272.

68. "The Special Representative of the United States in Israel (McDonald) to President Truman," Secret, Urgent, Tel Aviv, October 17, 1948—4 p.m., *FRUS 1948*, p. 1486.

69. "Editorial Note," *FRUS 1948*, p. 688. The embassy reports were written in January and February 1949.

70. "Palestine Refugee Problem," Annex I, Secret, Washington, April 22, 1949, *FRUS 1949*, p. 938.

71. "Policy Paper Prepared in the Department of State," Palestine Refugees, Secret, Washington, March 15, 1949, *FRUS 1949*, p. 835.

72. "The Consul at Jerusalem (Burdett) to the Secretary of State," Secret, Jerusalem, February 28, 1949—11 a.m., *FRUS 1949*, p. 780.

73. "Memorandum by the Director of the Office of Near Eastern and African Affairs (Satterthwaite) to the Secretary of State," Necessity for early liquidation of Arab refugee problem, Secret, Washington, March 1, 1949, *FRUS 1949*, p. 782.

74. "The Minister in Lebanon (Pinkerton) to the Secretary of State" [from Ethridge], Top Secret, NIACT, Beirut, March 28, 1949, *FRUS 1949*, pp. 876–77.

75. "Policy Paper Prepared in the Department of State," Palestine Refugees, Secret, Washington, March 15, 1949, *FRUS 1949*, pp. 828–42.

76. Segev, *1949*, p. 30.

77. Khalidi (ed.), *All That Remains*, Appendix III.

78. *New York Times*, 17 February 1949. Also see Beryl Cheal, "Refugees in the Gaza Strip, December 1948–May 1950," *Journal of Palestine Studies* 18, no.1 (Autumn 1988), pp. 138–57.

79. Resolution 212 (III). The text is in Tomeh, pp. 17–18.

80. The text is in *New York Times*, 12 December 1948, and Tomeh, pp. 15–16.

81. The PCC effort paralleled negotiations between the parties conducted by Acting UN Mediator Bunche on Rhodes, which began 13 January 1949. The Rhodes talks were limited to formalizing the end of the fighting with armistices, which came on 24 February between Egypt and Israel; 25 March with Lebanon; 3 April with Jordan, and 20 July with Syria. Texts of the armistice agreements are in Sydney D. Bailey, *Four Arab-Israeli Wars and the Peace Process* (London: Macmillan, 1990), pp. 97–106. Iraq refused to enter into talks, thus becoming the only combatant not to sign an armistice with Israel; see Sachar, pp. 347–51; and Walid Khalidi, "The Palestine Problem: an Overview," *Journal of Palestine Studies* 21, no.1 (Autumn 1991), pp. 5–16.

82. David P. Forsythe, *United Nations Peacemaking: The Conciliation Commission for Palestine* (Baltimore: Johns Hopkins University Press, 1972), pp. 30, 48. For an excellent study of the Lausanne Conference and the commission's problems, see Shlaim, *Collusion Across the Jordan*, pp. 461–88.

83. "The Acting Secretary of State to Mr. Mark F. Ethridge," signed Robert A. Lovett, Top Secret, Washington, January 19, 1949, *FRUS 1949*, pp. 681–83.

84. Khalidi (ed.), *All That Remains*, pp. xxxi–xxxii.

85. Don Peretz, "The Arab Refugee Dilemma," *Foreign Affairs* (October 1954); and idem, "The Question of Compensation," *Palestinian Refugees: Their Problem and Future* (Washington, D.C.: The Center for Policy Analysis on Palestine, 1994), p. 16. See also David K. Shipler, *Arab and Jew: Wounded Spirits in a Promised Land* (New York: Times Books, 1986), pp. 32–36; Segev, *1949*, pp. 69–71.

86. Forsythe, pp. 117–19.

87. Peretz, "The Question of Compensation," p. 16.

88. Anne O'Hare McCormick, *New York Times*, 10 January 1949. This was one of a series of ten penetrating articles McCormick wrote from Israel at this time.

89. Anne O'Hare McCormick, *New York Times*, 17 January 1949.

90. Kermit Roosevelt, letter, *New York Times*, 11 February 1949.

91. "Policy Paper Prepared in the Department of State," Palestine Refugees, Secret, Washington, March 15, 1949, *FRUS 1949*, p. 838.

92. Ronald Sanders, *Shores of Refuge: A Hundred Years of Jewish Emigration* (New York: Henry Holt and Co., 1988), pp. 567–68.

93. "Policy Paper Prepared in the Department of State," Palestine Refugees, Secret, Washington, March 15, 1949, *FRUS 1949*, p. 836.

94. "The Special Representative of the United States in Israel (McDonald) to the Secretary of State," Secret, Tel Aviv, February 22, 1949, *FRUS 1949*, pp. 761–64.

95. "Policy Paper Prepared in the Department of State," Palestine Refugees, Secret, Washington, March 15, 1949, *FRUS 1949*, pp. 828–42.

96. "Report by the National Security Council on United States Policy Toward Israel and the Arab States," Top Secret, Washington, October 17, 1949, *FRUS 1949*, pp. 1430–40.

97. "The Consul at Jerusalem (Burdett) to the Secretary of State," Secret, Jerusalem, February 28, 1949—10 a.m., *FRUS 1949*, pp. 776–78.

98. "The Consul at Jerusalem (Burdett) to the Secretary of State," [from Ethridge?] Secret, Jerusalem, February 28, 1949—9 a.m., *FRUS 1949*, pp. 775–76.

99. Segev, *1949*, p. 30.

100. *FRUS 1949*, p. 806, fn 3.

101. "The Minister in Lebanon (Pinkerton) to the Secretary of State" (from Ethridge), Top Secret, NIACT, Beirut, March 28, 1949, *FRUS 1949*, pp. 876, 878.

102. "Mr. Mark F. Ethridge to the Secretary of State," Secret, April 13, 1949—1 p.m., *FRUS 1949*, pp. 911–16.

103. "Mr. Mark F. Ethridge to the President," Secret, Jerusalem, April 11, 1949, *FRUS 1949*, pp. 905–06.

104. "The President to Mr. Mark F. Ethridge, at Jerusalem," Washington, April 29, 1949, *FRUS 1949*, p. 957.

105. "Memorandum by the Acting Secretary of State to the President," Top Secret, Washington, May 27, 1949, *FRUS 1949*, pp. 1060–61.

106. "The Acting Secretary of State to the Embassy in Israel," Top Secret, Priority, NIACT, Washington, May 28, 1949—11 a.m., *FRUS 1949*, pp. 1072–74.

107. "Memorandum of Telephone Conversation, by the Director of the Office of Near Eastern and African Affairs (Satterthwaite)," Secret, Washington, June 8, 1949, *FRUS 1949*, pp. 1094–95.

108. "The Government of Israel to the Government of the United States," Top Secret, Tel Aviv, June 8, 1949, *FRUS 1949*, pp. 1102–06.

109. "Memorandum by William J. McWilliams, Assistant to the Director of the Executive Secretariat," Secret, Washington, August 26, 1949, *FRUS 1949*, p. 1332; also see pp. 1375, 1389, 1455.

110. George McGhee, *Envoy to the Middle World: Adventures in Diplomacy* (New York: Harper & Row, 1983), p. 37.

111. "The Consul at Jerusalem (Burdett) to the Secretary of State," Secret, Jerusalem, July 6, 1949, *FRUS 1949*, p. 1205.

112. James G. McDonald, *My Mission to Israel* (New York: Simon and Schuster, 1951), p. 184.

113. "Mr. Stuart W. Rockwell to the Secretary of State," Secret, Priority, Lausanne, September 10, 1949—2 p.m., *FRUS 1949*, p. 1375.

114. "The Ambassador in France (Bruce) to the Secretary of State," From Ethridge, USDel at Lausanne commenting separately on Israel note, Top Secret, Paris, June 12, 1949—1 p.m., *FRUS 1949*, pp. 1124–25. In their reports from the region, a number of State Department officials repeatedly referred to Israel's "voracious territorial appetite," "expansionist ambitions," its threats of force and to its "take it or leave it attitude." The consul in Jerusalem reported that "the favorable opportunity for settlement" generated at the time of the February 24 Israel-Egypt armistice agreement "has now passed" because of Israel's "harsh terms;" see "The Consul at Jerusalem (Burdett) to the Secretary of State," Secret, Jerusalem, July 6, 1949, *FRUS 1949*, p. 1203.

115. Segev, *1949*, p. 31n.

116. Resolution 302 (IV). The text is in Tomeh, pp. 18–20. The resolution accepted the 18 November 1949 report by the PCC's Economic Survey Mission, which put the figure of the refugees at 726,000.

117. "Editor's Note," *FRUS 1949*, p. 1529.

118. Norbert Scholz (ed.), *U.S. Official Statements: The Palestinian Refugees* (Washington, D.C.: Institute for Palestine Studies, 1994), pp. 165, 167.

119. Sachar, p. 457.

120. Scholz, p. 127.

121. Brecher, p. 194; and Kennet Love, *Suez: The Twice-Fought War* (New York: McGraw-Hill Book Co., 1969), pp. 12, 60.

122. Scholz, p. 48. The speech was the public unveiling of the top secret Operation Alpha, a joint U.S.-British effort to find a practical peace plan; see chapter 5 for details.

123. "Telegram from the Department of State to the Embassy in Israel," Top Secret, Prior-

ity, Alpha, Washington, 24 August 1955—4:01 p.m., *FRUS 1955–1957*, p. 385.

124. "Points of Agreement in London Discussions of Arab-Israel Settlement," Top Secret, Alpha, Limited Distribution, London, March 10, 1955, *FRUS 1955–1957*, p. 103.

125. Tab A "Possibility of Settlement of Principal Israel-Arab Issues," Top Secret, Alpha, May 18, 1955, *FRUS 1955–1957*, p. 203.

126. Benny Morris, *Israel's Border Wars: 1949-1956* (Oxford: Clarendon Press, 1993), p. 364.

127. Joseph E. Johnson, "Arab vs. Israel: A Persistent Challenge to Americans," *Middle East Journal* 18, no.1 (Winter 1964).

128. Forsythe, pp. 124–25.

129. Ibid., pp. 133–34.

130. Ibid., p. 127.

131. Zaha Bustami, "The Kennedy-Johnson Administrations and the Palestinian People," in Suleiman (ed.), p. 104.

132. Steven L. Spiegel, *The Other Arab-Israeli Conflict: Making America's Middle East Policy, from Truman to Reagan* (Chicago: University of Chicago Press, 1985), p. 113. See also Bustami, in Suleiman (ed.), pp. 107–08; and Forsythe, pp. 134–35.

133. Forsythe, p. 137.

134. Ibid.; and Spiegel, p. 115.

135. Bustami, in Suleiman (ed.), pp. 110–11.

136. UN A/6797*, "Report on the Mission of the special Representative to the occupied territories, 15 Sept. 1967."

137. Scholz, p. 167.

138. Ibid., p. 73. The phrase was used by U.S.-UN Ambassador Arthur Goldberg in the UN General Assembly on 19 June 1967. As an active Zionist, he may have been referring mainly to Jewish refugees.

139. Ibid., pp. 78, 116.

140. Graham Usher, "The Demise of UNRWA?" *Middle East International*, 6 January 1995.

Notes to Chapter 4: *Borders*

1. "The Acting Secretary of State to the Embassy in Israel," Top Secret, Priority, NIACT, Washington, May 28, 1949—11 a.m., *FRUS 1949*, pp. 1072–74.

2. Henry Kissinger, "The Path to Peaceful Coexistence in the Middle East," *Washington Post*, Outlook section, 2 August 1992.

3. Louis, pp. 345–46.

4. Ibid., p. 369.

5. Shlaim, *Collusion Across the Jordan*, p. 139.

6. Louis, p. 369.

7. "Memorandum by Mr. Robert M. McClintock," Top Secret, Washington, June 23, 1948, *FRUS 1948*, pp. 1134–37.

8. "The Secretary of State to the Embassy in the United Kingdom," Top Secret, Washington, June 25, 1948—6 p.m., *FRUS 1948*, pp. 1148–49.

9. "Text of Suggestions Presented by Count Bernadotte, at Rhodes, to the Two Parties on June 28, 1948," *FRUS 1948*, pp. 1152–54.

10. "Editorial Note," *FRUS 1948*, p. 1192.

11. "The Acting United States Representative of the United Nations (Jessup) to the Secretary of State," Top Secret, Urgent, New York, June 30, 1948—8:30 p.m., *FRUS 1948*, pp. 1161–71.

12. Ibid.

13. Trevor N. Dupuy, *Elusive Victory: The Arab-Israeli Wars, 1947–74* (New York: Harper & Row, 1978), p. 75; Morris, *Birth of the Palestinian Refugee Problem*, p. 197.

14. Dupuy, pp. 86–87.

15. "Report by the Central Intelligence Agency," Secret, Washington, July 27, 1948, *FRUS 1948*, pp. 1240–48.

16. "The Secretary of State to the Embassy in the United Kingdom," Top Secret, Washington, August 12, 1948—1 p.m., *FRUS 1948*, pp. 1303–06.

17. "The Secretary of State to the Embassy in the United Kingdom," Top Secret, Washington, August 13, 1948—1 p.m., *FRUS 1948*, pp. 1308–10.

18. "Memorandum by Mr. Robert M. McClintock to the Director of the Office of United Nations Affairs (Rusk)," Top Secret, Washington, September 3, 1948, *FRUS 1948*, pp. 1371–72.

19. "The Secretary of State to the Special Representative of the United States in Israel (McDonald)," Top Secret, US Urgent, Washington, September 1, 1948—6 p.m., *FRUS 1948*, pp. 1366–69.

20. "The Acting United States Representative of the United Nations (Jessup) to the Secretary of State," Top Secret, Urgent, New York, June 30, 1948—8:30 p.m., *FRUS 1948*, pp. 1161–71.

21. "The Ambassador in the United Kingdom to the Secretary of State," Top Secret, London, September 3, 1948—4 p.m., *FRUS 1948*, pp. 1373–75.

22. "The Ambassador in Egypt (Griffis) to the Acting Secretary of State," Top Secret, Urgent, NIACT, Cairo, September 15, 1948—midnight, *FRUS 1948*, pp. 1398–1401.

23. "Progress Report of the United Nations Mediator in Palestine," [Extracts], undated but signed and sent to the UN on 16 September 1948, *FRUS 1948*, pp. 1401–06.

24. "The Ambassador in Egypt (Griffis) to the Acting Secretary of State," Secret, Cairo, October 13, 1948—3 p.m., *FRUS 1948*, pp. 1471–72.

25. "Memorandum for the Files by Mr. Robert M. McClintock," Top Secret, Washington, September 30, 1948, *FRUS 1948*, pp. 1437–38.

26. "Memorandum of Telephone Conversation, by the Acting Secretary of State," Top Secret, Washington, September 29, 1948, *FRUS 1948*, pp. 1430–31.

27. "The President's Special Counsel (Clifford) to the acting Secretary of State (Lovett)," Top Secret, Aboard Presidential Special Train, October 11, 1948—11:30 p.m., *FRUS 1948*, p. 1467.

28. "The Secretary of State to the Acting Secretary of State," Top Secret, NIACT, Eyes Alone, Paris, October 13, 1948—midnight, *FRUS 1948*, pp. 1470–71.

29. "The Ambassador to the United Kingdom (Douglas) to the Secretary of State," Top Secret, NIACT, US Urgent, London, October 14, 1948—3 p.m., *FRUS 1948*, pp. 1474–76.

30. "The Acting Secretary of State to the Secretary of State, at Paris," Top Secret, US Urgent, NIACT, Eyes Only, Washington, October 23, 1948—1 p.m., *FRUS 1948*, pp. 1507–08.

31. "The Acting Secretary of State to the Secretary of State, at Paris," Top Secret, US Urgent, NIACT, Eyes Only, Washington, October 24, 1948—7 p.m., *FRUS 1948*, pp. 1512–14.

32. "The Acting Secretary of State to the Secretary of State, at London," Top Secret, US Urgent, NIACT, Eyes Only, Washington, October 29, 1948—3 p.m., *FRUS 1948*, p. 1528.

33. Sydney Gruson, *New York Times*, 23 October 1948.

34. Dana Adams Schmidt, *New York Times*, 25 November 1948.

35. "The Minister in Syria (Keeley) to the Acting Secretary of State," Secret, Damascus, November 3, 1948—8 p.m., *FRUS 1948*, p. 1542.

36. "The Acting Secretary of State to the Secretary of State, at Paris," Top Secret, Urgent, NIACT, Eyes Only, Washington, October 29, 1948—1 a.m., *FRUS 1948*, p. 1527.

37. "The Acting Secretary of State to the Secretary of State, at Paris," Top Secret, US Urgent, NIACT, Eyes Only, Washington, October 31, 1948—5 p.m., *FRUS 1948*, p. 1535.

38. "The Acting Secretary of State to the Secretary of State, at Paris," Top Secret, US Urgent, NIACT, Eyes Only, Washington, October 30, 1948—12 noon, *FRUS 1948*, pp. 1533–34.

39. "The Secretary of State to the Acting Secretary of State," Top Secret, US Urgent, NIACT, Paris, November 15, 1948—noon, *FRUS 1948*, pp. 1595–97.

40. Associated Press, *New York Times*, 30 December 1948; and Gene Currivan, *New York Times*, 11 January 1949.

41. "The Acting Secretary of State to the Special Representative of the United States in Israel (McDonald)," Top Secret, December 30, 1948, 5 p.m., *FRUS 1948*, p. 1704.

42. Shlaim, *Collusion Across the Jordan*, pp. 367–68.

43. Segev, *1949*, pp. 4–5.

44. Ezer Weizman, *On Eagles' Wings: The personal story of the leading commander of the Israeli Air Force* (Tel Aviv: Steimatzky's Agency Ltd., 1976), pp. 79–81.

45. Tab A "Possibility of Settlement of Principal Israel-Arab Issues," Top Secret, Alpha, Washington, May 18, 1955, *FRUS 1955–1957*, p. 202.

46. Epp, p. 195; and Sachar, p. 350. For details of Israel's plans for occupying Palestinian territory, see Khalidi (ed.), *From Haven to Conquest*, pp. lxxv– lxxxiii, 755–61; and idem, "The Palestine Problem: an Overview." For an excellent study of Jewish land ownership, see John Ruedy, "Dynamics of Land Alienation," in Abu-Lughod (ed.), pp. 119–138. See also Uri Davis and Norton Mezvinsky, *Documents from Israel 1967–73: Readings for a Critique of Zionism* (London: Ithaca Press, 1975), pp. 43–54; Morris, *Birth of the Palestinian Refugee Problem*, pp. 155, 179; Nakhleh, pp. 305–45; Shipler, pp. 32–36; and Segev, *1949*, pp. 69–71.

47. Morris, *Birth of the Palestinian Refugee Problem*, pp. 155, 179.

48. Peretz, "The Arab Refugee Dilemma." See also Shipler, pp. 32–36; and Segev, *1949*, pp. 69–71.

49. Palumbo, p. 146.

50. Ian Lustick, *Arabs in the Jewish State: Israel's Control of a National Minority* (Austin, Tex.: University of Texas Press, 1980), p. 59.

51. The parallel runs about fifteen miles south of Beersheva, meaning Israel was expected to give up most of the Negev, including the port of Aqaba.

52. "The Acting Secretary of State to Mr. Mark F. Ethridge," signed by Robert A. Lovett, Top Secret, Washington, January, 19, 1949, *FRUS 1949*, pp. 681–83.

53. Texts of the all the agreements are in Meron Medzini, *Israel's Foreign Relations: Selected Documents, 1947–1974*, vol. 1 (Jerusalem: Ministry of Foreign affairs, 1976). For a good review of the negotiations and the environment in which they took place, see Neil Caplan, "A Tale of Two Cities: The Rhodes and Lausanne Conferences, 1949," *Journal of Palestine Studies* 21, no. 3 (Spring 1992); and Shlaim, *Collusion Across the Jordan*, pp. 386–433. See also Dupuy, pp. 114–16; "The Consul at Jerusalem (Burdett) to the Secretary of State," Top Secret, Jerusalem, April 20, 1949—4 p.m., *FRUS 1949*, pp. 928–30; Glubb, *A Soldier with the Arabs*, p. 231; Sachar, p. 349; and Tannous, pp. 684–731.

54. Glubb, *A Soldier with the Arabs*, p. 231.

55. "The Consul at Jerusalem (Burdett) to the Secretary of State," Top Secret, Jerusalem, April 20, 1949—4 p.m., *FRUS 1949*, pp. 928–30.

56. Michael Bar-Zohar, *Ben-Gurion: A Biography* (New York: Delacorte Press, 1978), p. 161.

57. "Memorandum by the Acting Secretary of State to the President," Top Secret, Washington, May 27, 1949, *FRUS 19449*, pp. 1060–63.

58. "The Acting Secretary of State to the Embassy in Israel," Top Secret, Priority, NIACT, Washington, May 28, 1949—11 a.m., *FRUS 1949*, pp. 1072–74.

59. "The Government of Israel to the Government of the United States," Top Secret, Tel Aviv, June 8, 1949, *FRUS 1949*, p. 1102.

60. "The Acting Secretary of State to the Secretary of State, at Paris," Top Secret, Priority, NIACT, June 12, 1949—10 p.m., *FRUS 1949*, p. 1127.

61. Louis, p. 568.

62. "The Consul at Jerusalem (Burdett) to the Secretary of State," Secret, Jerusalem, July 6, 1949, *FRUS 1949*, pp. 1203–05.

63. Albion Ross, *New York Times*, 24 April 1950. The text of the Jordanian annexation order is in Medzini, *Israel's Foreign Relations*, vol. 1, pp. 242–43. See also Feintuch, p. 95; Quigley, p. 153; and Shlaim, *Collusion Across the Jordan*, pp. 550–58.

64. Peter Snow, *Hussein* (London: Barrie & Jenkins, 1972), pp. 35–36; and Shlaim, *Collusion Across the Jordan*, p. 605. See also "The Consul at Jerusalem (Burdett) to the Secretary of State," Secret, Jerusalem, October 29, 1949, *FRUS 1949*, pp. 1456–59.

65. "U.S. Efforts to Obtain a Settlement Between Egypt and Israel; the Beginnings of Operation Alpha, January 1-August 26, 1955," *FRUS 1955–1957*, p. 1.

66. "Points of Agreement in London Discussions of Arab-Israel Settlement," Top Secret, Alpha, Limited Distribution, March 10, 1955, *FRUS 1955–1957*, p. 102.

67. Tab A "Possibility of Settlement of Principal Israel-Arab Issues," Top Secret, Alpha, Washington, May 18, 1955, *FRUS 1955–1957*, p. 203.

68. "Letter from the Secretary of State to the President," Top Secret, Alpha, Washington, August 19, 1955, *FRUS 1955–1957*, p. 369.

69. The idea of an international guarantee was resurrected in 1970 by Democratic Senator J.W. Fulbright of Arkansas, chairman of the Senate Foreign Relations Committee and generally a foe of U.S. commitments abroad. He proposed in a 15,000-word speech titled "Old Myths and New Realities—the Middle East" that the UN Security Council seek to have the parties negotiate a peace and if they failed to then impose a fair settlement. Israel's anxieties would be dealt with by having the United States enter into a bilateral treaty with Israel promising to use military force if necessary to "guarantee the territory and independence of Israel within the borders of 1967," adding: "the agreement would also obligate Israel, firmly and unequivocally, never to violate those borders herself." Fulbright's proposal also called for self-determination for the Palestinians and an international status for Jerusalem. Israel showed no interest and the idea died; see Tad Szulc, *New York Times*, 23 August 1970; excerpts are in the same edition.

70. "Letter from the Secretary of State to the President," Top Secret, Alpha, Washington, August 19, 1955, *FRUS 1955–1957*, p. 369.

71. Brecher, p. 112.

72. Bar-Zohar, pp. 223–24.

73. Abba Eban, *An Autobiography* (Tel Aviv: Steimatzky's Agency Ltd., 1977), p. 184.

74. *New York Times*, 17 June 1955.

75. "Telegram from the Department of State to the Embassy in Jordan," Secret, Washington, 2 October 1955—6:07 p.m., *FRUS 1955–1957*, p. 541.

76. "Telegram from the Secretary of State to the Department of State," Secret, NIACT, No Distribution, Geneva, November 8, 1955—noon, *FRUS 1955–1957*, p. 717.

77. "Documents and Source Material," *Journal of Palestine Studies* 14, no. 4 (Summer 1985), p. 220.

78. Benjamin Beit-Hallahmi, *The Israeli Connection* (New York: Pantheon Books, 1987), p. 5; also see Bar-Zohar, p. 236; and Moshe Dayan, *Story of My Life* (New York: William Morrow and Co., 1976), p. 215.

79. Transcripts of Dulles telephone conversations on 11, 12 and 19 February 1957, quoted in Donald Neff, *Warriors at Suez: Eisenhower takes America into the Middle East* (New York: Linden Press/Simon & Schuster, 1984), p. 433.

80. Love, p. 666.

81. The text is in State Department, *American Foreign Policy Current Documents 1957*, pp. 923–28.

82. Neff, *Warriors at Suez*, pp. 433–35.

83. Richard F. Nyrop (ed.), *Israel: a Country Study*, 2d ed. (Washington, D.C.: U.S. Government Printing Office, 1979), p. xix; Epp, p. 185; and Foundation for Middle East Peace, *Report on Israeli Settlement in the Occupied Territories*, Special Report, July 1991.

84. The text of Resolution 242 in full:

> *The Security Council,*
> *Expressing* its continuing concern with the grave situation in the Middle East,
> *Emphasizing* the inadmissibility of the acquisition of territory by war and the need to work for a just and lasting peace in which every State in the area can live in security,
> *Emphasizing further* that all Member States in their acceptance of the Charter of the United Nations have undertaken a commitment to act in accordance with Article 2 of the Charter,
> 1. *Affirms* that the fulfillment of Charter principles requires the establishment of a just and lasting peace in the Middle East which should include the application of both the following principles:
> (i) Withdrawal of Israeli armed forces from territories* occupied in the recent conflict;
> (ii) Termination of all claims or states of belligerency and respect for and acknowledgement of the sovereignty, territorial integrity and political independence of every State in the area and their right to live in peace within secure and recognized boundaries free from threats or acts of force;
> 2. *Affirms further* the necessity
> (a) For guaranteeing freedom of navigation through international waterways in the area;

(b) For Achieving a just settlement of the refugee problem;

(c) For guaranteeing the territorial inviolability and political independence of every State in the area, through measures including the establishment of demilitarized zones;

3. *Requests* the Secretary-General to designate a Special Representative to proceed to the Middle East to establish and maintain contacts with the States concerned in order to promote agreement and assist efforts to achieve a peaceful and accepted settlement in accordance with the provisions and principles in this resolution;

4. *Requests* the Secretary-General to report to the Security Council on the progress of the efforts of the Special Representative as soon as possible.

* The French version said "des territoires occupes."

85. Nina J. Noring (of the Office of the Historian) and Walter B. Smith II (director of the Office of Israeli and Arab-Israeli Affairs, Department of State), *The Withdrawal Clause in UN Security Council Resolution 242 of 1967*, February 1978; Secret/Nodis, p. 24. The study was based on contemporaneous secret U.S. reports from 1967 and was undertaken at the request of the Carter Administration to determine if there was any justice to the Israeli position that the resolution did not include all the occupied territories; it concluded there was not. See also Donald Neff, *Warriors Against Jerusalem*, chapter 15, "Passage of U.N. Resolution 242," which discusses in detail U.S. tactics used in gaining passage of the resolution.

86. Noring and Smith, pp. 12–13.

87. Ibid., p. 13; also author interview with King Hussein, Amman, Jordan, 7 August 1983.

88. Noring and Smith, p. 14.

89. Ibid., p. 23.

90. Norman G. Finkelstein, "To Live or Perish: Abba Eban 'Reconstructs' the June 1967 War," unpublished manuscript, 1993, p. 19.

91. Ibid.

92. Jody A. Boudreault et al., *U.S. Official Statements regarding UN Resolution 242* (Washington, D.C.: Institute for Palestine Studies, 1992), p. 123.

93. Letter to the author, 23 August 1983.

94. Dean Rusk, *As I Saw It* (New York: W.W. Norton and Co., 1990), p. 389.

95. Lord Caradon et al., *UN Security Council Resolution 242* (Washington, D.C.: Georgetown University, 1981), p. 9.

96. Henry A. Kissinger, *White House Years* (New York and Boston: Little, Brown and Co., 1979), p. 345.

97. See, for instance, his article "Hussein's Misreading of History," *Jerusalem Post*, 28 May 1983.

98. Interview with Lucius D. Battle, Washington, DC, 7 July 1993.

99. One such reference came in Carter's 9 March 1977, press conference; the text is in

Meron Medzini, *Israel's Foreign Relations: Selected Documents, 1974–1977*, vol. 3 (Jerusalem: Ministry of Foreign Affairs, 1982), p. 543.

100. The text is in *New York Times*, 28 June 1977.

101. William B. Quandt, *Camp David: Peacemaking and Politics* (Washington, D.C.: The Brookings Institution, 1993), p. 81. See also Zbigniew Brzezinski, *Power and Principle: Memoirs of the National Security Adviser* (New York: Farrar, Strauss, Giroux, 1983), p. 100, who reports the same account.

102. *New York Times*, 14–15 June 1978; and Seth Tillman, *The United States in the Middle East: Interests and Obstacles* (Bloomington, Ind.: Indiana University Press, 1982), p. 184. See also Ahmad Beydoun, "The South Lebanon Border Zone: A Local Perspective," *Journal of Palestine Studies* 21, no. 3 (Spring 1992), p. 44.

103. Hussein A. Amery, "Israel's Designs on Lebanese Water," *Middle East International*, 10 September 1993.

104. Boudreault et al., *U.S. Official Statements regarding UN Resolution 242*, p. 132.

105. Henry Kissinger, "The Path to Peaceful Coexistence in the Middle East," *Washington Post*, Outlook section, 2 August 1992.

106. Texts of the papers are in "Documentation," *Middle East Journal* 2, no. 2 (1993)), pp. 155–56, 158–60.

Notes to Chapter 5: *Palestinians*

1. "The Acting Secretary of State to Certain Diplomatic Offices," October 2, 1948—1 a.m., *FRUS 1948*, pp. 1447–48.

2. John M. Goshko, *Washington Post*, 17 September 1988.

3. Shlaim, *Collusion Across the Jordan*, pp. 116–21.

4. P. Mattar, pp. 118, 138, 148.

5. Ibid., p. 64.

6. Ibid., pp. 71–72.

7. Ibid., p. 74.

8. Nur Masalha, *Expulsion of the Palestinians: The Concept of "Transfer" in Zionist Political Thought, 1882–1948* (Washington, D.C.: Institute for Palestine Studies, 1992), pp. 60–61; Sachar, pp. 204–205. Excerpts are in Laqueur and Rubin (eds.), pp. 56–58. A third independent region was to be reserved for Britain between Jerusalem and Bethlehem with British rule continuing in the main towns in the north and a corridor to the sea between Jaffa and Jerusalem.

9. Cleveland, p. 241.

10. Neff, *Warriors at Suez*, pp. 439–40.

11. P. Mattar, p. 106.

12. "Mr. Moshe Shertok to the Under Secretary of State (Lovett)," Washington, February 22, 1948, *FRUS 1948*, pp. 645–48.

13. P. Mattar, p. 131.

14. Ibid., p. 121; and Robert W. Macdonald, *The League of Arab States: A Study in the Dynamics of Regional Organization* (Princeton, N.J.: Princeton University Press, 1965), pp. 42–43.

15. P. Mattar, p. 118.

16. Dan Kurzman, *Genesis 1948: The First Arab-Israeli War* (New York: The World Publishing Co., 1970), p. 21.

17. Quigley, p. 38.

18. P. Mattar, p. 132.

19. "The Consul General at Jerusalem (Macatee) to the Secretary of State," Secret, Jerusalem, February 9, 1948, *FRUS 1948*, pp. 609–11.

20. Dupuy, pp. 12–14.

21. *New York Times*, 3 October 1948; P. Mattar, pp. 131–33; and Tannous, pp. 655–60. See also Avi Shlaim, "The Rise and Fall of the All–Palestine Government in Gaza," *Journal of Palestine Studies* 20, no. 1 (Autumn 1990), pp. 37–53.

22. "The Ambassador in Egypt (Griffis) to the Acting Secretary of State (Lovett), Received October 2, 1948—12:53 p.m., *FRUS 1948*, p. 1447.

23. Ibid.

24. Ibid., p. 1447, fn. 1.

25. Shlaim, *Collusion Across the Jordan*, p. 298.

26. "Developments of the Quarter: Comment and Chronology," *Middle East Journal* 3, no. 1 (January 1949), p. 78.

27. "The Acting Secretary of State to Certain Diplomatic Offices," October 2, 1948—1 a.m., *FRUS 1948*, pp. 1447–48.

28. P. Mattar, pp. 133–34.

29. Hedrick Smith, *New York Times*, 16 April 1964.

30. David Hirst, *The Gun and the Olive Branch: The Roots of Violence in the Middle East* (New York: Harcourt Brace Jovanovich, 1977), p. 264, quoting the *Sunday Times* of London, 15 June 1969.

31. Tessler, p. 127; Neville J. Mandel, *The Arabs and Zionism Before World War I* (Berkeley: University of California Press, 1976), p. 21; and L.M.C. Van Der Hoeven Leonhard, "Shlomo and David: Palestine, 1907," in Khalidi (ed.), *From Haven to Conquest*, p. 119.

32. The text of the PLO charter is in Y. Harkabi, *The Palestinian Covenant and its Meaning* (Totowa, N.J.: Vallentine, Mitchell & Co., Ltd., 1979), Appendix B2, pp. 119–24. See also Alan Hart, *Arafat: Terrorist or Peacemaker?* (London: Sidgwick & Jackson, 1985), p. 265.

33. *Time*, 13 June 1969, p. 42.

34. Texts of the following resolutions are in Tomeh (ed.).

35. Hirst, *The Gun and the Olive Branch*, p. 335.

36. Interview with Harold Saunders, Washington, D.C., 25 May 1994.

37. The text is in Edward R.E. Sheehan, *The Arabs, Israelis, and Kissinger: A Secret History of American Diplomacy in the Middle East* (New York: Reader's Digest Press, 1976), p. 257; and Lukacs (ed.), pp. 60–61. The commitment said the United States would not "recognize or negotiate with the Palestine Liberation Organization as long as the Palestine Liberation Organization does not recognize Israel's right to exist and does not accept Security Council Resolutions 242 and 338." An additional condition that the PLO renounce terrorism was added in 1985 by Congress when it passed into law the Kissinger pledge; the act, "Codification of Policy Prohibiting Negotiations with the Palestine Liberation Organization," added the condition that the PLO must "renounce the use of terrorism;" see U.S. Senate and U.S. House of Representatives, Committee on Foreign Relations and Committee on Foreign Affairs, *Legislation on Foreign Relations Through 1987*, vol. 1, (Washington, D.C.: U.S. Government Printing Office, March 1988), pp. 529–30.

38. Donald Neff, "Nixon's Middle East Policy: From Balance to Bias," *Arab Studies Quarterly* 12, nos. 1–2 (Winter/Spring 1990).

39. Yitzhak Rabin, *The Rabin Memoirs* (Boston: Little, Brown and Co., 1979), p. 261.

40. Kenen, pp. 108–10.

41. Eventually AIPAC went so far as to publish a blacklist in 1983 titled "The Campaign to Discredit Israel," listing thirty-nine individuals and twenty-one groups that it said were dedicated to opposing Israel's close ties with the United States. Among those listed were former senator James Abourezk; former undersecretary of state George W. Ball; Frederick G. Dutton, a Washington attorney representing Saudi Arabia; and former ambassadors Talcott W. Seelye and John C. West. The groups included Americans for Middle East Understanding; see "Washington Talk," *New York Times*, 13 July 1983.

42. Richard B. Parker, "The Arabists," *Journal of Palestine Studies* 24, no. 1 (Autumn 1994), p. 72.

43. Joseph Kraft, "Those Arabists in the State Department," *New York Times Magazine*, 7 November 1971.

44. *Washington Post*, 24 October 1993.

45. The text is in Lukacs, pp. 61–64.

46. *New York Times*, 17 November 1975.

47. Interview with Harold Saunders, Washington, D.C., 25 May 1994. See also William B. Quandt, *Decade of Decisions: American Policy towards the Arab-Israeli Conflict, 1967–1976* (Berkeley: University of California Press, 1977), p. 278. That Saunders had acted with Kissinger's support became clear the next month when Saunders was promoted in December 1975 to assistant Secretary of State in charge of Intelligence and Research.

48. Quandt, *Decade of Decisions*, p. 279. See also Marwan R. Bubeiry, "The Saunders Document," *Journal of Palestine Studies* 8, no. 1 (Autumn 1978).

49. Kathleen Christison, "Blind Spots: Official U.S. Myths About the Middle East," *Journal of Palestine Studies* 17, no. 2 (Winter 1988), p. 57.

50. Ismail Fahmy, *Negotiating for Peace in the Middle East* (Baltimore: Johns Hopkins University Press, 1983), pp. 196–97. A similar concern was expressed by President Ford; see Quandt, *Camp David*, p. 33.

51. Brzezinski, p. 108; and Quandt, *Camp David*, p. 129.

52. Brzezinski, p. 91; Lukacs, p. 71; Quandt, *Camp David*, p. 48; and Cheryl A. Rubenberg, *Israel and the American National Interest: A Critical Examination* (Chicago: University of Illinois Press, 1986), pp. 210–11.

53. *New York Times*, 13 May 1977; the text is in same edition.

54. *New York Times*, 10 March 1978; and Tillman, p. 222. When an early effort to deal with the PLO through third parties sputtered to an end in the latter half of 1977, Carter's National Security Advisor Zbigniew Brzezinski flippantly dismissed the group by saying, "Bye-bye, PLO." After U.S. policy was delivered a major setback in 1979 with the fall of the shah of Iran, Arafat taunted: "Bye-bye to American interests in the region." See Aryeh Y. Yodfat and Yuval Arnon-Ohanna, *PLO: Strategy and Tactics* (London: Croom Helm, 1981), p. 119.

55. Interview with Harold Saunders, Washington, D.C., 25 May 1994.

56. Quandt, *Camp David*, pp. 255–56; and Fred J. Khouri, *The Arab Israeli Dilemma*, 3d ed. (Syracuse, N.Y.: Syracuse University Press, 1985), pp. 407–08. See also Adel Safty, *From Camp David to the Gulf: Negotiations, Language & Propaganda, and War* (New York: Black Rose Books, 1992), pp. 78–84.

57. Tillman, p. 132. See also Rubenberg, pp. 138–39.

58. *Washington Post*, 20 September 1978.

59. *Washington Post*, 16 August 1979; and Victor Ostrovsky and Claire Hoy, *By Way of Deception* (New York: St. Martin's Press, 1990), pp. 279–82.

60. U.S. Department of State, *American Foreign Policy, 1977–1980* (Washington, D.C.: U.S. Government Printing Office, n.d.), p. 701.

61. Quandt, *Camp David*, p. 322.

62. The text is in *New York Times*, 1 December 1981; Institute For Palestine Studies, *International Documents on Palestine 1981* (Washington, D.C.: Institute for Palestine Studies, 1983), pp. 405–406; and John Norton Moore (ed.), *The Arab-Israeli Conflict: Volume IV: The Difficult Search for Peace (1975–1988)*, part 1 (Princeton, N.J.: Princeton University Press, 1991), pp. 1065–66.

63. Khouri, pp. 426–27; and Quigley, pp. 217–18. Official Arab reaction is in *Journal of Palestine Studies* 11, no. 2 (Winter 1982), p. 194. See also Rubenberg, pp. 268–69, who claims Washington saw the relationship as having Israel act as its proxy around the world.

64. Partial text is in *International Documents on Palestine 1981*, p. 414; it gives the release date as 12 December, but that is two days before Israel's action.

65. The text is in Mallison and Mallison, p. 444.

66. *New York Times*, 19 December 1981. See also "US Assistance to the State of Israel, Report by the Comptroller General of the United States," GAO/ID-83-51, June 24, 1983, US Accounting Office, pp. 154–57. The report is the most comprehensive survey ever made of the extraordinary special arrangements provided for Israel's profit. When it was released, the report was heavily censored but uncensored versions quickly leaked to such organizations as the American-Arab Anti-Defamation Committee. An uncensored early draft of the report can be found in Mohammed El-Khawas and Samir Abed-Rabbo, *American Aid to Israel: Nature and Impact* (Brattleboro, Vt.: Amana Books, 1984), pp. 114–91.

67. *New York Times*, 21 December 1981. See also Silver, pp. 245–46.

68. *New York Times*, 30 November 1983. See also Bernard Gwertzman, "Reagan Turns to Israel," *The New York Times Magazine*, 27 November 1983.

69. Thomas L. Friedman, *From Beirut to Jerusalem* (New York: Farrar, Strauss, Giroux, 1989), pp. 152–53.

70. Zeev Schiff and Ehud Ya'ari, *Israel's Lebanon War* (New York: Simon and Schuster, 1984), pp. 74–75, 211; Cockburn and Cockburn, pp. 327–29; and Noam Chomsky, *The Fateful Triangle* (Boston: South End Press, 1983), pp. 388–92. During the summer of slaughter, the United States maintained its strong support of Israel and cast three vetoes in the UN Security Council to shield Israel, two of them involving Lebanon and the other on Israel's occupation policies: 8 June, 26 June, and 6 August.

71. Excerpts of Shultz's confirmation hearings testimony on 13 July 1982 are in *Journal of Palestine Studies* 11–12, nos. 4 & 1 (Summer/Fall 1982), pp. 333–35.

72. The arms export act was invoked 10 June 1981 and again on 15 July 1982; the Reagan peace plan was introduced 1 September 1982.

73. Bernard Gwertzman, *New York Times*, 20 February 1983.

74. Michael Getler, *Washington Post*, 24 April 1983.

75. William Safire, *New York Times*, 16 June 1983. See also Donald Neff, "The remarkable feat of George Shultz," *Middle East International*, 5 March 1988. For a description of Shultz's style henceforth on dealing with the Israelis, see T. Friedman, *From Beirut to Jerusalem*, pp. 500–501.

76. *New York Times*, 31 May 1984.

77. Interview with State Department sources who wished to remain anonymous, Washington, D.C., 9 December 1982.

78. *New York Times*, 2 October 1985. The Israeli bombs hit the home but Arafat was away.

79. *New York Times*, 27 November 1988.

80. The text is in *Journal of Palestine Studies* 14, no. 4 (Summer 1985), pp. 122–28.

81. The text of Dine's speech, "The Revolution in U.S.-Israel Relations," is in *Journal of Palestine Studies* 15, no. 4 (Summer 1986), pp. 134–43.

82. Richard B. Straus, *Washington Post*, 27 April 1986.

83. *New York Times*, 7 August 1986; and Quigley, p. 146.

84. The text of Dine's speech is in *Journal of Palestine Studies* 16, no. 4 (Summer 1987), pp. 95–106; the same issue also carries the text of AIPAC's 1987 policy statement, pp. 107–14.

85. Middle East Policy and Research Center, May/June 1987, 5/6–IV–3–Page 12.

86. David K. Shipler, *New York Times*, 6 July 1987.

87. Christison, "Blind Spots," p. 50.

88. Ibid.

89. Official text of the "Political Communique" is in *Journal of Palestine Studies* 18, no. 2 (Winter 1989), pp. 216–28.

90. *New York Times*, 27 November 1988, includes text of the State Department statement. See also Kathleen Christison, "The Arab-Israeli Policy of George Shultz," *Journal of Palestine Studies* 18, no. 2 (Winter 1989).

91. *New York Times*, 14 December 1988. The text of Arafat's 80-minute speech is in *Journal of Palestine Studies* 18, no. 3 (Spring 1989), pp. 161–71.

92. The text of Arafat's statement is in *Journal of Palestine Studies* 18, no. 3 (Spring 1989), pp. 180–81.

93. The text is in *Department of State Bulletin*, No. 2143, February 1989.

94. *New York Times*, 15 December 1988.

95. Clyde Haberman, *New York Times*, 24 December 1988.

96. Associated Press, *Wall Street Journal*, 9 January 1989.

97. Thomas L. Friedman, *New York Times*, 21 June 1990. The text of Bush's remarks is in the same edition.

98. Thomas L. Friedman, *New York Times*, 23 May 1989.

99. Clyde Haberman, *New York Times*, 15 May 1992.

100. The text is in *New York Times*, 1 September 1993. For an analysis, see Burhan Dajani, "The September 1993 Israeli-PLO Documents: A Textural Analysis," *Journal of Palestine Studies* 23, no. 3 (Spring 1994).

101. Resolution 48/40A. See Jules Kagian, "Rewriting Resolutions," *Middle East International*, 17 December 1993; and Scholz, p. 161. The General Assembly repeated the rights of Palestinians to return or compensation in forty subsequent resolutions between 1950 and 1993 in UNGA numbers: 394, 818, 916, 1018, 1191, 1315, 1456, 1604, 1725, 1856, 1912, 2052, 2154, 2341, 2452, 2535, 2672, 2792, 2963, 3089, 3331, 3419, 32/90, 33/112, 34/52, 35/13, 36/120, 36/146, 37/120, 38/83, 39/99, 40/165, 41/69, 42/69, 43/57, 44/47, 45/73, 46/46, 47/69.

102. Kagian, "Rewriting Resolutions."

Notes to Chapter 6: *Jerusalem*

1. "The Acting Secretary of State to Mr. Mark F. Ethridge," signed Robert A. Lovett, Top Secret, Washington, January 19, 1949, *FRUS 1949*, pp. 681–83.

2. U.S. State Department, *Settlement Report*, quoted in Foundation for Middle East Peace, *Report on Israeli Settlement in the Occupied Territories*, July 1993.

3. Its members were Australia, Britain, China, France, Mexico and the United States.

4. Resolution 181 (II), 29 November 1947.

5. Michael C. Hudson, "The Transformation of Jerusalem: 1917–1987 A.D.," in *Jerusalem in History*, ed. by K.J. Asali (New York: Olive Branch Press, 1990), p. 257.

6. Ibid., p. 258; and Kurzman, *Genesis 1948*, p. 41.

7. Feintuch, p. 1.

8. *Village Statistics*, Jerusalem Palestine Government, 1945. Map published as UN map no. 94(6) in August 1950.

9. Hudson, in Asali (ed.), p. 258.

10. Henry Cattan, *Jerusalem* (New York: St. Martin's Press, 1981), pp. 45, 61; and Hirst, *The Gun and the Olive Branch*, p. 232.

11. It remained in existence until 1950 when, on 14 June, it finally admitted its impotence and returned the Jerusalem issue back to the General Assembly; see Feintuch, p. 98.

12. Feintuch, p. 41.

13. Eban, pp. 124–25.

14. Persson, p. 204. See also Kurzman, *Genesis 1948*, pp. 555–56; and Avishai Margalit, "The Violent Life of Yitzhak Shamir," *The New York Review of Books*, 14 May 1992.

15. "The Acting Secretary of State to the Secretary of Defense (Forrestal)," Top Secret, Washington, October 18, 1948, *FRUS 1948*, pp. 1488–89.

16. "Progress Report of the United Nations Mediator in Palestine," Extracts, September 16, 1948, *FRUS 1948*, pp. 1401–06.

17. "The Consul General at Jerusalem (Macdonald) to the Secretary of State," Confidential, Jerusalem, July 11, 1948—4 p.m., *FRUS 1948*, pp. 1212–13.

18. Cattan, *Jerusalem*, pp. 51, 61, 63.

19. Hudson, in Asali (ed.), p. 260.

20. Meron Benvenisti, *Jerusalem: The Torn City* (Jerusalem: Isratypeset Ltd., 1976), p. 6. The text is in Medzini, vol. 1, pp. 219–20. See also "The Acting United States Representative at the United Nations (Jessup) to the Secretary of State," Confidential, US Urgent, New York, July 29, 1948—5:35 p.m.; and "The Acting Special Representative of the United States in Israel (Knox) to the Secretary of State," Tel Aviv, August 3, 1948, *FRUS 1948*, pp. 1256–57, 1273–74.

21. "The Acting Special Representative of the United States in Israel (Knox) to the Secretary of State," Tel Aviv, August 3, 1948, *FRUS 1948*, p. 1273.

22. Brecher, p. 24.

23. Benvenisti, *Jerusalem*, p. 9.

24. David Ben Gurion, *Israel: A Personal History* (New York: Funk & Wagnalls, Inc., 1971), p. 331; Sachar, pp. 356–57; and Segev, *1949*, p. 6.

25. Bailey, pp. 64–65. See also Eban, pp. 140–42.

26. The text is in Tomeh (ed.), p. 18.

27. Brecher, p. 26.

28. Feintuch, p. 62.

29. Michael I. Hoffman, *New York Times*, 7 September 1949. For background on the commission, see chapter 3.

30. "Memorandum by the Secretary of State to the President," Washington, December 20, 1949; *FRUS 1949*, p. 1552.

31. Brecher, p. 25; and Feintuch, p. 69. See also Bailey, p. 107; and Benvenisti, *Jerusalem*, p. 11.

32. Feintuch, p. 74.

33. Ibid., pp. 75–76. Dulles lost the race, although not necessarily just because of this one issue.

34. Louis L. Gerson, *John Foster Dulles* (New York: Cooper Square Publishers, 1967), p. 57.

35. Camille M. Cianfarra, *New York Times*, 16 April 1949. The text is in the same edition.

36. *New York Times*, 16 November 1949.

37. "Memorandum by the Secretary of State to the President," Washington, November 21, 1949, *FRUS 1949*, pp. 1498–99.

38. Benvenisti, *Jerusalem*, pp. 11–12. The text is in Medzini, vol. 1, pp. 223–24.

39. "The Ambassador in Israel (McDonald) to the Secretary of State," Secret, Tel Aviv, December 5, 1949, *FRUS 1949*, p. 1521.

40. Thomas J. Hamilton, *New York Times*, 10 December 1949. Resolution No. 303 (IV). The text is in Tomeh (ed.), pp. 20–21.

41. "The Ambassador in Israel (McDonald) to the Secretary of State," Secret, NIACT, Tel Aviv, December 11, 1949—1 p.m., *FRUS 1949*, pp. 1532–33.

42. *New York Times*, 21 December 1949.

43. Benvenisti, *Jerusalem*, p. 12; and Feintuch, p. 88.

44. "The Secretary of State to the Embassy in Israel," Secret, Washington, December 20, 1949—1 p.m., *FRUS 1949*, p. 1555.

45. Resolution 114 (S–2). The text is in Tomeh (ed.), p. 176.

46. *New York Times*, 21 December 1949; and "Memorandum by the Acting Assistant Secretary of State for Near Eastern, South Asian, and African Affairs (Hare) to the Secretary of State," Secret, Washington, December 17, 1949, *FRUS 1949*, pp. 1547–48.

47. *New York Times*, 1 January 1950.

48. *New York Times*, 24 January 1950; and Brecher, p. 32. At the same time, the Knesset voted down an amendment by Menachem Begin's opposition Herut party that would have made the proclamation applicable to all of Jerusalem, including Arab East Jerusalem and the Old City.

49. McDonald, p. 223; and "Acheson to the Embassy in Israel," Washington, January 4, 1950, *FRUS 1950*, pp. 667–68.

50. Feintuch, pp. 103–104.

51. Albion Ross, *New York Times*, 24 April 1950. It also changed its name to Jordan. The text of the Jordanian annexation order is in Medzini, vol. 1, pp. 242–43. See also Feintuch, p. 95; Shlaim, *Collusion Across the Jordan*, pp. 550–58; and Quigley, pp. 146, 153.

52. Brecher, pp. 33–35.

53. The text of his report is in *New York Times*, 2 June 1953. See also Gerson, pp. 246–55; and Rubenberg, p. 63.

54. Dana Adams Schmidt, *New York Times*, 11 July 1953; *New York Times*, 16 July 1953; the Israeli decision was announced on 7/10/53. The U.S. position on the matter was spelled out in two State Department statements on 29 July 1953, and 3 November 1954; see Department of State, *American Foreign Policy 1950–1955*, pp. 2254–55. See also Brecher, p. 34; and Feintuch, p. 109.

55. Feintuch, pp. 112–16.

56. Ibid., p. 117.

57. James Feron, *New York Times*, 31 August 1966; and Ben Gurion, p. 746.

58. Feintuch, pp. 116, 121.

59. Ibid., p. 116.

60. Ibid., p. 117.

61. Mordechai Gur, *The Battle For Jerusalem* (New York: Popular Library, 1974), p. 362.

62. J. Robert Moskin, *Among Lions: The Battle for Jerusalem, June 5–7, 1967* (New York: Arbor House, 1982), p. 308.

63. Ibid., p. 324; Neff, *Warriors Against Israel*, pp. 230–34. The text of Dayan's remarks is in Medzini, vol. 1, pp. 243–44.

64. Rafik Halabi, *The West Bank Story* (New York: Harcourt Brace Jovanovich, 1981), pp. 35–36. See also David Hirst, "Rush to Annexation: Israel in Jerusalem," *Journal of Palestine Studies* 3, no. 4 (Summer 1974); and Donald Neff, *Warriors For Jerusalem: The Six*

Days the Changed the Middle East (New York: Linden Press/Simon & Schuster, 1984), pp. 289–90. The text of East Jerusalem Mayor Rouhi Khatib's statement before the UN Security Council meeting of 3 May 1968 about Israel's actions in Jerusalem during the first two weeks of occupation is in Nakhleh, pp. 374–77. Nakhleh also carries extensive quotes from other witnesses about Israel's actions in Jerusalem as stated in UN Document S/13450 and Add. 1 of 12 July 1979. The commission was established by the Security Council resolution 446 on 22 March 1979 "to examine the situation relating to settlements in the Arab territories occupied since 1967 including Jerusalem."

65. Ronald Storrs, *Orientations* (London: Nicholson & Watson, 1945), p. 347.

66. Ibid., p. 346. See also Vincent Sheean, "Holy Land 1929," in Khalidi (ed.), *From Haven to Conquest*, pp. 273–302. Sheean was an American foreign correspondent who witnessed the bloody 1929 riots sparked by Jewish claims to the wall and later wrote about them in *Personal History*, published in 1934.

67. Ann Lesch, "Israeli Settlements in the Occupied Territories," *Journal of Palestine Studies* 8, no. 1 (Autumn 1978). See also Ghada Talhami, "Between Development and Preservation: Jerusalem Under Three Regimes," *American-Arab Affairs*, Spring 1986, pp. 93–107.

68. Neff, *Warriors For Jerusalem*, p. 307; the text is in *New York Times*, 20 June 1967.

69. Interview with Lucius D. Battle, Washington, D.C., 27 May 1993.

70. Ibid.

71. Mahmoud Riad, *The Struggle for Peace in the Middle East* (New York: Quartet Books, 1981), p. 62. Jerusalem's deputy (Jewish) mayor, Meron Benvenisti, reported in his memoirs how close relations were between U.S. and Israeli officials: "Privately, the Americans advised their Israeli friends more or less as follows: do what you like in Jerusalem...;" Benvenisti, *Jerusalem*, p. 123. Similarly, Israeli scholar Feintuch, after interviewing Goldberg, wrote that "the Americans intimated to the Israelis: 'You are there, and you will be there,' thus minimizing the possibility that Israel would be dislodged from Eastern Jerusalem by an external imposition of UN resolutions"; see Feintuch, p. 126.

72. Interview with Lucius D. Battle, Washington, D.C., 27 May 1993.

73. Feintuch, p. 126.

74. Neff, *Warriors For Jerusalem*, p. 307.

75. "Marvin to the President," 6:30 p.m., 19 June 1967, LBJ Library.

76. *Washington Post*, 19 June 1967.

77. Benvenisti, *Jerusalem*, p. 117; and Brecher, pp. 39–40. The text of the two enabling amendments, No. 6 and 11, to the Municipalities Ordinance and the Law and Administration Ordinance 5708–1948, respectively, is in Medzini, vol. 1, pp. 245–46; both amendments were adopted by the Knesset on 27 June 1967. See also Henry Cattan, "The Status of Jerusalem under International Law and United Nations Resolutions," *Journal of Palestine Studies* 10, no. 3 (Spring 1981), pp. 3–15, as well as Cattan's book, *Jerusalem*; Ibrahim Dakkak, "The Transformation of Jerusalem: Juridical Status and Physical Change," in *Occupation: Israel over Palestine*, ed. by Naseer H. Aruri (Belmont, Mass.: Association of

Arab-American University Graduates, 1983), pp. 67–96; Hirst, "Rush to Annexation," pp. 3–31; Mallison and Mallison, pp. 207–39; and Talhami, pp. 93–107.

78. Cattan, *Jerusalem*, p. 72. See also Joseph Judge, "This Year in Jerusalem," *National Geographic*, April 1983, pp. 479–514.

79. Foundation for Middle East Peace, *Report on Israeli Settlement in the Occupied Territories*, Special report, Winter 1991–1992.

80. Benvenisti, *Jerusalem*, p. 251.

81. Ibrahim Mattar, "From Palestinian to Israeli: Jerusalem 1948–1982," *Journal of Palestine Studies* 12, no. 4 (Summer 1983), pp. 57–63.

82. Benvenisti, *Jerusalem*, p. 251.

83. *New York Times*, 30 June 1967; and Benvenisti, *Jerusalem*, p. 124.

84. Feintuch, p. 130.

85. UN A/6793. Excerpts are in "Documents Concerning the Status of Jerusalem," *Journal of Palestine Studies* 1, no. 1 (Autumn 1971), pp. 178–82; and Medzini, vol. 1, pp. 251–53.

86. The texts are in U.S. Department of State, *American Foreign Policy: Current Documents 1967*, pp. 563–64. See also Feintuch, pp. 127–29.

87. Resolution 2253 (ES-V); the text is in Tomeh (ed.), pp. 67–68. See also Mallison and Mallison, p. 215.

88. Resolution 2254 (ES-V); the text is in Tomeh (ed.), p. 68.

89. Bernard Gwertzman, *New York Times*, 13 March 1980; Feintuch, p. 137.

90. The text is in Sheehan, Appendix Two.

91. Brecher, pp. 481–83.

92. Resolution 298. The text is in Tomeh (ed.), p. 148; and Cattan, *Jerusalem*, pp. 187–88.

93. USUN Press Release #147 (71), 25 September 1971.

94. Brecher, p. 40.

95. *Facts on File 1971*, p. 749.

96. Rowland Evans and Robert Novak, *Washington Post*, 1 October 1971.

97. Kissinger, *White House Years*, p. 1285.

98. Richard M. Nixon, *The Memoirs of Richard Nixon* (New York: Grosset & Dunlap, 1978), p. 481.

99. *New York Times*, 25 March 1976. Excerpts of Scranton's speech are in the same edition.

100. Ibid.

101. The text of the draft resolution is in *New York Times*, 26 March 1976.

102. *New York Times*, 12 November 1976.

103. Resolution No. 33/113 A; the text is in Regina S. Sherif (ed.), *United Nations Resolutions on Palestine and the Arab-Israeli Conflict, 1975–1981* (Washington, D.C.: Institute for Palestine Studies, 1988), pp. 78–79. See also Department of State, Office of the Legal Adviser, *Digest of United States Practice in International Law 1978*, pp. 1575–83. For a detailed discussion, see Mallison and Mallison, chapter 6.

104. Resolution No. 446; the text is in Sherif (ed.), p. 188.

105. Resolution 452; the text is in ibid., p. 190.

106. Ibid., p. 191; and Mallison and Mallison, pp. 474–76.

107. Tillman, p. 167. See also Brzezinski, p. 442. Brzezinski reports the reversal of the vote was "shattering for [Secretary of State Cyrus] Vance." The text of Carter's remarks is in *New York Times*, 5 March 1980.

108. Resolution No. 476; the text is in Sherif (ed.), p. 195.

109. Resolution ES-7/2; the text is in ibid., pp. 110–11; and *New York Times*, 30 July 1980.

110. Geoffrey Aronson, Creating Facts: Israel, Palestinians and the West Bank (Washington, D.C.: Institute for Palestine Studies, 1987), pp. 137–39. The text is in *New York Times*, 31 July 1980. See also Quigley, p. 172.

111. The background on annexation can be found in David Shipler, *New York Times Magazine*, 14 December 1980. See also Cattan, *Jerusalem*, p. 223. Lengthy excerpts of a letter from Egypt's Anwar Sadat to Israel's Menachem Begin protesting the annexation are in *Journal of Palestine Studies* 10, no. 1 (Autumn 1980), pp. 202–204.

112. Resolution 478; the text is in Sherif (ed.), p. 196; Khouri, pp. 418–19; and Cattan, *Jerusalem*, pp. 219–20.

113. See, for instance, excerpts of AIPAC's policy statement in *Journal of Palestine Studies* 14, no 4 (Summer 1985), pp. 220–24; and *Near East Report*, 13 April 1992.

114. For details, see chapter 8.

115. Bernard Gwertzman, *New York Times*, 3 October 1984.

116. The text is in *New York Times*, 18 July 1984.

117. Martin Gellman, *Washington Post*, 28 October 1994.

118. Francis A. Boyle memorandum to Rep. Lee Hamilton, 21 July 1989, *Arab-American Affairs*, Fall 1989, p. 126.

119. The text of Helms' remarks is in *Congressional Record—Senate*, SS9919, 26 July 1988.

120. Boyle to Hamilton, *Arab-American Affairs*, Fall 1989, pp. 125–38.

121. Rowland Evans and Robert Novak, *Washington Post*, 2 February 1995.

122. Transcript, president's remarks in Palm Springs, CA, *New York Times*, 3 March 1990.

123. Jackson Diehl, *Washington Post*, 6 March 1990. See also Thomas L. Friedman, *New York Times*, 13 March 1990.

124. John M. Goshko, *Washington Post*, 7 March 1990.

125. Sabra Chartrand, *New York Times*, 13 April 1990.

126. Joel Brinkley, *New York Times*, 22 April 1990.

127. Al Kamen, *Washington Post*, 24 April 1990.

128. Thomas L. Friedman, *New York Times*, 25 April 1990.

129. Clyde Haberman, *New York Times*, 13 December 1991; Stirh O'Sullivan, *Washington Times*, 13 December 1991; and Paul Adams, "Passions Ignited," *Middle East International*, 20 December 1991.

130. Jackson Diehl, *Washington Post*, 10 October 1991.

131. Bardley Burton, *Washington Times*, 29 August 1991; and Jackson Diehl, *Washington Post*, 8 September 1991, 25 September 1991.

132. Foundation for Middle East Peace, *Report on Israeli Settlement in the Occupied Territories*, March 1993.

133. Foundation for Middle East Peace, *Report on Israeli Settlement in the Occupied Territories*, January 1992.

134. *Forward*, 21 May 1993.

135. U.S. Department of State, *Settlement Report*, quoted in Foundation for Middle East Peace, *Report on Israeli Settlement in the Occupied Territories*, July 1993.

136. The text is in Foundation for Middle East Peace, *Report on Israeli Settlement in the Occupied Territories*, May 1993.

137. *Washington Times*, 16 January 1995.

Notes to Chapter 7: *Settlements*

1. Jody A. Boudreault et al. (eds.), *U.S. Official Statements: Israeli Settlements* (Washington, D.C.: Institute for Palestine Studies, 1992), p. 15.

2. Foundation for Middle East Peace, "U.S. Official Revises Government View of Settlements," *Report on Israeli Settlement*, May 1994.

3. See chapter 4 for details of Israel's conquests.

4. Halabi, pp. 35–36; and Paul Findley, *Deliberate Deceptions: Facing the Facts about the U.S.-Israeli Relationship* (Brooklyn, N.Y.: Lawrence Hill Books, 1993), pp. 172–73.

5. Aronson, p. 16. See also Israel Shahak, "Memory of 1967 'Ethnic Cleansing' Fuels Ideology of Golan Settlers," *Washington Report on Middle East Affairs*, November 1992.

6. Israeli Housing Minister Zeev Sharef revealed details of the Jerusalem settlements on 18 February 1971; see *Facts on File 1971*, p. 123.

7. Benvenisti, *Jerusalem*, p. 233. See also Dayan, *Story of My Life*, p. 372.

8. *New York Times*, 29 October 1953.

9. Dana Adams Schmidt, *New York Times*, 28 February 1957.

10. Terence Smith, *New York Times*, 25 September 1967.

11. Ibid.

12. Khalidi, "The Palestine Problem: An Overview," p. 9.

13. Aronson, p. 16. See also Shahak, "Memory of 1967."

14. Hedrick Smith, *New York Times*, 27 September 1967.

15. In Hebrew, Eretz Yisrael means the Land of Israel as occupied by ancient Israelites, a phrase invested with strong nationalist and messianic significance.

16. Ehud Sprinzak, *The Ascendance of Israel's Radical Right* (New York: Oxford University Press, 1991), p. 38. See also Ammon Rubinstein, *The Zionist Dream Revisited* (New York: Schocken Books, 1984), p. 103; and Sachar, pp. 708–09.

17. Sprinzak, pp. 39–40.

18. Rael J. Isaac, Israel Divided: Ideological Politics in the Jewish State (Baltimore: Johns Hopkins University Press, 1977), pp. 3–13; and Rubinstein, *The Zionist Dream Revisited*, p. 103.

19. Jody A. Boudreault et al. (eds.), *U.S. Official Statements: Israeli Settlements/The Fourth Geneva Convention* (Washington, D.C.: Institute for Palestine Studies, 1992), p. 127.

20. Terence Smith, *New York Times*, 12 May 1976.

21. Boudreault et al., *U.S. Official Statements: Israeli Settlements*, p. 15.

22. The text of the draft resolution is in *New York Times*, 26 March 1976; and Jody A. Boudreault (ed.), *United Nations Resolutions on Palestine and the Arab-Israeli Conflict: 1987–1991* (Washington, D.C.: Institute for Palestine Studies, 1993), pp. 413–14.

23. Resolution 446; the text is in Sherif, p. 188.

24. UN Document S/13450 and Add. 1 of 7/12/79. The report is extensively quoted in Nakhleh, pp. 483–93.

25. Meron Benvenisti, *The West Bank Data Project: A Survey of Israel's Policies* (Washington, D.C.: American Enterprise Institute for Public Policy Research, 1984), p. 52.

26. Aronson, p. 17.

27. For a report on violent frictions with the Arabs of Hebron caused by the settlement, see Sprinzak, p. 89. See also Robert I. Friedman, *Zealots for Zion: Inside Israel's West Bank Settlement Movement* (New York: Random House, 1992), pp. 18–19; Grace Halsell, *Prophesy and Politics: Militant Evangelists on the Road to Nuclear War* (Westport, Conn.: Lawrence Hill & Co., 1986), pp. 106–12; J. Abu-Lughod, in I. Abu-Lughod (ed.), pp. 139–64; David McDowall, *Palestine and Israel: The Uprising and Beyond* (Berekely: University of California Press, 1989), p. 170; and Quigley, pp. 174–81.

28. Samaria is the biblical name of northern Palestine and was publicized by ultranationalists as a way to establish their ancient claim to the land.

29. Aronson, p. 39.

30. Peretz Merhav, *The Israeli Left: History, Problems, Documents* (New York: A.S. Barnes & Co., Inc., 1980), p. 342.

31. Aronson, p. 46.

32. Foundation for Middle East, *Report on Israeli Settlement in the Occupied Territories*, Special Report, July 1991; and Aronson, p. 70.

33. Silver, p. 254.

34. Author interview with Geoffrey Aronson, Washington, D.C., 24 January 1994.

35. Associated Press, *Washington Times*, 9 May 1992.

36. Quandt, *Camp David*, pp. 80–83.

37. Clifton Daniel (ed.), *Chronicle of the Twentieth Century* (New York: Prentice Hall, 1988), p. 1127.

38. Boudreault et al., *U.S. Official Statements: Israeli Settlements*, p. 14; and *New York Times*, 29 July 1977.

39. Quandt, *Camp David*, p. 83.

40. Silver, p. 168.

41. Quandt, *Camp David*, p. 83n.

42. *New York Times*, 18 August 1977.

43. Quandt, *Camp David*, p. 100.

44. *New York Times*, 2 and 3 September 1977; and Aronson, pp. 70, 85. See also Uzi Benziman, *Sharon: An Israeli Caesar* (New York: Adama Books, 1985), pp. 206–07; and *Journal of Palestine Studies* 8, no. 2 (Winter 1978), p. 130.

45. Foundation for Middle East, *Report on Israeli Settlement in the Occupied Territories*, Special Report, July 1991.

46. Aronson, p. 85.

47. Quandt, *Camp David*, p. 161; and Safty, pp. 70–71.

48. Quandt, *Camp David*, p. 161.

49. Rubenberg, p. 224.

50. *The Arabs Under Israeli Occupation 1978* (Beirut: Institute for Palestine Studies, 1979), p. 10.

51. U.S. Department of State, *American Foreign Policy 1977–80* (Washington, D.C.: U.S. Government Printing Office, 1983), p. 650. See also Moshe Dayan, *Breakthrough* (New York: Alfred A. Knopf, 1981), pp. 115–19.

52. *The Arabs Under Israeli Occupation 1978*, pp. 10–11; the text is in *New York Times*, 13 February 1978.

53. *The Arabs Under Israeli Occupation 1978*, p. 11.

54. *New York Times*, 27 February 1978.

55. Jimmy Carter, *Keeping Faith: Memoirs of a President* (New York: Bantam Books, 1982), pp. 312–13. See also Safty, pp. 74–75.

56. Department of State, Office of the Legal Adviser, *Digest of United States Practice in International Law 1978*, pp. 1575–83. The text is in Boudreault et al., *U.S. Official Statements: Israeli Settlements*, pp. 7–11. For a detailed discussion, see Mallison and Mallison, chapter 6.

57. SC 465, 1 March 1980; GA 34/90 C, 12 December 1979; and GA 33/113 B, 18 December 1978.

58. GA 35/122 B, 11 December 1980; SC 452, 20 July 1979; SC 446, 22 March 1979; and GA 32/5, 28 October 1977.

59. SC 465. The text is in Sherif, p. 191; and Mallison and Mallison, pp. 474–76.

60. The text of Carter's remarks is in Jody A. Boudreault and Yasser Salaam (eds.), *U.S. Official Statements: Status of Jerusalem* (Washington, D.C.: Institute for Palestine Studies, 1992), pp. 46–47.

61. Tillman, p. 167.

62. *The Arabs Under Israeli Occupation 1980* (Beirut: Institute for Palestine Studies, 1981), pp. 7, 21, 25; and maps on pp. 6, 20, 24.

63. *New York Times*, 3 February 1981; and Boudreault et al., *U.S. Official Statements: Israeli Settlements*, p. 19.

64. David A. Korn, letter, *New York Times*, 10 October 1991.

65. *New York Times*, 16 March 1989.

66. Quigley, p. 176.

67. Boudreault et al., *U.S. Official Statements: Israeli Settlements*, p. 48.

68. Jackson Diehl, *Washington Post*, 25 January 1990.

69. Paul Taylor, *Washington Post*, 16 January 1990; and Larry Cohler, *Washington Jewish Week*, 8 February 1990.

70. Joel Brinkley, *New York Times*, 5 February 1990.

71. Al Kamen, *Washington Post*, 2 March 1990. The text of Baker's remarks is in *Journal of Palestine Studies* 19, no. 3 (Summer 1990), pp. 175–79.

72. Associated Press, *New York Times*, 3 October 1990. Texts of Israel's 2 October letter to Baker and a clarifying letter dated 18 October are in *Journal of Palestine Studies* 20, no. 2 (Winter 1991), pp. 190–92.

73. Jackson Diehl, *Washington Post*, 8 October 1990.

74. Al Kamen, *Washington Post*, 21 February 1991.

75. Resolution 672; the text is in *New York Times*, 14 October 1990.

76. Foundation for Middle East Peace, *Report on Israeli Settlement in the Occupied Territories*, November 1991.

77. Jackson Diehl, *Washington Post*, 5 April 1991.

78. Thomas L. Friedman, *New York Times*, 18 September 1991.

79. Jackson Diehl, *Washington Post*, 8 September 1991.

80. John M. Goshko and John E. Yang, *Washington Post*, 7 September 1991.

81. Thomas L. Friedman, *New York Times*, 7 September 1991.

82. Jackson Diehl, *Washington Post*, 9 September 1991.

83. Adam Clymer, *New York Times*, 15 September 1991.

84. The text is in *New York Times*, 13 September 1991.

85. Clyde Haberman, *New York Times*, 14 September 1991.

86. Thomas L. Friedman, *New York Times*, 6 October 1991. See also Thomas R. Mattair, "The Arab-Israeli Conflict: The Madrid Conference, and Beyond," *American-Arab Affairs*, Summer 1991.

87. *New York Times*, 5 January 1993.

88. Thomas L. Friedman, *New York Times*, 19 October 1991.

89. Clyde Haberman, *New York Times*, 24 October 1991.

90. Clyde Haberman, *New York Times*, 27 June 1992; and David Hoffman, *Washington Post*, 27 June 1992.

91. Jackson Diehl, *Washington Post*, 20 January 1992.

92. Clyde Haberman, *New York Times*, 21 January 1992.

93. Rowland Evans and Robert Novak, *Washington Post*, 24 January 1992.

94. General Accounting Office, "Israel: U.S. Loan Guaranties for Immigrant Absorption," GAO/NSIAD-92-119, 12 February 1992.

95. Edward T. Pound, *Wall Street Journal*, 13 March 1992; and David Hoffman and R. Jeffrey Smith, *Washington Post*, 14 March 1992.

96. Bill Gertz and Rowan Scarborough, *Washington Times*, 12 and 13 March 1992.

97. David Hoffman, *Washington Post*, 2 April 1992.

98. Associated Press, *Washington Times*, 9 May 1992.

99. Sammy Smooha and Don Peretz, "Israel's 1992 Knesset Elections: Are They Critical?" *Middle East Journal* 47, no. 3 (Summer 1993).

100. Don Oberdorfer, *Washington Post*, 25 June 1992.

101. See Rabin's 1992 inaugural address; the text is in *Foreign Broadcast Information Service*, 14 July 1992, pp. 23–27. See also Findley, *Deliberate Deceptions*, p. 123.

102. Thomas L. Friedman, *New York Times*, 5 February 1995.

103. Ann Devroy and Don Oberdorfer, *Washington Post*, 12 August 1992.

104. Amendment to the 1993 Foreign Aid Bill, pp. 197–206. See also Helen Dewar, *Washington Post*, 2 October 1992; and Gene Bird, "How Israel Got the Loan Guarantees Opposed by 89 Percent of Americans," *The Washington Report on Middle East Affairs*, November 1992. The text of the legislation is in *Journal of Palestine Studies* 22, no. 2 (Winter 1993), pp. 158–60.

105. David Hoffman, *Washington Post*, 10 June 1993.

106. Clyde Haberman, *New York Times*, 6 October 1993.

107. Israel Shahak, "The Israeli Government and the Settlements," *Middle East International*, 7 January 1994.

108. Jules Kagian, "Rewriting Resolutions," *Middle East International*, 17 December 1993.

109. Foundation for Middle East Peace, "U.S. Official Revises Government View of Settlements," *Report on Israeli Settlement*, May 1994.

110. Ibid., July 1994.

Notes to Chapter 8: *Arms*

1. U.S. State Department, *American Foreign Policy 1960*, "Reply Made by the President (Eisenhower) to a Question Asked at a News Conference, February 17, 1960 (Excerpt)," p. 497.

2. Elaine Sciolino, *New York Times*, 16 March 1993; excerpts are in *Journal of Palestine Studies* 22, no. 4 (Summer 1993), pp. 140–43.

3. "The Secretary of State to the Acting United States Representative at the United Nations (Jessup)," Secret, Washington, June 21, 1948—2 p.m., *FRUS 1948*, p. 1126. See also Cockburn and Cockburn, pp. 24–25; Grose, pp. 210–11; Dan Raviv and Yossi Melman, *Every Spy a Prince: The Complete History of Israel's Intelligence Community* (Boston: Houghton Mifflin Co., 1990), pp. 326–30; "The Secretary of State to Certain Diplomatic Offices," Confidential, Washington, July 1, 1948—4 p.m., *FRUS 1949*, p. 1179; and "The Acting Secretary of State to the Special Representative of the United States in Israel (McDonald), Secret, US Urgent, Washington, November 13, 1948—1 p.m., p. 1580.

4. The text is in *New York Times*, 15 July 1948.

5. "Memorandum by the Secretary of State to the President," Policy with respect to Arms Shipments to the Arab States and Israel, Confidential, Washington, September 1, 1949, *FRUS 1949*, p. 1341.

6. Donovan, p. 358.

7. "The Ambassador in the United Kingdom (Douglas) to the Acting Secretary of State,"

Top Secret, London, October 29, 1948—7 p.m., *FRUS 1948*, p. 1531.

8. Ibid.

9. "The Acting United States Representative at the United Nations (Jessup) to the Secretary of State," Top Secret, Priority, New York, July 1, 1948—4:16 p.m., *FRUS 1948*, p. 1182.

10. Cockburn and Cockburn, pp. 21–22.

11. Ibid., pp. 29–30; and "Report by the National Security Council on United States Policy Toward Israel and the Arab States," Top Secret, Washington, October 17, 1949, *FRUS 1949*, pp. 1430–40.

12. Anne O'Hare McCormick, *New York Times*, 14 January 1949. See also see Ben Gurion, p. 339; Uri Bialer, *Between East and West* (New York: Cambridge University Press, 1990), p. 213; Brecher, p. 166; Cockburn and Cockburn, p. 21; and Conor Cruise O'Brien, *The Siege: The Saga of Israel and Zionism* (New York: Simon & Schuster, 1986), p. 371. However, some critics argued that Ben Gurion all along planned an alliance with the West; see Shlaim, *Collusion Across the Jordan*, pp. 231–38.

13. Anne O'Hare McCormick, *New York Times*, 14 January 1949.

14. C.C. O'Brien, p. 370.

15. Ben Gurion, p. 339.

16. Bialer, p. 15.

17. Ibid., p. 213.

18. Brecher, p. 166; and C.C. O'Brien, p. 371. The actual breakthrough was reported to come in May 1951 with a secret agreement between the intelligence services of the two countries, the Mossad and CIA; see Cockburn and Cockburn, p. 49; and Raviv and Melman, p. 76.

19. Anthony Leviero, *New York Times*, 26 May 1950; the text is in the same edition. For a discussion of the background, see Louis, pp. 583–90.

20. Beit-Hallahmi, p. 7; and Neff, *Warriors at Suez*, pp. 162–63.

21. E.L.M. Burns, *Between Arab and Israeli* (New York: Ivan Obolensky, 1962), pp. 18, 99–101.

22. "Memorandum of Conversation with the Secretary of State," Washington, October 18, 1955, *FRUS 1955–1957*, p. 612.

23. Morris, *Israel's Border Wars*, p. 364.

24. U.S. Department of State, *American Foreign Policy 1960*, "Reply Made by the President (Eisenhower) to a Question Asked at a News Conference, February 17, 1960 (Excerpt)," p. 497.

25. Max Frankel, *New York Times*, 27 September 1962; and Zeev Schiff, *A History of the Israeli Army (1870–1974)* (San Francisco: Straight Arrow Books, 1974), pp. 257–59.

26. Max Frankel, *New York Times*, 27 February 1962.

27. Riad, p. 39.

28. Leonard S. Spector, *Nuclear Proliferation Today* (New York: Vintage Books, 1984), p. 121.

29. For more on the Johnson Plan, see chapter 3.

30. Spiegel, p. 113. See also Bustami, in Suleiman (ed.), pp. 107–08; and Forsythe, pp. 134–35.

31. Seymour M. Hersh, *The Samson Option: Israel's Nuclear Arsenal and American Foreign Policy* (New York: Random House, 1991), pp. 111, 210–11.

32. Cockburn and Cockburn, p. 91.

33. Sheehan, p. 199.

34. Spector, p. 119.

35. Charles DeGaulle, *Memoirs of Hope, Renewal and Endeavor* (New York: Simon & Schuster, 1971), p. 266.

36. *Washington Post*, 2 March 1978; David Burnham, *New York Times*, 2 March 1978; and Hersh, *The Samson Option*, p. 188. See also Robert Manning and Stephen Talbot, "American Cover-Up on Israeli Bomb," *The Middle East*, June 1980; Gary Milhollin, "Israel's Nuclear Shadow," Wisconsin Project on Nuclear Arms Control, University of Wisconsin, 10 November 1986; and Steve Weissman and Herbert Krosney, *The Islamic Bomb: The Nuclear Threat to Israel and the Middle East* (New York: Times Books, 1981).

37. *New York Times*, 25 June 1981. The document was released under a Freedom of Information Act request; the CIA later said the release had been a "mistake."

38. Arthur Kranish, *Washington Post*, 15 March 1976. The unnamed official was widely reported to be the CIA's Carl Duckett; see for instance Spector, p. 130; and Cockburn and Cockburn, pp. 93–94.

39. Spector, p. 132.

40. Ibid., p. 129.

41. *New York Times*, 25 June 1981.

42. Spector, p. 126. See also Beit-Hallahmi, pp. 129–36; and Hersh, *The Samson Option*, pp. 52–58.

43. Julia Preston, *Washington Post*, 28 January 1995.

44. Mohamed Heikal, *The Sphinx and the Commissar: The Rise and Fall of Soviet Influence in the Middle East* (New York: Harper & Row, 1978), p. 139.

45. Alvin Z. Rubinstein, *Red Star on the Nile: the Soviet-Egyptian Influence Relationship since the June War* (Princeton, N.J.: Princeton University Press, 1977), pp. 30–31.

46. Lawrence L. Whetten, *The Canal War: Four-Power Conflict in the Middle East* (Cambridge, Mass.: MIT Press, 1974), p. 395.

47. Rubinstein, *Red Star on the Nile*, pp. 46–47. See also CIA, "Mediterranean Strategy

and Force Structure Study (extract)," 19 August 1970, cited in Neff, *Warriors Against Israel*, p. 61.

48. Rubinstein, *Red Star on the Nile*, p. 109.

49. CIA, "Mediterranean Strategy and Force Structure Study (extract)," 19 August 1970. A ship-day equals one ship in the Mediterranean for one day whether at sea, in port or at anchor.

50. Ibid.; see also Whetten, p. 391.

51. CIA, "Mediterranean Strategy and Force Structure Study (extract)," 19 August 1970.

52. Ibid.

53. International Security Affairs, Office Assistant Secretary of Defense. "US Policy and Strategy in the Mediterranean Basin, February 1970;" Secret, p. 6; see also Neff, *Warriors Against Israel*, p. 61.

54. Nixon, p. 484.

55. Kissinger, *White House Years*, p. 623.

56. Rabin, p. 189.

57. Kissinger, *White House Years*, p. 631.

58. Quandt, *Decade of Decisions*, p. 124; Hart, pp. 319–20, quotes Fatah official Khalad Hassan as saying that "the only thing the Soviets did as the crisis approached was to send a stream of urgent messages, mainly through Nasser, asking us all to cool it and to avoid a confrontation in Jordan at all costs." See also Yodfat and Arnon-Ohanna, p. 88. John K. Cooley, *Green March, Black September: The Story of the Palestinian Arabs* (Princeton, N.J.: Princeton University Press, 1982), has an interesting discussion in chapter 8 on Moscow's ambivalent attitude toward the guerrilla groups. See also Donald Neff, "Nixon's Middle East Policy: From Balance to Bias," *Arab Studies Quarterly*, Winter/Spring 1990.

59. Quandt, *Decade of Decisions*, p. 124.

60. Seelye letter to author, 23 October 1987.

61. "US Assistance to the State of Israel, Report by the Comptroller General of the United States," GAO/ID-83-51, June 24, 1983, US Accounting Office, p. 43.

62. Whetten, pp. 205–06. See also Quandt, *Decade of Decisions*, p. 132; and Neff, "Nixon's Middle East Policy."

63. Defense Department, Middle East Arms Transfer Panel, "Review of Israel's Military Requirements, 1979–84"; secret; August 1979.

64. Quandt, *Decade of Decisions*, p. 132.

65. Whetten, p. 165.

66. Quandt, *Decade of Decisions*, p. 131.

67. Kissinger, *White House Years*, p. 1247.

68. Quandt, *Decade of Decisions*, p. 141; and Neff, *Warriors Against Israel*, p. 67.

69. Lacey, p. 399.

70. Marvin Kalb and Bernard Kalb, *Kissinger* (Boston: Little Brown and Co., 1974), p. 475.

71. J.B. Kelley, *Arabia, the Gulf & the West* (New York: Basic Books, 1991), p. 396.

72. Neff, *Warriors Against Israel*, p. 221.

73. Henry A. Kissinger, *Years of Upheaval* (Boston: Little Brown and Co., 1982), p. 536.

74. Kelley, p. 397.

73. Kissinger, *Years of Upheaval*, pp. 538, 541.

75. Lacey, p. 413; and Nixon, p. 932.

76. Lacey, p. 413; State Department Middle East Task Force, "Situation report #51," 21 October 1973, secret; declassified 31 December 1981.

77. Rubenberg, p. 173.

78. Kissinger, *Years of Upheaval*, pp. 587–88. See also Mohamed Heikal, *The Road to Ramadan: The Inside Story of How the Arabs Prepared for and Almost Won the October War of 1973* (London: Collins, 1975), pp. 254–55; and Rubinstein, *Red Star on the Nile*, p. 275. Widespread media reports at the time of a Soviet ship carrying nuclear warheads to Egypt did not play any part in the declaration of the alert. These reports first emerged on 25 October, after the alert was ordered. Neither Kissinger nor Nixon mentions the reports in his memoirs and they were likely false. A Rand Corporation study of the issue concluded that "there is no reliable evidence that nuclear weapons ever entered Egypt"; see letter from Shmuel Meir of the Tel Aviv Jaffee Center for Strategic Studies in *The International Herald Tribune*, 18 August 1985.

80. Clyde R. Mark, "Israel: US Foreign Assistance Facts," Congressional Research Service, updated 5 November 1986.

81. Robert Byrd, *Congressional Record—Senate*, 4/1/92.

82. *New York Times*, 20 March 1981. See also Rubenberg, pp. 264–65; and Tillman, p. 37, for a brief discussion of Haig's strategic ideas.

83. *New York Times*, 1 December 1981. The text is in the same edition. Ultimately, it did not go into effect until 29 November 1983. For details, see chapter 5.

84. Sharon, p. 414.

85. A. Craig Murphy, "Congressional Opposition to Arms Sales to Saudi Arabia," *American-Arab Affairs*, Spring 1988, p. 106. A good analysis of the incident is in Hendrick Smith, *The Power Game* (New York: Ballantine Books, 1989), pp. 215–20.

86. Tillman, p. 121.

87. Both houses must defeat the proposal to kill a military sale. To gain the Senate's support, President Reagan sent a detailed letter to Majority Leader Senator Howard Baker Jr. outlining unusual restrictions on the use of the AWACS to preserve security of the AWACS' systems; see *International Documents on Palestine 1981*, pp. 365–68, and A. Craig Murphy, pp. 100–12.

88. Rubenberg, p. 258; see also Smith, pp. 220–24.

89. *Weekly compilation of Presidential Documents*, Government Printing Office, Washington, DC, 22 February 1982, p. 177.

90. Elaine Sciolino, *New York Times*, 16 March 1993.

91. Fred J. Khouri, "Major Obstacles to Peace: Ignorance, Myths and Misconceptions," *American-Arab Affairs*, Spring 1986, p. 47.

92. Bernard Gwertzman, "Reagan Turns to Israel," *The New York Times Magazine*, 27 November 1983. See also John M. Goshko, *Washington Post*, 22 November 1983; Charles R. Babcock, *Washington Post*, 5 August 1986; *Mideast Observer*, "Free Trade Area for Israel Proposed," 15 March 1984; and Khouri, *The Arab-Israeli Dilemma*, pp. 449–500.

93. Bernard Gwertzman, *New York Times*, 16 December 1983.

94. Clyde Mark, "The Israeli Economy," Foreign Affairs and National Defense Division, Congressional Research Service, 31 October 1986.

95. Bernard Gwertzman, *New York Times*, 14 March 1984.

96. Bernard Gwertzman, *New York Times*, 21 March 1984, and 3 October 1984.

97. John Newhouse, "Politics and Weapon Sales," *The New Yorker*, 9 June 1986, pp. 41–61. See also Briget Bloom and Richard Johns, *The Financial Times* of London, 19 February 1986.

98. R. Jeffrey Smith, *Washington Post*, 29 October 1990.

99. John M. Goshko, *Washington Post*, 22 November 1994; and Michael Wines, *New York Times*, 22 November 1994.

100. General Accounting Office, "U.S.–Israel Arrow/Aces program: Cost, Technical, Proliferation, and Management Concerns," GAO/ NSIAD-93-254, 23 August 1993; and Duncan L. Clarke, "The Arrow Missile: The United States, Israel and Strategic Cooperation," *Middle East Journal* 48, no. 3 (Summer 1994).

101. Reuters, *International Herald Tribune*, 25 August 1993.

Notes to Conclusion:

1. From Washington's Farewell Address.

2. John M. Goshko, *Washington Post*, 8 January 1988.

3. Judith Miller, *New York Times*, 9 December 1981.

4. Findley, *Deliberate Deceptions*, pp. 192–94.

5. Robert Byrd, *Congressional Record—Senate*, 4/1/92.

6. Keith Brasher, *New York Times*, 23 September 1991.

7. Robert W. Gibson, *Los Angeles Times*, 20 July 1987.

8. For details, see chapter 8.

9. Edward T. Pound, *Wall Street Journal*, 13 March 1992; David Hoffman and R. Jeffrey Smith, *Washington Post*, 14 March 1992; Bill Gertz and Rowan Scarborough, *Washington Times*, 12–13 December 1992.

10. The Middle East Justice Network, "The Israel-PLO Deal and the Question of Compliance," *Breaking the Siege*, October/November 1994.

11. Youssef M. Ibrahim, *New York Times*, 31 July 1994; Thomas L. Friedman, *New York Times*, 8 February 1995.

12. Quoted in Haim Baram, "International Affairs," *Middle East International*, 9 September 1994, p. 6.

13. The effort actually began under the Bush Administration but it was limited to revoking the assembly's "Zionism is racism" resolution. Washington was successful on 16 December 1991 in rescinding the Zionism resolution with passage of a one-line resolution that declared the assembly "decides to revoke the determination contained in its Resolution 3379 of 10 November 1975." The U.S. argument at the time for spearheading this action was, in the words of Deputy Secretary of State Lawrence S. Eagleburger, because it was "time to consign one of the last relics of the Cold War to the dustbin of history;" see John M. Goshko, *Washington Post*, 17 December 1991.

14. Madeleine K. Albright letter to members of the UN General Assembly, 8 August 1994.

15. "Arab Newspapers Decry U.S.-Israeli Moves to Tamper with UN Mideast Resolutions," *Mideast Mirror*, 22 September 1994.

16. *Reuter*, #0226, 21 September 1994; Reuters, *Washington Times*, 2 October 1994.

17. Graham Usher, "The Demise of UNRWA?" *Middle East International*, 6 January 1995.

SELECTED BIBLIOGRAPHY

Abu Iyad with Eric Rouleau. *My Home, My Land: A Narrative of the Palestinian Struggle.* New York: Times Books, 1978.

Abu-Lughod, Ibrahim (ed.). *Transformation of Palestine* (2d ed.). Evanston, Ill.: Northwestern University Press, 1987.

Abourezk, James G. *Advise & Dissent.* Chicago: Lawrence Hill Books, 1989.

Abourezk, James G. and Hyman Bookbinder. *Through Different Eyes.* Bethesda: Adler & Adler, 1987.

Acheson, Dean. *Present at the Creation.* New York: Signet New American Library, 1970.

Arkadie, Brian Van. *Benefits and Burdens: A Report on the West Bank and Gaza Strip Economies since 1967.* New York: Carnegie Endowment for International Peace, 1977.

Aronson, Geoffrey. *Creating Facts: Israel, Palestinians and the West Bank.* Washington, D.C.: Institute for Palestine Studies, 1987.

Aruri, Naseer H. (ed.). *Occupation: Israel over Palestine.* Belmont, Mass.: Association of Arab-American University Graduates, Inc., 1983.

Asali, K.J. (ed.). *Jerusalem in History.* New York, Olive Branch Press, 1990.

Avineri, Shlomo. *The Making of Modern Zionism: The Intellectual Origins of the Jewish State.* New York: Basic Books, Inc., 1981.

Azcarate, Pablo de. *Mission in Palestine, 1948–1952.* Washington, D.C.: Middle East Institute, 1966.

Bailey, Sydney D. *Four Arab-Israeli Wars and the Peace Process.* London: Macmillan, 1990.

Ball, George W. *Error and Betrayal in Lebanon.* Washington, D.C.: Foundation for Middle East Peace, 1984.

Ball, George W. and Douglas B. Ball. *The Passionate Attachment: America's Involvement with Israel, 1947 to the Present.* New York: W.W. Norton & Company, 1992.

Barbour, Nevill. *Nisi Dominus: A Survey of the Palestine Controversy.* Beirut: Institute of Palestine Studies, 1969.

Bar-Zohar, Michael. *Ben-Gurion: A Biography.* New York: Delacorte Press, 1978.

Beit-Hallahmi, Benjamin. *The Israeli Connection.* New York: Pantheon Books, 1987.

———. *Original Sins: Reflections on the History of Zionism and Israel.* New York: Olive Branch Press, 1993.

Bell, J. Bowyer. *Terror Out of Zion*. New York: St. Martin's Press, 1977.

Ben Gurion, David. *Israel: A Personal History*. New York: Funk & Wagnalls, Inc., 1971.

Benvenisti, Meron. *The West Bank Data Project: A Survey of Israel's Policies*. Washington, D.C.: American Enterprise Institute for Public Policy Research, 1984.

———. *Jerusalem: The Torn City*. Jerusalem: Isratypeset Ltd., 1976.

Bethell, Nicholas. *The Palestine Triangle: The Struggle for the Holy Land, 1935–48*. New York: G.P. Putnam's Sons, 1979.

Bialer, Uri. *Between East and West*. New York: Cambridge University Press, 1990.

Bin Talal, Hassan. *Palestinian Self-Determination: A Study of the West Bank and Gaza Strip*. New York: Quartet Books, 1981.

———. *Search For Peace*. New York: St. Martin's Press, 1984.

Black, Ian, and Benny Morris. *Israel's Secret Wars: A History of Israel's Intelligence Service*. New York: Grove Weidenfeld, 1991.

Boudreault, Jody A. (ed.). *United Nations Resolutions on Palestine and the Arab-Israeli Conflict: 1987–1991*, vol. 4. Washington, D.C.: Institute for Palestine Studies, 1993.

Boudreault, Jody, et al. (eds.). *U.S. Official Statements Regarding U.N. Resolution 242*. Washington, D.C.: Institute for Palestine Studies, 1992.

Boudreault, Jody, and Yasser Salaam (eds.). *U.S. Official Statements: Status of Jerusalem*. Washington, D.C.: Institute for Palestine Studies, 1992.

Boudreault, Jody, and Emma Naughton, and Yasser Salaam (eds.).

U.S. Official Statements: Israeli Settlements and The Fourth Geneva Convention. Washington, D.C.: Institute for Palestine Studies, 1992.

Boudreault, Jody and Eric Fortin (eds.). *U.S. Official Statements: The Golan Heights*. Washington, D.C.: Institute for Palestine Studies, 1993.

Brecher, Michael. *Decisions in Israel's Foreign Policy*. London: Oxford University Press, 1974.

Brenner, Lenni. *Zionism in the Age of the Dictators*. Westport, Conn.: Lawrence Hill, 1983.

———. *The Iron Wall: Zionist Revisionism from Jabotinsky to Shamir*. London: Zed Books Led., 1984.

Brzezinski, Zbigniew. *Power and Principle: Memoirs of the National Security Adviser*. New York: Farrar, Strauss, Giroux, 1983.

Bull, Odd. *War and Peace in the Middle East: The experiences and views of a U.N. Observer*. London: Leo Cooper, 1976.

Burns, Lt. Gen. E. L. M. *Between Arab and Israeli*. New York: Ivan Obolensky, 1962.

Caradon, Lord et. al. *U.N. Security Council Resolution 242*. Washington, D.C.: Georgetown University, 1981.

Carter, Jimmy. *The Blood of Abraham*. Boston: Houghton Mifflin Company, 1985.

———. *Keeping Faith: Memoirs of a President*. New York: Bantam Books, 1982.

Cattan, Henry. *Palestine, The Arabs and Israel: The search for justice*. London: Longman, 1969.

———. *Jerusalem*. New York: St. Martin's Press, 1981.

Chomsky, Noam. *The Fateful Triangle*. Boston: South End Press, 1983.

———. *Pirates & Emperors: International Terrorism in the Real World*. Brattleboro, Ver.: Amana Books, 1986.

Cleveland, William L. *A History of the Modern Middle East*. Boulder: Westview Press, 1994.

Clifford, Clark. *Counsel to the President: A Memoir*. New York: Random House, 1991.

Cobban, Helena. *The Palestinian Liberation Organization*. New York: Cambridge University Press, 1984.

Cockburn, Andrew and Leslie. *Dangerous Liaison: The Inside Story of the U.S.-Israeli Covert Relationship*. New York: HarperCollins Publishers, 1991.

Cohen, Michael J. *Palestine and the Great Powers 1945–1948*. Princeton, N.J.: Princeton University Press, 1982.

Collins, Larry and Dominique Lapierre. *O Jerusalem!* New York: Simon and Schuster, 1972.

Cooley, John K. *Green March, Black September: The story of the Palestinian Arabs*. London: Frank Cass, 1973.

———. *Libyan Sandstorm*. New York: Holt, Rinehart and Winston, 1982.

———. *Payback: America's Long War in the Middle East*. New York: Brassey's (U.S.), Inc., 1991.

Crosbie, Sylvia Kowitt. *A Tacit Alliance: France and Israel from Suez to the Six Day War*. Princeton, N.J.: Princeton University Press, 1974.

Curtiss, Richard. *A Changing Image: American Perceptions of the Arab-Israeli Dispute* (2d ed.). Washington, D.C.: American Educational Trust, 1986.

———. *Stealth PACs: How Israel's American Lobby Seeks to Control U.S. Middle East Policy*. Washington, D.C.: American Educational Trust, 1990.

Davenport, Elaine et. al. *The Plumbat Affair*. New York: J.B. Lippincott Company, 1978.

Davis, John H. *The Evasive Peace*. London: John Murray, 1970.

Davis, M. Thomas. *40 Km into Lebanon: Israel's 1982 Invasion*. Washington, D.C.: National Defense University Press, 1987.

Davis, Uri & Norton Mezvinsky. *Documents from Israel 1967–73: Readings for a Critique of Zionism*. London: Ithaca Press, 1975.

Dayan, Moshe. *Story of My Life*. New York: William Morrow and Company, Inc., 1976.

DeGaulle, Charles. *Memoirs of Hope: Renewal and Endeavor*. New York: Simon and Schuster, 1971.

Derogy, Jacques and Hesi Carmel. *The Untold History of Israel*. New York: Grove Press, Inc., 1979.

Donovan, Robert J. *Conflict and Crisis: The Presidency of Harry S. Truman, 1945–1948*. New York: W.W. Norton, 1977.

Dupuy, Colonel Trevor N. *Elusive Victory: The Arab-Israeli Wars, 1947–74*. New York: Harper & Row, 1978.

Eban, Abba. *An Autobiography*. Tel Aviv: Steimatzky's Agency Ltd., 1977.

El-Khawas, Mohammed and Samir Abed-Rabbo. *American Aid to Israel: Nature and Impact*. Brattleboro, Ver.: Amana Books, 1984.

Eisenhower, Dwight D. *Waging Peace: 1956–61*. Garden City, N.Y.: Doubleday & Company, Inc., 1965.

Epp, Frank, H. *Whose Land is Palestine?* Grand Rapids, Mich.: William B. Eerdmans Publishing Company, 1974.

Evans, Lawrence. *United States Policy and the Partition of Turkey, 1914–1924*. Baltimore: Johns Hopkins Press, 1965.

Eveland, Wilbur Crane. *Ropes of Sand: America's Failure in the Middle East*. New York: W.W. Norton & Co., 1980.

Fahmy, Ismail. *Negotiating for Peace in the Middle East*. Baltimore: The Johns Hopkins University Press, 1983.

Feintuch, Yossi. *U.S. Policy on Jerusalem*. New York: Greenwood Press, 1987.

Feuerlicht, Roberta Strauss. *The Fate of the Jews: A People Torn between Israeli Power and Jewish Ethics*. New York: Times Books: 1983.

Findley, Paul. *They Dare to Speak Out: People and Institutions Confront Israel's Lobby*. Westport, Conn.: Lawrence Hill & Co., 1985.

———. *Deliberate Deceptions: Facing the Facts about the U.S.-Israeli Relationship*. Brooklyn, N.Y.: Lawrence Hill Books, 1993.

Fisk, Robert. *Pity the Nation: The Abduction of Lebanon*. New York: Atheneum, 1990.

Flapan, Simha. *The Birth of Israel: Myths and Realities*. New York: Pantheon Books, 1987.

Forsythe, David P. *United Nations Peacemaking: The Conciliation Commission for Palestine*. Baltimore: The Johns Hopkins University Press, 1972.

Friedman, Robert I. *The False Prophet: Rabbi Meir Kahane*. Brooklyn, N.Y.: Lawrence Hill Books, 1990.

———. *Zealots for Zion: Inside Israel's West Bank Settlement Movement*. New York, Random House, 1992.

Friedman, Thomas L. *From Beirut to Jerusalem*. New York: Farrar, Strauss, Giroux, 1989.

Gerson, Louis L. *John Foster Dulles.* New York: Cooper Square Publishers Inc., 1967.

Gilbert, Martin. *Jersulam History Atlas.* New York: Macmillan Publishing Co., 1977.

————. *The Arab-Israeli Conflict: Its History in Maps.* London: Weidenfeld and Nicolson, 1981.

Glubb Pasha (Sir John Bagot Glubb). *A Soldier with the Arabs.* London: Hodder and Stoughton, 1957.

————. *The Great Arab Conquests.* London: Quartet Books, 1963.

Green, Stephen. *Taking Sides: America's Secret Relations with a Militant Israel.* New York: William Morrow and Company, Inc., 1984.

————. *Living by the Sword: America and Israel in the Middle East, 1968–87.* Brattleboro, Ver.: Amana Books, 1988.

Grose, Peter. *Israel in the Mind of America.* New York: Alfred A. Knopf, 1983.

Gur, Mordechai. *The Battle for Jerusalem.* New York: Popular Library, 1974.

Halabi, Rafik. *The West Bank Story.* New York: Harcourt Brace Jovanovich, 1981.

Halsell, Grace. *Journey to Jerusalem.* New York: Macmillan Publishing Co., Inc., 1981.

————. *Prophesy and Politics: Militant Evangelists on the Road to Nuclear War.* Westport, Conn.: Lawrence Hill & Company, 1986.

Harkabi, Y. *The Palestinian Covenant and its Meaning.* Totowa, N.J.: Vallentine, Mitchell & Co. Ltd., 1979.

————. *Israel's Fateful Hour.* New York: Harper & Row, Publishers, 1988.

Hart, Alan. *Arafat: Terrorist or Peacemaker?* London: Sidgwick & Jackson, 1985.

Heikal, Mohamed. *Autumn of Fury: The Assassination of Sadat.* New York: Random House, 1983.

————. *Nasser: The Cairo Documents.* London: New English Library, 1973.

————. *The Road to Ramadan: The Inside Story of How the Arabs Prepared for and Almost Won the October War of 1973.* London: Collins, 1975.

————. *The Sphinx and the Commissar: The Rise and Fall of Soviet Influence in Middle East.* New York: Harper & Row, 1978.

Hersh, Seymour M. *The Price of Power: Kissinger in the Nixon White House.* New York: Summit Books, 1983.

————. *The Samson Option: Israel's Nuclear Arsenal and American Foreign Policy.* New York: Random House, 1991.

Hirst, David. *The Gun and the Olive Branch: The Roots of Violence in the Middle East.* New York: Harcourt Brace Jovanovich, 1977.

Howard, Harry N. *The King-Crane Commission.* Beirut: Khayats, 1963.

Howe, Irving. *World of Our Fathers*. New York: Harcourt Brace Jovanovich, 1976.

Irani, George E. *The Papacy and the Middle East: The Role of the Holy See in the Arab-Israeli Conflict, 1962–1984*. Notre Dame, Ind.: University of Notre Dame Press, 1986.

Isaac, Rael J. *Israeli Divided: Ideological Politics in the Jewish State*. Baltimore: Johns Hopkins University Press, 1977.

Jabber, Fuad. *Israel and Nuclear Weapons*. London: Chatto and Windus, 1971.

Jackson, Elmore. *Middle East Mission: The Story of a Major Bid for Peace in the Time of Nasser and Ben-Gurion*. New York: W.W. Norton & Company, 1983.

Jiryis, Sabri. *The Arabs in Israel*. New York: Monthly Review Press, 1976.

Kenen, I.L. *Israel's Defense Line: Her Friends and Foes in Washington*. Buffalo, N.Y.: Prometheus Books, 1981.

Kerr, Malcolm H. *The Arab Cold War: Gamal 'Abd Al-Nasir and His Rivals 1958–1970* (3d ed.). New York: Oxford University Press, 1971.

———. *America's Middle East Policy: Kissinger, Carter and the Future*. Beirut: Institute for Palestine Studies, 1980.

——— (ed.). *All That Remains: The Palestinian Villages Occupied and Depopulated by Israel in 1948*. Washington, D.C.: Institute for Palestine Studies, 1991.

———. *Before Their Diaspora: A Photographic History of the Palestinians 1876–1948*. Washington, D.C.: Institute for Palestine Studies, 1984.

Khalidi, Walid (ed.). *From Haven to Conquest: Readings in Zionism and the Palestine Problem until 1948*. Washington, D.C.: Institute for Palestine Studies, second printing, 1987.

Khouri, Fred J. *The Arab Israeli Dilemma* (3d ed.). Syracuse, N.Y.: Syracuse University Press, 1985.

Kissinger, Henry A. *White House Years*. New York: Boston: Little, Brown and Company, 1979.

———. *Years of Upheaval*. Boston: Little, Brown and Company, 1982.

Klieman, Aaron S. *Foundations of British Policy in the Arab World: The Cairo Conference of 1921*. Baltimore: The Johns Hopkins Press, 1970.

Kurzman, Dan. *Ben Gurion: Prophet of Fire*. New York: Simon and Schuster, 1983.

———. *Genesis 1948: The First Arab-Israeli War*. New York: The World Publishing Company, 1970.

Lacey, Robert. *The Kingdom*. London: Hutchinson & Co. (publishers) Ltd., 1981.

Laqueur, Walter and Barry Rubin (eds.). *The Israel-Arab Reader* (revised and updated). New York: Penguin Books, 1987.

Lenczowski, George. *The Middle East in World Affairs* (3d ed.). Ithaca, N.Y.: Cornell University Press, 1962.

————. *Soviet Advances in the Middle East.* Washington, D.C.: American Enterprise Institute for Public Policy Research, 1971.

Lilienthal, Alfred M. *The Zionist Connection: What Price Peace?* New York: Dodd, Mead & Company, 1978.

————. *What Price Israel?* Chicago: Henry Regnery Company, 1953.

Louis, Wm. Roger. *The British Empire in the Middle East 1945–1951.* Oxford: Clarenden Press, 1988.

Love, Kennett. *Suez: The Twice-Fought War.* New York: McGraw-Hill Book Company, 1969.

Lucas, Noah. *The Modern History of Israel.* London: Weidenfeld and Nicolson, 1974.

Lukacs, Yehuda (ed.) *The Israeli-Palestinian Conflict: A Documentary Record.* New York: Cambridge University Press, 1992.

Lustick, Ian. *Arabs in the Jewish State: Israel's Control of a National Minority.* Austin, Tex.: University of Texas Press, 1980.

Macdonald, Robert W. *The League of Arab States: A Study in the Dynamics of Regional Organization.* Princeton, N.J.: Princeton University Press, 1965.

Magnus, Ralph H., ed. *Documents on the Middle East.* Washington, D.C.: American Enterprise Institute, 1969.

Mallison, Thomas and Sally V. *The Palestine Problem in International Law and World Order.* London: Longman Group Ltd., 1986.

————. *Armed Conflict in Lebanon, 1982: Humanitarian Law in a Real World Setting.* Washington, D.C.: American Educational Trust, 1985.

Mandel, Neville J. *The Arabs and Zionism Before World War I.* Berkeley: University of California Press, 1976.

Mansour, Camille. *The Palestinian-Israeli Peace Negotiations.* Washington, D.C.: Institute of Palestine Studies, 1993.

————. *Beyond Alliance: Israel in U.S. Foreign Policy.* New York: Columbia University Press, 1994.

Manuel, Frank E. *The Realities of American-Palestine Relations.* Washington, D.C.: Public Affairs Press, 1949.

Masalha, Nur. *Expulsion of the Palestinians: the Concept of "Transfer" in Zionist Political Thought, 1882–1948.* Washington, D.C.: Institute of Palestine Studies, 1992.

Mattar, Philip. *The Mufti of Jerusalem: Al-Hajj Amin Al-Husyni and the Palestinian National Movement.* New York: Columbia University Press, 1993.

McCarthy, Justin. *The Population of Palestine: Population Statistics of the Late Ottoman Period and the Mandate.* New York: Columbia University Press, 1990.

McDonald, James G. *My Mission to Israel.* New York: Simon and Schuster, 1951.

McDowall, David. *Palestine and Israel: The Uprising and Beyond*. Berkeley: University of California Press, 1989.

McGhee, George. *Envoy to the Middle World: Adventures in Diplomacy*. New York: Harper & Row, Publishers, 1983.

Medzini, Meron. *Israel's Foreign Relations: Selected Documents, 1947–1974* (vols. 1 and 2). Jerusalem: Ministry of Foreign Affairs, 1976.

———. *Israel's Foreign Relations: Selected Documents, 1974–1977* (vol. 3). Jerusalem: Ministry of Foreign Affairs, 1982.

———. *Israel's Foreign Relations: Selected Documents, 1977–1979* (vols. 4 and 5). Jerusalem: Ministry of Foreign Affairs, 1981.

Merhav, Peretz. *The Israeli Left: History, problems, documents*. New York: A.S. Barnes & Company, Inc., 1980.

Moore, John Norton (ed.). *The Arab-Israeli Conflict: Volume IV: The Difficult Search for Peace (1975–1988)*, part 1. Princeton, N.J.: Princeton University Press, 1991.

Morris, Benny. *The Birth of the Palestine Refugee Problem*. New York: Cambridge University Press, 1987.

———. *Israel's Border Wars: 1949–1956*. Oxford, Clarendon Press, 1993.

Moskin, J. Robert. *Among Lions: The Battle for Jerusalem June 5–7, 1967*. New York: Arbor House, 1982.

Murphy, Bruce Allen. *The Brandeis/Frankfurter Connection: The Secret Political Activities of Two Supreme Court Justices*. Garden City, N.Y.: Anchor Press/Doubleday & Company, Inc., 1983.

Nakhleh, Issa. *Encyclopedia of the Palestine Problem* (2 vols). New York: Intercontinental Books, 1991.

National Lawyers Guild. *Treatment of Palestinians in Israeli-Occupied West Bank and Gaza: Report of the National Lawyers Guild—1977 Middle East Delegation*. New York: National Lawyers Guild, 1978.

Nazzal, Nafez. *The Palestinian Exodus from Galilee 1948*. Beirut: Institute for Palestine Studies, 1978.

Neff, Donald. *Warriors at Suez: Eisenhower takes America into the Middle East*. New York: Linden Press/Simon and Schuster, 1981.

———. *Warriors for Jerusalem: The Six Days that Changed the Middle East*. New York: Linden Press/Simon and Schuster, 1984.

———. *Warriors Against Israel: How Israel Won the Battle to Become America's Ally 1973*. Brattleboro, Ver.: Amana Books, 1988.

Nixon, Richard M. *The Memoirs of Richard Nixon*. New York: Grosset & Dunlap, 1978.

Nyrop, Richard F. (ed.). *Israel: a Country Study* (2d ed.). Washington, D.C.: U.S. Government Printing Office, 1979.

O'Brien, Conor Cruise. *The Siege: The Saga of Israel and Zionism*. New York: Simon and Schuster, 1986.

O'Brien, Lee. *American Jewish Organizations & Israel*. Washington, D.C.: Institute for Palestine Studies, 1986.

Ostrovsky, Victor and Claire Hoy. *By Way of Deception*. New York: St. Martin's Press, 1990.

Palumbo, Michael. *The Palestinian Catastrophe: The 1948 Expulsion of a People from their Homeland*. Boston: Faber and Faber, 1987.

Parker, Richard. *The Politics of Miscalculation in the Middle East*. Indianapolis: Indiana University Press, 1993.

Patai, Raphael (ed.) *The Complete Diaries of Theordor Herzl*. Translated by Harry Zohn. New York: Herzl Press and Thomas Yoseloff, 1960.

Peck, Juliana S. *The Reagan Administration and the Palestinian Question: The First Thousand Days*. Washington, D.C.: Institute for Palestine Studies, 1984.

Peres, Shimon. *David's Sling: The Arming of Israel*. London: Weidenfeld and Nicolson, 1970.

Persson, Sune O. *Mediation & Assassination: Count Bernadotte's Mission to Palestine in 1948*. London: Ithaca Press, 1979.

Petran, Tabitha. *Syria*. New York: Praeger Publishers, 1972.

———. *Camp David: Peacemaking and Politics*. Washington, D.C.: The Brookings Institution, 1986.

Quandt, William B. *Decade of Decisions: American Policy toward the Arab-Israeli Conflict, 1967–1976*. Berkeley: University of California Press, 1977.

———. *Peace Process: American Diplomacy and the Arab-Israeli Conflict since 1967*. Washington, D.C.: The Brookings Institution, 1993.

Quigley, John. *Palestine and Israel: A Challenge to Justice*. Durham, N.C.: Duke University Press, 1990.

Rabin, Yitzhak. *The Rabin Memoirs*. Boston: Little, Brown and Company, 1979.

Raviv, Dan and Yossi Melman. *Every Spy a Prince: The Complete History of Israel's Intelligence Community*. Boston: Houghton Mifflin Company, 1990.

Rearden, Steven L. *History of the Office of the Secretary of Defense: The Formative Years—1947–1950*. Washington, D.C.: Historical Office, Office of the Secretary of Defense, 1984.

Riad, Mahmoud. *The Struggle for Peace in the Middle East*. New York: Quartet Books, 1981.

Rodinson, Maxime. *Israel and the Arabs*. New York: Pantheon Books, 1968.

———. *Israel: A Colonial-Settler State?* New York: Monad Press, 1973.

Rokach, Livia. *Israel's Sacred Terrorism: A Study based on Moshe Sharett's Personal Diary and Other Documents*. Belmont, Mass.: Association of Arab-American University Graduates, Inc., 1980.

Roy, Sara. *The Gaza Strip Survey*. Boulder, Col.: Westview Press, 1986.

Rubenberg, Cheryl A. *Israel and the American National Interest: A Critical Examination*. Chicago: University of Illinois Press, 1986.

Rubinstein, Alvin Z. *Red Star on the Nile: The Soviet-Egyptian Influence Relationship since the June War*. Princeton, N.J.: Princeton University Press, 1977.

Rubinstein, Ammon. *The Zionist Dream Revisited*. New York: Schocken Books, 1984.

Rusk, Dean. *As I Saw It*. New York: W.W. Norton and Company, 1990.

Sachar, Abram Leon. *A History of the Jews*. New York: Alfred A. Knopf, 1974.

Sachar, Howard M. *A History of Israel: From the Rise of Zionism to Our Time*. Tel Aviv: Steimatzky's Agency Ltd., 1976.

Safty, Adel. *From Camp David to the Gulf: Negotiations, Language & Propaganda, and War*. New York: Black Rose Books, 1992.

Said, Edward W. *The Question of Palestine*. New York: Times Books, 1980.

———, and Christopher Hitchens (eds.). *Blaming the Victims*. New York: Verso, 1988.

Sanders, Ronald. *Shores of Refuge: A Hundred Years of Jewish Emigration*. New York: Henry Holt and Company, 1988.

———. *The High Walls of Jerusalem: A History of the Balfour Declaration and the Birth of the British Mandate for Palestine*. New York: Holt, Rinehart and Winston, 1983.

Schiff, Zeev. *A History of the Israeli Army (1870–1974)*. San Francisco: Straight Arrow Books, 1974.

———, and Ehud Ya'ari. *Israel's Lebanon War*. New York: Simon and Schuster, 1984.

Schleifer, Abdullah. *The Fall of Jerusalem*. New York: Monthly Review Press, 1972.

Scholz, Norbert (ed.). *U.S. Official Statements: The Palestinian Refugees*. Washington, D.C.: Institute for Palestine Studies, 1994.

Segev, Tom. *1949: The First Israelis*. New York: The Free Press, 1986.

———. *The Seventh Million: The Israelis and the Holocaust*. New York: Hill & Wang, 1993.

Sheehan, Edward R.E. *The Arabs, Israelis, and Kissinger: A Secret History of American Diplomacy in the Middle East*. New York: Reader's Digest Press, 1976.

Sherif, Regina S. (ed.) *United Nations Resolutions on Palestine and the Arab-Israeli Conflict: 1975–1981*, vol. 2. Washington, D.C.: Institute for Palestine Studies, 1988.

Shipler, David K. *Arab and Jew: Wounded Spirits in a Promised Land*. New York: Times Books, 1986.

Shlaim, Avi. *Collusion Across the Jordan: King Abdullah, the Zionist Movement, and the Partition of Palestine.* New York: Columbia University Press, 1988.

———. *War and Peace in the Middle East: A Critique of American Policy.* New York: Viking, 1994.

Silver, Eric. *Begin: The Haunted Prophet.* New York: Random House, 1984.

Simpson, Michael (ed.). *United Nations Resolutions on Palestine and the Arab-Israeli Conflict: 1982–1986* (vol. 3). Washington, D.C.: Institute for Palestine Studies, 1988.

Smith, Hendrick. *The Power Game.* New York: Ballantine Books, 1989.

Snow, Peter. *Hussein.* London: Barrie & Jenkins, 1972.

Spector, Leonard S. *Nuclear Proliferation Today.* New York: Vintage Books, 1984.

Spiegel, Steven L. *The Other Arab-Israeli Conflict: Making America's Middle East Policy, from Truman to Reagan.* Chicago: University of Chicago Press, 1985.

Sprinzak, Ehud. *The Ascendance of Israel's Radical Right.* New York: Oxford University Press, 1991.

Stevens, Art. *The Persuasion Explosion.* Washington, D.C.: Acropolis Books, Ltd., 1985.

Stevens, Stewart. *The Spymasters of Israel.* New York: Macmillan Publishing Co., Inc., 1980.

Stewart, Desmond. *Herzl.* London: Hamish Hamilton, 1974.

Stone, Michael J. *Truman and Israel.* Berkeley: University of California, 1990.

Storrs, Ronald. *Orientations.* London: Nicholson & Watson, 1945.

Suleiman, Michael W. *U.S. Policy on Palestine from Wilson to Clinton.* Normal, Ill.: Association of Arab-American University Graduates, Inc., 1995.

Sykes, Christopher. *Crossroads to Israel, 1917–1948.* Bloomington: Indiana University Press, 1973.

Tannous, Izzat. *The Palestinians: A Detailed Documented Eyewitness History of Palestine under British Mandate.* New York: I.G.T. Company, 1988.

Tessler, Mark. *A History of the Israeli-Palestinian Conflict.* Indianapolis: Indiana University Press, 1994.

Teveth, Shabtai. *Ben Gurion—The Burning Ground: 1886–1948.* Boston: Houghton Mifflin Company, 1987.

Thorpe, Merle Jr. *Prescription for Conflict: Israel's West Bank Settlement Policy.* Washington, D.C.: Foundation for Middle East Peace, 1984.

Tillman, Seth. *The United States in the Middle East: Interests and Obstacles.* Bloomington: Indiana University Press, 1982.

Tivnan, Edward. *The Lobby: Jewish Political Power and American Foreign Policy.* New York: Simon and Schuster, 1987.

Tomeh, George J. (ed.). *United Nations Resolutions on Palestine and the Arab-Israeli Conflict: 1947–1974* (vol. 1). Washington, D.C.: Institute for Palestine Studies, 1975.

Truman, Harry S. *Memoirs by Harry S. Truman* (2 vols). Garden City, N.J.: Doubleday & Company, 1955 and 1956.

U.S. Department of State. *Foreign Relations of the United States 1943* (vol. 4), The Near East and Africa. Washington, D.C.: U.S. Printing Office, 1967.

———. *Foreign Relations of the United States 1945* (vol. 8), The Near East and Africa. Washington, D.C.: U.S. Printing Office, 1969.

———. *Foreign Relations of the United States 1946* (vol. 7), The Near East and Africa. Washington, D.C.: U.S. Printing Office, 1970.

———. *Foreign Relations of the United States 1947* (vol. 5), The Near East and Africa. Washington, D.C.: U.S. Printing Office, 1971.

———. *Foreign Relations of the United States 1948* (vol. 5), The Near East, South Asia, and Africa. Washington, D.C.: U.S. Printing Office, 1975.

———. *Foreign Relations of the United States 1949* (vol. 6), The Near East, South Asia, and Africa. Washington, D.C.: U.S. Printing Office, 1977.

———. *Foreign Relations of the United States 1955–1957* (vol. 14), Arab-Israeli Dispute 1955. Washington, D.C.: U.S. Printing Office, 1989.

———. *American Foreign Policy, 1950–1955: Basic Documents* (vol. 2). Washington, D.C.: U.S. Government Printing Office, 1957.

———. *American Foreign Policy: Current Documents, 1967*. Washington, D.C.: U.S. Government Printing Office, 1971.

Urofsky, Melvin. *We Are One! American Jewry and Israel*. Garden City, N.Y.: Anchor Press/ Doubleday, 1978.

Von Horn, Carl. *Soldiering for Peace*. New York: David McKay Company, Inc., 1967.

Whetten, Lawrence L. *The Canal War: Four-Power Conflict in the Middle East*. Cambridge, Mass.: The MIT Press, 1974.

Wilson, Evan M. *Decision on Palestine: How the U.S. came to Recognize Israel*. Stanford, Cal.: Hoover Institution Press, 1979.

Yale, William. *The Near East: A Modern History*. Ann Arbor: The University of Michigan Press, 1958.

Yodfat, Aryeh Y. and Yuval Arnon-Ohanna. *PLO: Strategy and Tactics*. London: Croom Helm, 1981.

INDEX

Abdul Aziz, Faisal ibn, 35, 177
Abdul Aziz ibn Saud, 25–26, 34, 38, 42–43, 57
Abdullah ibn Hussein, 30, 95, 109; territorial ambitions in Palestine, 84–85, 88, 96, 107–108, 111
Abir Yaacov, 148
Abu Dhabi, 177
Abu Dis, 130
Abu Maydan waqf, 138
Acheson, Dean, 32–33, 40–41, 43, 96, 134, 135, 136
Acre, 52; conquest by Israel of, 65, 72; population of, 65; terrorism in, 34
Adam, 148
Aden, 53
Affula, 34
Agency for Relief for Palestine Refugees, 70
American Israel Public Affairs Committee (AIPAC), 116, 119–20, 122–24, 159, 161, 180, 181; goals of, 99, 124, 145. *See also* Jewish lobby
Albright, Madeleine K., 55, 186
Alexandria, 35; British naval base at, 37; Soviet naval base at, 174
Algeria, 169, 177
All Palestine Government, 110–112
Almon, 148
America, 73
American Colony, 147
American Emergency Committee for Zionist Affairs, 23
American Federation of Labor (AFL), 12, 24
American Jewish Committee, 8, 26
American Jewish Conference, 22

American Jewish Trade Union Committee for Palestine, 24
American Jews. *See* Jewish Americans
American Palestine Committee, 23–24
American Zionism and Zionists, 7–26, 36, 84, 89, 93, 115, 117, 133–34, 170; leaders of, 8, 10–12, 28. *See also* Jewish lobby
American Zionist Council, 80–81
American Zionist Emergency Council, 23
American Zionist Organization. *See* Zionist Organization of America
Anglo-American Committee of Inquiry, 33–39, 64; membership of, 35; opposition to, 33–34; report of, 37–38
Aqaba, 97
Arab Government of Palestine. *See* All Palestine Government
Arab Higher Committee, 39, 47, 48, 52, 108, 110
Arab-Israeli armistices, 92, 93–94, 119, 152
Arab-Israeli truces, 86–87, 91, 92, 99
Arab League, 31–32, 51, 74, 110, 186
Arab Legion, 84, 94, 107, 111
Arab Revolt of 1936–39, 108–109
Arabists, 13, 64, 116–17, 123
Arabs, 30, 38, 39, 77, 119; aid to refugees, 69; Anglo-American Committee and, 34, 38; Bernadotte and, 86, 89; immigration and, 31; oppose Johnson Plan, 80–81; partition and, 29–32, 42, 47, 52; Peel plan and, 109; relations with U.S., 29, 32, 35, 60, 95, 101, 112, 114, 120, 173, 177, 179–81; relations with USSR, 170, 171, 173–74, 179. *See also* Egypt,

Near East Report, 116
Near Eastern Affairs Department. *See*
    Office of Near Eastern Affairs
Negev, 152; as part of border settle-
    ments, 93, 94, 95, 97; Bernadotte
    plan and, 86, 88, 89;
military activity in, 91; partition and,
    46, 49, 52; population of, 52; settle-
    ments in, 87
New Leader, 73
New York Post, 73
New York Times, 8, 53, 72, 73, 121, 124,
    133, 161, 164, 169
New York Times Magazine, 116
Newsweek, 121
Niebuhr, Reinhold, 24
Niles, David K., 29, 35, 38, 41, 50
1948 war, 65–66, 80; armistice, 92–94;
    truces, 86–87, 91
1956 war. *See* Suez War
1967 war, 100, 138, 151
1973 war, 114, 176, 184
Nixon, Richard M., 97, 115, 120, 143,
    174–76; administration, 81; refugees
    and, 81
Norton, Augustus Richard, 117
Novak, Robert, 121, 143
Nuclear capability, 3, 123, 171–73, 183
Nuclear Non-Proliferation Treaty, 173
Nuqrashi, Mahmud, 109

Office of Near Eastern Affairs, 32, 42,
    57, 64, 117
Office of Near Eastern and African Af-
    fairs, 42, 46, 64
Office of United Nations Affairs, 54, 59
Oil, 24, 57, 60, 61, 89, 174, 184; con-
    cessions, 37; embargo, 176–77
Old City, 93, 152; demography, 130;
    expulsions from, 138; Jordan and,
    132, 133. *See also* Jerusalem
Operation Alpha, 97–98
Ottoman Empire, 7, 9, 10, 12, 113. *See
    also* Turkey

Pakistan, 96
Palestine, borders, 3, 83–105; civil war,
    53, 55; demography, 1, 7, 9, 15, 18,
    37, 49, 51, 52, 56, 61–62, 65, 69–
    70, 74, 93, 130, 132, 138–39, 140,
    148, 153, 155–56, 161, 162–63, *see
    also* Demography; Israeli occupa-
    tion of, 3, 71–72, 93, 100, 102, 103,
    130–33, 134, 136, 138, 139, 140,
    144–47, 148, 151–52, 154, 159;
    refugees, 1, 4, 55–82, 91, 92, 121,
    126. *See also* Gaza Strip, Jerusalem,
    West Bank
Palestinians, identity, 18–19, 71, 117;
    negotiations involving, 2, 80, 93,
    125–26; refugees, 1, 4, 55–82, 91,
    92, 121, 126; rights, 19, 112, 113–
    14, 118–19, 126, 184, 186; U.S.
    policy towards, 4, 16–17, 107–27
Palestine Conciliation Commission,
    70–71, 74, 75, 76, 80, 133–34
Palestine, Land of Promise, 23
Palestine Liberation Organization, 118,
    119, 123–25; accord with Israel, 2,
    81, 105, 119, 186; Charter, 113; dia-
    logue with U.S., 124–25, 126; estab-
    lishment, 112; factions, 112, 113;
    Israeli invasion of Lebanon and, 121;
    observer status at UN, 114; re-
    nounces terrorism, 119, 124; repre-
    sentative of Palestinians, 114, 115.
    See also Arafat, Yasser
Palestine National Council, 124
Palestine Post, 35, 76
Palestinian National Authority, 81
Parker, Richard B., 116
Partition, 2, 3, 27–54, 56–59, 60, 61,
    70, 83–84, 107–108, 109. *See also*
    United Nations General Assembly,
    Resolution 181
Patterson, Jefferson, 66
Peel Commission, 108–109
Peel, Lord Robert, 108
Pelletreau, Robert H., 151, 165

ABOUT THE AUTHOR

DONALD NEFF was a foreign correspondent for the *Los Angeles Times* and *Time* magazine, where he also served as a senior editor. His previous works include the *Warriors* trilogy—an examination of U.S. policy during the Middle East wars of 1956, 1967 and 1973—as well as the unpublished data base *Middle East Handbook*, from which much of the material for this book was taken.